"十四五"职业教育国家规划教材
"十三五"职业教育国家规划教材
21世纪应用型人才培养规划教材

21世纪实用国际商务英语口语

（第三版）

Practical International Business Spoken English
(Third Edition)

陈宁 池玫 陈鹏南 著

图书在版编目(CIP)数据

21世纪实用国际商务英语口语/ 陈宁，池玫，陈鹏南著 .—3版. — 北京：北京大学出版社，2018.3
（21世纪全国高校应用人才培养规划教材）
ISBN 978-7-301-28908-2

Ⅰ.①2… Ⅱ.①陈…②池…③陈… Ⅲ.①国际商务—英语—口译—高等学校—教材 Ⅳ.①H315.9

中国版本图书馆CIP数据核字（2017）第252330号

书　　名	21世纪实用国际商务英语口语（第三版）
	21 SHIJI SHIYONG GUOJI SHANGWU YINGYU KOUYU
著作责任者	陈 宁 池 玫 陈鹏南 著
责任编辑	成 淼
标准书号	ISBN 978-7-301-28908-2
出版发行	北京大学出版社
地　　址	北京市海淀区成府路205号　100871
网　　址	http://www.pup.cn 　　新浪微博：@北京大学出版社
电子信箱	zyjy@ pup.cn
电　　话	邮购部 010-62752015　发行部 010-62750672　编辑部 010-62704142
印 刷 者	北京虎彩文化传播有限公司
经 销 者	新华书店
	787毫米×1092毫米　16开本　22.75印张　600千字
	2007年4月第1版　2012年8月第2版
	2018年3月第3版　2023年7月重排　2024年7月第7次印刷
定　　价	52.00元（含光盘）

未经许可，不得以任何方式复制或抄袭本书之部分或全部内容。
版权所有，侵权必究
举报电话：010-62752024　电子信箱：fd@pup.pku.edu.cn
图书如有印装质量问题，请与出版部联系，电话：010-62756370

第三版前言

新时代，新形势，实施科教兴国战略，强化社会主义现代化建设人才支撑，加快建设教育强国、科技强国、人才强国，这对商务英语口语课程的学习提出了新的更高的要求。本书深入贯彻党的二十大精神，以习近平新时代中国特色社会主义思想为指导，准确把握教育事业发展面临的新形势、新任务，以培养学生的商务英语口语能力为核心，把英语语言能力培养与商务知识学习有机结合起来，希望为高等院校的商务英语、国际贸易和经济等专业的学生以及外贸工作者提供了一本有针对性和实用价值的商务英语口语教材。

本书在编写过程中，坚持培育和践行社会主义核心价值观，坚持深化教育改革创新，坚持用社会主义核心价值观立德树人，书中融入了展示中华文明等内容，突出知识掌握、能力培养与价值塑造的协同发展。从第一版到第三版，编者不断在书中充实新知识、完善新内容，体现与时俱进，与时代发展同步。

本书具有以下特色：

1. 理论与实践一体化结合。

本书集商务和英语理论知识、实际运用及实训于一体。本书以能力培养为目标，以国际贸易实际工作项目为载体，以学生为中心，以交易磋商任务驱动学生完成知识和技能的学习，以国际贸易交易实际操作环节为章节，每个章节都是独立的商务活动场景，把理论知识的学习与语言能力的培养放在具体的商务情景中，形成了适应一体化教学的模式。本书将理论学习与实践相结合，可促进学生认知能力的发展和商务英语口语的提高。第三版在教材Part C部分强化了理论与实践一体化结合的内容。

2. 融入思政元素，体现鲜明的时代特色。

本书应用现代流行、生动地道的国际商务英语口语的表达方式，摒弃过时的商务知识和行话，便于开展互动式商务英语口语训练；融合于各章节中的国际商务观念和技巧贴近时代脉搏，具有强烈的时代感；涉及的内容贴近现代国际商务实际，满足了当前国际商务的交际需求。本书结合时代发展，通过例句融入思政元素，拓展学生关于"一带一路"、国际进口博览会、开放合作、中华民族伟大复兴、北京奥运会、小康社会等新思维，以及数字经济等新话题，以调动学生的学习兴趣和求知欲望，用潜移默化的方式培养学生的国际视野和中国情怀，提高学生的学习效果。

3. 架构完整，内容丰富。

本书以国际商务交际活动为中心，展示如何处理实际交易环节中出现的各类问题，内容涉及国际贸易的各个实战环节和相关商务活动两大主线，涵盖客户介绍、寻找贸易机会、商务安排、参加交易会、商务拜访、营销策略、商务会议、商务促销、商务谈判、技术创新和自主品牌战略等。从开展国际贸易实务，如询盘、报盘、还价、接受、签约、支付、包装、商检、发货和索赔等各个实战环节入手，其中还涉及许多外贸的知识细节，如商标、专利、保险、普惠制和独家经营等，让学生在逼真的贸易情景中学习国际商务知识和模仿体验如何开展国际贸易，应用国际商务英语口语，提高商务交际技能。

4. 突出实用性和实战技能。

本书所包含的国际商务知识、英语口语技能、商务业务技巧、商务礼仪和流行口语、情景对话、经典句型等，让学生接触到生动真实的国际商务英语口语信息；通过模拟操练、角色扮演、讨论和辩论等方法，可调动学生学习的积极性，培养学生熟练运用英语从事商务活动的能力，启迪学生在逼真的贸易情景中学习国际商务知识，模仿体验如何开展国际贸易，应用国际商务英语口语，提高商务交际技能。

本书由具有丰富教学和外贸实践经验的资深教师精心撰写，许多章节情景就是现实国贸业务的片段再现。课文的音频材料由外国专家朗读，便于学生模仿和进行听说练习。学生可用微信扫描二维码或使用光盘方式获取学习材料。本书教学课件可提供给教师教学参考。本书可供一学年商务英语口语学习，若只安排一学期教学，教师可根据商务程序和课文的深浅酌情选择学习内容。

最后，衷心希望读者能学有所获。另外，书中还有很多不尽如人意之处，恳请专家、学者、同行等批评指正。

编　者

2023年7月

Contents

Chapter 1 Welcoming Clients ··· 1
    Part A Situational Dialogue ··· 2
        Communicative Scene 1 ··· 2
        Communicative Scene 2 ··· 2
        Communicative Scene 3 ··· 3
    Part B Practical Key Sentences ··· 6
    Part C Integration of Theory and Practice ··· 8
    Part D Practice ··· 10

Chapter 2 Seeking Business Opportunity ··· 13
    Part A Situational Dialogue ··· 14
        Communicative Scene 1 ··· 14
        Communicative Scene 2 ··· 15
        Communicative Scene 3 ··· 16
    Part B Practical Key Sentences ··· 21
    Part C Integration of Theory and Practice ··· 22
    Part D Practice ··· 24

Chapter 3 Making Inquiries ··· 27
    Part A Situational Dialogue ··· 28
        Communicative Scene 1 ··· 28
        Communicative Scene 2 ··· 29
        Communicative Scene 3 ··· 30
    Part B Practical Key Sentences ··· 34
    Part C Integration of Theory and Practice ··· 36
    Part D Practice ··· 38

Chapter 4 Business Appointment and Arrangement ··· 41
    Part A Situational Dialogue ··· 42
        Communicative Scene 1 ··· 42
        Communicative Scene 2 ··· 43
        Communicative Scene 3 ··· 44
    Part B Practical Key Sentences ··· 48
    Part C Integration of Theory and Practice ··· 49
    Part D Practice ··· 51

Chapter 5 Offer and Counter Offer ··· 55
    Part A Situational Dialogue ··· 56
        Communicative Scene 1 ··· 56

	Communicative Scene 2	57
	Communicative Scene 3	57
Part B	Practical Key Sentences	60
Part C	Integration of Theory and Practice	63
Part D	Practice	65

Chapter 6 At China Import and Export Fair ... 67
    Part A Situational Dialogue ... 68
        Communicative Scene 1 ... 68
        Communicative Scene 2 ... 69
        Communicative Scene 3 ... 69
    Part B Practical Key Sentences ... 72
    Part C Integration of Theory and Practice ... 74
    Part D Practice ... 76

Chapter 7 Business Visit ... 79
    Part A Situational Dialogue ... 80
        Communicative Scene 1 ... 80
        Communicative Scene 2 ... 81
        Communicative Scene 3 ... 82
    Part B Practical Key Sentences ... 86
    Part C Integration of Theory and Practice ... 87
    Part D Practice ... 89

Chapter 8 Innovative and Power Brand Strategy ... 93
    Part A Situational Dialogue ... 94
        Communicative Scene 1 ... 94
        Communicative Scene 2 ... 95
        Communicative Scene 3 ... 96
    Part B Practical Key Sentences ... 100
    Part C Integration of Theory and Practice ... 102
    Part D Practice ... 104

Chapter 9 Packing and Quality Inspection ... 107
    Part A Situational Dialogue ... 108
        Communicative Scene 1 ... 108
        Communicative Scene 2 ... 109
        Communicative Scene 3 ... 110
    Part B Practical Key Sentences ... 113
    Part C Integration of Theory and Practice ... 114
    Part D Practice ... 116

Chapter 10 Acceptance and Orders ... 119
    Part A Situational Dialogue ... 120
        Communicative Scene 1 ... 120

	Communicative Scene 2	121
	Communicative Scene 3	122
Part B	Practical Key Sentences	125
Part C	Integration of Theory and Practice	127
Part D	Practice	129

Chapter 11 Business Telephone Calls ·············· 133
    Part A Situational Dialogue ·············· 134
        Communicative Scene 1 ·············· 134
        Communicative Scene 2 ·············· 135
        Communicative Scene 3 ·············· 136
    Part B Practical Key Sentences ·············· 138
    Part C Integration of Theory and Practice ·············· 140
    Part D Practice ·············· 142

Chapter 12 Terms of Payment ·············· 145
    Part A Situational Dialogue ·············· 146
        Communicative Scene 1 ·············· 146
        Communicative Scene 2 ·············· 147
        Communicative Scene 3 ·············· 148
    Part B Practical Key Sentences ·············· 153
    Part C Integration of Theory and Practice ·············· 154
    Part D Practice ·············· 156

Chapter 13 Business Negotiation ·············· 159
    Part A Situational Dialogue ·············· 160
        Communicative Scene 1 ·············· 160
        Communicative Scene 2 ·············· 161
        Communicative Scene 3 ·············· 162
    Part B Practical Key Sentences ·············· 166
    Part C Integration of Theory and Practice ·············· 168
    Part D Practice ·············· 170

Chapter 14 Sign a Contract ·············· 173
    Part A Situational Dialogue ·············· 174
        Communicative Scene 1 ·············· 174
        Communicative Scene 2 ·············· 175
        Communicative Scene 3 ·············· 176
    Part B Practical Key Sentences ·············· 180
    Part C Integration of Theory and Practice ·············· 181
    Part D Practice ·············· 183

Chapter 15 Cargo Delivery ·············· 187
    Part A Situational Dialogue ·············· 188
        Communicative Scene 1 ·············· 188

Communicative Scene 2 ········188
    Communicative Scene 3 ········189
  Part B Practical Key Sentences ········193
  Part C Integration of Theory and Practice ········194
  Part D Practice ········196

Chapter 16 Business Conference ········201
  Part A Situational Dialogue ········202
    Communicative Scene 1 ········202
    Communicative Scene 2 ········203
    Communicative Scene 3 ········204
  Part B Practical Key Sentences ········208
  Part C Integration of Theory and Practice ········209
  Part D Practice ········212

Chapter 17 Sales Promotion ········215
  Part A Situational Dialogue ········216
    Communicative Scene 1 ········216
    Communicative Scene 2 ········217
    Communicative Scene 3 ········219
  Part B Practical Key Sentences ········222
  Part C Integration of Theory and Practice ········224
  Part D Practice ········226

Chapter 18 Interview ········229
  Part A Situational Dialogue ········230
    Communicative Scene 1 ········230
    Communicative Scene 2 ········230
    Communicative Scene 3 ········231
  Part B Practical Key Sentences ········235
  Part C Integration of Theory and Practice ········236
  Part D Practice ········240

Chapter 19 Complaints ········243
  Part A Situational Dialogue ········244
    Communicative Scene 1 ········244
    Communicative Scene 2 ········244
    Communicative Scene 3 ········245
    Communicative Scene 4 ········246
  Part B Practical Key Sentences ········250
  Part C Integration of Theory and Practice ········251
  Part D Practice ········253

Chapter 20 Banquet and Parting ········257
  Part A Situational Dialogue ········258

		Communicative Scene 1	258
		Communicative Scene 2	260
		Communicative Scene 3	260
	Part B	Practical Key Sentences	263
	Part C	Integration of Theory and Practice	265
	Part D	Practice	267

Appendix 1　Translation to Situational Dialogues 270
　　　　　（情景对话参考译文）
Appendix 2　Suggested Key to Practice 316
　　　　　（实践操练参考答案）

Chapter 1
Welcoming Clients

Learning Objectives
Upon completion of this chapter, you will be able to

- get used to the process for customs formality.
- welcome the guests at the airport.
- learn how to introduce yourself and someone else politely.
- perform the functions of skills of communication.
- conduct the activities related to the theme of greeting and introduction.

课文范读

Part A Situational Dialogue

 Communicative Scene 1

Going through Formalities (Going abroad on Business)

(Mr. Peng is a manager of China Machinery Import & Export Company. He goes abroad to the United States for the first time. Having claimed the luggage, he goes to the customs service desk.)

Officer: Good afternoon. May I have a look at your passport and customs declaration form?
  Peng: Certainly. Here you are.
Officer: Thank you. And your health declaration form, please?
  Peng: All right. Just a moment. Oh, here it is.
Officer: What nationality are you?
  Peng: I am Chinese.
Officer: Would you mind telling me the purpose of your visit?
  Peng: No, not at all. We are going to have business negotiations with some machinery companies. We are planning to import some equipment from your country.
Officer: I see. How long do you plan to stay in the United States?
  Peng: Only a couple of weeks.
Officer: Is this all your baggage, sir?
  Peng: That's right.
Officer: Have you anything particular to declare?
  Peng: I suppose not, except a digital camera, some samples and personal effects. Are they duty free?
Officer: You needn't pay duty on samples and personal belongings.
  Peng: I am taking USD 20,000 with me. Do I need to declare?
Officer: Yes. Please fill out this Currency Declaration Form.
  Peng: OK. I'll do it.
Officer: Thank you.
  Peng: Is that all for customs formalities?[1]
Officer: Yes, sir. You are through now. Go ahead. This way, please.
  Peng: Thanks.

■ Welcoming Clients

 Communicative Scene 2

Meeting at the Airport

(Sherry, the secretary of China Import and Export Corporation, is at the airport to meet Mr. Jones from Brazilian Company.)

Sherry: Excuse me. Aren't you Mr. Jones from Brazilian Company?
Jones: Yes, you are right. I don't believe we've met before.
Sherry: No, I don't think so. Allow me to introduce myself to you. I am Sherry, the secretary of China Import and Export Corporation.
Jones: How nice to meet you!
Sherry: Glad to meet you too. Welcome to Beijing!
Jones: Thank you. It's my pleasure to have an opportunity to visit China again.
Sherry: Our CEO was planning to pick you up at the airport in person, but it is a pity that he is tied up in important business affairs today.
Jones: That's all right. <u>I know he is somebody.</u>[2]
Sherry: You may well say so. He has been very successful in his job. What is more, he is never flashy and <u>he is really a team player, too.</u>[3]
Jones: He is doing a great job for our business. <u>I am dying to meet him.</u>[4]
Sherry: How was the flight? <u>You must be very tired after such a long journey.</u>[5]
Jones: Oh, no, the flight was comfortable and I had a very pleasant journey. But I could not sleep on the plane. I am feeling a little jet lag now.
Sherry: Please take a good rest before we have a business negotiation.
Jones: Things couldn't be better.
Sherry: We have made a reservation at a very nice hotel near a beautiful lake. I hope you'll have a pleasant stay in Beijing.
Jones: It's very kind of you to do so.
Sherry: Let's go to the hotel, shall we?
Jones: Terrific.

 Communicative Scene 3

Introducing Each Other

(Zheng Dongxiao is meeting Milton Walter, the president of a multinational corporation. <u>He also wants to make the acquaintance of marketing manager, Mr. Sam Auden.</u>[6])

Zheng: Good morning. If I'm not mistaken, you must be Mr. Walter, president of the multinational corporation. <u>May I take the liberty to introduce myself to you?</u>[7] My name is Zheng Dongxiao.
Walter: How do you do? I'm Milton Walter.

Zheng: How do you do? I have often heard about you. I've been looking forward to meeting you for a long time.

Walter: By the way, how to spell your name? It's hard for me to remember Chinese names.

Zheng: Z-h-e-n-g D-o-n-g-x-i-a-o. It's right here on my card. Here's my name card.

Walter: Good. I remember now. And here's mine.

Zheng: Thank you. Will you introduce me to your marketing manager over there?

Walter: Haven't you met yet?

Zheng: No, I don't think so.

Walter: I'm glad to introduce him to you.

Zheng: Yeah. Why not?

Walter: Sam, come and meet Dongxiao. This is Sam, my colleague.

Zheng: Hello, Mr. Sam Auden. It's a pleasure to finally meet you after so many e-mails, telephone calls and fax contacts.

Auden: <u>Wow! In the flesh!</u>[8] It's good to meet you.

Zheng: Let me help you with the baggage.

Auden: Thank you so much.

Zheng: It's my pleasure. I'd like to make an arrangement for tomorrow.

Walter: <u>Suppose we meet at 10 a.m. tomorrow.</u>[9]

Zheng: Here is a copy of the agenda I have worked out for you and Mr. Auden. I hope it will meet your requirements.

Walter: Fine. I'll have a look at it in the hotel.

Zheng: <u>It was nice meeting all of you.</u>[10] See you!

Walter: See you!

Words and Expressions

1. claim the luggage		领取行李
2. the customs service desk		海关服务台
3. declaration form		申报单
declare	*v.*	向海关申报进口应纳税物品
Currency Declaration Form		货币申报单
4. digital camera		数码相机
5. personal effects		个人用品
6. fill out		填写
7. CEO *abbr.* Chief Executive Officer		首席执行官，执行总裁
8. flashy	*adj.*	华而不实的，浮华的
9. be tied up		无法脱身，忙碌
10. terrific	*adj.*	好极了
11. jet lag		飞行时差反应
12. reserve	*v.*	预定，make a reservation 预定

13. meet the requirements of		满足要求
14. have a business negotiation		商务谈判，商洽
15. a multinational corporation		跨国公司
16. agenda/agendas	n.	议事日程（复数形式）
agendum	n.	议事日程（单数形式）
17. work out		制定

1. Is that all for customs formalities?

   海关手续办完了吗？

   ① go through formalities 办理手续

   ② customs formality and requirement 报关手续和规定

   ③ export formality 出口手续

   ④ transit formality 过境手续

   You are through now. 您的手续办好了。

2. He is somebody.

   他可是个人物。

   ① somebody 有影响力的重要人物

   ② VIP即very important person 贵宾或重要人物

   ③ nobody 平庸之辈

3. He is really a team player.

   他确实是个容易合作的人。

4. I am dying to meet him.

   很久以来一直期望与他相见。

   be dying for 非常渴望

   People around the world are dying for a complete success of Beijing 2022 Winter Olympic Games.

   世界人民期盼着北京2022年冬季奥运会的圆满成功。

   We are dying for the good cooperation with multinational companies.

   我方非常渴望与跨国公司的良好合作。

5. You must be very tired after such a long journey.

   长途旅行后您一定很累了。

   must 此处表示肯定的猜测，必定、非常可能发生，表示逻辑推断的可能性和必然性。

   You must be Mr. Walter.

   您一定是沃尔特先生吧。

   If the light was on, Dr. Bailey must have been in the office.

   如果灯亮着，贝利博士一定在办公室。

否定用 can not be，而 could not have done 表示对过去否定的猜测。

6. He also wants to make the acquaintance of marketing manager, Mr. Sam Auden.

   他还想结识公司的营销部经理山姆·奥登先生。

   ① make the acquaintance of sb. 结识某人

   ② make sb.'s acquaintance 结识某人

   ③ pick acquaintance with 偶然结识

   ④ have no acquaintance with 不熟悉，不了解

   ⑤ have a nodding acquaintance with sb./the subjects 与某人有点头之交/对某学科略知一二

7. May I take the liberty to introduce myself to you?

   我可以冒昧地自我介绍吗？

   ① liberty *n.* 冒昧，自由

   ② take the liberty to do sth. / take the liberty of doing sth. 冒昧行事

   May we take the liberty of asking you to make out the business negotiation agenda?
   我们可以冒昧地请您制定谈判的议事日程吗？

8. Wow! In the flesh!

   啊！终于见到真人了！

   ① in flesh 肥胖的

   ② in the flesh （习惯用语）活生生的，亲自

   Wow! In the flesh! You know she has not shut up about you ... you did something to impress her.
   哇，终于见到真人了！她总是谈到你……她对你的印象很好。（美国电影《蒙娜丽莎的微笑》中的一段对白）

9. Suppose we'll meet at 10 a.m. tomorrow.

   我建议明天上午十点相会。

   suppose 常用祈使语气表示：让我建议……

   Suppose we make an investment plan together.
   我建议我们一起制订投资计划。

10. It is nice to meet all of you.

    很高兴认识你们！（通常在见面介绍认识时用）

    It was nice meeting you.

    很高兴认识您！（通常在临别时用）

Part B Practical Key Sentences

1. **request the guests to show something**

   May I see your passport and customs declaration form?
   请您出示护照和报关申请表。

Certainly, here you are. 当然可以，给您。

替换表达：

Show me your passport, please.

Here it is.

Passport and declaration, please.

Certainly.

Would you show me your documents, please?

Sure.

2. introduce oneself

May I take the liberty to introduce myself to you? I am ... (Formal usage)

我可以冒昧地自我介绍吗？我是……

替换表达：

Allow me to introduce myself to you. My name is ... (Formal usage)

May I introduce myself to you? I am ... (Basic usage)

Hello! I am Peter. (Informal usage)

Let me introduce myself to you. (Basic usage)

3. introduce others

Sam, come and meet Dongxiao. This is Sam, my colleague.

山姆，来见见东晓。这位是山姆，我的同事。(Informal usage)

替换表达：

I'd like you to meet our manager. (Basic usage)

Hello, this is Mr. Forest. (Informal usage)

I'd like to introduce our manager to you. (Formal usage)

Please let me introduce Mr. James to you. (Formal usage)

Allow me to present my colleague to you. (Formal usage)

I am honored to introduce... (Formal usage)

It is with great pleasure to present Mr. Brown, our CEO. (Formal usage)

4. respond to an introduction

How do you do? 您好！（初次见面招呼用语）

How do you do? 您好！（回应用语）

替换表达：

How nice to meet you.

Glad to meet you.

It's good to meet you, too. (Basic usage)

It's a pleasure to know you.

Pleased to meet you.

I am happy to have the opportunity to meet you. (Formal usage)

I am delighted to make your acquaintance. (Formal usage)

5. get acquainted

Have you met before?

你们见过面吗？（介绍别人相识）

No, I don't think we have.

不，我想没有。

Yes, I think so.

是的，我们见过面。（此表达比No, I don't. 或Yes, I do. 更委婉）

替换表达：

Do you know each other?

Have we been introduced? (Basic usage)

Your name, please?

May I have your name, please?

Haven't you met before?

Yes, I think we have, haven't we?

I think I have seen you somewhere. You look familiar.

Part C Integration of Theory and Practice

【知识点】介绍是国际贸易中一个非常重要的环节，是商务交际之桥。介绍缩短了人际交流间的距离。得体的介绍将引导和缓和业务伙伴之间的关系，创造一种良好的印象，从而导致成功的交易。

1. first impression　第一印象

【知识点】在商务活动中，初次会面印象的好坏将关系到未来业务的开展。恰当得体的介绍将给贸易伙伴留下美好印象，主动自我介绍是自信的表现。不断认识新的贸易客户，第一印象和良好的介绍会给客户留下宝贵的形象，有利于开创新的贸易商机。

【技能训练句型】

Allow me to introduce myself to you. My name is ...

请允许我自我介绍，我叫……

May I take the liberty to introduce myself to you?

我可以冒昧地自我介绍吗？

2. order of introduction　介绍顺序

【知识点】介绍别人时，原则是尊者居后。有礼貌的方法是，向年长者介绍年轻者，把主人介绍给客人，将男士介绍给女士，把年轻人介绍给长者，把职位低者介绍给职务高者。

【技能训练句型】

Miss Taylor, may I introduce my friend Mr. Lee to you?

泰勒小姐，我能否向您介绍我的朋友李先生？

在商务活动中注重将职务低的人介绍给职务高的人。例如：

Mr. President, I'm glad to introduce her to you.

总裁先生，我很高兴将她介绍给您。

3. order of introduction for group people　集体相见介绍顺序

【知识点】在商务活动中，双方公司成员集体相见介绍时，先介绍主人方面成员，之后客方作介绍。顺序以职位高为先介绍。

【技能训练句型】

Hosting side: Song Dalian, Design manager; Wang Ming, President of ABC Computer Company; Ma Yuelin, Design Engineer（主方：宋大连，设计部经理；王明，ABC计算机公司总裁；马越林，设计工程师）

Introduce hosting side first to the visiting side（向客方介绍主方）:

This is Wang Ming, the President of ABC Computer Company, and this is Song Dalian, Design manager, and this is Ma Yuelin, Design Engineer. He has been very successful in his job.

这位是王明，ABC计算机公司总裁；这位是宋大连，设计部经理；这位是马越林，设计工程师，他的工作做得非常出色。

Then the visiting side will do the self-introduction to the hosting side in turn.（客方一一作自我介绍）

4. welcome new clients　迎接新客户

【知识点】迎接新客户，通常在迎宾处高举写着公司名称和客人姓名的牌子，遇到看似你的新客户，可向前询问加以确认。

【技能训练句型】

If I'm not mistaken, you must be Mr. Walter, from artificial intertigence company.

如果我没搞错的话，您一定是沃尔特先生吧。

Excuse me. Aren't you Mr. Jones from Brazilian Company?

请问，您是来自巴西公司的琼斯先生吗？

You are Milton Walter, president of the company, aren't you?

您是公司总裁密尔顿·沃尔特，对吗？

5. introduction　引见

【知识点】在商务活动中，要积极主动地认识客户和商务界人士，为避免唐突，不妨请客户帮助介绍。

【技能训练句型】

Will you introduce me to your marketing manager over there?

请替我引见那位营销部经理好吗？

I would like to meet Chairman of Council for the Promotion of International Trade.

我想结识一下国际贸易促进委员会的会长。

6. express the willingness of getting acquainted　表达想结识的意愿

【知识点】表达想结识的意愿，增进亲切友好的感觉，自然地缩小与客户的距离，有助于开展业务。

【技能训练句型】

I've heard a lot /so much about you.

久仰大名。
I have often heard of you.
久闻大名。
He always talks about you.
他常提及您。
I've been looking forward to meeting you for a long time.
久仰。
Your company is very reputed, I heard much praises for it.
贵公司信誉很好，我久仰大名。
I am dying to meet him.
我真想见到他。
It's nice to finally meet you.
终于见面了! 见到您真好。

7. remember other's names　听清并记住对方的姓名

【知识点】被介绍人要听清并记住对方的姓名，否则叫错客人姓名，有失礼仪。若未听清楚，可马上请求对方再说一遍。

【技能训练句型】

What is your name again? I beg your pardon.
请再说一遍。

如对方的姓名很长而且难记，可要求拼写方法。例如：

By the way, how do you spell your name? It's hard for me to remember Chinese names.
顺便问一下，如何拼读你的名字？对我来说很难记住中国人的姓名。

8. popular greeting　地道流行招呼语

【知识点】熟人见面打招呼问好，如果只会用在以往教科书最常用的How are you? I am fine. Thank you. And you? 显然过时了。

当今美语流行How are you doing?（近来好吗？）（例如：美国电视剧《老友记》里的Joey，每次见到美女都会上前搭讪问How are you doing?）

【技能训练句型】
回答可根据实际情况用：

I am doing good. 或I am pretty good.（我很好。）
Not so good.
不怎样。
Uh, nothing much.
哦，老样子。

英美国家人士还常喜欢用：

What's up? (Informal usage)
嗨，怎么样?
How's everything?
一切都好?
What's new?
有什么新鲜事?
What's happening?

在忙什么?
How is it going?
近来好吗?

Part D Practice

I. Complete the Following Dialogues

(1)

Zhang: May I introduce ___1___ to you? My name is Zhang Hua.

George: Glad to meet you. I am George. How do you ___2___ your name? It is difficult for me to remember Chinese ___3___.

Zhang: Z-h-a-n-g H-u-a. Here's my name ___4___.

George: Good. I ___5___ now. Here is my card. By the way, do you know Zhang Ziyi?

Zhang: Yes, I know a lot about her. Why do you ___6___?

George: That is impossible. You are kidding, I am afraid. Do you ___7___ know her?

Zhang: Certainly. Zhang Ziyi is a famous film star.

George: How do you know her? Can you ___8___ her to me?

Zhang: Oh, I realize that I ___9___ a mistake. Just now my answer to your question means "Do you ___10___ who Zhang Ziyi is?"

(2)

A: Excuse me. ___1___ and your vaccination certificate, please?

B: Yeah, here is my passport. But what do you mean ___2___ vaccination certificate?

A: Vaccination certificate ___3___ the report of health condition.

B: I see. Oh, here ___4___ is.

A: Is this all your baggage, Sir?

B: That's right.

A: Do you have anything to ___5___?

B: No, Sir. I am just bringing in personal ___6___ and some fruits.

A: Sorry, rotten fruit is not allowed to bring ___7___.

B: But it is not rotten. Would you ___8___ allow me to bring in Lichi? It is my wife's favorite ___9___.

A: I am afraid not. Perishables are ___10___, too.

B: Oh, my poor wife!

II. Interaction Activities

Task 1

The teacher divides students into groups. Each group is suggested to be 5 students. Students make dialogues and role-play them:

Introduce the delegation to the hosts according to the following hints. Give the title of each person and make a brief introduction. Try to use the introductory phrases in the unit and respond to the introduction. The words or phrases suggested below might be helpful:

(1) Mr. Steve Singer, Sunshine Group Ltd.

(2) Mr. Robinson, Chief Executive Officer, a somebody

(3) Mr. Bright, export manager, a team player

(4) Miss Howard, attractive, smile

(5) Ms Morley, secretary, kind-hearted

Task 2

Short conversations.

(1)

Suppose you meet your client whom you have never met before at the airport. Introduce each other, express your welcome on behalf of your company and leave a good impression on the client.

(2)

Meet your old clients with an informal greeting.

III. Actual Practice

Work in pairs.

Use the business card to practice the following situation with your partner:

> Fruits & Vegetable Corp.
> Henry Brown
> Managing Director
> 10 Hero Street, Toronto, Canada
> Tel: (416)480-480
> Fax: (416)480-481

(1) Introducing himself to Jake Tompkins

(2) Greeting

(3) Exchanging business cards

(4) Exchanging information about the company

IV. Creative Discussion

The teacher divides the class into groups and asks them to discuss, then choose the representatives of each group after discussion. The student who expresses well will be the winner.

Topic:

It is said that first impression is very important, especially in business activity. What do you think of first impression? Do you think it does matter? Please discuss with your partners about how to create a good impression on the customers that you first meet.

Chapter 2　Seeking Business Opportunity

Learning Objectives
Upon completion of this chapter, you will be able to

- get to know the channels through which importers and exporters establish business relations.
- learn the ways to get ready for getting into business relations.
- perform the functions of skills of communication.
- conduct the activities related to the theme of seeking business opportunities.

课文范读

Part A Situational Dialogue

 Communicative Scene 1

Tips for Seeking Business Opportunities

(*Miss Fan Xin has just graduated from the university. She works in China Tea Export Corporation and is desirous of starting business. She is asking Liu Tao, a veteran businessman for some advice.*)

Liu: Fan Xin, you seem troubled. Is anything the matter?

Fan: Oh, Mr. Liu. I'd like to ask you some questions.

Liu: Yes, go ahead.[1]

Fan: You see, I'm really green.[2] I lack experience here. I wonder if you could give me some advice about how to seek business opportunities.

Liu: By all means,[3] there are tricks in every trade.[4]

Fan: I am eager to learn.[5]

Liu: Since we entered into the 21st century, great changes have taken place in the way of doing business. We may establish business relations with companies thousands of miles away through many channels.

Fan: It sounds interesting.

Liu: I'd like to introduce to you some main channels. From my point of view, nowadays the most effective way to find clients is surfing the Internet. Its advantage is fast and inexpensive. You may make a search on the web for prospective clients.

Fan: It is a good idea. It's a pity that I haven't learnt much about it in the classroom.

Liu: E-commerce plays an important part in modern business. It is easier and time-saving to find potential customers from the Internet. We needn't travel here and there to find customers and we still know a lot.

Fan: Oh, I can't wait to try it.

Liu: A Chamber of Commerce is an important channel to get the information and contact businessmen.

Fan: What is Chamber of Commerce?

Liu: Chamber of Commerce is an organization of businessmen. One of the main tasks for this organization is to help the companies or members get the business information and seek opportunities.

Fan: I remember now. Anything more?

Liu: Looking up in the Trade Directory is helpful, too.

Fan: What shall I do?
Liu: You will find companies by checking the specific categories. Then you'll get the name, address and telephone number of the desired companies.
Fan: I learned from a textbook that banks usually supply the names and addresses of companies for businessmen.
Liu: Actually, it's not always the case. <u>Banks help companies for credit investigation. But they should keep the information of customers confidential, too.</u>[6] As a matter of fact, you can't rely on their finding clients for you in the foreign trade now.
Fan: Oh, really?
Liu: Some points in the trade books published long time ago may be out of date. You should be careful when you read and don't follow the old idea.
Fan: <u>You said it.</u>[7]
Liu: Necessary information can be obtained from <u>Commercial Counselor's Office stationed abroad</u>[8] and advertisement in the newspapers and magazines. Going to business fairs may be a good way to get in touch with customers but the cost is too high.
Fan: Um, I see your point.
Liu: After you get the desired names and addresses, you may begin to send e-mail, fax or telephone to start business.
Fan: Oh, yes.
Liu: Thanks to the development of the means of communication we no longer need to go to post office to send telegram or telex.
Fan: Yeah, the modern development ends its function.
Liu: Nowadays the most common and quickest way of communication is by sending e-mail, fax and telephone call.
Fan: True enough.
Liu: We can get in touch with whomever we want within seconds by using the Internet and computer.
Fan: It seems that we can probably make sure of business in the office. I am confident to start the business now.

 Communicative Scene 2

Contact the Client

(Miss Fan Xin is contacting a foreign company for business opportunities.)

Fan: Hello, May I speak to import manager?
Rance: <u>This is Mr. Rance of the Import Department. Who is it, please</u>?[9]
Fan: This is Fan Xin of China Tea Export Corporation.
Rance: What can I do for you?

Fan: I have come to know your company by making a search on the Internet. Your website shows that you are one of the leading importers of tea business in the European market. <u>I am glad to introduce my corporation to you as a professional one, specializing in the line of tea products.</u>¹⁰

Rance: Oh, I am interested. Would you tell me more about your business scope?

Fan: Certainly, we are exporters of high reputation, trading in various kinds of Black Tea, White Tea, Green Tea, Oolong Tea and Jasmine Tea. We have been in this line of business for more than fifty years.

Rance: Nice to hear that. How about the quality of tea?

Fan: <u>You may rest assured.</u>¹¹ Our tea products are very popular for their superb quality. We have our own processing factory and a lot of experienced technicians. Our Grade-A Jasmine Tea has won international high quality medals.

Rance: That's very inspiring. <u>So far the teabags cater to modern consumption habit.</u>¹² Can you supply them?

Fan: Yes, we are going all out to exploit new markets and push our new products. We are producing teabags in order to meet the need of world market.

Rance: What a coincidence! It seems to be what we are looking for.

Fan: We are also producing ice tea and Oolong liquor. They gain the character of quick and convenient drinking.

Rance: Fine. It would be very helpful if you could send us your catalogue or brochures for our further study.

Fan: <u>In order to let you have a general idea of all our products, I am going to send you our latest</u> illustrated catalogue by EMS for your perusal.¹³

Rance: Please send some samples of your teabags and new tea products.

Fan: No problem.

Rance: We'll let you know the result as soon as we study them.

Fan: I am looking forward to your favorable news soon.

 Communicative Scene 3

Establish Business Relations

(Mr. Rance is contacting Miss Fan Xin for establishing business relations.)

Rance: Hello, Miss Fan. This is Rance speaking.

Fan: Oh, hi, Mr. Rance.

Rance: We have got your pamphlet, samples of your teabags and new tea products sent by express mail.

Fan: What do you think of our items?

Rance: After careful examination, we find that your tea is excellent in quality and beautifully packed as you described in the last talk.

Fan: Exactly. We always adhere to the principle of keeping the promise and honoring the contract.

Rance: <u>We made a market research on your teabags and new tea products and find there is a ready market for them.</u>[14]

Fan: It's quite good.

Rance: As your tea products fall within the range of our business activities, we would like to express our wish to set up trade relations with your corporation.

Fan: <u>Your desire to establish business relations coincides with ours.</u>[15] Building up direct business relations between our companies will be mutually beneficial.

Rance: I have no doubt that it will bring about closer ties between our two companies.

Fan: It is our policy to trade with businessmen all over the world on the basis of equality and mutual benefit.

Rance: I know what you mean. We are considering expanding our business with you.

Fan: I'd be so pleased if you would.

Rance: Oh, yes. <u>We are prepared to trade with you in this line.</u>[16]

Fan: Sounds great!

Rance: I think I'll discuss with you more details about our business by e-mail.

Fan: I am for you. Our mutual understanding and cooperation will certainly result in more business.

Rance: Good-bye.

Fan: Bye.

Words and Expressions

1.	lack of experience		缺乏经验，不熟练
	lack	n.	常与 of 连用，表示缺乏，也可作动词
2.	veteran	n.	老手，经验丰富的人
		adj.	经验丰富的，熟练的
3.	trick	n.	诀窍，窍门，诡计
		v.	欺骗
4.	from my point of view		依我的观点看来
5.	effective	adj.	有效的，生效的，显著的
6.	client	n.	客户，顾客
	prospective clients		预期的客户
	potential customers		潜在的客户
7.	surf the Internet		网络搜索
8.	prospective	adj.	预期的，未来的
9.	Trade Directory		同业名录，行名录
10.	specific categories		具体的行业分类
11.	credit investigation		资信调查
12.	as a matter of fact		实际上

13. professional	adj.	专业的，职业的
	n.	专业人员
14. telegram	n.	cable电报
15. telex	n.	电传
16. cater	v.	迎合，满足需要
17. go all out		全力以赴
18. Oolong Tea		乌龙茶
Oolong liquor		乌龙浓缩液
19. Jasmine Tea		茉莉花茶
20. superb	adj.	极好的，超等的
21. processing	n.	加工，处理
22. exploit	v.	开发，开拓
23. push out		推出，使突出
24. gain the character of		博得……名声
25. catalogue	n.	目录
26. brochure	n.	pamphlet小册子（常包括推销材料或产品信息）
27. sample	n.	样品
28. bring about		使发生，致使，造成

1. go ahead

   ① 可以，干吧，表示毫不犹豫地开始做某事。

   I'd like to ask you some questions.

   我想问你几个问题。

   Yes, go ahead.

   请说吧。

   ② 常单独用于口语，当某人讲话欲言又止时，可用来催促大胆地说。

   Go ahead and tell us what you want.

   大胆说，告诉我们你要什么。

   ③ 前进，走在前面

   Go ahead. This way, please.

   请往前走，这边请。

   ④ 继续前进press ahead

   Chinese people sweated and we toiled as we pressed ahead with concrete efforts for achievements.

   中国人民用汗水浇灌收获，以实干笃定前行。

2. I'm really green.

   我是新手。

green 除众所周知绿色的意思之外，还有未成熟的、无经验的含义。

green hand 新手，刚入门某一行的人就可被称之为green hand.

3. by all means

① 当然可以

② 一定，务必

相似的词组：

by means of 借助于

by any means 用一切手段和办法

by some means 通过某种办法

by this means 用这种办法

by no means 决不

not by any means 绝对不

by what means 怎样

4. There are tricks in every trade.

行行都有诀窍。

trick 诀窍，窍门，诡计

5. I am eager to learn.

我渴望着学会。

相似的词组：

be eager for success

be eager about one's progress

6. Banks help companies for credit investigation. But they should keep the information of customers confidential，too.

银行帮助公司进行资信调查，但应该对客户的信息保密。

① keep confidential, be confidential, in confidence（保密）

Any information that you supplied to us would be held in strict confidence.

您为我们提供的任何信息都将严格保密。

② confident *adj.* 有信心的

I am confident to start the business now.

我现在对开展贸易充满了信心。

We are making confident strides on the path toward the great rejuvenation of the Chinese nation.

我们正昂首阔步行进在实现中华民族伟大复兴的道路上。

7. You said it.

说得是！表示随声附和。

8. Commercial Counselor's Office stationed abroad 驻外使馆商务处

9. This is Mr. Rance of Import Department. Who is it, please?

我是进口部的兰斯，请问谁找我？

汉语中一般不自称我是某先生，而当用英语自我介绍时若在名字前冠以Mr., Mrs., Miss 等称呼，便于辨别性别或身份。

10. I am glad to introduce my corporation to you as a professional one, specializing in the line of tea

products.

我很高兴地向您介绍本公司,我们是专业从事茶叶产品生产和出口的公司。

① specializing in 是现在分词短语作定语,修饰a professional one, specializing 与in搭配表示专营某产品。

11. You may rest assured.

您尽可放心。

① assured *adj.* 放心的,确信的

You can rest assured that our business relationship will be expanded continuously.

您尽可放心,我们的业务关系将不断扩展。

12. So far the teabags cater to modern consumption habit.

目前袋泡茶很适应现代消费的习惯。

① cater to/for 迎合,投合

The producers are catering to the taste of consumers.

生产者正设法迎合消费者需求。

13. In order to let you have a general idea of all our products, I am going to send you our latest illustrated catalogue by EMS for your perusal.

为了让贵方对我方的产品有个大概的了解,特打算寄上我方最新附图目录,以供细阅。

① have a general idea 有个大概的了解

14. We made a market research on your teabags and new tea products and find there is a ready market for them.

我方就贵方的袋泡茶和茶叶新产品做了市场调查,发现很受市场欢迎。

① make a market research 开展市场调查

② There is a ready market. 很受市场欢迎。

15. Your desire to establish business relations coincides with ours.

贵公司同我方建立业务关系的愿望与我们是一致的。

① coincide with 一致,完全相应,相符

What he said coincided with the facts.

他所说的事情与事实相符合。

② coincidence *n.* 巧合,同时发生,一致

What a coincidence! 真巧!

16. We are prepared to trade with you in this line.

我方愿意在这行业与贵司开展业务。

① be prepared to 表示愿意,并且能够做好

We are prepared to set up business relations with your company.

* 我方愿意与贵司建立业务关系。

17. be desirous of 渴望的

Many clients are desirous of establishing business relationship with you.

许多客户渴望与贵方建立业务关系。

① be desirous to do sth.

* ② be desirous that...
18. EMS *abbr.* Express Mail Service 邮政特快专递

    世界四大著名快递公司：DHL敦豪速递；Fedex（Federal Express）联邦快递；TNT（TNT Express）TNT快递；UPS（Universal Postal Service）联合包裹服务

    ① illustrated catalogue 附图目录

    ② for your perusal 供细阅

Part B Practical Key Sentences

1. asking for advice

I wonder if you could give me some advice about how to seek business opportunities.

您可否告诉我如何寻找贸易机会？

替换表达：

I was wondering if you could possibly give me some ideas.

Do you have any suggestions?

Would you recommend me whether it is a good way to make a business contact?

I hope you don't mind my asking your opinion.

I need your good suggestions.

What do you reckon I should do next?

What is your view about the seeking business opportunities?

Would you be so kind to give us some advice?

2. giving suggestions

From my point of view, nowadays the most effective way to find more clients is surfing the Internet.

依我看来，当今寻找更多客户最有效的方法是通过网络查寻。

替换表达：

Looking up in the Trade Directory is helpful too.

I advise you strongly to find companies by checking the specific categories.

I'd like to suggest that you make a market research.

If I were you, I would send a fax instead of telephone call.

Perhaps you'd better make a search on the net for prospective clients.

Why not adhere to the principle of keeping the promise and honoring the contract?

3. agreement

（1）Entire agreement

True enough. 太对了。

替换表达：

It is a good idea.

I am for you.
You said it.
It's quite good.
That's quite true.
What you said is true.
You are right.
I couldn't agree more!

（2）Partial agreement

I know what you mean but I need your samples right now.
我明白您的意思，但我急需您的样品。

替换表达：

I more or less agree with you.
I agree with much of your idea but ...
I don't entirely agree with you.
To a certain degree, yes, but ...

4. **communicate with businessmen**

We can get in touch with whoever we want within seconds by using the Internet and computers.
我们可以通过国际互联网和电脑在片刻间与任何人联系。

替换表达：

Miss Fan Xin is contacting a foreign company for business opportunities.
Mr. Robinson communicates with his new business partner by e-mail.
I'll convey my manager's intention of establishing business relations to him.
Would you connect me with the Marketing Department for Mr. Robert?

5. **line of business**

We are exporters of high reputation, trading in various kinds of Black Tea, White Tea, Green Tea, Oolong Tea and Jasmine Tea. We have been in this line of business for more than 50 years.
我们的公司是信誉卓越的出口企业，经营各种各样的红茶、白茶、绿茶、乌龙茶和茉莉花茶。公司在此行业已有50多年之久的经营历史。

We are prepared to trade with you in this line.
我方愿意在这行业与贵司开展业务。

替换表达：

As the item falls within the line of our business, we shall like to enter into business relations with your firm.
Our range of business coincided with yours.
We have learnt that you are the exporter of Chinese Tea, which comes within the frame of our business scope.

Part C Integration of Theory and Practice

【知识点】寻找贸易机会可以通过许多渠道进行,主要是通过网络、商会、通信录、跨境电商平台、驻外使馆商务处、报纸杂志的广告、朋友或公司介绍等途径获得必要的信息;介绍自己公司情况,了解对方,发现彼此间的共同点;参加交易会则可能有机会与客户直接会面。

1. the channel to get acquainted 告知认识对方的渠道

【知识点】初次与新客户联系,为了避免唐突,应告知对方是通过何种方式认识对方,尽可能给对方留下一个较好的印象。

【技能训练句型】

(1) By making a search on Internet

I have come to know your company by making a search on Internet. Your website shows that you are one of the leading importers of tea business in European market.

通过国际互联网搜索,我结识了贵公司。您的网站显示贵公司是欧洲市场主要的茶业进口商之一。

(2) By looking up in the Trade Directory

We have obtained your name and address by looking up in the Trade Directory.

我们是通过查看商业名录获知贵方的姓名与地址。

(3) Through the courtesy of Chamber of Commerce

Through the courtesy of Chamber of Commerce, we have learnt your corporation.

承蒙商会的介绍,获悉了贵公司。

(4) By Commercial Counselor's Office

Your company has been recommended from the Commercial Counselor's Office of the Chinese Embassy in Singapore.

中国驻新加坡大使馆的商务处向我方推荐了贵公司。

(5) By ads in the newspapers and magazines

Having had your name and address from ads in the newspapers and magazines, we avail ourselves of the opportunity to contact you.

从报纸杂志的广告得知你们的名字和地址,借此机会与贵方联系。

(6) By the introduction of friends or companies

Your name and address have been kindly introduced to us by Mr. Cade.

承蒙凯德先生的介绍,我们得知贵公司的名称和地址。

(7) By Cross-Border Electronic Commerce platforms.

Foreign consumers often buy Chinese merchandise from Alibaba's, Amazon and Ebay's platforms.

外国消费者常通过阿里巴巴、亚马逊、易趣等跨境电商平台购买中国产品。

Founded in 2004, Dunhuang is a leading B2B cross-border e-commerce trading service platform in China.

敦煌网成立于2004年,是中国领先的B2B跨境电商交易服务平台。

2. introducing company and business scope 介绍公司的经营情况和经营范围

【知识点】先让公司双方了解彼此的经营情况、经营能力和资信状况以及产品情况后,再进行实质性业务探讨。

【技能训练句型】

I am glad to introduce my corporation to you as a professional one, specializing in the line of tea products.

我很高兴地向您介绍本公司是专门从事茶叶产品生产和出口的专业公司。

We are exporters of high reputation, trading in various kinds of Black Tea, White Tea, Green Tea, Oolong Tea and Jasmine Tea. We have been in this line of business for more than 50 years.

我们的公司是信誉卓越的出口企业，经营各种各样的红茶、白茶、绿茶、乌龙茶和茉莉花茶。公司在此行业已有50多年之久的经营历史。

Our tea products are very popular for their superb quality. Our Grade-A Jasmine Tea has won international high quality medals.

我方经营的茶叶以其优异的品质深受广大消费者的喜爱。我方的一级茉莉花茶荣获国际优质奖。

3. establishing trade relations 建立业务关系

【知识点】在相互了解的基础上，公司双方的经营范围一致，可以确定贸易对象，建立业务关系。建立业务关系可促进双方密切合作，顺利进行交易。

【技能训练句型】

As your tea products fall within the range of our business activities, we would like to express our wish to set up trade relations with your corporation.

由于贵方的茶叶产品与我方的经营范围一致，我们愿意同贵公司建立业务关系。

Your desire to establish business relations coincides with ours. Building up direct business relations between our companies will be to our mutual benefit.

你方想同我方建立业务关系的愿望与我方是一致的。建立直接的业务关系，双方将互利互惠。

We are willing to establish direct business relationship with your company on the basis of equality and mutual benefit.

我们愿在平等互利的基础上与贵公司建立直接的业务关系。

We shall be pleased to enter into business relations with you.

我们很乐意同贵公司建立业务关系。

4. sending catalogues and samples 寄产品目录和样品等

【知识点】为了进一步了解对方经营的产品具体品种，需要对方提供附图目录等材料，寻找合适的品种、型号或规格。对方如有产品的网站信息可要求提供网址，可免去邮寄。如光看图片不能了解产品的品质，还需邮寄样品。

【技能训练句型】

In order to let you have a general idea of all our products, I am going to send you by air our latest catalogue for your perusal.

为了让贵方对我方的产品有个大概的认识，特打算航空邮寄我方最新附图目录，以供细阅。

Please send some samples of your teabags and new tea products.

请寄一些袋泡茶和茶叶新产品的样品。

It would be very helpful if you could send us your catalogue or brochures and give us your website for our further study.

如果你能寄给我们产品目录或小册子并提供网址供我们进一步研究将很有帮助。

5. expressing wishes 表达愿望

【知识点】在信件最后，表达对今后贸易的希望和期待。

【技能训练句型】

Our mutual understanding and cooperation will certainly result in more business.
我们之间的相互了解与合作必将促成今后的生意。
We look forward to trading with you and exchange of needed goods.
希望与贵方开展贸易，互通有无。

Part D Practice

I. Complete the Following Dialogues

A: Good afternoon. Import Department. Can I help you?

B: Hello, Can I ___1___ to Mr. Smith?

A: This is ___2___. Who is calling?

B: This is Pan Guoqiang speaking. We have obtained your name and address by ___3___ up in the Trade Directory.

A: Oh, hello. May I ask you what ___4___ of business you are ___5___?

B: I am glad to introduce my company to you as a ___6___ one, ___7___ in glass products. Our main ___8___ are constructive glass and pile glassware.

A: Oh, I think some of them will be of ___9___ to us.

B: Great! As your glass products ___10___ within the range of our business activities, we are ___11___ to establish ___12___ business relationship with your esteemed company on the ___13___ of equality and mutual benefit.

A: That's a good ___14___. We always ___15___ to the principle of keeping the promise and honoring the contract.

II. Interaction Activities

Divide students into pairs. Students make short dialogues and role-play them.

Task 1

Asking for advice on how to communicate with businessmen.

Ask for and get the advice form each other politely and express the agreement or partial agreement. Use the following expressions:

(1) I hope you don't mind

(2) Could you give me some advice about...

(3) Get in touch

(4) From my point of view...

(5) To a certain degree, yes, but...

(6) I know what you mean but...

(7) What is your view about...

(8) If I were you...

(9) That's quite true.

Task 2

Talking about how to ask for sending samples politely.

Ask and get the advice each other and express the agreement or partial agreement. Use the following expressions:

(1) I need...

(2) What's your opinion about...

(3) Don't hesitate to...

(4) I agree with much of your idea but...

(5) Ask for samples

(6) True enough.

(7) What do you reckon I...?

(8) I'd like to suggest that...

(9) I don't entirely agree with you but...

III. Actual Practice

Work in pairs and role-play the conversation.

You work in a trade company. You are contacting the exporter in order to seek business opportunities. By what means can you successfully establish business relations?

Use the hints below to practice with your partner:

(1) Inform the seller how you get to know the firm.

(2) Tell your intention.

(3) Tell the line of your business.

(4) Get some more information from prospective client.

(5) Express the desire to establish business relationship.

(6) Ask for catalogues and samples.

IV. Creative Discussion

The teacher divides the class into groups, and the students make a discussion with their partners and share their opinions with other pairs.

Topic:

Suppose you are working in an export department. You and your colleagues are desirous of seeking new business opportunities.

There are many channels to find the business opportunities. Discuss which one you prefer and show the reasons. If possible, discuss the advantages and disadvantages of each way.

V. Debate

The students are expected to give their own opinions freely on the following topic.

Topic:

Which channel is the best to find potential clients?

Chapter 3 Making Inquiries

Learning Objectives
Upon completion of this chapter, you will be able to

- understand that inquiries are made to seek the supply of products, services and information.

- learn the ways of making general inquiries and specific inquiries.

- perform the functions of skills of making inquiries.

- conduct the activities related to the theme of making inquiries.

课文范读

Part A　Situational Dialogue

 Communicative Scene 1

Making General Inquiries

(*Mrs. Hanna, the Import Manager of Robinson Textiles Import Company, is making a general inquiry with Textiles Limited Corporation.*)

Hanna: Good afternoon. Is this Textiles Limited Corporation?

Xue: Yes, it is. May I help you?

Hanna: This is Anna Hanna from Robinson Textiles Import Company. We have seen your advertisement in China Daily. Your textile products in the advertisement look really marvelous.

Xue: Oh, really?

Hanna: We are importers of fabrics. We have made a market research and found a promising market in our country for the textiles you listed in your advertisement.[1] So we are considering to broaden our business in Chinese market.[2]

Xue: Um. What a great idea! May I ask what kinds of products you are interested in?

Hanna: We are interested in the piece goods and made-up goods.[3]

Xue: Er, you know, we are a large textiles manufacturing corporation turning out high quality dyed fabric, printed fabric and 100% cotton garments.[4] We are making a variety of garments such as jackets, shirts, skirts, pants, jeans, pajamas and sport suits for men, women and children.[5]

Hanna: Wow! That's really something![6]

Xue: After China entered the WTO, our textiles have become more and more competitive in the world market.

Hanna: This is the reason we are getting in touch with you.

Xue: We are willing to enter into business relations with your firm.

Hanna: I think so, too. I believe that our trade relationship will be expanded continuously through our joint efforts.

Xue: I couldn't agree more.

Hanna: Would you please send us catalogues and necessary information for our reference?

Xue: Certainly. We are going to send you illustrated catalogues and some free samples by EMS for your consideration.

Hanna: We shall appreciate it if you will give us your price list for these garments.

Xue: OK. We are glad to do that. But these prices are subject to our final confirmation because the prices of raw materials keep rising recently.⁷

Hanna: Oh, goodness! We hope they are reasonable prices.

Xue: Don't worry, Mrs. Hanna. Our prices are still very competitive in spite of the rising prices of raw materials.

Hanna: I wouldn't mind knowing about your normal export terms.

Xue: We usually make an offer on basis of FOB on our price list.⁸ If we know your destination, we'll quote CIF or CFR as the clients required.

Hanna: Fine. Do you allow commission?

Xue: No problem.

Hanna: OK. Let's get the ball rolling.⁹

 Communicative Scene 2

Making Specific Inquiries

(*Mr. Penn, who comes from a Canadian Import Company, is making a specific inquiry.*)

Penn: Miss Yang, I'd like to thank you for your leaflet together with the sample which I received on Monday.

Yang: My pleasure.

Penn: We are particularly interested in well-favored electric irons.

Yang: Very good. Which model do you prefer?

Penn: We are in the market for your Model E013 and Model E016. Its power source is AC 220V, 1000W, but I am not clear about the type of steam generation.

Yang: They are drip type.

Penn: Do you have them in stock now?¹⁰

Yang: Yeah. They are available for export.

Penn: That is exciting! As Thanksgiving Day is drawing near, we need these products urgently. When will you be able to make shipment for these goods?

Yang: Don't worry. We'll make prompt shipment according to your requirement.

Penn: Fine. I'll be grateful to you for quoting me competitive prices CIF Vancouver, for these two models.

Yang: Okay. But could you tell me the quantity you want so that we can work out the quotation for you?

Penn: We are going to order 100,000 sets of electric irons, that is, 50,000 pieces each of the two models.¹¹

Yang: I see. The total electric irons you need are 100,000 sets.

Penn: Exactly.

Yang: I guess you must have noticed the soaring prices of raw materials in the world market recently.

Penn: Oh goodness! I hope you're not kidding. Can you keep competitive prices?

Yang: I'm not going to kid you. However, in view of our newly established good relationship, we'll keep our prices unchanged in spite of the rising prices of raw material.

Penn: I'm delighted to hear it. By the way, could you kindly send us a Proforma Invoice for electric irons?

Yang: Oh, you need Proforma Invoice?

Penn: Yeah. It will enable us to make the necessary preliminary import arrangements.

Yang: I understand.

Penn: We're looking forward to your reply to our inquiry soon.

Yang: I will.

 Communicative Scene 3

A First Inquiry

(*Mr. Hart is making a first inquiry to the supplier whom he has not previously dealt with.*)

SEC: Good afternoon. Furniture Enterprise Company.

Hart: Hello. Could I speak to Mr. Fu, please?

SEC: Just a sec., please.

Fu: Hello, Fu speaking.

Hart: This is Hart speaking. Chamber of Commerce in our country has recommended your name and firm to us. We are glad to note that you specialize in handling new types of furniture.

Fu: Yes, that's good. What particular items do you need?

Hart: We are very interested in your rattan furniture.

Fu: Good. We have been in this line for 25 years. We are making new designs of wood, rattan, bamboo and wicker furniture and products. Our rattan furniture enjoys good reputation in the world market.

Hart: Yes, I believe your rattan furniture may find a ready market in our area.[12]

Fu: I feel the same way.[13]

Hart: We shall be pleased if you quote us competitive prices in Eurocurrency CFR EMP for rattan furniture.

Fu: Thank you for your inquiry.

Hart: We'd like to stress the importance of the competitive prices since our customers are very sensitive to the prices.[14]

Fu: We assure you that the prices we quote are competitive enough to induce business.

Hart: Thanks. If the prices are workable, we are planning to place a trial order with you for the first time.[15]

Fu: I see.

Hart: The large orders will follow when our clients see your rattan furniture.

Fu: I hope so.

Hart: Could you do me a favor by sending us more copies of your relevant brochures?[16] We need them to send out to our customers.

Fu: Certainly.

Hart: We are expecting your offer.

Fu: We'll calculate and let you know as soon as possible.

Words and Expressions

1. dyed fabric		色布
2. printed fabric		花布
3. garment	n.	服装，cotton garments 全棉服装
4. pajama	n.	睡衣
5. FOB (Free on Board)		船上交货价
6. quotation	n.	报价
7. CIF (Cost, Insurance and Freight)		成本加保险费和运费
8. CFR (Cost and Freight)		成本加运费
9. leaflet	n.	活叶说明
10. brochure	n.	小册子
11. well-favored		漂亮的，吸引人的
12. electric iron		电熨斗
13. steam generation		蒸汽发生方式
14. drip type		滴下式
15. Proforma Invoice		形式发票
16. preliminary arrangements		预先安排
17. SEC (Secretary)		秘书
18. EMP (Europe Main Port)		欧洲主要港口
19. rattan furniture		藤制家具
20. wicker	n.	柳条
	adj.	柳条的
21. calculate	v.	计算
22. fabric	n.	织物，布

Notes

1. We have made a market research and found a promising market in our country for the textiles you listed in your advertisement.
   近来我们做了市场调查，发现你方刊登的纺织品广告在我国市场前景广阔。

promising market 市场前景广阔

相关表达：

booming market 市场繁荣

brisk market 市场景气

bull market 多头市场，市场行情看涨

bullish market 牛市

declining market 市场衰退

depressed market 市场萧条

dull market 市场呆滞

2. We are considering to broaden our business in Chinese market.

我们想把生意扩大到中国市场。

① broaden *vt. & vi.* 扩大，拓宽，扩大影响。主要指拓宽、增长（知识）等。

The college students broadened their experience by taking part-time job.

大学生通过兼职工作增长经验。

Good films broaden / widen our outlook / mind / horizon.

好影片使我们视野开阔。

② broad *adj.* 宽广的

The two countries make efforts to pursue stronger political trust, broader practical cooperation and closer cultural exchanges.

两国要努力夯实政治互信，扩大务实合作，密切人文交流。

③ widen *vt. & vi.* 使变宽，扩大

但 widen the opportunity（扩大机会）不能用 broaden the opportunity。

④ expand *v.* 扩展。主要指范围、数量、重要性、尺寸、体积方面的扩大。

We discuss the plan to expand business. 我们商议扩展业务的计划。

3. We are interested in the piece goods and made-up goods.

我们对布匹和纺织成品很感兴趣。

① made-up goods 本文指纺织成品

② made-up 性格，气质；组成，构成；化妆（品）

4. We are a large textiles manufacturing corporation turning out high quality dyed fabric, printed fabric and 100% cotton garments.

我们是一家大型纺织品生产公司，生产高质量的色布、花布和全棉服装。

① turn out 生产，证实，发觉是，原来是，关闭

② manufacture / produce / make 生产

The survey shows that Chinese families prefer electrical appliances turned out by Chinese companies rather than foreign-made ones.

调查表明中国家庭喜欢购买国产家电而不是国外制造的产品。

③ to be found to be 证实是，发觉是

That kind gentleman turned out to be an industry analyst.

那个慈祥的绅士原来是个行业分析家。

④ turn off 关闭

Please make sure to turn off the computer before you leave.

在离开时请务必关机。

5. We are making a variety of garments such as jackets, shirts, skirts, pants, jeans, pajamas and sport suits for men, women and children.

    我们生产多种男女服装和童装，例如：夹克衫、衬衫、裙装、裤子、牛仔服、睡衣和运动装。

    a (considerable, great, wide) variety of 品种繁多

    相关表达：

    various kinds of

    all kinds of

    a range of

6. Wow! That's really something!

    哇，真了不起！

    ① be something 了不起，重要

    口语中something 表示重要的人物或事情（非正式用法）

    He thinks he is something but actually he is nothing.

    他自以为是个重要的人物，可是其实没啥了不起。

7. But these prices are subject to our final confirmation because the prices of raw material keep rising recently.

    但由于近期原料价格不断上涨，这些价格应以我方最后确认为准。

    ① be subject to 依……而定的，以……为准

    The price of the export commodity is subject to the fluctuation exchange rate.

    出口商品的价格视外汇波动而决定。

8. We usually make an offer on basis of FOB on our price list.

    我们在价格单上通常报FOB价格。

    ① on (the) basis of FOB/on FOB basis 在FOB的基础上

    It is our usual practice to do business on the basis of L/C.

    在信用证的基础上做生意是我方的惯例。

9. Let's get the ball rolling.

    那就开始干吧。

    ① Get the ball rolling. 这是一句谚语，意思是开始某事并使之运作起来。

    Let's get the ball rolling on the performance. 让我们开始表演吧。

    一旦有了良好的开端，则可使用Keep the ball rolling表示继续的意愿。

10. Do you have them in stock now?

    你现在有现货吗？

    ① in stock 现货，库存

    The new type of computer is out of stock, but the similar one is in stock.

    这种新型电脑缺货，但类似的型号有现货。

    相似词组：

    from stock 现货供应

    come into (to) stock 库存有货

a stock of 一批……现货

out of stock 缺货，无货

no stock on hand 手头无存货

11. We are going to order 100,000 sets of electric irons, that is, 50,000 pieces each of the two models.

我们打算订100,000台电熨斗，即两种型号各50,000台。

① that is 即，也就是

Could I have your firm price quotation CFR Oslo, that is, the final and firm offer?

何时能得到贵方到奥斯陆（挪威首都，港口）的CFR实盘，即最后一次有效的报盘？

② 同义词namely, specifically, that is to say 即，那就是说，明确地

12. I believe your rattan furniture may find a ready market in our area.

我相信贵方的藤制家具在我国市场会旺销。

① find a ready market 旺销，畅销

② be in the market for 想购买

We are in the market for your electronic appliances.

我们想购买贵方的家用电器。

13. I feel the same way.

我有同感。

当你完全同意别人的观点，可以用I feel the same way. 这句话，不但让你避免把同样的话再重复一次，帮你省了不少口舌，还可以让对方感受到自己的意见被尊重。

14. We'd like to stress the important of the competitive prices since our customers are very sensitive to the prices.

需要特别强调的是竞争性的价格，因为我方客户对价格特别敏感。

sensitive

（1）敏感

She is sensitive to what people think of her.

她对别人如何想她很敏感。

（2）易波动的（价格，行情）

sensitive price 价格波动

sensitive stocks 行情起落的股票

15. If the prices are workable, we are planning to place a trial order with you for the first time.

若价格可行，我们准备首次向贵方下试订单。

① place a trial order with sb. 向某人下试订单

② place an initial order with sb. 初次向某人下订单

16. Could you do me a favor by sending us more copies of your relevant brochures?

能否帮忙寄上更多相关宣传小册子，以便我们分发给客户？

请人帮忙比较正式而礼貌的表达，常用Could you do me a favor?/ Could you give me a hand? / May I ask a favor of you?

有时候请别人帮忙不太好意思说时，可以婉转地说：

Could you do me a little favor？能不能帮我一个小忙？

Part B Practical Key Sentences

1. asking for some information in a formal way

I wouldn't mind knowing about your normal export terms.

我想知道你们一般采取什么出口条件?

"I wouldn't mind ..."是客套语,婉转表达本人的想法、愿望和请求。常用于表达想获取某种信息。译成"我希望了解……""我想要……""要是知道……就好了"。

I wouldn't mind learning the facts. 我想了解真相。

替换表达:

May I ask what kinds of products you are interested in?

I wonder which model you prefer.

I'd particularly like to find out the correct answer.

"I wonder if ..."表示说话人以试探的口气婉转表达本人的想法和请求。当不知道对方是否愿意提供某种信息时,动词用过去时或过去进行时,试探性更强。

I wonder if you can give me some idea about the purpose of Proforma Invoice now.

您现在可否告知形式发票的用途。

I was wondering if you could send me some information about your credit standing now.

不知您现在能否发送一些关于贵方资信的信息。

替换表达:

I wonder if you could give me a rough price of the oil in your market now.

I was wondering if you could tell us about the plan of this business project now.

2. expressing curiosity in an informal way

I am most curious about the new sales plan.

我非常想知道新的销售计划。

好奇是人之常情,可以询问想了解的事情,但不要涉及别人的隐私,如年龄、婚姻、工资和财产等隐私。

替换表达:

Hey, I wish I knew more about your trip.

I could hardly wait to know the result.

3. show interest

May I ask what kinds of products you are interested in?

请问您对什么产品感兴趣?

We take interest in Internet of Things Engineering.

我们对物联网工程很感兴趣。

We are in the market for your high quality products.

我们欲购贵方高质量的产品。

Are you particularly interested in cloud computing?

你们对云计算特别感兴趣吗？

试用下列短语造句：

take (an) interest in

show (an) interest in

have an interest in

hold sb.'s interest

in the interest(s) of

with interest

be keen on

be crazy about

4. **show no interest**

Nothing interests me less than going shopping.

我最不感兴趣的就是逛街买东西。

Business management isn't all that interesting as far as I am concerned.

工商管理对我来说没意思。

替换表达：

find ... rather uninteresting

lose interest

have no interest in

have no interest to

5. **express thanks in a formal way**

We shall be pleased if you quote us competitive prices in Eurocurrency CFR EMP for rattan furniture.

如果您能报藤制家具欧洲主要港口成本加运费有竞争性的价格，我们会感到十分高兴。

本句型是传统商务活动时，正式表达谢意的常见方式。

替换表达：

I'll be grateful to you for quoting me competitive prices CIF Vancouver, for these two models.

We shall appreciate it if you will give us your pricelist for these garments.

I'll be obliged if you would give the matter your close attention.

It would be appreciated if you would give us some catalogues for our reference.

I'd like to express my gratitude for your help.

6. **express disagreement in a direct way with familiar persons**

I hope you are not kidding. Can you keep competitive prices?

我想您不会开玩笑吧。能保持具有竞争力的价格吗？

替换表达：

Are you kidding?

You must be joking!

Sorry, I can't go along with your view.

on the contrary

Do you really mean it?

Part C Integration of Theory and Practice

【知识点】询盘是国际贸易的重要环节之一，买方在交易之初需要了解许多与贸易相关的信息，因此，一般由买方不受约束地提出询盘。询盘可通过面谈、电话、电子邮件等方式进行。询盘分为一般（普通）询盘和具体询盘。

1. general inquiries 一般（普通）询盘

【知识点】买方告知对某类商品感兴趣，通过询盘，简明扼要地向卖方了解一般的商品信息和生产经营情况。

【技能训练句型】

We take interest in Chinese electromobile.
我们中国生产的电动汽车很感兴趣。
买方进一步询问有关交易的信息。
I wouldn't mind knowing about your normal export terms.
我想知道你们一般采取什么出口条件？
Do you allow commission?
可以付佣金吗？

2. specific inquiries 具体询盘

【知识点】买方具体询问某种产品，不仅具体询问商品名称（name of the commodity），而且通过具体询盘，向卖方了解商品规格（specifications）、装船期（time of shipment）、付款方式（terms of payment）等细节。买方可告知购买的数量（quantity），请求卖方报价（make an offer）。

【技能训练句型】

We are in the market for your backup powers.
我们欲购买充电宝。
When will you be able to make shipment for these goods?
贵方何时可以装运？
I'll be grateful to you for quoting me competitive prices CIF Vancouver, for these two models.
请报这两种型号的CIF温哥华竞争性价格，我们将不胜感激。

3. a first inquiry 初次询盘

【知识点】首次向新客户询价，为了避免唐突，最好告知对方通过何种方式认识对方，并介绍自己公司情况，以便双方了解彼此的经营情况以及产品情况，以寻找商机。

【技能训练句型】

Chamber of Commerce in our country has recommended your name and firm to us. We are glad to note that you specialize in handling new types of furniture.
我国的商会把您的大名和公司介绍给我们。我们高兴地注意到贵方专门经营新型家具。

4. inquiry guide 询盘指南

【知识点】初次询盘既可以作一般询盘，也可具体询盘。

为了更好地了解对方经营的产品或分发给潜在的客户，询盘可要求索取商品资料，如附图目录（illustrated catalogues）、报价单（price-list）、宣传小册子（brochures）以及样品（samples）等。

【技能训练句型】

Would you please send us catalogues and necessary information for our reference?

请寄给我们产品目录和所需信息，供我们参考。

Could you do me a favor by sending us more copies of your relevant brochures to us? We need them to send out to our customers.

可否帮忙寄上更多相关宣传小册子，以便我们分发给客户？

【知识点】询盘要具体（specific）、简洁（brief）和得体（to the point）。虽然询盘无法律约束，但不要轻易许下订货承诺，以免未订购而引起麻烦。但可加上某种条件，若卖方给予价格优惠等，将向其订货。

【技能训练句型】

If the prices are workable, we are planning to place a trial order with you for the first time.

若价格可行，我们准备首次向贵方下试订单。

【知识点】卖方对询盘的反应要快（prompt）、诚恳（sincere）和有助（helpful）。详细告知经营情况和具体的产品，可了解买方的具体要求，尽快计算出合理的价格，促使交易获得成功。

【技能训练句型】

We'll calculate and let you know as soon as possible.

我们计算后尽快通知您。

5. proforma Invoice　形式发票

【知识点】在国际贸易中，形式发票是一种为了形式而发送的发票，形式发票的内容可与商业发票相同，常包含商品名称、规格、数量、价格等，但形式发票的名称为Proforma Invoice而不是Invoice或Commercial Invoice。形式发票与商业发票主要区别在于对买卖双方皆无约束力。

形式发票的主要作用：

（1）进口方申请进口许可证等；

（2）办理进口手续；

（3）作为正式报价。

注意：并不是每笔交易都要形式发票，其实大部分交易不需要形式发票。可在形式发票上注明有效期。

Part D　Practice

I. Complete the Following Dialogues

(1)

Fill in the blank with the proper words.

A: Mr. Wang, we take ___1___ in your electric meters.

B: Fine, we ___2___ out a considerable ___3___ of electric meters. They are both good in

____4____ and reasonable in price. Our company has ____5____ a market research and found it may be a promising ____6____ in your area.

A: That is why we are thinking to ____7____ our trade in Chinese market.
B: Yeah, indeed.
A: We would like to make an ____8____ for detecting instruments.
B: Which price term do you prefer?
A: We'd like you to ____9____ the price CIF Melbourne.
B: OK, we'll do it on the ____10____ of CIF Melbourne.

(2)

Fill in the blanks with the following useful expressions.

keep rising	interested in	in view of	wouldn't mind
place an order	in the market	in spite of	a great pleasure to
firm offers	conclude business	be helpful	subject to
in particular	get the ball rolling	from stock	

A: It is ____1____ have the opportunity of meeting you. I do hope to ____2____ with you.
B: What is it ____3____ you are ____4____ ?
A: We are ____5____ for your jackets and shirts for young men. Can you supply the goods soon after we ____6____ ?
B: I believe the jackets and shirts for young men can be supplied ____7____ recently.
A: Good. Er, I ____8____ knowing price terms of your products.
B: Thank you for your inquiry. Here are our FOB price lists. We hope they will ____9____ to you.
A: Are all prices on the list ____10____ ?
B: No, these prices are ____11____ our final confirmation because nowadays the prices of raw material ____12____ greatly.
A: Can I have your lowest prices?
B: Sure, ____13____ our new established good relationship, we'll keep our prices unchanged ____14____ the rising prices of raw material.
A: I am glad to hear it. Let's ____15____ immediately.

II. Interaction Activities

Divide students into pairs. Make short dialogues and role-play them.

Task 1

Inquire about the availability of the air conditioners.
The following expressions should be included in your dialogue:
(1) I wouldn't mind knowing about
(2) enjoy good reputation
(3) in the market for

(4) inquire about

(5) that is

(6) in stock

(7) out of stock

(8) Do you really mean it?

(9) Could you do me a favor by ...

(10) We shall appreciate it if you will ...

Task 2

Make an inquiry about the prices.

Use all of the following expressions in your dialogue:

(1) inquiry list

(2) You will find that the required items including ...

(3) I was wondering if ...

(4) competitive prices

(5) stress the important of

(6) find ... attractive

(7) place an order

(8) price list

III. Actual Practice

Work in pairs and role-play the conversation.

Suppose you show interest in importing mobile phones. You may make a specific inquiry for the following items with a new trade company:

(1) the specification of mobile phones

(2) competitive price

(3) superior quality

(4) terms of price

(5) shipment time

IV. Creative Discussion

The teacher divides the class into groups, and the Students make a discussion with their partners and share their opinions with other pairs.

Topic:

Inquiries are usually made by the importers without engagement to get the information about the commodity to be ordered. prices is one of the most important items to be inquired. Ordering large quantity usually makes prices cheaper. Some buyers may exaggerate their quantity for lower prices and promise to make substantial orders in order to get the lowest quotation.

Do you think it is a good way to get reasonable prices? Please discuss the issue with the members in your group.

Chapter 4 Business Appointment and Arrangement

Learning Objectives
Upon completion of this chapter, you will be able to

- make appointments with your clients.
- know how to make arrangements for your clients.
- make friends with your clients.
- know the importance of business appointment and arrangement.

课文范读

Part A Situational Dialogue

 Communicative Scene 1

Making a Business Appointment

(Miss Lin is calling Mr. Wade to make an appointment at Canton Fair.)

Lin: Hello, Mr. Wade. This is Lin, calling from Fuzhou, China.

Wade: Hello, Miss Lin. Pleased to hear from you.

Lin: As Canton Fair is approaching, I'd like to know if you have any plan to visit the fair this spring.

Wade: Yes, we are planning to visit the fair. We would appreciate it if you could meet us there.

Lin: I'm eager to meet you because we have a lot of things to discuss with you face to face.[1] Do you have any opening? Could you tell me the schedule of your visit so that we can make arrangement beforehand?[2]

Wade: Yes. We'll be there from April 14 to 25. What time would suit you?

Lin: We think we will be in Guangzhou during April 16~18. We are expecting you any time during that period.

Wade: Good. Would 6:00 p.m., April 17 be all right with you?

Lin: OK. Let's make it 6:00 p.m., April 17 in your hotel lobby. Have you booked your hotel in Guangzhou?[3]

Wade: Not yet. Could you do us a favor and book a hotel for 12 days from April 14?

Lin: Yes, of course. How many rooms should we book for you? Any special requirements for the hotel?

Wade: Nothing special. My colleague Mr. Brandon will go with me. So please make reservations for two standard rooms for us.

Lin: We will make a reservation for you immediately.

Wade: Oh, please book the hotel with convenient transportation to the Fair, because we are not familiar with the city and we don't want to spend too much time on the way back and forth everyday.[4]

Lin: Please don't worry about it. We will try our best. I think Overseas Chinese Hotel is a nice option.[5] It is within walking distance to the fair. You don't have to take any taxi, shuttle or other vehicles.

Wade: It is very considerate of you to do so.

Lin: That's all right. What projects should we discuss this time?

Wade: We'd like to talk about BBQ Oven, Grill Steel and BBQ set. Please bring all the related samples if possible.

Lin: Sure. Anything else?

Wade: We will bring some samples of new items, such as cutlery, wine bottle openers, etc. As you know, we are dealing with all kinds of kitchenware and bathroom appliances. We hope the cooperation between us will be expanded step by step.

Lin: I'm glad to hear that. I'll call you again when the reservation is made.

Wade: Thank you for calling, Miss Lin. Bye!

Lin: Thank you! Bye.

 Communicative Scene 2

Making Changes for the Appointment

(Mr. Wade is calling back to Miss Lin for the change of appointment.)

Wade: Hello! Miss Lin, this is Wade from Mexico City.

Lin: Hi! Mr. Wade. Nice to hear from you again.

Wade: I appreciated very much your effort for hotel reservation in Overseas Chinese Hotel. However, I'm terribly sorry to inform you that we have to cancel the reservation.

Lin: Is anything wrong? Are you going to cancel your trip to China?

Wade: No, no. <u>Our visiting itinerary remains the same.</u>⁶ The delegation from our country will stay in Garden Hotel. We prefer to stay with all the members of our delegation.

Lin: Got it. It's no problem. I'll cancel your reservation.

Wade: <u>Thank you all the same and I'm very sorry for the inconvenience caused by us.</u>⁷ I apologize for that.

Lin: Not at all. Shall we meet at 6:00 p.m., April 17 in the lobby of Garden Hotel as planned?

Wade: I am afraid I've to postpone our appointment because of something unexpected.

Lin: No worries. Let's say 7:30 p.m., all right?

Wade: <u>It's a date.</u>⁸

Lin: Why not have dinner together? We'd like to invite you to dinner in the Garden Hotel. We can have a discussion while we are having dinner.

Wade: It's very kind of you. By the way, does your company have a display stand in Canton Fair?

Lin: <u>Naturally.</u>⁹ You may see our new products during the fair.

Wade: Um, who is going to take care of the business and production of our orders while you are absent? <u>Please make sure our products are shipped without delay because they are strongly seasonal goods.</u>¹⁰ Even a little delay will cause big trouble.

Lin: My colleagues will take care of the orders. I'll stay in Guangzhou for only 3 days. It is only a one-hour flight from Guangzhou to our city. <u>I guarantee that your orders will be fulfilled in time for delivery.¹¹

Wade: Thanks a lot. My mobile phone number is 555-753-9900. It is on 24 hours. You can call me when necessary.

Lin: Fine. My mobile phone number is 013905622789.

Wade: Let's meet in Guangzhou. Have a nice day.

Lin: Have a nice day. Bye.

 Communicative Scene 3

Making Arrangements

(*Miss Xue is making arrangements for Mr. More.*)

More: Hello, Miss Xue. How are you?

Xue: I'm fine. Thank you! What can I do for you?

More: Yes, as you know, I'm going to visit Canton Fair next week. I'll stay there for more than two weeks. During the first and second sections, there is a break of 4 days. I may have nothing to do but stay in the hotel as I have been in Guangzhou many times.

Xue: Are you going to travel somewhere else?

More: Yes, you are right. I am planning to bring my wife with me this time.

Xue: Is this your wife's first trip to China?

More: Yes.

Xue: What kinds of places are you going to visit?

More: I don't have any idea as I always stay in Guangzhou for business though I have been to China so many times.

Xue: Oh. I understood the situation now. As you know, China is a large country and 4 days is not long enough for travel in China. If you and your wife would like to have a relaxing break, I suggest you to visit Hainan Island or Guilin City, where you will enjoy the beauty of nature.¹² If you are interested in historic sites, you can fly to Xi'an, I suppose.¹³

More: Could you tell me more about the island? We are from the inland country. We prefer to stay on the island during that time.¹⁴

Xue: OK. Hainan Island is the second largest island in China. Its tropical weather is mild and nice during April. You will enjoy the sunshine on the seashore and have fun there.¹⁵

More: It sounds marvelous. How can we get there?

Xue: You can get there by air. It is only about an hour's trip by air. If you agree, I can make the arrangement with a travel agent, which is the most convenient way to make your trip easy and comfortable.

More: It's really a good idea. Could you make a reservation for us? All the expenses will be on us.

Xue: No problem, it is my pleasure to help you. I'll send you an e-mail for the itinerary when it's fixed after I make the arrangement with the travel agency.

More: I can't thank you enough.

Xue: Please don't mention it. You are always welcome. Bye.

More: So long.

Words and Expressions

1.	beforehand	adv.	预先
2.	lobby	n.	门厅，门廊
3.	shuttle	n.	短程穿梭运输工具（如往返展览会和宾馆之间的大巴）
4.	convenient	adj.	便利，方便
	inconvenience	n.	不方便，麻烦
5.	option	n.	选择
6.	BBQ oven		烧烤炉
7.	grill steel		烧烤架
8.	BBQ set		烧烤用具
9.	cutlery	n.	（西餐的）刀叉餐具
10.	kitchenware	n.	厨房用品
11.	bathroom appliances		洁具
12.	itinerary	n.	旅程，旅行计划
13.	delegation	n.	代表团
14.	display stand		摊位
15.	guarantee	vt. & n.	保证，担保
16.	fulfill	vt.	完成，履行，满足
17.	release	vt. & n.	释放，解放，免除
	have a releasing break		有休闲的间隙
18.	island	n.	岛屿
	inland	n.	内陆，内地，国内
		adj.	内陆的，国内的
		adv.	向内地
19.	tropical	adj.	热带的

Notes

1. I'm eager to meet you because we have a lot of things to discuss with you face to face.

   我迫切希望见到您，因为我们有许多事情要和您面谈。

   face to face

（1）面谈，直接交流

The manufacturers are talking face to face with the consumers.

厂家与消费者正在进行直接交流。

（2）直接面对

Your financial investment option depends on whether you are face to face with a bullish or bearish market.

你的金融投资选择取决于你是直接面对牛市还是熊市。

2. Could you tell me the schedule of your visit so that we can make arrangement beforehand?

能否告知您的日程，以便我们预先做出安排？

make arrangement beforehand 预先做出安排

beforehand

（1）预先

Here is a copy of itinerary we have worked out for you beforehand.

这是我们为你预先拟定的活动日程安排。

（2）提前

The buyer have to be beforehand with his payment because he needs his goods urgently.

因为买主急需产品，不得已提前支付货款。

2. back and forth *adv.* 来回地，前前后后地，来来去去地

同义短语：

backward and forward

to and fro

from side to side

3. Have you booked your hotel in Guangzhou?

您在广州的宾馆预定了吗？

① book the hotel 预订房间

Make a reservation for a room overlooking the sea, please.

请预定一间临海的房间。

He booked a standard room for business fair.

他为参加交易会预定标准房。

4. Oh, please book the hotel with convenient transportation to the Fair, because we are not familiar with the city and we don't want to spend too much time on the way back and forth everyday.

噢，请订方便去交易会的宾馆，因为我们对广州不熟悉，不想每天在来回的路上花太多的时间。

① convenient transportation 便捷的交通

② convenient food 方便食品

③ convenient locations 便利地点

5. I think Overseas Chinese Hotel is a nice option. It is within walking distance to the fair.

华侨饭店就是很好的选择，步行就可到达交易会。

① option 选项，选择权，买卖的特权

There are quite a lot options open to me.

我有很多选择。

He has no option but to apply for a mortgage loan.

他别无选择，只好申请抵押贷款。

② within walking distance 步行距离，步行能达到的地方，在……附近

China Council for the promotion of International Trade is within walking distance.

中国国际贸易促进委员会就在附近。

within touch 在……能达到的地方，在……的附近，可以接近的

6. Our visiting itinerary remains the same.

我们的访问日程不变。

As a special accommodation, our discount will remain unchanged for you.

作为特殊照顾，我们给你的折价保持不变。

7. Thank you all the same and I'm very sorry for the inconvenience caused by us. I apologize for that.

太感谢了，对此造成的不便深表歉意，我为此道歉。

① be terribly /very sorry for 深表歉意

I'm terribly sorry to inform you that we have to cancel the reservation.

我非常抱歉地通知你，我们不得不取消这个预订。

② apologize 道歉

No reason to apologize.

不必道歉。

8. It's a date.

那就说定了。（非正式口语用法）

9. naturally *adv.* 必然地，自然地

表示肯定的用语。

同义词：surely，certainly，of course，as expected

10. Please make sure our products are shipped without delay because they are strongly seasonal goods.

请一定保证我们的货物按时发运，因为这些产品的季节性很强。

① without delay 立即

同义词：at once，soon

② strongly seasonal goods 季节性很强的产品

11. I guarantee that your orders will be fulfilled in time for delivery.

我保证你们的订单会按时完工并发送。

① guarantee *n. & vt.* 保证，担保

He guaranteed that he would keep appointments unchanged.

他保证会守约。

② fulfill *vt.* 履行，执行

fulfill the orders 按时完成订单

fulfill the task 完成任务

fulfill the plan 完成计划

China will fulfill its plan to finish building a moderately prosperous society in all respects and realize the first centenary goal.

中国将全面建成小康社会，实现第一个百年奋斗目标。

12. If you and your wife would like to have a relaxing break, I suggest you to visit Hainan Island or Guilin City, where you will enjoy the beauty of nature.

    如果您和夫人喜欢轻松休闲，我建议去海南岛或者桂林，在那儿，你们可以享受美丽的大自然。

    ① have a releasing break 有个休闲的间隙

13. If you are interested in historic sites, you can fly to Xi'an, I suppose.

    如果你们对历史名胜感兴趣，我想可以去西安。

    historic sites 历史古迹

    注意以下二词的用法有所不同：

    ① historic *adj.* 历史上著名的，指历史上有重要意义的

    ② historical *adj.* 历史上的，有关历史的

14. We are from the inland country. We prefer to stay on the island.

    我们来自内陆国家，更愿意到岛上去。

    注意inland（内陆，内地，国内）和island（岛屿）的区别。

15. You will enjoy the sunshine on the seashore and have fun there.

    您可以在海边享受阳光，在那里玩得开心。

    ① have fun there 在那里玩得开心

    ② be fun 玩得开心

    Chinese historic sites are great fun. 中国历史古迹真好玩。

    You are no fun. 你这人真没劲。

Part B Practical Key Sentences

1. **making appointments**

    make appointments with your clients 与客户约会

    make arrangements for your clients 为客户作安排

    替换表达：

    We are having an appointment with our clients.

    The client asked me to reserve a single room with a private bath.

    They are making an arrangement for business visit.

2. **finding suitable time**

    询问对方，找到双方合适的时间。

    What time would suit you?

    你们什么时间方便呢?

    Would next Tuesday be convenient for you?

    下周二您方便吗?

替换表达：
What is the most convenient time for you?
What time is good for you?
We are expecting you any time during that period.
Would 10:00 a.m., July 1 be all right with you?
Let's say 7:30 p.m., all right?
How about meeting at 12 o'clock this afternoon?
Will you be available this evening, say from 7 to 11?

3. **expression of appreciation formally**

    It is very considerate of you to do so.
    你这样做考虑得真周到。
    That's most thoughtful of you.
    你想得真周到。
    替换表达：
    That's very nice of you.
    It's very kind of you.
    That was extremely good of you.
    That's very helpful of you to offer.

4. **got it**

    Got it.
    明白。（口语用法，可省略主语）
    替换表达：
    询问：You got it, didn't you?
    Do you take me?
    Do you understand?
    Are you there yet?
    回答：I see.
    That's clear to me now.
    I know.

5. **something unexpected**

    something修辞语的位置在something之后。
    I am afraid I have to postpone our appointment because of something unexpected.
    恐怕因未预料之事，我还得推迟约会。
    替换表达：
    The appointment has to be canceled for I have something important to do.
    Something urgent has come up. It looks as if our arrangement has to be changed.
    You still have something to do before we come to trade conclusion.

6. **All the expenses will be on us.**

    The dinner is on me today.
    今天这顿饭我请客。
    I'll get the check.

我来付账。

替换表达：

Let me pay this time.

I'll pay the bill.

The boarding and lodging per day is on our boss.

Part C Integration of Theory and Practice

【知识点】现代国际商务活动特别崇尚效率，讲究时间观念，每日商务活动通常经过精心安排，无论商务洽谈还是社交活动都事先约定好，随意拜访必然会碰钉子。

1. making appointment beforehand 预先约定

【知识点】（1）与客户或其他与业务有关的人之间进行的商务活动要预先约定，约会方式一般通过电话预约。预约时可开门见山，直奔主题，告诉约会的目的和计划，了解对方是否有兴趣见面。

【技能训练句型】

A: We are planning to visit the fair. We would appreciate it if you could meet us there.

我们打算参加这次广交会。如能在会上与你见面，我们将非常荣幸。

B: I'm eager to meet you because we'd like to exchange views with you about promoting sales face to face.

我也迫切希望见到您，因为我们想就推销事宜和您面谈，交换意见。

【知识点】（2）商务活动前常客气地征求意见，询问对方是否有空，找到双方合适的时间。

【技能训练句型】

Do you have any opening?

您是否有空？

Could you tell me the schedule of your visit so that we can make arrangement beforehand?

能告诉我您的日程安排，以便我们预先做出安排吗？

Will you be available this weekend?

您本周末有事吗？

Any time will suit me.

我随时有空。

【知识点】（3）若对方不愿意见面可婉言谢绝或告知原因。

【技能训练句型】

I am afraid all the appointments are filled.

恐怕全部预约时间都已排满。

I had a careful check with my secretary and suddenly realized I had another appointment beforehand.

我与秘书仔细核对了一下，发现我已有其他约会。

【知识点】（4）若对方表示忙，不能确定，可随后找时间再打电话约，也许会有收获。

【技能训练句型】

A: I suppose you would be free tomorrow.

我想您明天有空吧？

B: Yes, I can manage to come then.

有，到时候我一定来。

【知识点】（5）当对方表示愿意时，接着用商量的口气，约定合适的时间。

【技能训练句型】

Could you arrange it for us?

您能帮我们安排一下吗？

We'll be in Guangzhou during the fair. We are expecting you any time during that period.

我们将参加广交会，在此期间随时都可以与你会面。

Would 8:00 p.m., Oct. 18 be all right with you?

那10月18日晚上8点如何？

【知识点】（6）双方同意后，定下约会确定时间。

【技能训练句型】

OK. Let's make it 8:00 p.m., Oct. 18 in your hotel restaurant.

行，那就10月18日晚上8点在您下榻宾馆的餐厅见。

That's settled then.

就这么定了。

It's a date.

好的。

2. keeping an appointment 遵守约定

【知识点】预先约定完毕后，要遵守约定，按时到达，因迟到让人久等是不礼貌的。当然，过早到达影响别人也不可取。

如果约会时隔太久，不妨赴约前再确认一次。

【技能训练句型】

A: I am calling to confirm my appointment with you at 9:00 tomorrow morning.

我想与您确认明天上午的约会。

B: I'll be expecting you.

明天上午我等您。

A: I hope you could come at 7.

希望你7点能到。

B: I'll be there right on time.

我会准时到达。

3. changing or canceling an appointment 更改约会或取消约会

【知识点】因特殊情况，无法守约，应及时告诉对方，讲明失约的具体原因，表示道歉，请求谅解。征求是否更改约会时间或者取消约会。

【技能训练句型】

I am afraid I've to postpone our appointment because of something unexpected.

恐怕因未预料之事,我得推迟约会。

Sorry. I stood you up. I had something urgent so I had to cancel the appointment.

对不起,我失约了。我有紧急公务不得已取消约会。

A: I'm terribly sorry to inform you that we have to change the appointment. I am tied up recently.

十分抱歉,我们不得不更改约会时间,因为我最近抽不开身。

B: It doesn't matter.

没关系。

A: Can we make it another time?

其他时间行吗?

B: Let's say 7:30 p.m., all right?

那么,晚上7:30行吗?

A: It's a date. Sorry again for the inconvenience caused by us.

那就说定了。对此造成的不便再次深表歉意。

Part D Practice

I. Complete the Following Dialogues

Fill in the blanks with the following useful expressions.

a releasing break	Got it	keep him long
have an appointment	be filled	do me a favor
be convenient for	have a try	look at his schedule
something urgent	be available	Let's make it
be very kind of	be afraid	for business activities

　　Lee: Good morning. I'd like to have a business discussion with Mr. White.

Secretary: Do you ___1___ with Mr. White?

　　Lee: No, I ___2___ not. I have ___3___ to talk with him.

Secretary: But all the appointments ___4___.

　　Lee: Could you ___5___ and arrange it for me?

Secretary: It is very important to make an appointment beforehand ___6___.

　　Lee: ___7___. But it is really something unexpected.

Secretary: I'll ___8___ and have a ___9___.

　　Lee: I guarantee that I won't ___10___.

■ Business Appointment and Arrangement

Secretary: There is ___11___ at 11:30. I'll ask him if he ___12___ at the moment.

Lee: It ___13___ you to do so.

Secretary: Mr. White asks if the talking at 11:50 ___14___ you?

Lee: Fine. ___15___ at 11:50.

II. Interaction Activities

Task 1

Students role play and make a dialogue according to the situation.

Mr. Smith is going to pay a business visit to your company. Make a reservation for hotel and arrange everything well to make his visit comfortable.

Use the following expressions:

Role A	Role B
pay a business visit	book your hotel
make a hotel reservation	have your business schedule
be very considerate of	any special requirements
Just make reservation for	Let's fix it.
visit natural wonders	strongly recommend
a nice option	have a lot of fun there

Task 2

You have to break an appointment with your client because you have pressing business to attend to. You are calling the client to say sorry for the changing of time and explain the reason.

Use all of the following expressions in your dialogue:

(1) I'm terribly sorry

(2) keep the appointment with you

(3) What's up

(4) I have pressing business

(5) put off the meeting

(6) make it another time

(7) How about...

(8) be tied up then

(9) When is the most convenient time for you?

(10) be expecting

(11) be settled

III. Actual Practice

Students make up a dialogue according to the following situation with partners.

Mr. James is an Australian trader of chemical fertilizer. He is going to attend China Technology and Projects Fair and makes an appointment beforehand to meet Mr. Tao, director of the factory. Mr. Tao wants to know the itinerary in order to make arrangement. They discuss the purpose of the meeting and the proper time to meet.

IV. Creative Discussion

The teacher divides the class into groups, and the students make discussions with their partners and share their opinions with other pairs.

Topic:

Making appointments is very common in business activity. How should you make an appropriate appointment politely with the managing director of your client when he is very busy?

If the managing director tells you that he is tied up recently and contact him sometime later, how can you tell whether he is telling the real thing or declining your offer by an excuse? Please discuss the topic with the members in your group.

Chapter 5 Offer and Counter Offer

Learning Objectives
Upon completion of this chapter, you will be able to

- get used to the process for offer and counter offer.
- learn how to persuade clients to accept the offer.
- learn how to make a counter offer.
- form the functions of skills of communication.
- conduct the activities to the theme of offer and counter offer.

课文范读

Part A Situational Dialogue

 Communicative Scene 1

Making an Offer

(*Mr. Smith is a purchaser from Italy. Miss Arenas is Mr. Smith's assistant. Jane is the sale manager of a garment manufacturing company. They are talking about the prices.*)

Jane: Mr. Smith, did you have a good time yesterday?

Smith: Oh, yes. We climbed the Great Wall and had a great time up there.

Jane: Good! How about you, Miss Arenas? Have you enjoyed your first visit to China?

Arenas: Oh yes. I've enjoyed everything about it!

Jane: I'm glad to hear that. Well, since you both have had a good time, maybe it's time to talk business now.[1]

Smith: I think so.

Jane: Terrific. Now let's get down to business. Your e-mail of August 24 says you want to buy bathrobes from us.

Smith: That's correct. Here are the designs.

Jane: Thanks. Fleece, 260 g/m², one size fits all. Quantity: 6,000 pcs.[2]

Smith: I was wondering if you would give us a response to our inquiry.[3]

Jane: Certainly. We are pleased to offer you 6,000 pcs micro-fibre fleece bathrobe, 100% polyester at USD 5.90 each, FOB Shanghai.

Smith: Packing?

Jane: The bathrobes will be packed in plastic bags, each four dozen in a corrugated cardboard box.

Smith: How to make delivery?

Jane: Well, according to your requirement, the goods will be delivered in two consignments of 3,000 each, the first by September 30 and the second by October 15.

Smith: How about terms of payment?

Jane: The terms of payment will be the same as those in the previous contract, that is, sight letter of credit.

Smith: Thank you very much for your offer, and we'll give it serious consideration. As it'll take us some time to calculate, may I suggest we take a 20-minute break? Then we'll give you an answer.

Jane: Fine.

Communicative Scene 2

Counter Offer

(They are negotiating. Smith tries hard to buy at a lower price, but Jane persuades the opposite to accept their price by bargaining hard.)

Smith: Well, Jane. I've discussed your offer with Miss Arenas, and I'm afraid we found it rather on the high side.⁴

Jane: Why do you think so?

Smith: To tell you the truth, just before we left for China, we were approached by a Guangdong garments manufacturer. Their offer was USD 4.50 FOB Guangzhou each bathrobe, so we don't see why we should pay more for your bathrobe.

Jane: USD 4.50 each bathrobe? Really?

Smith: That's right, USD 4.50.

Jane: That's really cheap. I guess you must have bought a lot from this manufacturer.⁵

Smith: We bought 200 pieces.

Jane: Only 200?

Smith: Well, as we don't know much about that firm, we just placed a trial order.

Jane: Right, it takes time to find out whether a business partner is trustworthy.

Smith: This is why we sent our inquiry to you. I believe you are not only trustworthy but also competitive in price.⁶

Jane: You bet.⁷

Smith: But your offer is obviously far from competitive.⁸

Jane: Then what do you think a competitive price would be?

Smith: USD 4.50, the price we paid the Guangdong Manufacturer.

Jane: Oh, come on, our bathrobe certainly deserves more than that.

Smith: Oh, why?

Jane: It's true that our price is higher, but isn't it equally true that our quality is better? Mr. Smith, you wouldn't disagree on that, would you?⁹

Smith: You may have a point there.¹⁰ But, how can you prove your bathrobe is better than the Guangdong ones?

Jane: Well, we have won a gold medal from the General Association of Textiles. Here is the certificate.

Smith: Oh, thank you.

 Communicative Scene 3

Reaching an Agreement

(The final transaction has been concluded. Both parties have made some concession.)

Smith: All right, Jane. What about USD 5.00 each bathrobe? To be frank, I've increased it more by 11%.

Jane: I appreciate your effort toward reaching an agreement, but I'm afraid your concession is too moderate.

Smith: Oh come on, Jane. You'll drive us bankrupt if you raise the price any further.

Jane: You can't be serious, Mr. Smith. As an expert in garments business, you know our bathrobe is worth much more than your counter offer.

Smith: Thanks for the compliment. <u>But as an expert, I don't think your offer is in alignment with the prevailing price in the market.</u>[11]

Jane: <u>I'm afraid I can't go along with you on that.</u>[12] However, to show our goodwill to an old friend, let me cut my offer by 40 cents and make it USD 5.50. What do you say to that?

Smith: Well, I have to say we still can't afford to pay at that price. Jane, I hate to say this, but I am already in a tight corner and can't move any more.

Jane: <u>Well, it seems to be a real hard nut to crack.</u>[13] Mmm, well, I've got an idea. I suggest that you increase your quantity to 10,000 pcs, and we'll manage to make it USD 5.00.

Smith: <u>I'm afraid I'm not authorized to make such a compromise.</u>[14] I'll have to contact my boss and see what he says.

Jane: OK, please go ahead.

(Mr. Smith calls his boss, then comes back to Jane twenty minutes later.)

Smith: Well, after communicating with my boss, we'll make it happen although it is a little bit out of our budget plan.

Jane: That's all right. Shall we discuss the details of your delivery?

Smith: Sure.

Words and Expressions

1. polyester	n.	涤纶
2. on the high side		价格偏高
3. gold medal		金牌
4. concession	n.	让步
5. moderate	adj.	适度的，轻微的
6. bankrupt	adj.	破产
7. counter offer		还盘
8. compliment	n.	称赞，恭维
9. in alignment with		与……一致
10. in a tight corner		处于困境
11. micro-fiber fleece		摇粒绒（一种布料）
12. consignment	n.	货物，运送
13. trustworthy	adj.	值得信赖
14. deserve	vt.	应该得到

15. prevail	vi.	流行
16. corrugated cardboard box		瓦楞纸板箱
17. sight letter of credit		即期信用证
18. quantity	n.	数量
19. 100% polyester		全涤
20. budget plan		预算计划

1. Well, since you both have had a good time, maybe it's time to talk business now.
   既然你们玩儿得很愉快,那么现在该谈生意了吧!
   ① It's time to do sth. 该做某事了
   It's time for me to make an offer.
   我该报价了。
   It's time to have another meeting.
   该开另一场会议了。

2. Fleece, 260 g/m^2, one size fits all. Quantity: 6,000 pcs.
   摇粒绒,260克每平方米,单码,数量6,000件。
   ① fleece 摇粒绒(布料名称)
   ② 260g/m^2 指每平方米的质量为260克
   ③ one size fits all 单码(单一尺码)

3. I was wondering if you would give us a response to our inquiry.
   我想知道你是否对我们的询价给一个答复。
   I wonder who he is.
   我想知道他是谁。
   I was wondering how to establish business relation with clients from abroad.
   我想知道如何与来自国外的客户建立业务关系。

4. I'm afraid we found it rather on the high side.
   恐怕你所报的价格太高。
   ① on the high side 高价
   If the price is on the high side, it's hard to conclude the transaction.
   若价格太高,生意是很难成交的。

5. I guess you must have bought a lot from this manufacturer.
   我想您一定从此制造商买进大批的货品。
   ① must +现在完成时,表示对过去事情的推测。
   You must have drunk a lot.
   你一定喝多了。

6. I believe you are not only trustworthy but also competitive in price.

我相信你们不仅可靠，而且价格有竞争力。

① not only ... but also ... 不但……而且……

The bike is not only cheap but also attractive in its design.

这款自行车不仅价格便宜，而且设计新颖。

7. You bet. 请您放心。

8. But your offer is obviously far from competitive.

不过，你们的报价可是明显没有竞争力啊。

① be far from 远非

Your work is far from satisfactory.

你的工作一点也不令人满意。

The newspaper accounts are far from being true.

报纸的报道远非事实。

9. Mr. Smith, you wouldn't disagree on that, would you?

史密斯先生，你对这点不会不同意吧？

wouldn't ..., would you? 反意疑问句子

10. You may have a point there.

你说的也许有点道理。

11. But as an expert, I don't think your offer is in alignment with the prevailing price in the market.

不过作为行家，我觉得你的报价与市场的主流价格不太相符。

① be in alignment with ... 与……相符……

It is not in alignment with our company's regulations.

它与我们公司的规定不相符。

12. I'm afraid I can't go along with you on that.

恐怕在这一点上我不敢苟同。

13. Well, it seems to be a real hard nut to crack.

这似乎真是个难题啊。

14. I'm afraid I'm not authorized to make such a compromise.

恐怕我无权做出如此大的让步。

*15. qty.＝ quantity

Part B Practical Key Sentences

1. **light talk before formal negotiation**

   Did you have a good time yesterday?

   昨天玩得开心吗？

   正式谈话前，说一些轻松的话题。

   替换表达：

Did you have a pleasant flight?

Yes, the flight was smooth. The service was good, too.

How do you like the weather here? It's nice. It is really sunny.

What do you think of your hotel?

Do you like the food here?

2. starting the negotiation

Well, since you both have had a good time, maybe it's time to talk business now.

既然你们都过得愉快，那现在该谈生意了吧！

替换表达：

Well, shall we get down to business?

Well, I understand that you want to buy some leather shoulder bags from us.

OK, let's get down to our main point.

May I know what line of business you are in?

Could you give me a general picture of your company?

Well, the purpose of my visiting your company is to inquire about the possibility of establishing business relationships with you.

This is the outline of our proposal. Now, let's talk about business.

I'm glad to hear that you've overcome jet-lag. Now let's talk business.

3. making an offer

We are pleased to offer you ...

我们很高兴向您报……的价格。

替换表达：

We would like to offer you ...

As requested, we are pleased to make you a firm offer.

Our offer is a non-firm offer. It is subject to our final confirmation.

Could you make an offer on FOB basis?

We were thinking of making you an offer.

4. counter offer

I'm afraid we found it rather on the high side.

我们觉得价格仍然偏高。

替换表达：

In reply, we regret to inform you that your price is out of line with the market here.

I don't think your price is in alignment.

We can not close negotiations at that price.

Your price is too high for us to accept.

Your quotation is beyond our reach.

Yet on the other hand, your price is not as competitive as theirs.

It's true that our price is higher, but isn't it equally true that our quality is better?

5. making a concession

I suggest that you increase your quantity to 10,000 pcs, we'll manage to make USD 5.00.
若您能将数量提高到1万件，我们就把价格定在每件5.00美元。

替换表达：

We are prepared to allow you a 5% discount if you can increase the quantity of your order to 2,000 dozen.

May I suggest we go fifty-fifty and close the gap?

I think we should fill the gap by compromise.

Shall we meet half way? Each makes a further concession so that business can be done.

We agree to grant you a 5% discount.

With an eye to future business, we'll make an exception and allow you a 2% discount.

In order to promote our business, we are prepared to give you a 3% discount.

For the sake of encouraging future business, we may grant you a special discount of 1%.

From a sincere desire to increase trade between us, we are going to reduce our price by 2%.

6. sentence patterns for price negotiation

Business is closed at this price.
交易就按此价敲定。

Your price is acceptable (unacceptable). 你方价格可接受（不可接受）。

Your price is feasible (infeasible). 你方价格是可行（不可行）的。

Your price is workable. 你方出价可行。

Your price is realistic (unrealistic). 你方价格合乎实际（不现实）。

Your price is reasonable (unreasonable). 你方价格合理（不合理）。

The goods are (not) competitively priced. 此定价有（无）竞争力。

The goods are priced too high. 定价太高。

Your price is prohibitive. 你方价格高得令人望而却步。

Your price is rather stiff. 你方价格相当高。

7. expressions for rising and falling of price

Price is turning high (low). 价格上涨（下跌）。

Price is high (low). 价格高（低）。

Price is rising (falling). 价格上升（下降）。

Price is up (down). 价格上涨（下跌）。

Price is looking up. 价格看涨。

Price has skyrocketed. 价格猛涨。

Price has shot up. 价格飞涨。

Price has risen in a spiral. 价格螺旋上升。

Price has hiked. 价格急剧抬高。

Price has risen perpendicularly. 价格直线上升。

Price has advanced. 价格已上涨。

Price is leveling off. 价格趋平。

Part C Integration of Theory and Practice

1. offer   报盘

【知识点】在商务活动中，报盘也称报价（offer），是一个重要的环节。通常卖方应买方询盘要求发出，也可主动报盘。报盘还可分为实盘和虚盘。实盘是指报盘人明确表示其签发实盘，一旦被受盘人所接受，报盘者必须承担严格依照发盘条件向对方供货的法律责任，是有约束力的报盘，因此报盘者应对盘中的每个细节给予重视。报盘通常用以下方式表达：

【技能训练句型】

We offer you our best price, at which we have done a lot of business with other customers.
我们向你们所报的是最优惠价，按此价我们已经与其他客户做了大量交易。
Can you make an offer, CFR London, at your earliest convenience?
您能尽快报一个伦敦港成本加运费价格吗？
Please make us a cable offer for 5 metric tons of walnut.
请电报5吨核桃仁的价格。
Our offer is USD 30 per set of tape-recorder, FOB Tianjin.
我们的报价是每台收录机30美元，天津离岸价。
We quote lowest lithium battery at USD 2500 per set CFR New York.
我们报锂电池最优惠的纽约成本加运费价每套2500美元。
All your prices are on CIF basis.
你们所有价格都是成本加保险费运费价格。
We'll let you have the official offer next Monday.
下星期一就向您正式报盘。
This offer is based on an expanding market and is competitive.
此报盘着眼于扩大销路，很有竞争性。

2. firm-offer   实盘

【知识点】清晰而准确的实盘应包括以下诸点：
（1）a detailed description of the item   对货物的具体描述
（2）price, currency   价格，货币
（3）packaging   包装
（4）minimum or maximum quantity   最大或最小数量
（5）quality   质量
（6）shipping date, mode   装运日期，方式（指海运、空运或其他方式）
（7）terms of payment   付款方式
（8）a time frame during which your offer is available   发盘的有效期

3. indefinite offer / non-firm offer   虚盘

【知识点】虚盘是指报盘人未明确指出其接受意向的发盘。与实盘相比，虚盘对发盘人并无约束力，虚盘通常不一定像实盘那样，包括交易所需要的所有细节。虚盘常会有"subject to our final confirmation"（以我方最后确认为准），或"for reference only"（仅供参考）等说法，以示发盘者有所保留。

【技能训练句型】

发盘时常说：

We quote our best price, and we hope it will interest you.

我们提供最优惠的报价，希望你们有兴趣。

We can offer you a quotation based upon the international market.

我们可以按国际市场价格给您报价。

We are in a position to offer tea from stock.

我们现在可以报茶叶现货。

The offer is for your reference only, subject to our final confirmation.

此报盘仅供参考，以我方最后确认为准。

4. counter-offer 还盘

【知识点】当受盘人对报盘中的某些条款不满意时，可以提出一套新的条款或通过对报盘做些修改来有条件地接受报盘，这就是还盘。事实上，一个还盘就是一个取代原报盘的新的报盘，还盘一经提出，原来的受盘人就成了新的报盘人，而原来的报盘人就成了新的受盘人。新的受盘人可选择拒绝还盘、再次还盘或接受还盘。

【技能训练句型】

In reply, we regret to inform you that our buyers in Paris find the price you offered much too high.

我方很遗憾地通知贵方，我方巴黎买主觉得贵方的报价太高了。

Your offer is too high to be acceptable.

你方报价太高，不能接受。

Your price is out of line with the market here.

你方定价高出我方市场价。

I wish to point out that yours are about 9% higher than the quotation I have received from your competitors.

我方得指出你方的报价比从其他竞争商家收到的报价高约9%。

We can't accept your offer unless the price is reduced by 5%.

除非你们减价5%，否则我们无法接受报盘。

My offer was based on reasonable profit, not on wild speculations.

我方的报价以合理利润为依据，不是漫天要价。

Moreover, we've kept the price close to the costs of production.

再说，这已经把价格压到生产费用的边缘了。

5. strategy of making an offer 报价策略

【知识点】（1）报价时机：报价之前把商品的使用价值介绍清楚，待对方对其产品已有所了解之后，再提出价格。

（2）价格分割策略：报价时可利用对方的求廉心理，用较小的计价单位报价，造成需方心理上的便宜感。

（3）价格优惠策略：报价时可把价格和商品的优越性或优惠条件联系起来。

（4）价格比较策略：提出己方价格时，可联系另一种商品的价格进行比较，突出相同使用价值的不同价格，或突出相同价格的不同使用价值。

（5）价格差异策略：根据商品的流向、买方的需求急缓程度、购买次数、购买时间、付款方式的不同，可采取不同的价格。

6. tips of making concession while negotiating 谈判中的让步技巧

【知识点】（1）在让步的最后阶段，让出全部可让利益。

（2）等额地让出可让利益。

（3）让步先大后小，逐步提高。

（4）让步从大到小，然后微升。

（5）让步从大到小，渐次缩小。

（6）出让全部可让利益后赔利相让，然后再讨回赔利。

Part D Practice

I. Complete the Following Dialogues

(1)

Li: How are you, Mr. Morer? It's very ___1___ of you to see us in ___2___.

Morer: Hello. It's good to see you in person in the Canton Fair as we have a lot of written ___3___ in the ___4___ years.

Li: Yeah, and I think through your ___5___ we can settle the price for beach chair one way or ___6___. How I wish to point ___7___ that due ___8___ sharp increase of raw material we'll be ___9___ need to adjust our export prices before ___10___.

(2)

Li: I think it ___1___ for either of us to insist ___2___ his own price. How about meeting each other ___3___? I only ask you to make a ___4___ of 3% on your quotation. That's ___5___, isn't it?

Morer: To tell you the ___6___, the price we ___7___ you last is ___8___ the lowest and we cannot stand any cuts. Had it not been for an old ___9___, like you, we would not ___10___ made you such a low offer in the first place.

II. Role-plays

Task 1

Students work in pairs and make a dialogue based on the following situation.

Jack is going to import 20,000 pcs T-shirt from China to America. But he finds the price quoted by Miss Wang on the high side. He tries his best to persuade Miss Wang to reduce her price with good reasons. The words or phrases suggested below might give you a hand:

(1) Your price is beyond our reach / rather out of line.

(2) Our price is most moderate / favorable in line with the prevailing market.

(3) This price has been reduced to the limit from 5% to 6% lower than others.

(4) If you insist on your price, we can hardly come to terms.

(Hang on the previous quotation, business is impossible.)

(5) With an eye to future business, for the sake of encouraging future business.

(6) We agree to grant you a 2% discount, if you increase your quantity from 5,000 pcs to 10,000 pcs.

Task 2

Short conversations.

(1) Suppose you bargain with your client.

(2) Describe your offer.

III. Guided Talking

Students work in pairs.

Talk about offers in details. The following information can be used for reference:

(1) soccer money box

(2) size (15 cm / diameter)

(3) logo (2 color / 1 position, 3 colors / 1 position)

(4) material: polyresin(树脂)

(5) quantity: 50,000 pcs

IV. Creative Discussion

The teacher divides the class into groups and asks them to discuss one of the following to pics, then choose a representative form each group to present their discussion. The student who expresses well will be the winner.

Topic:

What are a firm offer and a non-firm offer?

What are the main differences between firm offer and non-firm offer?

How to make a satisfactory offer?

Chapter 6 At China Import and Export Fair

Learning Objectives
Upon completion of this chapter, you will be able to

- ☑ know the words and expression related to business fair.
- ☑ describe your products in detail.
- ☑ establish business relations with customers.
- ☑ know how to promote sales in the fair.

课文范读

Part A Situational Dialogue

 Communicative Scene 1

At China Import and Export Fair

(*Helen, a representative of a Greek company, is now in the bag booth of Canton Fair. Jack is the salesman who works for JOY Bag Company.*)

Jack: Good morning. <u>Welcome to our booth.</u>[1]

Helen: Good morning. Nice to meet you. I'm Helen from Greece. Here is my card. We are one of the leading importers at our end. <u>I wish to have a discussion with you about those backpacks on display.</u>[2]

Jack: Thank you. Here is my card. <u>It's a pleasure to have a chance to talk business with you personally.</u>[3] We appreciate your interest. I have some catalogues, and I'd like you to have a look at them.

Helen: Thanks! <u>Do these cover all products displayed on your booth?</u>[4]

Jack: Yes, of course.

Helen: Well, we are managing to import some satchels for the coming season. Would you recommend some for our reference?

Jack: Well. How about these? Item number YX-01 to YX-10. The series of satchels are specially designed for pupils. We use transferring printing to make the logo with vivid cartoon figures which will be popular among pupils.

Helen: Could you tell us the material of those satchels?

Jack: Some of them are 600D × 600D polyester, some are micro fibre.

Helen: Could you give me more details about them?

Jack: <u>Well, here are the specifications for the satchels: 16″ length × 10″ width, and 5″ depth; backing PVC sheet lining; U shaped main compartment entry; removable and adjustable shoulder strap.</u>[5]

Helen: All right. What's the minimum quantity of each item?

Jack: Usually the minimum quantity of each item is 1,000 pcs.

Helen: MOQ?

Jack: 3,000 pcs.

Helen: May I have your price-list ?

Jack: Here you are.

Helen: Oh, it's very considerate of you. If you excuse me, I'll go over your price-list first. Then come back again.

Jack: Take your time. Hope to see you

■ At China Import and Export Fair

 Communicative Scene 2

Talking about Products

(*Miss Lin, Manager of Sales Department. Mr. Brown is a client from abroad.*)

Lin: Good afternoon! My name is Lin, Manager of Sales Department.
Brown: Nice to see you, Miss Lin.
Lin: Nice to see you too, Mr. Brown. Please have a seat. What would you like, tea or coffee?
Brown: I'd prefer coffee if you don't mind.
Lin: Not in the least. What do you think of the Fair?
Brown: Well, there is a great change about the Fair. I have attended three of your fairs, but I find the business scope this time has been broadened, and there are more businessmen than ever before.
Lin: Really. Did you find anything interesting?
Brown: Yes, quite a few. We have special interest in your products, particularly in your kid's shoes. These shoes are fashionable and suit our market. If they are of high quality and the prices are reasonable, we'll purchase large quantities of them.[6]
Lin: Our shoes are in various colors and sizes. All products have to go through five checks in the whole process. They are not only superior in quality but also attractive in designs as well.[7] They are well-received overseas and are always in great demand.
Brown: That sounds nice.
Lin: Well, for your information, there is an upward tendency on the world market and our prices are likely to rise at any moment. We have specially made out a price-list which covers the most saleable products in your market.[8] Here is our price sheet and catalogues.
Brown: Oh, that's nice. By the way, how long will your offer hold good?
Lin: 15 days. Our prices compare most favorably with quotations you can get from other manufacturers. You'll see that from our price sheet. The prices are subject to our confirmation.
Brown: Well, I sincerely hope to establish good business relationship with you and I'd like to have a further discussion with you.
Lin: Me too.

 Communicative Scene 3

Making Acquaintance with Business Customer

(*Nancy is a purchaser from America. Park is a salesman of an electronic household corp.*)

Park: Good morning. May I help you?
Nancy: I wonder if you can give me more information about this refrigerator model you're showing.

Park: I'd be glad to help. Would you like a packet of our promotional literature?

Nancy: Thank you. <u>We've been thinking of placing an order if they are of the types we want and their prices are reasonable.</u>[9]

Park: <u>We also take special orders. That is to say, we can make refrigerators according to samples and specifications.</u>[10]

Nancy: These models seem to be quite small.

Park: Yes, one of the problems that we were trying to solve when working on this model was to do away with the freezer. This refrigerator is only USD 50. Its appearance has been designed in the shapes of animals, such as pandas, bears, and so on.

Nancy: Remarkable! There's nothing quite like seeing a problem and solving it to create a good product. Are all the components made here in Shanghai?

Park: Yes, we do some subcontracting, but only in Shanghai. These are made here. May I ask what company you work for?

Nancy: I represent Electronic Supply Company from the United States.

Park: Would you like to tour our factory and perhaps even one or two of our subcontractors?

Nancy: Yes, if it wouldn't take too long to arrange. <u>I'm due to fly back to the States on Friday.</u>[11]

Park: I'm sure we can arrange it before then. How about meeting the founder of our company? Would you be interested in talking with him about our ideas for upcoming models?

Nancy: That's a good idea. To tell you the truth, we're looking for ways to outperform our competitors. In the past few months, we've been considering the possibility of transferring some of our manufacturing to China as a way to reduce production cost. Our marketing people have done some studies, but their data is mostly second hand.

Park: I guess this is why you came to this fair.

Nancy: You're right. I'd like to have face-to-face contact with people like you.

Park: I see. Why not contact the founder of our company right away?

Nancy: Yes, I think that would be useful. Thank you for your help.

Words and Expressions

1. booth	n.	展摊
2. leading importer		主要进口商
3. at our end		在我方市场
4. logo	n.	标识语
5. polyester	n.	涤纶面料，聚酯纤维
6. micro fibre		超细纤维
7. MOQ =Minimum Order Quantity		最小订购量
8. satchel	n.	书包
9. compartment	n.	分隔的口袋
10. transferring printing		热移印（一种印花技术名称）

11. sales department		销售部
12. superior in quality		质量上乘
13. subcontracting	n.	转包合同
14. specification	n.	规格
15. freezer	n.	冷冻室（冰箱）
16. component	n.	成分
17. outperform	vt.	胜过
18. face-to-face contact		面对面接触

1. Welcome to our booth.
   欢迎参观我们的展摊。

2. I wish to have a discussion with you about those backpacks on display.
   我想同您谈谈所展出的背包。

3. It's a pleasure to have a chance to talk business with you personally.
   我很高兴有机会与你面谈。
   ① to have a chance to do sth. 有机会做某事
   I'm glad to have a chance to cooperate with you.
   我很高兴有机会与您合作。
   I'm glad to have the chance to call on you.
   我很高兴有机会拜访您。

4. Do these cover all of your products displayed on your booth?
   您展摊上展出的产品都在目录上吗？
   displayed on your booth 过去分词短语作定语，修饰products

5. Well, here are the specifications for the satchels: 16″ length × 10″ width, and 5″ depth; backing PVC sheet lining; U shaped main compartment entry; Removable and adjustable shoulder strap.
   书包的规格：长度16英寸，宽度10英寸，厚度是5英寸，PVC背胶，U形口袋，可调整肩带。
   ① Shall we talk about the specification of the products?
   我们能否谈谈产品的规格？
   ② on display 展出
   A great variety of new products are on display at the fair, which offers a variety of attractions.
   交易会上陈列着多种新产品，很有吸引力。

6. If they are of high quality and the prices are reasonable ...
   如果质量好，价格合理……
   ① Our price is most favorable.
   我们的价格是最优惠的。

② both reasonable and practical 既合理又可行

③ closely calculated 经过仔细核算

7. They are not only superior in quality but also attractive in designs as well.

   它们不仅质量上乘而且设计新颖。

   It's not only durable but also competitive in price.

   此产品不仅经久耐用，而且价格上很有竞争力。

8. We have specially made out a price-list which covers the most saleable products in your market.

   我们专门做了一个报价表，上面的产品都是你方市场上畅销的。

   I'm sure the goods will be readily saleable in your market at this price.

   我相信此价格在贵方市场上是很好销的。

9. We've been thinking of placing an order if they are of the types we want and their prices are reasonable.

   如果是我们要的类型，价格又合理的话，我们会考虑下订单。

   ① we want 定语从句，修饰types

   They are of the types = they are the types

10. We also take special orders. That is to say, we can make refrigerator according to samples and specifications.

    我们还接特殊订单。也就是说，我们可以根据客户的样品及规格生产冰箱。

11. I'm due to fly back to the states on Friday.

    我定于星期五飞回美国。

    ① be due to 将要做

    China International Import Expo is due to show a civilized, open and inclusive China to the rest of the world.

    中国国际进口博览会，将向世界展示一个文明、开放、包容的中国。

    ② in the due time 在规定的时间

    ③ due to bad weather 由于坏天气

Part B Practical Key Sentences

1. talking about the products on display

I wish to have a discussion with you about those backpacks on display.

我想同您谈谈展出的背包。

替换表达：

I'd like to have a further discussion on the import of hardware with you.

Is there any way of ensuring we'll have enough time for our talks about the aquatic products business?

We'd have to compare notes on what we've discussed on the products displayed on your booth during the day.

2. I'd like to know whether you manufacture ...

I'd like to know whether you have photocopier XXC830?

贵公司是否经营XXC830复印机？

替换表达：

Do you have digital answering phones?

I'm thinking of purchasing /ordering / buying trays.

I'd go for projectors which are mainly used in conferences.

3. I have some catalogues ...

I have some catalogues and I'd like you to have a look at them.

我有一些产品目录，请您看一看。

替换表达：

Here is a copy of the itinerary we have worked out for you and your friends. Would you please have a look at it?

Could I have a set of catalogues of all your products?

Here is my business card and some of the catalogues of our products.

These drawings on the wall are process sheets and they describe how each process goes on to the next.

4. Our company specializes in ...

Our company specializes in manufacturing office furniture.

我们公司主要生产办公用品。

替换表达：

We are in the line of stationery. We are a state-owned corporation.

Their line of business is light industrial products.

Our company is one of the leading exporters of MP4.

5. Which appeals to you more ...

Which appeals to you more, the type of NN1 or the type of NN2?

您想要哪种型号，NN1型还是NN2型？

替换表达：

These photo supplies may interest a lot of foreign traders.

You may find packing machinery interesting /of interest.

Which type would you prefer?

6. introduce the characteristics of the dealings

First of all, I will outline the characteristics of our sales.

首先，我将简略说明我们销售经营的特性。

We have adopted much more flexible methods in our dealings.

我们在经营的具体做法上灵活多了。

替换表达：

We have adopted some usual international practices in our trade.

We represent Electronic Products Company and our trade policy has always been based on equality and mutual benefit and exchange of needed goods.

Part C Integration of Theory and Practice

1. attending the fair   参展

【知识点】参展是企业与客户建立和保持业务联系的最有效的方式之一。与前来展摊的客户进行交谈绝非易事。如同在参展前准备样品、布置展摊一样,这种交谈需要一定的技巧。某些客户可能成为企业产品的未来买主,企业代表在展台对他们的接待将决定着参展的成功与否。

【知识点】(1) 与客户接洽的第一步是鼓励他们在你处展台驻足,要显得热忱,让人感到你们乐意与他们交谈。

【技能训练句型】

Have you seen our latest innovation?
你们见过我们最近的新产品吗?

Do you import products from China?
您从中国进口产品吗?

【知识点】(2) 取得客户的资料,这对企业日后与客户保持联系是很重要的。通常这么说:

【技能训练句型】

May I have your business card, please?
您能否给一张名片?

【知识点】(3) 呈上自己的名片(上面须有详细的资料,如公司名称、姓名、电话号码、手机号和E-mail,有的背面还注明了企业的经营范围及企业网址)。名片要设计新颖,以吸引客户。

【技能训练句型】

Hello, I'm Bill, here is my card.
您好,我是Bill,这是我的名片。

【知识点】(4) 保留交谈记录,以便日后与参观者进一步联系,增加业务的可能性;记录内容为客户名片、经营范围、对哪些产品感兴趣、产品的资料。

【知识点】(5) 同时要注意以下三点:

① 要自信。② 要熟悉自己的产品。因为买家可能非常专业,这就要求我们也要专业。③ 要注意礼节,因为各个国家的习俗是不一样的。

2. introduction of products   产品介绍

【知识点】企业参展的目的是推销自己的产品,产品介绍得成功与否直接影响交易的成败。

【技能训练句型】

通常我们可以这样介绍产品:

Let me tell you about its special features. It's made of leather/wood/steel/aluminium. It weighs just 2.3 kilos. It comes in a wide range of colors.
让我来介绍一下产品的特色之处吧。它是用真皮/木头/钢材/铝制成的。重量只有2.3千克。有多种颜色可供选择。

It has several special features. The most useful feature is the energy-saving design. Another advantage is its very small size.
它有几个特点,最有用的是它的节能设计,另一个长处是它的体积非常小。

Yet on the other hand, our products are hundred percent natural.

不过，我们的产品可是100%全天然的。

This new type of electromobile car can drive 200 kilometers per hour with a built-in air-conditioner.
这种新款电动汽车每小时可行驶200公里，自带空调。

The electric fan needs no lubrication and will not heat up if left on around clock.
这种电扇不用润滑，全天运行也不会发热。

Try this notebook computer. It features a dictionary with 60,000 entries and can store 12,000 addresses.
试一下这种笔记本电脑。它带一部60,000个条目的词典，并能存储12,000个地址。

3. make acquaintance with business customers　接触和认识客户

【知识点】中国进出口商品交易会是中国规模最大，到会国外客户最多，成交效果最好的综合性国际贸易盛会。来自全世界的客商云集，洽谈业务，增进友谊，这是认识客户、建立贸易关系的好机会。

展览的重要任务是接触和认识客户，确定贸易对象，发展客户关系，包括巩固现有客户的关系和发展潜在客户的关系，尤其是后者。潜在客户往往意味着公司的未来发展希望，但是由于展览会时间短、客户多，展览接待工作大多是尽可能多地接触和认识客户。展览会期间的客户工作应重数量，而展览会之后的客户工作则应重质量。要加深与客户的相互了解，建立相互信任关系，使之发展成伙伴关系和买卖关系。

在整个展会中，如何同客人打招呼是很重要的，当客人走到你的展位前停留时，有两种情况。一种是感兴趣的，一种只是随便看看的。一定要注意观察客人的视线停留在哪一类型的产品上，并主动上前同客人打招呼。简单地说"Hi"、"Morning"或"Hello"，有时甚至一个眼神就可以了，只要引起客人的注意，让他知道你在关注他！

真正的客户，他们一般都会主动和你打招呼的。这时，你就可以开始介绍你公司的产品了。对于无礼的或者傲慢的客人，一定要不卑不亢。

【技能训练句型】

Perhaps you've heard our product's name. Would you like to know more about it?
也许您已听说过我们的产品。您想进一步了解吗？

The purpose of my coming here is to inquire about possibilities of establishing trade relations with your company.
我此行的目的正是想探询与贵公司建立贸易关系的可能性。

If you are interested, I will prepare a list of them.
如果您感兴趣的话，我可以列表让您参考。

I'd like to introduce you to our company. Is there anything in particular you'd like to know?
我将向您介绍我们的公司，您有什么特别想了解的吗？

I'd like to know something about the current investment environment in your country.
我想了解一下贵国的投资环境。

Part D Practice

I. Complete the Following Dialogues

(1)

A: Hello, my ___1___ is Jimmy. Here is my card. Yesterday, I took ___2___ in your demo and found myself particularly ___3___ in your drapery system.

B: Thank you. Here is my ___4___ card and some of the ___5___ of our products.

A: I'm a leading ___6___ at our end. We found your ___7___ are salable in our ___8___.

B: Good. Our drapery system is patented ___9___ its unique design.

A: By the way, are you licensed to ___10___?

B: Yes, of course, we have a licensed exporter since 1989.

(2)

A: Good afternoon, ladies and gentlemen, welcome to Y&X mobile phone booth. Today, I take ___1___ in presenting to you one of our ___2___ developed mobile phone, YX192. The new ___3___ incorporates multiple functions.

B: My name is John Smith. I'm the sales manager of G&X Company. Could you ___4___ your products' multiple functions?

A: The remote control can control ___5___ functions individually. It is a unique design. The timer can preset times open/close with 24 hours.

B: Could I ___6___ a set of catalogue of all your products?

A: Yes, of course. Could you ___7___ me your ___8___ card, please?

B: OK.

II. Role-plays

Task 1

Question and answer.

At the Q&A session, some visitors ask a lot of questions, such as: Could you specify the function of your unique design? Could I have a set of catalogues of all your products?

Students work in pairs to give as many questions as possible. Then the teacher chooses two members to be the chairpersons of the Q&A session and others work as visitors questioning the chairpersons.

Task 2

Short conversation.

Suppose you are a stationery purchaser from Australia. You visit Canton Fair. You go to talk with the sales promoters of the stationary booths. Make 3 dialogues according to the following topics:

(1) establishing a business relationship

(2) asking for the product catalogue

(3) inquiring about the price

III. Guided Talking

Students work in pairs.

Topic: At the show

Use the following to practice with partner:

(1) Establish or consolidate business relationship

(2) Solve specific problems

(3) Find a new market

(4) Appoint agents /seek principals

(5) Discuss specific terms /conditions

(6) Seek the latest products

(7) Obtain new technical knowledge

(8) Discuss business needs in a neutral environment

IV. Creative Discussion

The teacher divides the class into groups and asks them to discuss and choose the representatives of each group after discussion. The student who expresses well will be the winner.

Topic:

1. Have you ever attended any show? What are your reasons for attending it?

2. What is your impression at China Import and Export Fair?

Chapter 7 Business Visit

Learning Objectives
Upon completion of this chapter, you will be able to

- get to know the process of welcoming visitors.
- learn how to introduce your company or factory.
- conduct the activities related to be a host.
- discuss more details with clients at working site.

课文范读

Part A Situational Dialogue

 Communicative Scene 1

Visiting the Factory

(*Mrs. Elizabeth Gage, General Manager of Union Supplies Company from the United States of America, is paying a visit to Mr. Huang's factory for the first time.*)

Huang: I am so happy to meet you again in our factory, Mrs. Gage. How are things going with you and your family?

Gage: Fine, just fine. Thank you. Since we are old friends, please call me Lisa. May I call you "Huang"?

Huang: Sure, Lisa. How is your lovely boy, Tom? He must have grown up a lot since I saw him last time in the States.

Gage: Yes, he is now a high school student. I should say he is a handsome young boy.

Huang: Good! How is Mr. Gage? Why didn't he come this time?

Gage: Fine, just fine. Thank you. He is fully occupied by his work.

Huang: It's a pity. Please extend my sincere wishes to him.[1]

Gage: I will. In fact, I am fully responsible for the business between our two companies now.

Huang: I'm very happy to work with you. I believe the cooperation between us will be more delightful and fruitful.

Gage: Me too.

Huang: May I give you a tour of the factory?

Gage: Sounds great.

Huang: As you may know, it is now the peak season for nanometer antibacterial shoes, so our factory is working at full capacity.[2] We have a production capacity of 10 thousand pairs of shoes per day.

Gage: Good. One of our purposes to visit is to see how well our order is carrying out. The quality of the products is always the most important matter and the delivery time is also a vital point, especially for the seasonal products.

(*While talking, they are approaching the production line where the products for Union Supplies Company are under processing.*)[3]

Huang: I fully agree with you. I'm sure that our products will meet the standards specified in our contract and your requirement. According to our working schedule, your order will be completed in time for delivery. Don't worry about it.

Gage: Could you complete all the orders from other customers at the same time besides our company?

Huang: Basically yes, our workers will work overtime 2 hours every day in peak season, though we have to pay double overtime payment.

Gage: How do you control the quality?

Huang: Here is the Quality Inspection Section. All shoes are made under an extremely tight quality control.

Gage: I am very interested in learning more about it.

Huang: The finished products will flow to this section before they continue their trip to the packing area. The products are 100% checked here and defective ones will be thrown out to these boxes for the head of the workshop and technicians to analyze what the problems are and find out the ways to prevent the occurrence again.[4]

Gage: Is that your Design Department?

Huang: Yes, look at our revolutionary new nanometer products. We always make great efforts to keep the novelty of products. What's your overall impression of our factory?

Gage: Wow, excellent! Seeing is believing. Mr. Gage told me a lot about what he had seen in your factory. Now I have seen with my own eyes. I will report everything I saw here and I believe our orders will be placed immediately after the delivery of this batch.

Huang: Thanks a lot!

 Communicative Scene 2

Meeting in the Showroom

(Miss Jin, Sales Manager of Broad Arts & Crafts Company accompanies Mr. Brian from a Canadian company to look around the showroom of the company.)

Brian: How nice your showroom is!

Jin: Thank you! Please feel free to look around our showroom, which is fully opened to you.

Brian: I'm glad to hear you say so. As I introduced to you last night in my hotel room, our company is one of the major dealers of arts and crafts in Canada. We are handling various kinds of art products. The variety of numbers is up to 1 500. Most of them are imported from China because the Chinese arts and crafts are well appreciated by our customers.

Jin: What particular products are you looking for?

Brian: I'm seeking arts porcelain, ornaments for display, imitation antique porcelain, and so on.

Jin: You have found the right place because our main products are ceramic arts and crafts. With rich raw materials, fine workmanship, up-to-date patterns and featuring great varieties,[5] our products enjoy a good reputation at home and abroad.

Brian: Great!

Jin: Let's look around all the display of arts and crafts first. Then sit down and have a detailed talk on quality, quantity, price and other issues.

Brian: OK. Can you provide us with some samples?

Jin: Sure. Are you going to take them with you? If so, I'll pack them now.

Brian: No, they are heavy and I'll travel some other places. Could you send them back to my office directly?

Jin: No problem. However, you may have to pay for the postage. I'll send them by postage due.

Brian: That will be fine. Thank you for your kind help. Here is a new design from our company. Can you make a counter-sample for us? I hope I'll take this one back with me.

Jin: We'll make the counter sample in about ten days. When are you leaving?

Brian: Saturday. I don't think there is enough time before I leave. Will you send it together with your samples? We hope your counter sample can meet all the requirements indicated in this description sheet.

Jin: You can rest assure. I believe that <u>well begun is half done</u>.[6] I hope the counter sample is a satisfactory beginning of the new business between us.

Brian: I hope so, too.

 Communicative Scene 3

Discussion on Investment

(Mr. Dong is discussing an investment proposal with Mr. Watt, CEO of a foreign company.)

Dong: Mr. Watt, to our regret, we are unable to supply the bearing you are asking since it is the busiest season and our factory has been operating in three shifts. We are totally booked up until next March.

Watt: Sorry to hear that. However, I'm coming not only to push you to make the best arrangement of our order, but also to discuss the possibility of our investment on a new machine line to produce bearing for us.

Dong: We appreciate your timely help. But you know to build up a new production line takes a long time. How can we have our production capacity doubled overnight?

Watt: We had a manufacturing line in Korea before. As the labor cost got higher and higher, the products manufactured there lost their competitive ability. If we ship the existing line here, it won't take too much time. <u>The new production capacity will come into being in two or three months.</u>[7]

Dong: It is an interesting proposal. Do you have a more detailed plan to carry out your proposal?

Watt: Sure. It takes about two weeks to disassemble and pack the line. Another two or three weeks are needed to ship the goods and one more week for customs declaration. If we lose no time, we can reassemble and adjust the machine line in three weeks. And then the line can be put into production by the end of this year, which means we can save more than two months than just waiting for the present production lines.

Dong: Are you sure the line can be rebuilt up and put into use in such a short time?

Watt: I'm quite confident because we can bring the engineers and workers who had worked in this factory before. They knew the line very well just as their own children.

Dong: How are you going to charge for this line?

Watt: We don't want to have additional charge for the line itself. We request the line must be used for our orders only. The cost of daily maintenance of the machine line should be covered by your side.

Dong: Please let me think it over.

Watt: Our company won't pay any down payment for our orders, because we'll have deposited our machines in your factory.[8] Of course, we will pay full amount when the orders are completed. It is your responsibility to keep the machines in good condition. During the period while our line is used in your factory, we will possess the complete right to dispose our properties.

Dong: It sounds very reasonable. We will provide necessary assistances for customs declaration, local transportation, and assembly in our workshop. We will give you a final reply in two days after our board meeting tomorrow. By my personal opinion, I am certain that our board meeting will approve this "win-win" proposal.[9]

Watt: I'm glad to hear that and look forward to having your positive decision.

Words and Expressions

1. simplify	vt.	使简单，简化
2. delightful	adj.	令人高兴的，使人快乐的
3. fruitful	adj.	多产的，富有成效的
4. nanometer antibacterial shoes		纳米抗菌鞋
5. vital	adj.	极其重要的；必不可少的；致命的
6. peak	adj.	最高的，高峰的
7. approach	vt.	接近，靠近
8. overtime	adj.	超时；加班
9. defective	adj.	有缺陷的
10. occurrence	n.	发生，出现
11. novelty	n.	新颖，新奇，新鲜
12. batch	n.	批，次
13. accompany	vt.	陪，伴
14. arts and crafts	n.	工艺品
15. arts porcelain		美术陶瓷
16. ornaments for display		陈设（陶瓷）
17. imitation antique porcelain		仿古陶瓷
18. bearing	n.	轴承

19. shift	n.	轮班；转变
20. overnightad	adv.	一夜间，一下子，突然
	adj.	一夜间的，突然的
21. disassemble	vt.	拆卸，分解
22. maintenance	n.	维修；保养；维持，保持
23. responsibility	n.	责任，职责；责任心；任务
24. possess	vt.	拥有，占有
25. dispose	vt.	处理；布置；安排
26. property	n.	财产，资产；性质，特征
27. assistance	n.	帮助，援助
28. transportation	n.	运输，运送
29. workshop	n.	车间
30. positive	adj.	正面的；积极的；肯定的；明确的

1. Please extend my sincere wishes to him.

   请代我向他转达我的衷心祝福。

   ① extend *v.* 给予，提供；延伸，伸展；扩张

   We extend a warm welcome to Chairman of Chamber of Commerce.

   我们给予商会会长热烈的欢迎。

   Our factory intends to extend our production line.

   我们打算扩大生产线。

2. As you may know, it is now the peak season for nanometer antibacterial shoes, so our factory is working at full capacity.

   你可能了解，现在是纳米抗菌鞋的生产高峰期，我们的工厂正在满负载生产。

   ① peak season 高峰期，比 busy season 的程度更强，表示最繁忙。

   ② at peak periods 在最繁忙的时刻，在高峰期

   ③ at off-peak producing period 在低谷生产期

   ④ the peak output 最高产量

   ⑤ at full capacity 满负载，以全部力量，满功率

3. While talking, they are approaching the production line where the products for Union Supplies Company are under processing.

   谈话间，他们来到正在生产联合供应公司产品的生产线。

   （1） under processing 正在加工中

   ① under 表示过程，在……中

   The products quotation is under way.

   产品的报价正在进行中。

   The trade showroom of the factory is under construction.

工厂的展室正在建设之中。

（2）While talking...

本句中while 是连词，引导状语从句。while从句中要用延续性动词。

① 当……的时候

While (I am) making a business appointment, my secretary gets ready for taking notes.

当我正在联系商务约会的时候，我的秘书做好准备记录。

② 虽然，但是

While you have a point there, I can't agree with you.

虽然你说得有道理，但我还是不同意。

4. The head of the workshop and technicians analyze what the problems are and find out the ways to prevent from occurrence again.

车间主任和技术员分析问题原因，并找出防止再度发生的办法。

① find out 指通过观察和探索而发现真相，发现秘密和调查出原因。

The bank has helped us to find out the potential customer's credit standing.

银行已帮助我们调查潜在客户的资信状况。

② find 常指偶然发现，碰到。当表示了解、打听的意思时，与find out同义。

You'll find the right products in our factory.

你在我们工厂能找到想要的产品。

③ find与looking for、discover 的区别： find强调找到的结果，而looking for强调寻找的过程，discover强调发现客观事物的存在。

5. featuring great varieties 种类繁多

① feature *vt. & n.* 以……为特色；特征，特色

The automated production features largely in the factory.

自动化生产是这家工厂的一大特色。

6. Well begun is half done.

（谚语）良好的开端是成功的一半。

7. The new production capacity will come into being in two or three months.

将现在的生产线运到这儿来，可在两三个月内形成新的生产能力。

① come into being 产生，形成，成立

Before fax came into being, telex was a popular means of communication.

在传真还没出现以前，电传是流行的通信工具。

8. Our company won't pay any down payment for our orders, because we'll have deposited our machines in your factory.

我们公司将不再支付我方订单的预付款，因为我们的机器已经抵押在贵厂了。

① down payment 预付定金

② deposit *vt. & n.* 储蓄，寄存；定金，押金

9. By my personal opinion, I am certain that our board meeting will approve this "win-win" proposal.

但我个人认为我们的董事会定会批准这项"双赢"的建议。

① win-win 是指双方都有赢利，达到双赢。

Fair trade is a win-win situation because both producers and consumer benefit.
公平贸易达到双赢，生产者和消费者都有利可图。
② no-win 指在没有结果的情况下，各方皆有损失。

*10. by postage collect 采用邮费到付
  freight collect 运费到付
  collect call 受话方付费电话

Part B Practical Key Sentences

1. asking after somebody

见面询问家庭情况时的常用语：

How are things going with you and your family?

家里一切都好吗？

转达问候的常用语：

Please extend my best wishes to him.

请代我向他转达我的衷心祝福。

Please give my kind regards to him.

请向他转达我的问候。

替换表达：

How is everything with you and your family?

How is everything at home?

Please remember me to your husband.

Say hello to your colleagues for us.

2. showing around the factory

May I give you a tour of the factory?

我可以带您参观工厂吗？

Let me show you around the factory.

我带您参观一下工厂。

替换表达：

Let me take you to have a look of the production line.

Shall we go to the showroom?

3. be fully occupied

The producers are totally booked up until next March from now.

从现在到明年三月份的订单已经满了。

He employed himself in the design of up-to-date patterns.

他正忙着设计最新的款式。

He is fully occupied by his work.

他正忙着工作。

替换表达:

He occupied himself with touring a factory.

The manufacturers busied themselves preparing counter-samples.

The president is engaged. Can you call him an hour later?

4. **be fully responsible for**

I am fully responsible for the business between our two companies now.

我现在全权负责我们之间的业务。

take full responsibility 全权负责,对……负完全责任

General manager took full responsibility for the company affairs.

总经理负责公司的全部事务。

替换表达:

The inspectors are in charge of product inspection.

The manufacturer has an obligation to deliver the goods as required.

It is our duty to make good quality goods.

5. **make great efforts**

We always make great efforts to keep the novelty of products.

我们总是竭尽全力保持产品的新颖性。

The designers do their utmost to make the color of products more attractive.

设计师们全力以赴让产品的色彩更引人注目。

替换表达:

Our company goes all out to develop oversea market.

The manufacturers do their best to improve the quality of products.

Part C Integration of Theory and Practice

1. **enhancing close relationship　加深友情**

【知识点】拜访或接待客户时,先说些轻松的话题,拉拉家常,可增强彼此的亲切感。

【技能训练句型】

Since we are old friends, please call me Lisa. To be simplified, I'll call you "Huang", is it OK?

既然我们是老朋友了,请叫我丽莎。我可以简单点叫你小黄吗?

Sure, Lisa. How is your lovely boy, Tom? He must have grown up a lot since I saw him last time in the States.

当然可以,丽莎。您那可爱的儿子汤姆好吗?自从我上次在美国见到他以来,他一定长大了许多。

2. visiting the guest most concern section 考查客户最关心的环节

【知识点】客户来访最想了解产品生产过程、生产工艺、质量检验环节等，应妥善安排让客户一饱眼福，眼见为实。

【技能训练句型】

One of our purposes to visit is to see how well our order is carrying out. The quality of the products is always the most important matter and the delivery time is also a vital point, especially for the seasonal products.

我此行的目的之一就是想了解我们订单的执行情况。产品质量永远是最重要的，而交货期也是一个关键因素，尤其对于季节性产品来说。

【知识点】以本文的客户为例，当了解客人来访的目的后，可带他们到工厂看看，并针对来访目的多考查客户最关心的环节。

【技能训练句型】

They are approaching the production line where the products for Union Supplies Company are under processing.

他们来到正在生产联合供应公司纳米抗菌鞋产品的生产线。

Here is Quality Inspection Section. All shoes are made under an extremely tight quality control.

这里是质量检验区，所有的产品都经过极其严格的质量检测。

I'll show you around our Design Department.

我带你看看我们的设计部门。

3. introducing with specific detail 具体详细的介绍

【知识点】向客人介绍工厂或公司情况时，要重点介绍自己的特色。

【技能训练句型】

You have found the right place because our main products are ceramic arts and crafts. With rich raw materials, fine workmanship, up-to-date patterns and featuring great varieties, our products enjoy good reputation at home and abroad.

您算找对地方了，因为我们的主要产品就是工艺瓷器。由于资源丰富、工艺精湛、款式新颖和种类繁多，我们的产品在国内外市场上享有盛誉。

【知识点】向客人介绍工厂或公司情况时，要实事求是，不可过分拔高公司。

【技能训练句型】

We are the leading porcelain enterprise in China.

我们是中国陶瓷的龙头企业。

【知识点】我们对外宾作业务介绍时，常用上述的句子，但如果未达到龙头企业水准，就不要任意添油加醋。应该作具体详细的介绍，多用实际数字说话。

【技能训练句型】

We have a production capacity of 30 thousand pairs of shoes per day.

我们工厂的生产能力达到每天3万双鞋。

We are handling various kinds of art products. The total article numbers are up to 2,000.

我们经营着品种繁多的工艺产品，总数可达2,000种。

4. feeling satisfactory at the visit 让客户感到满意

【知识点】让客户对最关心的产品标准、按期交货、产品种类和款式新颖等感到满意。

【技能训练句型】

I'm sure that our products will meet the standards specified in our contract and your requirement. According to our working schedule, your order will be completed in time for delivery.

我确信我们的产品会符合合同规定的标准和您的要求。根据我们的工作日程安排，贵方的订单将按期完工交货。

Look at our revolutionary new nanometer products. We always make great efforts to keep the novelty of products.

请看我们的创新纳米产品。我们总是尽力保持产品的新颖性。

【知识点】考查结束后，及时询问其感觉，激起客户购买的欲望。如有不妥的地方进一步完善。

【技能训练句型】

What's your overall impression of our company?

您对本公司的总印象如何？

Seeing is believing. Mr. Gage told me a lot about what he had seen in your factory. Now I have seen with my own eyes. I will report everything I saw here I believe our orders will be placed immediately after the delivery of this batch.

真是眼见为实啊。盖德先生曾多次告诉我他在贵厂的所见所闻，现在是我亲眼所见。我将向公司报告我的所见所闻，我相信在这批产品发货后，后续订单会接踵而来。

5. please think it over 请考虑考虑

【知识点】与客户商谈时，若遇到重大事情切不可急急忙忙地做出决定。守信是商务活动的基本原则，答应的事情如反悔改变，会产生不良后果。因此，碰到重大决策时要认真思考，请客户给点时间考虑。

【技能训练句型】

Please let me think it over.

请让我考虑考虑。

I am not in a position to give you a decision now. I have to discuss it with my colleagues.

我无法现在就给你做决定，我不得不与同事共同商议。

Part D Practice

I. Complete the Following Dialogues

(1)

Ye: Hello, nice to see you again, Mr. William.

Bill: Hi, long time no see. To be ____1____, just call me Bill.

Ye: OK, Bill. Let me give you a ___2___ of the factory.

Bill: That's exactly what I want to do. There is nothing like ___3___ things with my own eyes.

Ye: What do you like to see in ___4___?

Bill: I'd like to see your production ___5___ first.

Ye: Come on. Please ___6___ me to the workshop.

Bill: I appreciate the engineers and workers do their ___7___ to make the high quality products.

Ye: Thank you.

Bill: I see that the automated production ___8___ largely in the factory.

Ye: Some machines are designed by our engineers.

Bill: Great. It is really a large factory. I think I have found the right ___9___ for my future orders.

Ye: I think you'll have a better idea about our factory now. I am ___10___ your order.

(2)

Yang: Martin, shall I give you a general ___1___ of the company?

Martin: Certainly. I couldn't ___2___ more.

Yang: Ours is a large washing machine company in the province. We have a good ___3___ in this field.

Martin: What is your production ___4___?

Yang: We have a production capacity of 80 thousand washing machines ___5___ month.

Martin: When is your ___6___ season?

Yang: Oh, we are fully ___7___ until next December from now.

Martin: My purpose to visit is to see how well our order is ___8___ out.

Yang: Don't worry. We ___9___ ourselves to meet the standards specified in our contract and your requirement.

Martin: I am glad to hear it.

Yang: Look! Your washing machines are ___10___ processing there.

II. Interaction Activities

Task 1

Ask students work in pair and make a dialogue according to the situation.

A and B talk about the new products.

Use the following expressions:

(1) design department

(2) revolutionary new nanometer products

(3) up-to-date patterns

(4) make great efforts

(5) have a new face

(6) upgrade products

(7) overall impression

(8) Seeing is believing.

Task 2

Talking about joint investment.

Use the following expressions in your dialogue:

(1) after looking around the plant

(2) While ... the production capacity is not large enough.

(3) enlarge the production scale

(4) double overnight

(5) be kidding

(6) prevent sb. from expansion

(7) out of funds

(8) joint investment

(9) in detail

(10) provide the existing line

(11) It's not incredible that ...

(12) come into being

III. Actual Practice

Make up a conversation and role-play the following practical situation.

1. Mr. Tang, director of the factory, is showing Mr. Watt around the factory.
2. Mr. Watt is seeking for arts porcelain, ornaments for display, imitation antique porcelain.
3. Mr. Tang believes his products will meet the client's demand.
4. The showroom displays a great variety of porcelain.
5. Mr. Tang introduces the features of the ceramic arts and crafts.
6. Mr. Watt wants to see everything with his own eyes instead of telling story by Mr. Tang.
7. After visit, Mr. Watt considers to place an initial order soon.

IV. Creative Discussion

The teacher divides the class into groups and asks students to discuss. Then each group takes turns presenting its conclusions.

Topic:

1. What are the important aspects to show the visiting clients?
2. How to make an appropriate introduction of the factory?
3. How to make clients feel satisfactory at the visit so as to induce them to place more orders?

Chapter 8 Innovative and Power Brand Strategy

Learning Objectives
Upon completion of this chapter, you will be able to

- learn the importance of innovative strategy and own brands.
- improve your communication skills on the technical discussion.
- discuss more specifically technical issues with your clients.
- avoid disputes on technical issues when you deal with a business transaction.
- make yourself more knowledgeable in more fields.

课文范读

Part A Situational Dialogue

 Communicative Scene 1

Discussion on Innovative Commodity

(*Mr.Nixon is visiting Miss Zhao's company and they are discussing the innovative products and own power brands.*)

Zhao: Hello, Mr. Nixon. It's so nice to meet you again.

Nixon: Hello, Miss Zhao. Have you received our fax regarding the issues of commodity innovation that we want to talk with you? To promote the sales in our market, our company wants to improve and modernize the design, quality and some other matters.

Zhao: Oh, yes. Shall we begin our discussion now?

Nixon: Sure, let's start from the design. As your products have been sold in the market for some time, there have been some copies from other manufacturers and importers. To lead the market, we'd like to show our customers some new faces of tools.[1] Do you have any good ideas for that?

Zhao: Yes. That is what we are worrying about. We have paid special attention to it for some time. Our company is adopting an innovative strategy. We'll try our best to create our own power brands.

Nixon: Great!

Zhao: Only through innovation and creation of our own power brands can our company hold market share in this intensified market competition.[2]

Nixon: Absolutely.

Zhao: Our designers have developed some new designs for you to choose from. We may start with one or two of them to see the response from the customers while we are selling the old items.

Nixon: That's a good idea. They all look very nice. I believe they will meet with great favor in our market. Also, to make our products look more fancy, our company is going to adopt a new series of color sleeves.[3]

Zhao: Printing these new sleeves is not a problem. We'll use brighter paper to print the sleeves to make them look brighter.

Nixon: I'm anxiously looking forward to seeing innovative products with the new series packing on the store shelves of our supermarkets. We have still received some complaints from our customers, though the quality of your tools are basically acceptable. We'd like to mention it again, because we don't want to lose our market and customers due to small quality problems.

Innovative and Power Brand Strategy

Zhao: We certainly appreciate your reminding us of quality. As a matter of fact, the quality is always a key point in our mind. For your information, our company has just passed ISO 9000 and our products are applying for a CE Certificate now. With CE Certificate, our products will stand higher in European market, which will specially benefit your company.

Nixon: I'm so glad to hear the good news. Last but not least, we request that all the tools should be heat-treated.[4]

Zhao: That will not be a problem from technical point of view. However, the overall price, due to production cost, will be some 20% higher than the present one in the case all the tools are heat-treated.

Nixon: I understand, but I'm sorry to say it is a must.[5] Meanwhile we don't like to force our customers to pay higher prices.

Zhao: In this case, may I suggest a compromise? Let us make easily worn-out screwdriver bits heat-treated instead of all the tools, so that we can increase the rank of our tools and keep the prices steady.

Nixon: Personally speaking, I accept your proposal. However, I'm not entitled to the decision in this matter. I'll[6] have to call my headquarter office to get their approval. Anyway, I'm very pleased to see everything being settled so smoothly. I appreciate your kind cooperation on almost every field.

Zhao: You are always welcome.

 Communicative Scene 2

Specific Technical Negotiation

(Technical negotiation between Mr. Chen and Mr. Marks is going on.)

Chen: Mr. Marks, we have carefully studied your prototype and related drawings of the ladder hooks. We are very interested in developing this new patent product with you.

Marks: I'm glad to hear that. What can I do for you now?

Chen: First of all, we'd like to discuss some technical issues with you. We tested your prototype and found that the plastic clip part bends easily, even breaks if the screw is tightened too much. To solve this problem, we suggest using metal parts to replace the plastic ones.

Marks: It is technically OK, but commercially not, because the metal part does not look as good as the plastic one.

Chen: Got it. We may have to make the plastic part thicker than the original design to strengthen the weak point.

Marks: That is what we want.

Chen: Before starting work on it, we'd like to see if we can find a ready market for ladder hooks.

Marks: I don't know for sure.

Chen: Do you have any idea how many pieces you are going to order for the first time?

Marks: Does that matter?

Chen: Yes. It certainly does. As you know, to produce the plastic portion for this product, we must build three injection molds. Each one will cost USD 1,000. Moreover, we need 5 dies and USD 200 for each. We shall invest at least USD 4,000 at the very beginning. If the order quantity were too small, the unit price for each product would be very high.

Marks: <u>Is there a better way out?</u>[7]

Chen: You may have to pay for the moulds and dies first. <u>We'll pay you back the cost for moulds and dies by deducting from the unit price when your future orders accumulate up to 100,000 pieces.</u>[8]

Marks: That means I'll have to take the risk of USD 4,000 investment until I can sell 100,000 pieces. Is there any way to minimize my risk?

Chen: Let me think...OK, let's share the risk by half and half. Our company will pay USD 2,000 and you'll pay the rest.

Marks: That's very kind of you. Thank you so much.

Chen: But, please note since we share the risk with you, we'll be unable to pay you back your portion no matter what quantity of products you are going to order in the future. Do you agree?

Marks: Sure, you are quite right. We will write it down in our contract.

Chen: Good! Let's move forward.

 Communicative Scene 3

Trademark and Patent

(Mr. Zhang and Mr. Brown are discussing an electronic product sales contract.)

Brown: What a relief after 3-days of tough negotiation on this contract! I'm so happy we finally come to a successful conclusion.

Zhang: <u>As a Chinese saying goes, "The road to happiness is always strewn with setbacks."</u>[9] Before celebrating victory, we still have two more points to discuss with you.

Brown: Two more "setbacks"? My goodness!

Zhang: Please don't worry. We believe they can be settled without any difficulties.

Brown: Really? What are they?

Zhang: As you mentioned in article 11 and 12, your high-tech product is a US patented product and we should sell your products with your trademark.

Brown: Is there any problem?

Zhang: No, not at all. <u>At first, we need you to provide us with copies of your patent certificate and trademark registration to show you are the owner of the patent and trademark.</u>[10] We also want to see that your patent and trademark are still valid.

Brown: OK. That is no problem. We will attach the copies to this contract as the appendixes.

Zhang: <u>At the same time, we strongly recommend you to apply for the trademark in China to protect yourself from offences.</u>[11] In case the trademark is registered by someone else, it'll be a headache.

Brown: You are absolutely right. Thank you for reminding me. We will register our trademark in China without any delay. By the way, as we are not familiar with related Chinese laws and regulations, could you help me to do this in someway?

Zhang: Certainly. To do this, we need an authorized letter from your company before we start.

Brown: Thank you ever so much.

Zhang: Now we can cheer for the conclusion of our business.

Words and Expressions

1. fancy	*adj.*	花哨的；奇特的；异样的
2. modernize	*v.*	使现代化
3. adopt	*vt.*	采用，采纳，采取；收养
4. innovative strategy		创新战略
5. intensify	*vi. & vt.*	加强，增强
6. sleeve	*n.*	体壳，color sleeve 彩套
7. shelf	*n.*	货架
8. complaint	*n.*	抱怨；投诉
9. as a matter of fact		实际上，其实
10. for your information		供参考
11. ISO	*abbr.*	International Organization for Standardization 国际标准化机构
12. compromise	*n., vi. & vt.*	妥协，折中，让步
13. worn-out	*adj.*	用坏的，穿旧的
14. screwdriver bits		螺丝刀头
15. entitle	*vt.*	给权力，有资格
16. prototype	*n.*	原型；模型；样板
17. ladder hook		梯用挂钩
18. clip	*n.*	夹子，回形针
19. bend	*vt.*	夹住；修剪
	v.	弯曲；屈服
20. injection	*n.*	注射；喷射；注塑
21. mould	*n.*	注塑模，压铸模
22. die	*n.*	冲压模
23. accumulate	*vt. & vi.*	积累，积聚
24. portion	*n.*	部分
25. tough	*adj.*	坚韧的，强硬的，严峻的
26. strew	*vt.*	撒，播；铺盖

27. setback	n.	挫折；失败；逆流；旋涡
28. appendix	n.	附件，附录
29. high-tech	n.	高科技
30. patent	n.	专利权
31. offend	vt.	冒犯；伤害
offense (Chiefly America)	n.	冒犯；伤害
offence (Chiefly British)	n.	冒犯；伤害
32. regulation	n.	规则，规章；调节
33. authorized letter		授权书

1. To lead the market, we'd like to show our customers some new faces of tools.

   为了引领市场，我们想让客户看到新面孔的工具产品。

   ① to lead the market 为了引领市场

   同义词：to direct the market, to guide the market

   ② show n.,v 指示；出示；引导；显示；说明；展出

   非正式用语，使用范围广，所表示的"显示"可以是有意的，也可以是无意的，或由于疏忽而暴露。而（display）是强调摆给别人看，特别把要给人家看的东西精心陈列出来，如精心陈列展品，以期收到良好的展示效果。

2. Only through innovation and creation of our own power brands can our company hold market share in this intensified market competition.

   只有通过产品创新和创立名牌，我们公司才能在激烈的市场竞争中占一席之地。

   ① 本句为倒装句，重点强调产品创新和创立名牌。Only在句子开头，can随其后，倒装句型提醒读者后边是一个条件句，起强调作用。

   Only through the introduction of competition can we cut down the prices.

   只有引入竞争机制，才能把价格降下。

   ② power brand 品牌

   ③ brand power strategy / brand strategies 品牌战略

3. To make our products look more fancy, our company is going to adopt new series of color sleeves.

   为了让我们的产品看上去更花哨，我们公司准备采用新系列的彩套。

   ① fancy adj. 超过的，不合理的

   Mr. Smith paid a fancy price for a computer.

   史密斯先生以过高的价格买下一部电脑。

   fancy vt. 设想，认为，爱好，自负 n. 爱好，迷恋，想象力

   Fancy meeting you here in the exhibition!

   想不到在展览馆见面！

   take / catch the fancy of 使……喜欢；吸引

The Commodity Fair catches the fancy of thousands of businessmen.

take a fancy to 喜欢上……

商品交易会吸引了数以千计的商人。

② adopt *vt.* 采用，采纳，采取；收养

Our company is adopting an innovative strategy.

我们公司正推行产品创新战略。

adopt new series of color sleeves 采用新系列的彩套

注意 adopt 与 adapt、adept 的区别：

adapt *v.* 使适应，改编

The manufacturers should adapt themselves to the market requirements.

生产厂家应使自己适应新的市场要求。

adept *n.* 内行；有很高技巧的人，专家

4. Last but not least, we request that all the tools should be heat-treated.

最后，很重要的一点是要求将所有工具进行热处理。

① Last but not least 是插入语，位于句首，起加强语气和承上启下的作用。翻译时注意不要照字面译成"最后，但并非不重要的一点"，而应译为"最后，很重要的一点"。

Last but not least, I'll have to make a report to the general manager to get the approval.

最后，很重要的一点是我不得不向总经理汇报以便得到批准。

5. I'm sorry to say it is a must.

我很抱歉，必须这么做。

① be a must 必须做

A good command of English is a must in foreign trade.

从事外贸，掌握好英语是必须的。

6. Personally speaking, I accept your proposal. However, I'm not entitled to the decision on this matter.

我个人可以接受你的建议。但在这个问题上，我无权决定。

① be entitled to 有权，给……权利或给……资格

② entitle sb. to do sth. 给某人做某事的权利

The seller is entitled to the payment on presenting documents.

卖方有权在递交单证后得到支付。

7. Is there a better way out?

有什么解决的办法？

Please find a way out

请找出路。

8. We'll pay you back the cost for moulds and dies by deducting from the unit price when your future orders accumulate up to 100,000 pieces.

当你的订货数量累计达到10万件时，我们将从单价中扣还模具的费用。

① deduct *v.* 扣除

② accumulate *v.* 积累

accumulate使用范围较广,强调经过一段较长的时间由少积多的积累,可以表示数量方面的积累增长。

③ up to 多至……;一直到;等于

9. As a Chinese saying goes, "The road to happiness is always strewn with setbacks."

正如中国话所说的,"好事多磨"。

① strew *vt.* 播,撒

Export documents were strewn all over the floor.

出口单证撒满了一地板。

同义词:distribute, spread, scatter

② setback *n.* 挫折

10. At first, we need you to provide us with copies of your patent certificate and trademark registration to show you are the owner of the patent and trademark.

首先我方需要贵公司提供专利证书和商标注册的复印件,以表明贵公司是这项专利和商标的所有权人。

① trademark registration 注册商标

同义词组:registered trademark, have trademark registered, apply for the registration

11. We strongly recommend you to apply for the trademark in China to protect yourself from offenses.

我们竭力建议贵公司在中国申请此商标以保护自己免受侵犯。

① recommend sb. to do sth. 建议……做……

The lawyer strongly recommended to prepare a lot of documents for trademark registration, and many of them must be notarized.

为了申请注册商标,律师强烈忠告要准备就绪大量凭证,许多凭证还要公证。

② recommend 后接从句结构时,用虚拟语气。

The manager strongly recommended that you notice the trademark to be limited by region.

经理强烈建议要注意商标受地域的限制。

*12. However, it greatly related with the matter of production cost.

然而,它与生产成本有很大关系。

① It greatly related with ... 与……有很大关系

② relate with / to 使联系

CFR prices relate the cost with freight.

成本加运费价涉及成本与运费。

Part B Practical Key Sentences

1. expressing the idea of good sale

Our newly designed artificial intelligence have met with great favor home and abroad.

Innovative and Power Brand Strategy

我们新设计的人工机器人产品在国内外很受欢迎。

find a ready market 畅销，好销路

find a market 找到销路

be popular 畅销，流行

be welcome 受欢迎

替换表达：

China's power brands are the best sellers all over the world.

The new style will be welcomed by our customers.

I believe they will find a ready market in our area.

There is a good market for our hand tools.

You'll find a promising market for our new products.

2. for your information

顺便告知，仅供参考

For your information, our company has just passed ISO 9000 and our products are applying for CE Certificate now.

顺便告诉你，我们公司已经通过了ISO 9000的认证，我们的产品也正在申请CE认证。

国际商务业务中常用此句型，婉转地传达有关信息。又如：

for your perusal 供你方斟酌，供你方细读

for you to study 供你方研究

替换表达：

For your information, computer sales have increased rapidly and will keep on rising in the years to come.

For your perusal, the price list gives referent prices for all our export products.

For you to study, we have sent you catalogues and samples.

3. replace sth. with sth.

replace是指代替他人或他物的相等物或替换物。

To solve this problem, we suggest using metal parts to replace the plastic ones.

为了解决这个问题，我们建议用金属部件来代替塑料部件。

替换表达：

instead of 代替，而不是

instead *adv.* 代替，顶替

Let us make the easily worn-out screwdriver bits heat-treated instead of all the tools.

substitute *n.* 用人或事来取代，替代品

The oil prices keep rising so people are trying to find substitute for petroleum.

take the place of another 用……替代

Moral power will take the place of physical force.

4. minimize the risk

They try to minimize the risk of their investment to zero.

他们试图把投资降到零风险。

He took out a patent in order to minimize the risk of innovation.

为了降低创新的风险,他申请获得了专利。

试用下列含risk的短语造句:

minimize the risk 把风险降到最低

share the risk by half and half 承担一半的风险

at risk 处境危险

at the risk of one's life 冒着生命危险

at all / any risks 无论冒什么危险

do business at one's own risk 自负盈亏

take / run a risk 冒险

5. **saying you are not sure**

I don't know for sure.

我没把握。

I am not quite sure about the exchange rate today.

我对今日外汇汇率不清楚。

替换表达:

I can't make out why you are making a compromise suggestion.

I am in two mind about ...

It is not certain that ...

It is hard to say.

6. **be valid**

We also want to see that your patent and trademark are still valid.

我们还需要有关证据来表明你们的专利和商标仍然有效。

be good 有效

remain valid 有效

The lawyer strongly recommended that apply for a renewal within 6 months before expiry. Each renewal is good for 10 years.

律师竭力建议在期满之前6个月内申请继续注册,每次继续注册有效期为10年。

替换表达:

The duration of patent right remains valid for at least 15 years.

How long will the registered trademark be valid?

Our firm offer is good for 10 days.

Part C Integration of Theory and Practice

1. **apply for CE Certificate 申请"CE"标志**

【知识点】"CE"标志是一种安全认证标志,被视为制造商打开并进入欧洲市场的护照。凡是贴有"CE"标志的产品就可在欧盟各成员国内销售,无须符合每个成员国的要求,从而实现了商品在欧盟成员国范围内的自由流通。

在欧盟市场，"CE"标志属于强制性认证标志，不论是欧盟内部企业生产的产品，还是其他国家生产的产品，要想在欧盟市场上自由流通，就必须加贴"CE"标志，以表明产品符合欧盟《技术协调与标准化新方法》指令的基本要求。这是欧盟法律对产品提出的一种强制性要求。

过去，欧共体国家对进口和销售的产品要求各异，根据某一国标准制造的商品到别国，也许不能上市，作为消除贸易壁垒之努力的一部分，CE应运而生，代表欧洲统一。事实上，CE还是欧共体许多国家语种中的"欧共体"这一词组的缩写，原来用英语词组EUROPEAN COMMUNITY的缩写EC，后因"欧共体"的法文是COMMUNATE EUROPEIA，意大利文为COMUNITA EUROPEA，葡萄牙文为COMUNIDADE EUROPEIA，西班牙文为COMUNIDADE EUROPE等，故改EC为CE。

欧（洲）共（同）体后来演变成了欧洲联盟（简称欧盟）。近年来，在欧洲经济区（欧洲联盟、欧洲自由贸易协会成员国，瑞士除外）市场上销售的商品中，CE标志的使用越来越多，CE标志加贴的商品表示其符合安全、卫生、环保和消费者保护等一系列欧洲指令所要表达的要求。

我国企业生产的产品若要成功进军欧盟市场就要特别注意申请"CE"标志（CE Certificate）。

2. strategy of power brands　自主品牌战略

【知识点】在商务交易中，商品是买卖双方首先需要明确和洽谈的事宜。

塑造自主品牌和技术创新，构建核心竞争力是当今我国出口商品的重要战略决策。企业要善于技术创新，提高产品质量和经营方式，促进产品升级换代，创立自主商品名牌，增加出口商品的国际竞争力。

企业积极申报，争取通过质量认证体系和质量标准，这等于获得了进军海外市场的许可证，对占领细分市场份额十分有利。

本文中出现不少有关品牌战略的句型，可实践操练：

【技能训练句型】

Our company is adopting innovative strategy. We'll try our best to have our own power brands.
我们公司正推行产品创新战略，力争创自主品牌。

Only through innovation and creation of our own power brands can our company hold market share in intensified market competition.
只有通过技术创新和创立名牌，我们公司才能在激烈的市场竞争中占一席之地。

Our company has just passed ISO 9000 and our products are applying for CE Certificate now. With CE Certificate, our products will stand higher in European market, which will specially benefit your company.
我们公司已经通过了ISO 9000的认证，我们的产品也正在申请CE认证。有了CE认证，我们的产品将以更高的身价进入欧洲市场，这对贵公司尤为有利。

3. trademark and patent　商标和专利

【知识点】（1）商标由品牌名称、符号、数字、图案和颜色等标志组成。一旦它在商标法下注册登记成功，生产商便在此商标上具有垄断权。商品名称和商标是商品不可分割的部分，名牌产品因其良好的质量深受消费者欢迎。

【技能训练句型】

Trademarks ensure the quality of products and encourage its improvement and it also enable the consumers to choose what is dependable in quality and reasonable in price to meet their demand.

商标确保产品质量并促进改善创新。商标促使消费者挑选质量可靠、价格合理的商品来满足他们的需要。

【知识点】（2）为确保产品在国外市场畅销，尤其是大宗重要出口产品，最好也在国外注册商标，维护商标持有者正当权利。按照中国与申请国关于商标互惠的双边协议，外国商标也允许在中国注册，受到保护。

【技能训练句型】

As you mentioned in article 11 and 12, your product is a US patented product and we should sell your products with your trademark.

正如您在条款11和12中提到的那样，你们的产品在美国享有专利，我们销售时必须使用你们的商标。

At the same time, we strongly recommend you to apply the trademark in China to protect yourself to be offended. In case the trademark registered by someone else, it will be a headache.

同时，我们竭力建议贵公司在中国申请此商标以保护自己免受侵犯。如果商标被别人注册，那将是很头疼的事。

We will register our trademark in China without any delay. By the way, as we are not familiar with related Chinese laws and regulations, could you help me to do this in someway?

我们将立即在中国注册我们的商标。请问，您能帮帮忙吗？因为我们对中国的法律法规不熟悉。

【知识点】（3）专利法（patent law）给予发明者使用以及授予他人使用其发明的独占性和排他性的权利。要使专利得到保护，需要将本国注册的专利在国外注册。

【技能训练句型】

The aim of our patent law is to encourage invention, advance science and technology and promote technical exchanges with other countries.

我国专利法目的是鼓励发明创造和先进的科学技术，促进与各国之间的技术交流。

At first, we need you to provide us with copies of your patent certificate and trademark registration to show you are the owner of the patent and trademark.

首先我方需要贵公司提供专利证书和商标注册的复印件，以表明贵公司是这项专利和商标的所有权人。

We also want to have the evidence to see your patent and trademark are still valid.

我们还需要有关证据来表明你们的专利和商标仍然有效。

To do this, we need an authorized letter from your company before we start.

办理此事之前，我们需要贵公司的授权书。

Part D Practice

I. Complete the Following Dialogues

(1)

Marks: Mr. Wang, the ___1___ is going on well. We have already ___2___ on many points. What shall we talk ___3___ this time?

Wang: First of all, we'd like to discuss some technical issues ___4___ you. This is the first time your products will be ___5___ in our market, they must be attractive and helpful to the sales. Do you have any good ideas for that?

Marks: That is what we ___6___ about. In order to ___7___ customers, our designers have ___8___ some new designs for your choice.

Wang: That is what we want to hear. Very nice looking! I believe they will be ___9___ by our ___10___.

(2)

be entitled to	do sb. a favor	promote technical exchanges
don't know for sure	be a must	enjoy the exclusive right
The aim of	authorized letter	so far as rights are concerned
take out		

Fill in the blanks with the following useful expressions:

A: I am going to ___1___ a patent on my new invention. But I ___2___ about Patent Law. Could you ___3___?

B: Certainly. ___4___ our patent law is to encourage invention, advance science and technology and ___5___ with other countries.

A: Got it.

B: Well, ___6___, the one who owns the patent rights ___7___ to exploit them. Nobody else ___8___ the invention without the owner's written ___9___.

A: Yes. I think it ___10___.

II. Interaction Activities

Task 1

Ask students work in pair and make a dialogue according to the situation.

A and B discuss the design and color of stationery.

Use the following expressions:

(1) it's high time

(2) to lead the market

(3) look more fancy

(4) pay special attention to

(5) looking forward to

Task 2

Talking about trademarks.

Use following expressions in your dialogue:

(1) strongly recommend that

(2) protect yourself to be offended

(3) have ... registered

(4) better way out

(5) for your information

(6) contact the Trademark Office

(7) go through the formality

(8) no opposition to

(9) be valid

(10) don't know for sure

III. Actual Practice

Practise with your partner and role-play the conversation.

Talking about the issues of commodity innovation. The conversation should be well organized with the following items you have learnt in the text:

1. introduce the development of innovative products

2. adopt innovative strategy

3. have own power brands

4. develop some new designs

5. hold market share in the world market

6. obtain CE Certificate

7. find a ready market

IV. Creative Discussion

Debate

Students choose one topic for debate.

Topics:

1. Chinese enterprises should adopt innovative strategy in order to be more competitive in the world market.

2. Do you think it is necessary to apply for trademark and patent?

The class is divided into several groups. The affirmative side is supposed to develop as many affirmative statements while the negative side is supposed to develop as many negative statements as possible. Giving the arguments with reasonable support.

Chapter 9 Packing and Quality Inspection

Learning Objectives
Upon completion of this chapter, you will be able to

- understand that quality is a key to business door.
- know the importance of packing in foreign trade.
- learn how to introduce the quality of your products.
- improve your communication skills on packing and quality related issues.
- perform the right role in quality inspection.

课文范读

Part A Situational Dialogue

 Communicative Scene 1

Quality Control

(*Mr. Zhou, Manager of QC Department of Jin Xin Loudspeaker Company, is introducing his company to Mrs. Carl, a quality inspection representative.*)

Zhou: Mrs. Carl, welcome to our company.

Carl: Hello, Mr. Zhou. It is my pleasure to visit your company. My boss, Mr. Albert Gordon sent me here for quality inspection.

Zhou: Oh, Mr. Gordon is an old friend of our company. I believe he must have told you something about our company.

Carl: He did. I'll appreciate if you can tell me more about your company before starting quality inspection on the products under our Contract #5406.

Zhou: To let you know more about us, I'd like to introduce our company, our products as well as our inspection department briefly.

Carl: Go ahead, please.

Zhou: Our company is one of the main manufacturers of loudspeakers in China with hundreds of different kinds of loudspeakers, which are mainly exported to over 30 foreign countries and regions. <u>We employ about 500 workers and staff. Among them, 150 members are engineers and technicians.</u>[1] The annual export is about 80 million US dollars.

Carl: <u>Real cool!</u>[2]

Zhou: <u>Our quality control department, directly under the general manager, is in charge of all quality control related matters.</u>[3]

Carl: <u>It's essential that your boss attach importance to the quality.</u>[4] How many people are there in your department?

Zhou: 25 people, plus 15 inspectors in every workshop.

Carl: What is their responsibility? Or what is their daily job?

Zhou: They spread out to every corner of the workshops. They check the products from the production lines, test and record the technical parameters of our products, put forward the ideas on how to improve the quality and minimize the defects and others.

Carl: Do you think their inspection in the first line is effective and workable?

Zhou: Strictly speaking, yes. Very effective and workable. <u>They do form the first line of our quality control. Few defective products in the warehouse are checked out. According to statistics, the average rate is less than 0.015%.</u>[5]

Carl: Thank you for your introduction. Should we go and meet these quality controllers and inspect the products?

Zhou: It's my pleasure. Let's go to the workshops.

 Communicative Scene 2

Packing

(After showing Mrs. Carl around the workshops, Mr. Zhou is talking about packing with her.)

Carl: Your efficient inspection work left a favorable impression on me. Generally speaking, our order is being carried out in a good manner. My boss will be satisfied with your products after reading my inspection report.

Zhou: Thanks a lot. I'm so delighted to hear your positive comments on our job. I always believe that quality is a key to business.

Carl: Absolutely! I don't have anything more to say for the loudspeaker itself, except for the matters I mentioned while we were walking around the production lines. But I'd like to emphasize the importance of packing to the general aspect of quality.

Zhou: Please don't hesitate to let us know the weak points of our packing.[6] We'll do our best to improve it.

Carl: All right. First, the poly-bag for wrapping up each loudspeaker could be a little thicker. I don't think it would cost more because the poly-bags seem too thin. Loudspeakers may scratch the thin poly-bay during the transportation and handling. The poly-bag is the final packing when our products reach the hands of our consumers, though its cost is very subtle compared with other parts of the entire products.[7]

Zhou: You're right. The bags with double thickness will be used for your order.

Carl: Good. We request the plastic recycle mark should be printed on the backside corner of the poly-bag. It is a necessity of environmental protection.

Zhou: We'll do it.

Carl: The next issue is the inner box. The size of the inner box should be unified. Being too tight or too loose may damage the inner box that is the outlook of our products on the shelves of the stores.

Zhou: We'll pay special attention to that point.

Carl: The last point is the master carton. Please do not use iron staples and plastic belts that are commonly used for outside packing.

Zhou: I believe that's also better for environment protection.

Carl: Correct. That's all for today.

Zhou: Thanks. Your kind and timely suggestions are very precious for us to improve the quality not only of your goods, but also of other products supplied to all our customers. We'll keep them in mind.

Communicative Scene 3

Commodity Inspection

(Mr. Zhou and Mrs. Carl are going on talking about commodity inspection.)

Carl: Mr. Zhou, we won't be able to send anyone else to your company before the goods are shipped. For this reason, we request the commodity inspection should be conducted for our order.

Zhou: No problem. Our export inspections are mainly made by Entry-Exit Inspection and Quarantine Bureau. It enjoys high international reputation all over the world.

Carl: I've heard about it.

Zhou: The inspection will be carried out within 5 days before delivery. The Bureau has branch offices in all port cities, such as ours, so it's very convenient to carry out the inspection.

Carl: What standards are they using?

Zhou: <u>The Chinese national standards will be applied, if the commodity is a compulsory inspected item.</u>[8] If not, the standards can be ones stipulated in applicant's commercial contract.

Carl: Since the certificate of quality and quantity issued by the Bureau will be an important document for L/C negotiation, can they issue the certificate in German?

Zhou: I don't think so. <u>As a rule, the inspection certificates are made in the form of Chinese and English.</u>[9]

Carl: All right. A copy in English would also be acceptable. Can we make re-inspection at the port of destination when the goods arrive?

Zhou: Theoretically yes, but I don't think it is necessary, because it may cause disputes. If you prefer an inspection agency other than Entry-Exit Inspection and Quarantine Bureau, it will be fine for us, as we are confident for our products. However, the expenses for inspection will be covered by your company.

Carl: OK. I hope there is no occasion for any disagreeable things to happen. <u>An eye finds more truth than two ears.</u>[10] I think I have completed all my tasks for this trip.

Zhou: <u>Why not take a trip to look around our city to relax?</u>[11]

Carl: Thank you. That sounds nice.

Words and Expressions

1.	loudspeaker	*n.*	扬声器，喇叭
2.	annual	*adj.*	每年的，一年一次的
3.	spread out		分布；展开
4.	put forward		提出（意见、建议）；推举出
5.	parameter	*n.*	参数
6.	statistics	*n.*	统计
7.	warehouse	*n.*	仓库

8. emphasize	vt.	强调，着重
9. poly-bag	n.	塑料包装袋
10. wrap	v.	包装，卷，裹
	n.	包装纸；披肩；外套，大衣
11. scratch	vt. & vi.	抓破，划伤
12. subtle	adj.	微小的，细微的
13. recycle	vt.	再循环
14. environmental	adj.	环境的
15. uniform	adj.	（与其他）一样的，统一的；一致的
16. tight	adj.	紧的
17. staple	n.	订书钉，U形钉
18. plastic belt		塑料打包带
19. precious	adj.	珍贵的，宝贵的
20. Entry-Exit Inspection and Quarantine Bureau		进出口检验检疫局
21. compulsory	adj.	强迫的；强制的；义务的
22. re-inspection	n.	复检
23. theoretically	adv.	理论上
24. dispute	n.	争论；争议；辩论
25. cover	vt.	支付，偿付
26. disagreeable	adj.	不合意的；不愉快的

1. We employ about 500 workers and staffs. Among them, 150 members are engineers and technicians.
   我们拥有员工500人，其中包括150名工程师和技术员。
   表示拥有员工，用employ最贴切，不用possess。
   ① possess v. 拥有，占有，possess一般不跟随人。
   Our company possessed valuable technical know-how.
   本公司拥有宝贵的技术诀窍。

2. Real cool！
   好极了，了不起。（俚语）

3. Our Quality Control Department, directly under the general manager, is in charge of all the quality control related matters.
   质量控制部由总经理直接领导，负责所有质量控制有关的事宜。
   directly under general manager 插入语

4. It's essential that your boss (should) attach importance to the quality.
   贵方老板重视产品质量至关重要。
   ① It's essential that … 至关重要的，紧要的

主语从句中的虚拟语气。一些表示important（重要的）、imperative（迫切的）、urgent（紧迫的）、necessary（必要的）、requested（要求）、proposed（建议）等意思的形容词和过去分词，在主语从句中，谓语动词用should加动词原形或仅用动词原形，表示虚拟。

It's appropriate that the factory upgrade the products every year.
工厂的产品每年升级换代很有必要。

It is vital that this tax be abolished.
废除这项税收是非常重要的。

5. They do form the first line of our quality control. Few defective products in the warehouse are checked out. According to statistics, the average rate is less than 0.015%.
他们的确形成我们质量控制的第一道防线。从库房中检出的次品非常少。据统计，次品平均比率不到万分之一点五。

① check out 检验，检测，合格，结账

Our products are made under reliable quality control and they are checked out seriously.
我们的产品经过认真检验，在严格的质量管理下生产。

② average *adj.* 平均

Frankly speaking, the quality of that kind of refrigerator is below average.
坦率地说，那种电冰箱的质量在一般水平之下。

6. Please don't hesitate to let us know the weak points of our packing.
请不必顾虑地告诉我们包装方面的缺点。

① don't hesitate to 不必顾虑地

Please don't hesitate to tell me if you need help.
如果你需要帮助，请告诉我。

Don't hesitate about pointing out the mistakes I made when calculating the prices.
若我计算价格有误，请大胆指出。

7. The poly-bag is the final packing when our products reach the hands of our consumers, though its cost is very subtle compared with other parts of the entire products.
虽然与整个产品的其他部分相比，塑料袋的成本是微不足道的，但却是我们的产品到达顾客手中时的最终包装物。

① compare with 与……相比

Your quotation seems a little too high compared with the offers from other similar companies.
与其他同类公司的报盘相比，贵方的报价似乎有点偏高。

8. The Chinese national standards will be applied, if the commodity is a compulsory inspected item.
如果是法定商检产品，将采用中国国家标准。

① apply to 适用于；运用于；关系到；把……运用于

We should apply the economic theory that we learned in the classroom to practice.
我们应当把课堂所学的经济学理论应用于实践。

② apply oneself to 致力于，集中精力做某事

③ apply one's mind to 专心于

9. As a rule, the inspection certificates are made in the form of Chinese and English.
通常，证书是用中文和英文的。

① in the form of 以……的形式，呈……状态

② form *n.* 强调 "形式"

The right of cargo is presented in the form of Bill of Lading.

货物所有权以提单的形式体现。

③ in shape 强调 "外形"、"形状"

④ in figure 强调 "外形"、"轮廓"

10. An eye finds more truth than two ears.

    百闻不如一见。

11. Why not take a trip to look around our city to relax?

    为何不到我们市转一转，放松一下？

    ① Why +not +动词原形，表示提出建议。

    ② Why +动词原形，表示不定式后的动作不必要做或毫无意义。

    Why not look around Quality Control Center with our inspectors?

    为什么不和我们的检验员一起到质量管理中心看看？

    Why spend so much time negotiating for the increase of price? There is no way to persuade him to accept your offer.

    为什么花这么多的时间洽谈提价？根本就无法劝说他接受你方的报盘。

Part B Practical Key Sentences

1. **strictly speaking**

   副词+speaking 形成的副词短语，位于句首。

   Strictly speaking, yes. Very effective and workable.

   严格说来，是的。行之有效。

   Frankly speaking, our company only accept L/C.

   坦率地说，我公司仅仅接受信用证付款。

   替换表达：

   Properly speaking, your prices are on the high side.

   Generally speaking, we are fully confident about the quality of our air conditioners.

   Roughly speaking, our factory produces more than 5,000 shoes everyday.

   Briefly speaking, our prices are in line with the prevailing market.

   Broadly speaking, your products are in standard quality.

2. **attach importance to**

   Our manager attached importance to the development of new products.

   我们的经理重视产品创新。

   emphasize the importance of 重视

   lay emphasis on 强调，突出重点

   The director of the factory laid particular emphasis on quality control.

   厂长特别强调质量管理的重要性。

替换表达：

The workers emphasized the importance of packing.

The workers think much of quality inspection.

The buyer put emphasis on terms of payment.

3. **according to statistics**

   According to statistics, the rate is less than 0.015% on average.

   据统计，次品平均比率不到万分之一点五。

   By estimate, our orders will exceed a total amount of USD 100,000 this month.

   据估计，本月我们的订单将超过十万美元。

   替换表达：

   By statistics, Mr. William's account was overdrawn USD 200 this week.

   At a rough estimate, your commission for trade will be 1,000 Pounds or over.

   It is estimated that the effective work will reduce cost by 20%.

4. **give sb. a favorable impression**

   Your efficient inspection work gave me a favorable impression.

   你们有效的检验工作给我留下美好的印象。

   The tight quality control of your factory made a deep impression on us.

   贵工厂严格的质量管理给我们留下深刻的影响。

   替换表达：

   Your excellent packing method impressed me a great deal.

   The attractive advertisement left a good impression on all customers.

   Your idea of environmental protection made an impression on the manufacturers.

5. **conduct the inspection**

   We request the commodity inspection should be conducted for our order.

   我们要求对我们订单项下的货物实施商品检验。

   conduct *v.* 进行；开展；实施；处理

   We are conducting an advertising campaign to make ourselves known by TV ads.

   我们大力开展广告宣传，让外界通过电视广告了解我们。

   替换表达：

   The production of ordered goods will be made as soon as the opening of L/C.

   The packing of products is carried out before shipment.

   The inspection should be done by Entry-Exit Inspection and Quarantine Bureau.

Part C Integration of Theory and Practice

1. **packing 商品包装**

   【知识点】科学、美观、适销和牢固的商品包装能保护商品，方便运输和增加商品价值。商品包装分为销售包装（内包装inner packing）和运输包装（外包装outside packing）。现代包装的发展日新月异，随着超市的发展，销售包装造型更美观大方，印刷条形码，讲究包装装潢，突出商标品牌，吸引顾客，提高有形商品的内外在质量。

【技能训练句型】

The size of the inner box should be unified. Too tight or too loose may damage the inner box that is the outlook of our products on the shelves of the stores.

内盒的尺寸必须一致，太松或太紧都可能损坏内盒。内盒是我们产品在货架上的形象展示。

Your kind and timely suggestions are very precious for us to improve the quality not only of your goods, but also of other products supplied to all our customers.

您中肯、及时的建议有利于我们产品质量的提高，这不仅有益于你们，也有益于其他客户。

2. environmental protection consciousness 环境保护意识

【知识点】现代商品包装充分体现了环境保护意识，使用环保材料，印制环保的标志，实现绿色包装。

【技能训练句型】

Please do not use iron staples and plastic belts that are commonly used for outside packing.

请不要使用通常用于外包装的订书钉和塑料打包带。

We request the plastic recycle mark should be printed on the backside corner of the poly-bag, which is a necessity of environmental protection.

我们要求在塑料袋背面的角落上印上可循环塑料的标志，这是环境保护的要求。

3. quality control 质量管理

【知识点】良好的产品质量是商品畅销的重要保证，生产企业一定要花大气力，严格把好质量关。出口商品要尽量采用国际标准，提升竞争能力。质量赢得市场，诚信铸就品牌。创立名牌，以质取胜。

【技能训练句型】

Our export commodity are all quality goods. The aim of our company is "Quality and Customers first".

我们的出口商品全是一级品，公司的宗旨是"质量第一，用户第一"。

All products are made under an extremely tight quality control.

所有的产品都经过极度严格的质量检测。

4. quality of goods 商品品质

【知识点】商品品质是合同首先要明确规定的交易条件，国际贸易中常见对商品品质的要求。

（1）凭样品买卖 (Sales by sample)。例如：

凭卖方样品买卖 Quality as per Seller's Sample

凭买方样品买卖 Quality as per Buyer's Sample

对等样品买卖 Quality as per Counter Sample

样品指从一批商品中抽出来，足以反映和代表整批商品品质的少量实物。

（2）凭规格、等级、标准买卖。例如：

凭规格买卖 Sale by Specification

凭等级买卖 Sale by Grade

凭标准买卖 Sale by Standard

（3）凭品牌或商标买卖 Brand Name or Trade Mark

（4）凭产地买卖 Name of Origin

（5）凭说明书和图样买卖 Sale by Descriptions and Illustrations

制定品质条款的诀窍：

（1）要根据生产实际，恰如其分，不可定得太高，否则导致无法履约。而定得太低，则影响声誉和价格。

（2）正确运用各种表示品质的方法，采用何种表示品质的方法，应视商品特性而定。凡能用科学的指标说明其质量的商品，适合凭规格、等级或标准买卖；有些难以规格化和标准化的商品，则适于凭样品买卖；名优产品，适于凭商标或品牌买卖；某些性能复杂的机器、电器和仪表，则适于凭说明书和图样买卖；凡具有地方风味和特色的产品，则可凭产地名称买卖。

（3）品质条件的规定应明确具体，不用"大约""左右"之类的含糊字眼，以免在交货品质上引起麻烦。

5. quality inspection 商品检验

【知识点】商品检验是外贸的重要环节之一，商品的品质关系重大，买方担心实际交货是否与样品保持一致。有些进口商为了确保产品质量可行，专门派人或委托专业检测部门来了解和验货，可详细向他们介绍本企业提高产品质量和质量检测的措施。

【技能训练句型】

The inspectors check the products from the production lines, test and record the technical parameters of our products, put forward the ideas on how to improve the quality and minimize the defects and others.

检验员检查生产线下来的产品，测试和记录产品参数，提出改进质量和减少次品的建议等。

The products are 100% checked here and defective ones will be thrown out to these boxes for the head of the workshop and technicians to analyze what the problems are and find out the ways to prevent from future occurrence.

百分百的产品都经这里检验，次品被扔到这些箱子里，由车间主任和技术员分析存在的问题，并找出防止再度发生的办法。

6. compulsory inspected item 法定商检

【知识点】列入国家质检总局颁布的实施出口质量许可、出口食品卫生注册登记"两证"管理目录的产品生产企业，必须获得"两证"，方可出口。国家法定商检项目，出口前须进行商检。商检部门对进出口商品的品质、数量、重量和包装等实施检验，根据需要出具检验证书（Inspection Certificate）。非法定商检产品的检验标准由买卖双方自行商定。

【技能训练句型】

The Chinese national standards will be applied to, if the commodity is a compulsory inspected item. If not, the standards can be ones stipulated in applicant's commercial contract.

如果是法定商检产品，将采用中国国家标准；若非法定商检产品，可采用申请人的商业合同中指定的标准。

Part D Practice

I. Complete the Following Dialogues

(1)

Fill in the blanks with proper words.

A: I understand packing is a ____1____ to business door.

B: That's why we always ___2___ importance to packing.
A: Proper ___3___ can protect the goods from ___4___ during transportation.
B: How many kinds of packing?
A: There are mainly two kinds of ___5___, inner and outside packing.
B: Could you tell me more about them?
A: Outside packing prevents the goods from damage of shipment. ___6___ packing is the final packing to reach the ___7___ of customers.
B: I think inner packing should be not only strong but also ___8___ to attract customers.
A: Quite right. The novel packing will help promote ___9___. We also take environmental protection into ___10___ when choosing the packing materials nowadays.
B: Thank you. I have learned a lot from you today.

(2)

Complete the following dialogue with expressions or sentences.
A: Why not ___1___ packing now, Mr. White?
B: Yes. ___2___ the usual way to pack Qingdao Beer?
A: Sure. We always lay ___3___ packing because the bottles of beer are easily broken
B: I agree.
A: Master cartons are used for ___4___ and nylon straps are used to strengthen them.
B: ___5___ they are not strong enough.
A: ___6___ use wooden cases?
B: Our master cartons are strong enough ___7___, but wooden cases ___8___ trans-portation and they will cost more.
A: Do you use warning marks for handling?
B: Yes. ___9___, we print "Handle With Care" in the outside cartons.
A: Great! I can ___10___ about it now.

II. Interaction Activities

Task 1

Mr. Zhu, from an inspection bureau, goes to the factory to inspect the export goods before shipment.

Students make conversations by using the following expressions.
(1) be ready for
(2) look round
(3) quality inspection
(4) attach importance to
(5) under strict quality control
(6) it's essential that
(7) form the first line
(8) spread out

(9) effective and workable

(10) checking out

(11) it's time to

(12) select a few goods at random

(13) don't hesitate to

(14) give sb. a favorable impression

Task 2

Students make up a conversation between Mr. Green and the manager of an export company.

Mr. Green is sent to inspect the quality of porcelain goods by his company. After inspection, he finds some problems for packing:

1. outside packing for improvement

2. poly-bag of inner packing

3. the outlook of box

Please find the solution to the problems including timely suggestions made by Mr. Green and promise for improvement made by manager.

III. Actual Practice

Students work in groups and try to give advice for the following business situations:

1. What standards of quality will he choose if Sam is going to import a large quantity of sugar from China? Give the reasons.

2. What standards of quality will she choose if Cindy is going to import some arts porcelain and imitation antique porcelain? Give the reasons.

3. What standards of quality will he choose if David is going to import Haier Washing Machine? Give the reasons.

4. What standards of quality will he choose if Mark is going to import local specialities? Give the reasons.

IV. Creative Discussion

It's known to all of us that there are heat competitions in the international market.

In order to dominate the market, Company A adopts strategy of lowering prices by sacrificing the quality.

In order to dominate the market, Company B adopts strategy of improving quality but keeping the prices on the high side comparing with other companies.

The class is divided into several groups to discuss which strategy is better according the situation in different countries. Every student gives his own idea about the propositions with reasonable support points.

Each group provides a summary to present in the class.

Chapter 10 Acceptance and Orders

Learning Objectives
Upon completion of this chapter, you will be able to

- acquire knowledge of skills of price negotiation.
- learn how to accept the orders from the clients.
- open the mind to differentiated marketing.
- improve the communication skills for business talks.
- conclude business transaction.

课文范读

Part A Situational Dialogue

 Communicative Scene 1

Showing an Interest in the Products

(*Ms. Liu, the General Manager of Hope Tool Enterprise is attending an international fair in Poznan, Poland. Mr. Mason, an import manager from a European company comes up Liu's booth, looking at samples at the show.*)

Liu: Good afternoon! Can I help you?

Mason: Yes. I am interested in 100 pc tool kits. Can you show me more samples?

Liu: Sure. <u>Here are some samples of different kinds of 100 pc tool sets.</u>[1] They contain different tools for different purposes.

Mason: They look wonderful.

Liu: This is for professional use, because the materials used for each individual tool are high quality steel and they are all heat-treated. <u>The 5-year warranty is granted.</u>[2]

Mason: What about this one?

Liu: These two items are for family use. They will be nice gifts for Father's Day.

Mason: Perfect. Oh, I guess this must be for Mother's Day.

Liu: Yes, you are right. We specially designed it for lady use. Look, the box and all plastic handles are light and clear pink. It is lady's color, don't you think so?

Mason: Yep, it is very thoughtful. I like it very much. What's the cost?

Liu: It is USD 2.49 per set FOB China port, and <u>this price is based on the FCL.</u>[3]

Mason: I don't think we can order so many for the first time. We have never dealt with the tools for ladies. It is a brand new idea for the market, too. Well, let me see. <u>Maybe we can combine some other tool kits, such as professional tools and family items in one container.</u>[4]

Liu: That's all right. However, as you may know, the production costs and handling fee for assorted goods will be much higher than just a single product.

Mason: That's understandable, but ...

Liu: OK. To establish business relations with your esteemed company, we'll consider making you a concession. Now, we offer you USD 2.59 per set FOB China port on condition that the minimum order quantity should reach 500 sets.

Mason: Thank you for your kindness. I will come back later.

Liu: Here is my business card with my mobile phone number and our booth number on it. You are always welcome to come back again. So long!

Mason: So long!

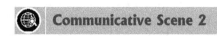

Communicative Scene 2

Detailed Business Bargain

(*Ms. Liu is negotiating with Mr. Mason on prices at the fair.*)

Liu: Nice to see you again, Mr. Mason. How are you doing?

Mason: Fine, thank you.

Liu: It has been two days since we met each other for the first time. Have you made up your mind?

Mason: Not really. Your tool kits look nice, but comparing them with others, they seem a bit overpriced. Could you reduce the price a little further? Let's say, USD 2.29 per set.

Liu: Frankly speaking, yes, our price is a little higher than others. However, if the new styles and features open up markets, aren't they worth the money? Moreover, our quality is superior to other manufacturers'. [5]

Mason: Sounds reasonable. Shall we come to the price again later on after we finish with the other terms and conditions? Firstly, please let me know the leadtime for 500 sets.

Liu: It will be about 30 days after your order confirmation and receipt of your down payment.

Mason: Could it be a little faster, say 20 days? You see, it will be midseason.

Liu: No problem.

Mason: Wow, you're a lot of help. What about the terms of payment?

Liu: We usually accept payment by L/C. That is our usual practice.

Mason: L/C payment requires a high fee and slows down our capital flow. We prefer T/T payment.

Liu: For T/T payment, we request a 30% down payment upon your order confirmation and the balance payment will be paid before shipment.

Mason: How about after shipment?

Liu: I'm afraid not.

Mason: Oh, there is one more important matter. Please tell me about the packing.

Liu: Every individual tool will be put in the pink box as the sample you saw two days ago. Each box will be covered by a 4-colour printed sleeve and then wrapped by shrinkage film. Five boxes are packed to one export carton. You can print your company's logo and description in different languages on the color sleeve. [6]

Mason: Everything sounds great aside from the price. [7]

Liu: To conclude the business and show our sincerity, we agree to cut 10 cents for each set.

Mason: USD 2.29/set?

Liu: Should we meet each other half way? USD 2.49 is already our bottom price.

Mason: Let's close a deal.

Liu: Thank you very much. I'll prepare the contract in a few minutes. Would you please wait here or walk around and come back in 20 minutes?

Mason: I prefer to wait here as I have stepped over to every corner of the exhibition hall.

Communicative Scene 3

Repeat Orders

(*Mr. Mason will place repeat orders with Ms. Liu.*)

Mason: How are you doing, Ms. Liu?

Liu: Fine, thank you. And you?

Mason: I'm fine, too. Thanks. I'm very happy to inform you that your goods are selling remarkably well in our market. Your new concept has been warmly welcome by our consumers. To meet the heavy demand from all the supermarkets where we are selling your tool kits, we'd like to place a new order with you immediately.

Liu: I'm glad to hear the good news. We'll do our best to meet your requirements.

Mason: To meet the rapidly growing demand, our quantity of order will be more than triple of the last one. Please give us your best offer based on the quantity of 2,000 sets.

Liu: That will be USD 2.48 / set FOB China port.

Mason: It is almost the same price as we had last time.

Liu: You are right. However, it actually is much cheaper than last time.

Mason: Why do you say that? Could you give me some more explanation?

Liu: The situation has changed a lot since your first order. We are facing pressures from at least two aspects. As you may know, the US dollar has been devaluing against Chinese currency since then. For this reason only, we have already lost 3%.

Mason: I'm sorry to hear that.

Liu: Worse still, affected by oil prices in the international market, steel and plastic prices in Chinese domestic market have increased tremendously. You see, steel and plastics are our main materials. Under such circumstances, we still offer you the same price, even a little lower. It means we are giving you a special favor on the price.

Mason: Understand. We'll not insist on our position anymore. We accept your price. In case the international oil price falls, we request our prices follow automatically.

Liu: Fully agreeable. We hope the situation will get better in the near future.

Words and Expressions

1. acquire knowledge of		获得知识
2. kit	*n.*	成套工具，工具箱
tool kit		成套工具，工具箱
3. warranty	*n.*	保证；理由；证书
4. professional	*adj.*	专业的
5. grant	*vt. & n.*	同意，准予，授予

6. Father's Day		父亲节（六月份的第三个星期日）
7. Mother's Day		母亲节（五月份的第二个星期日）
8. yep	adv.	是（俚语）
9. thoughtful	adj.	考虑周到的；体贴的；思考的
10. FCL abbr. Full Container Load		整集装箱货
11. assorted	adj.	各式各样的，混杂的
12. understandable	adj.	可理解的
13. on condition that ...		条件是……
14. esteemed	adj.	尊敬的；尊贵的
15. bargain	v.	讨价还价
	n.	（通过讨价还价）成交的商品；便宜货
16. make up (one's) mind		决定，下决心
17. feature	n.	特色，特征
18. lead time		交货期
19. midseason	n.	旺季
20. capital flow		资本流动
21. down payment		订金，预付款
22. balance payment		余款
23. T/T abbr. telegraphic transfer		电汇
24. sleeve	n.	袖子；外套；体壳
25. shrinkage	n.	收缩；缩水
26. conclude the business		成交
27. bottom price		底价
28. triplead	adv.	三倍
29. pressure	n.	压力
30. devalue	vt.	贬值
31. tremendously	adv.	极大地；惊人地

Notes

1. Here are some samples of different kinds of 100 pc tool sets.
   请看这些不同款式的100件组合工具。
   ① 100 pc tool sets 表示包含100件不同用途的各种工具。
   ② tool kits / tool sets 成套工具；工具箱
2. The 5-year warranty is granted.
   保质期五年。
   ① grant v. 准许，同意
   Warranty is granted for household appliances made by our factory.
   我们生产的家电有保修。

The manager granted the salesman permission to cut the price by 5%.

经理允许推销员降价5%。

3. This price is based on the FCL.

这价格是基于整货柜的订量。

根据集装箱货物装箱数量和方式可分为整箱和拼箱两种。

① FCL 整箱（Full Container Load）

指出口商自行将货物装满整个集装箱以后，以箱为单位托运的集装箱。一般在货主有充足货源装载一个或多个整箱时采用。

② LCL 拼箱（Less than Container Load）

指承运人接受出口商托运的数量不满整箱的货物后，根据货物运输的目的地和商品的特性进行分类整理。把运往相同目的地的货物，集中到足够数量，拼装入集装箱。一个集装箱内有不同货主的货拼装在一块，称为拼箱。

4. Maybe we can combine some other tool kits, such as professional tools and family items in one container.

也许我们可以和其他组合工具拼柜，比如专业工具和家用工具拼柜。

① combine *v.* 使结合，合并

指与其他组合工具拼柜，用的是拼箱的方法装入集装箱。

② combine with ... 把……与……相结合

We must combine international economy theory with trade practice.

我们把国际经济学理论与贸易实践相结合。

5. Moreover, our quality is superior to other manufacturers'.

而且，我们的质量比其他厂家更优越。

① be superior to 优良的，优越的，上等的，胜过……的(to, in)

The function of this kind of aerator is superior to that one made in Korea.

这种增氧机的功能在很多方面比韩国造的好。

6. Every individual tool will be put in the pink box as the sample you saw two days ago. Each box will be covered by a 4-colour printed sleeve and then wrapped by shrinkage film. Five boxes are packed to one export carton. You can print your company's logo and description in different languages on the color sleeve.

正如你两天前见到的样品那样，所有工具都放在粉红色工具盒里。每盒套上四色印刷的彩套，然后包上收缩膜。五盒装一个外纸箱。贵公司可在彩套上印上公司标志和不同语言的说明文字等。

包装的表示方法：

（1）be packed in 用某种包装物包装

We require live clam be packed in strong gunny bags.

我们要求活文蛤用结实的麻袋包装。

（2）be packed to 装入某种包装物

Toys are packed 2 pieces to a box and 10 boxes to a carton.

每2件玩具装一盒，10盒装一纸箱。

（3） each containing ... 每包装物内装……

Straw mushrooms are in polythene bag, each containing 500 g.

草菇装聚乙烯袋，每袋装500克。

（4） be packed in ... of ... each 用某种包装物包装，每包装物内装……

Women's blouses are packed in a carton of 12 dozen each.

女式衬衫使用纸箱包装，每箱装一打。

7. Everything sounds great aside from the price.

各项都很好，就剩下价格问题了。

① aside from prep./adv. 除……以外

I think we have discussed all details of the trade aside from claims.

除索赔外，我们已经讨论了交易的各个细节。

*8. OK与That's OK 的区别

众所周知OK是"好的"，但如果认为That's OK也是相同意思，则是有误。当别人问是否要做时，回答OK是"要"做，而回答That's OK却是"不要"。回答身体状况时，That's OK表示"我很好，不用操心。" That's OK意思是"没关系，无所谓。"

*9. Now we understood more about your situation. We are not going to insist on our position anymore. We accept your price.

现在我们明白了你的处境，就不再坚持自己的立场。我们接受你们的报价。

① insist on 坚持，主张（常与on、that连用）

If you insist that the payment be paid by D/A, I am afraid that we can't make a deal.

如果你坚持承兑交单支付，恐怕我们无法成交。

It is unwise of you to insist on maintaining your uncompetitive price.

坚持毫无竞争性的价格是不明智的。

*10. repeat orders 续订的订单（与上一订单商品一样，但有些条款不同）

duplicate orders 重复订单（与上一订单数量等条款相同）

Part B Practical Key Sentences

1. **be worth doing** +*n.*

    worth *adj.* 值……的，相等于……的价值

    用作表语，后接名词或动名词作宾语。

    How much is this antique of handicraft worth?

    这件手工艺品古董值多少钱？

    It is worth at least USD 6 million for its special value of age.

    它因其年代悠久而具有特殊价值，至少值六百万美元。

    It's worth buying, don't you think so?

你不认为值得买吗?

替换表达:

It's worth attending business fair.

The older its age, the more it's worth.

It is worth while to visit the factory.

It is worth while negotiating price before signing the contract.

2. keep one's mind though something reasonable

That is understandable, but ... 这可以理解,但……

That is understandable that you are short of workforce, but the products we need are seasonable. We can't miss it.

你方缺乏劳力可以理解,但我们要的产品是季节性的,不可错过。

替换表达:

It is a brand new concept, but it should be tested by the market.

While I appreciate your effort, I have to point out the problems of your quality.

Much as we are pleased to get your quotation, we are regretful that we still think your prices are not competitive enough.

3. let's say

Your prices seem a bit overpriced. Could you please reduce the price a little more? Let's say, USD 2.29 per set.

贵公司的定价偏高了些。能优惠一些,再降点价吗?比如每套2.29美元。

Considering your cooperation, we decide to cut the price by USD 10, i.e. to USD 190 per set.

考虑到你方的友好合作,我们决定降价10美元,即每台190美元。

替换表达:

To encourage business, we'll give you the reduction of price by 5%, that is, USD 6.00 per kg.

It's better for you to decrease the price, say HKD 5 per set.

4. buyers'reasons avoid using L/C

L/C payment requires high fee and slow down our capital flow. We prefer T/T payment.

信用证付款的费用挺高,并减缓资金周转。我们更赞成电汇付款。

替换表达:

An opening of L/C will add some extra cost to us.

The payment by letter of credit will cause both of us some inconvenience.

Our money will be tied up if you insist on L/C payment.

5. accept only L/C or other terms

Our company only accepts terms of payment by confirmed, irrevocable letter of credit. It assures the safe payment.

本公司只接受保兑的、不可撤销的信用证付款方式。它保证卖方收支安全。

但卖方若一直坚持信用证付款方式,可能会失去订单,不妨采取一些灵活但不影响收汇安全的方式。

For T/T payment, 30% down payment upon your order confirmation and balance payment will be paid before shipment.

采用电汇付款,合同确定后预付30%,发货前付清余款。

替换表达：

Only L/C is acceptable to us. That is our usual practice.

We agree to make an exception by accepting D/P at sight.

6. make no more price reduction

Let's meet each other half way. USD 2.49 is already our bottom price.

我们各让一半。2.49美元已是我们的底线。

We can't make further reduction because this is our floor price.

我们无法进一步减价，因为它是我们的地板价了。

替换表达：

We can't accept your counter offer for it is our rock-bottom quotation.

It is hard for us to decrease the price. We have lowered the price to the limit.

7. large quantity affects prices

Our quantity of order will be more than triple of the last one. Please give us your best offer based on the quantity of 2,000 sets.

我们的订量将是上次的三倍以上。请按2,000套的数量报个最优惠价格。

替换表达：

Now we quote you USD 5.00 per piece CFR Sydney on condition that the minimum order quantity should reach 10,000 pieces.

Further discount is possible if you place a large order.

We grant you a special discount if you increase the quantity by 10%.

Part C Integration of Theory and Practice

1. product warranty　产品保修

【知识点】产品出口必须使顾客感到放心。敢于承诺保修，表明产品质量可靠，如有损坏，卖主在一定期限内和一定条件下将免费维修或更换损坏的部分。良好的售后服务有利于交易。

对于出口商品，加强售后服务不可掉以轻心，尤其是机电产品，若无产品保修将对客户和消费者产生负面影响，使一些潜在的客户和消费者对你的产品望而却步。

现在出口电器等产品到欧美等地，须签订保修合同。欧美等国加紧了对电器产品质量的控制，对机电产品质量标准和保修要求更加严格。

当然中国产品出口，远离本国，要考虑到维修的不便，售后服务还要量力而行。非机电产品出口则大部分不保修。

让客户对最关心的产品标准、产品质量、按期交货、产品种类和款式新颖等方面感到满意。

【技能训练句型】

The 3-year warranty is granted for our electronic appliances.

我方的电器保修期3年。

The machine warranty assures customers of the reliability of the products.

机器保修确保了产品的可靠性。

Product warranty gives a guarantee to the quality of products. It will be helpful for product promotion.

产品保修使产品的质量有了保证,这有助于产品的促销。

2. marketing strategy　市场营销策略

【知识点】由于消费者的需求存在差异,哪家企业能够领先发现新的消费群体需求,根据市场细分对其产品进行开发和差异化营销(differentiated marketing),谁就能获得不菲的回报。

市场细分就是把一个看似完整的市场,划分成为多个存在着内在逻辑关系的、相对独立的、更小的市场。科学的市场细分能充分发挥市场营销的效率,从而更有效地占领目标市场。

企业可根据自己的产品特性,寻找不同的消费群体,开发不同的市场,并针对不同的市场进行不同的市场营销策划,使产品适销对路,提高经济效益。同时实施品牌战略,增强企业核心竞争力。例如,工具市场是一个完整的市场。公司可以根据自己的产品特点,按不同的用途和功能来细分为专业工具、家用工具、电动和手动工具等。按消费对象来细分为男式和女式工具等。这样可充分满足消费者多层次的需求。

【技能训练句型】

We specially designed the tools for lady use. Look, the box and all plastic handles are light and clear pink. It's lady's color, don't you think so?

我们是专为女性设计的。瞧,外盒及工具的手柄都用鲜艳亮丽的粉红色。那是女性专用的颜色,不是吗?

These two items are for family use. They will be nice gifts for Father's Day.

这两款是家用的,是父亲节的上好礼品。

3. acceptance　接受

【知识点】构成有效的接受(法律上称作承诺)要具备以下条件。

(1) 交易的一方在接到对方的报盘或还盘后,以声明或行为向对方表示同意。接受一定要由受盘人做出表示同意。

(2) 受盘人表示接受,要采取口头或书面的声明向报盘人明确表示出来。

(3) 应该是无条件的接受,接受的内容要与报盘的内容相符。如果对报盘的内容作了增加、限制或修改,则称为有条件的接受,不能成为有效的接受,而属于还盘。

【技能训练句型】

Let's close a deal. We'll accept your offer by sending fax soon.

成交!我们通过传真接受贵方的报价。

(4) 接受的通知要在报盘的有效期内送达报盘人才能生效。接受不可更改和撤销。

4. skills of price negotiation　洽谈价格技巧

洽谈价格时,客户经常用同类价格比较的方法压低价格,可尝试以下技巧。

【知识点】(1) 如果买方称价格太高,卖方可重点谈产品质量好,谈卖方产品和销售优势的方面,谈影响价格的不利因素,生产条件良好的话可带客户参观企业,增加价格的砝码。

【技能训练句型】

A: Comparing with others, your TV sets seem a bit overpriced. Could you give us more favor to reduce the price a little further?

与其他公司相比,贵方的定价有些偏高。您能给我们一些优惠,再降一点价吗?

B: The new styles and features to open markets are worth the money, aren't they? Moreover, our quality of TV sets is superior to other manufacturers'.

开辟市场的新时尚和新特色就值得这价格，不是吗？而且，我们的质量比其他厂家更优越。

【知识点】（2）不要和客户纠缠自己的价格和同类价格比较。为了避免这种比较，可岔开话题。

【技能训练句型】

Shall we come to the price again later on after we finish other terms and conditions?

那么我们先谈其他条款，回头再谈价格问题好吗？

【知识点】（3）当卖方降了价，而买方仍不满意，或在交易会上想货比三家时，买方可婉转表示过一会儿再来。

【技能训练句型】

Thank you for making a more competitive quotation. I'll look around and come back later.

谢谢报更优惠的价格。我想到周围转转，过一会儿再来。

【知识点】（4）价格是谈判中双方最敏感的主要问题。但国际贸易涉及方方面面，许多其他条件和方式也很重要。在谈判桌上多涉及几个问题，大家互相让步，找到交换条件，使双方有利可图，便于成交，达成双赢。

当买方要求T/T支付时，卖方采取灵活的方式，不坚持非信用证不可，在支付条件上先作了让步。

当回到最敏感的价格问题时，价格分歧较大，为了成交，卖方又作了让步。请双方各让一半，告知已是底价，几乎无利可图了。这样容易打动买方，欣然表示接受。

【技能训练句型】

We usually accept payment by L/C. That is our usual practice.

我们一般接受信用证付款，这是我们的惯例。

For T/T payment, 30% down payment upon your order confirmation and balance payment will be paid before shipment.

采用电汇付款，合同确定后预付30%，发货前付清余款。

To conclude the business and show our sincerity, we agree to cut 10 cents for each set.

为了促成生意，表示我方的诚意，我们同意每套降10美分。

Should we meet each other half way? USD 2.49 is already our bottom price.

我们各让一半好吗？2.49美元已是我们的底线了。

Part D Practice

I. Complete the Following Dialogues

(1)

Fill in the blanks with the proper prepositions.

A: We have talked about all terms aside ____1____ packing.

B: Well, I am eager to know the packing of vase as improper packing will result ___2___ the breakage of vase.

A: Each vase is packed ___3___ a plastic bag and 2 pairs ___4___ a box.

B: I see.

A: All vases are packed ___5___ cartons ___6___ 12 boxes each.

B: I worry ___7___ whether the cartons are strong enough.

A: We have taken ___8___ consideration and choose double cardboard to protect the goods.

B: Do you use warning mark ___9___ the cartons?

A: Sure. Warning mark ___10___ "Fragile" are painted outside the cartons.

B: Fine. We'll place an order ___11___ vases ___12___ you right now.

(2)

Fill in the blanks with the proper forms of following expressions.

assure sb. of	close a deal	place a duplicate order	push the sale
be superior to	insist on	tell something about	on condition that
It is understandable but		be inconvenient for	

A: Mr. Wu, could you ___1___ warranty of electronic toys?

B: I am afraid not. Our quality ___2___ other manufacturers'.

A: ___3___ product warranty gives a guarantee to the quality of products.

B: You are right.

A: Warranty ___4___ the reliability of the products.

B: But it ___5___ us to repair the electronic toys far away in your country.

A: Our customers ___6___ having product warranty before choosing the toys.

B: Well, I have an idea. Warranty is granted ___7___ you place a repeat order so that we can put additional toys for replacement.

A: OK. I am going to ___8___ each month.

B: Oh, you mean exactly the same orders every time?

A: Yes, you see, warranty will be helpful for us to ___9___.

B: Great! It's worth trying.

A: OK. Let ___10___.

II. Interaction Activities

Task 1

A foreign buyer is discussing prices for stainless wares with the seller. They can't reach the agreement on prices. At last, the seller agrees to meet each other half way on condition that the buyer increases the quantity of order.

Divide students into pairs. Make short dialogues and role-play them. The following expressions should be included in your dialogue.

(1) on the high side
(2) ask for a discount of 4%
(3) bad situation
(4) devaluation of the US dollar
(5) the increase of steel and plastic prices
(6) discount impossible
(7) seeking discount by large quantity
(8) more than triple, that is 3 FCL

Task 2

Imagine you are an importer. Try to persuade the seller to accept payment by T/T. Compose a conversation with your partner. Your conversation should cover the expressions below:

(1) terms of payment
(2) accept confirmed, irrevocable letter of credit at sight
(3) tied up capital flow
(4) cause some inconvenience
(5) protection of the banker's guarantee
(6) only a trial order
(7) It's not worth...
(8) costs less
(9) make an exception
(10) remit the payment before shipment

III. Actual Practice

Mr. John is having a negotiation with Mr. Xiao on the business of importing MP4.

Work in pairs and role-play the conversation.

Use the following background information:

(1) comparison with other suppliers
(2) prices on the high side
(3) superior quality
(4) beyond reach
(5) suggestion to discuss other terms and conditions first
(6) same thinking
(7) terms of payment
(8) suggestion to pay by D/A
(9) usual practice by L/C
(10) insist on payment by D/P
(11) In order to encourage business...
(12) make an exception

(13) ask for more reasonable prices

(14) carefully calculated

(15) rock-bottom prices

(16) no further reduction

(17) close a deal

IV. Creative Discussion

Divide the class into groups. Think first and then discuss in the group. Discuss the issue with your partners and share your opinions with other pairs.

Topic:

Suppose you are running a large shoes company. You are planning to adopt marketing strategy to occupy target markets. Make a market research first and find out what is the consumers' demand.

Then, according to the features of shoes, you fractionize the shoes markets to meet the demand of different consumers. How will you do to carry out the differentiated marketing?

Please discuss the issue with the members in your group.

Chapter 11
Business Telephone Calls

Learning Objectives
Upon completion of this chapter, you will be able to

- acquire some techniques of telephone conversation.
- acquaint with the etiquette on the phone.
- perform the functions of skills of communication on the phone.
- conduct the activities related to the theme of phone.

课文范读

Part A Situational Dialogue

 Communicative Scene 1

Hard to Reach Somebody

(*Mr. Sun met Miss Lin last week on an exhibition. He is trying to get her on the phone now. He dials the number, and <u>the telephone rings.</u>*[1])

Switchboard (*answering machine*): "Thanks for calling ABC Corporation, if you know your party's last name or extension, press 1. If you want to receive information of the corporation, press 2. If you want to talk to the operator, press pound sign or remain on the line."

(*Mr. Sun presses the button, and the music fades in ... The operator answers the call.*)

Operator: Hello? Thank you for waiting, what can I do for you?

    Sun: Can I speak to Miss Lin, please?

Operator: Would you like to tell me which department she works in? We have a couple of Miss Lins here.

    Sun: Er... I suppose it's in Purchasing Department.

Operator: Purchasing Department. Hold on please, I'll put you through.

(<u>*The extension is engaged.*</u>[2] *There comes the voice: the line is busy, hold on please... In a few seconds, Mr. Sun is through.*)

Lin: Hello, Purchasing Department, who's speaking?

Sun: Oh, hello, um...I'm an agent of shoes materials. May I speak to Miss Lin?

Lin: This is she.

Sun: Oh, good. Glad to hear you. This is Mr. Sun from Qing Shun Trading Company.

Lin: Mr. Sun?

Sun: Um...we met last week at the exhibition of shoes materials.

Lin: (*Silence*)

Sun: Er... You were quite interested in our synthetic and genuine leather and asked me to contact you later.

Lin: Exhibition? No...no, I haven't been there. You've probably made a mistake.

Sun: What? Sorry, er... maybe I got a wrong department.

Lin: I think so. The Technology Department of our company is in charge of affirming the materials for new products. You probably want Miss Lin in the Technology Department.

Sun: Oh, um...well...anyway, thank you, and <u>could you connect me back through the switchboard, please?</u>[3]

Lin: Well, let me try...

Communicative Scene 2

Taking a Message

(Miss Liu is making an international long-distance call to inform the relevant issues about the visiting delegation.)

Telephonist: Good afternoon, China Tiger Beverage Company.

Liu: Oh, good afternoon, this is Miss Liu calling from Malaysia. Could I speak to Mr. Zhang, chief manager of your company?

Telephonist: Certainly, Miss Liu, putting you through.

Secretary: Hello, Mr. Zhang's office.

Liu: Good morning, this is Miss Liu, I'm phoning from Malaysia, head office of the company. Is Mr. Zhang there?

Secretary: Sorry, he's in a conference now.[4] This is his secretary Wang Li. Can I help you?

Liu: Hello, Wang Li, it's about the visiting delegation to your plant. Would you please take a message for me?

Secretary: Sure, with pleasure.

Liu: The delegation from Malaysia is supposed to arrive in your city on Wednesday afternoon, but I'm sorry to inform that the schedule of the delegation has to be changed due to the temporary cancellation of this flight to your city.[5] The journey will be put off. They won't be arriving until this Saturday afternoon. And I want to make sure whether you are able to make adjustment accordingly.

Secretary: Right.

Liu: And also inform you that the members of the group have been trimmed down.[6] Five of them are otherwise engaged.[7]

Secretary: OK, let me double-check. The delegation will come on Saturday afternoon instead of Wednesday afternoon, and the size of groups will be smaller...by the way...can I have the exact number, please?

Liu: Um...a group of 11 in total.

Secretary: 11...in total, right?

Liu: Yes, wonderful, thanks. Could you please ask Mr. Zhang to fax or send me an e-mail to confirm that he is ready for the change?

Secretary: All Right, I'll take the message and inform Mr. Zhang when he's back. He'll be in touch with you.[8]

Liu: Thank you very much.

Communicative Scene 3

Something to Complain

(*Mr.Ma phones the Ads department to complain the slip of broadcasting their commercials.*)

Secretary: Good morning. Advertisement Department of Channel 9.
Ma: Good morning. I'd like to speak to Mr. Wang, deputy chief of your department.
Secretary: Whom am I speaking with, please?
Ma: Mr. Ma of Qinqin Foodstuff Company.
  One moment, please. (To Mr. Wang) Mr. Ma of Qinqin Foodstuff Company wants to speak to you.
Wang: Hello, Mr. Ma. This is Mr. Wang.
Ma: Good morning ,Mr. Wang. I'm calling about our commercials. <u>Yesterday evening we didn't see our ads film during the commercial break of the TV series.</u>[9]
Wang: I'm very sorry. I'm thinking to call you about this. We'll claim responsibility for this. Probably we could make up our slips by giving you another two times 30-second release free of charge. Do you agree?
Ma: Um... Well... What about the time?
Wang: The golden time, right after the news on the evening of Mar. 20 and 21.
Ma: Are you sure?
Wang: Sure, no problem.
Ma: OK, thank you. Goodbye.
Wang: Bye-bye.

Words and Expressions

1. etiquette	n.	礼节，礼仪
2. nuisance	n.	麻烦事
3. switchboard	n.	接线总机
4. answering machine	n.	电话答录机
5. pound sign	n.	#字键
6. fade in		（使）淡入；渐显
7. extension	n.	分机
8. engaged	adj.	使用中的
9. synthetic	adj.	合成的
10. genuine leather		真皮
11. delegation	n.	代表团
12. accordingly	adv.	从而
13. trim down		裁减

14. double-check		仔细检查
15. deputy chief		副总经理
16. foodstuff	*n.*	食品
17. commercial break		（电视）广告时间
18. claim	*vt.*	认领；（根据权利）要求
19. release	*vt.*	发行；发布

1. The telephone rings.
   电话铃响了。
   ring 在此处指电话铃响。ring在表示打电话时，多用于英式英语，美式英语中则用call来表示。ring 还可以指打电话，比如：
   Ring me up. 给我打电话。
   Ring me back. 给我回电话。

2. The extension is engaged.
   分机占线。
   be engaged 指电话占线，多用于英式英语，而美式英语则多用busy，如：The line is busy.
   engaged line / number 占线　　line in use 占线（美式英语）
   engaged tone 忙音　　　　　busy signal 忙音（美式英语）
   The line is free / open now. 现在不占线了。

3. Could you connect me back through the switchboard, please?
   请帮我转回总机好么？

4. Sorry, he is in a conference.
   很抱歉，他在开会。
   ① hold a conference 举行会议
   ② attend a conference 参加会议
   ③ press conference 新闻发布会

5. I'm sorry to inform that the schedule of the delegation has to be changed due to the temporary cancellation of this flight to your city.
   我很抱歉通知您由于飞往贵城的航班临时取消，我们只好改变了访问团的日程安排。
   ① schedule 日程/行程安排
   ② tight schedule 安排得很满的日程
   ③ ahead of schedule 提前于原定日程
   ④ due to / because of 因为，例如：We canceled the travel due to the bad weather.

6. And also inform you that the members of the group have been trimmed down.
   还要通知您，代表团的人数减少了。

① trim one's hair 修剪你的头发

② trim the budget 削减预算

7. Five of them are otherwise engaged.

其中有五个人另有安排（不能去了）。

be otherwise engaged 另有安排

8. He'll be in touch with you.

（就此事）他会和你联系的。

be in touch (with) 尤用于电话用语，也可用get in touch (with)替代，指就某事和某人在电话上联系。但 keep in touch (with) 则一般指两人经常没见面要保持联系。

9. Yesterday evening we didn't see our ads film during the commercial break of the TV series.

昨晚我们没看到电视剧中间播放我们的广告片。

① commercial break （电视节目中间的）广告时间

② ads film 广告片

Part B Practical Key Sentences

1. **This is ...**   我是……

Good morning. This is Miss Smith.

早上好，我是史密斯小姐。

替换表达：

This is Miss Smith, calling from the United States.

This is Miss Smith.

This is John speaking.

Peter speaking.

Speaking.

This is she / he.

当你正是电话那头要找的人，一般会回答：speaking或this is she / he，意即：我就是（你要找的人），后者多用于美式英语，使用时更要注意语气，否则会给人以唐突的感觉。

2. **One moment, please.**   请稍候

这句话用于话务员为来电者接入分机之前请来电者稍候的惯用语。或在接电话的人为来电者找人时使用。

替换表达：

One moment, please.

Just a second, please.

Could you hold a little longer?

Hold the line, please.

Hold on, please.

3. Connect me with...　请帮我接通……

Can you connect me with Quality Control Department?

请帮我接质检部好吗?

这句话是打电话要总机转某个分机时使用的一句惯用语。

替换表达：

Could you put me through to Public Relations Department?

Could you connect me with the extension 3336?

Extension 5096, please.

4. take a message or leave a message　带口信或留口信

Can I take a message for you?

能给您带个口信么?

She's out for lunch. Can I take a message for you?

她外出吃午饭，能给您带个口信吗?

Can I leave a message with you?

能帮我带个口信么?

替换表达：

May I take a message?

Do you want him to call you back?

Any message for him?

Would you like to leave a message?

5. putting you through　为您接通电话

I'll put you through.

我给您转接过去。

替换表达：

You're through.

I'll connect you immediately.

I'll get the extension for you.

I'm transferring your call.

I'm redirecting your call.

I'll put her on the phone. Just a second.

6. Could I speak to...　找某人接电话

Could I speak to Dr. Henderson?

亨德森博士在吗?

替换表达：

I'd like to speak to Ms. Chi.

Could I have a word with Jenny?

Is that Miss Chen?

Is Miss Hu there?

Is Mr. Watson available, please?

May I speak to Customer Service director?

I'm trying to get a hold of Miss Lin.

7. Contact me, please.　请和我联系。

You can reach me at this number.

拨这个号码能找到我。

替换表达：

I'm at 83517303.

My phone number is 87350510.

Contact me by telephone.

8. You are wanted on the phone.　有人找您。

Our manager would like to talk to you on the phone.

我们经理想与您电话交谈。

And you are...?

在给职位较高的人打电话时，负责转接电话的秘书可能会问：And you are...?（您是……？）这是一个很实用的句子。

替换表达：

You have a call from Mr. White.

Whom am I speaking with, please?

Part C　Integration of Theory and Practice

1. 用清晰而愉快的语调打电话。

【知识点】国际商务运作离不开电话这一便捷的通信工具，而你的声音在运用这一工具时是交流的唯一介质，因此充分体现语调的魅力至关重要。用清晰而愉快的语调接电话能显示出说话人的职业风度和可亲的性格。虽然对方无法看到你的面容，但你的喜悦或烦躁仍会通过语调流露出来。打电话时语调应平稳、柔和，这时如能面带微笑地与对方交谈，可使你的声音听起来更为友好热情。千万不要边打电话边嚼口香糖或吃东西。

2. 接电话时应注意得体的问答。

【知识点】（1）接商务电话时通常应先报公司的名字，然后再说："May I help you?"（我能帮您什么忙？）如果更客气一点的话，则可以说："How can I help you?"（我该怎么帮您？）因为这样的问法表示我"该"怎么帮您，而非我"需不需要帮您"。

【知识点】（2）接电话时，不要让铃声响得太久，应尽快接电话。若因为有急事或正在接另一部电话而耽搁时，应表示歉意。

【技能训练句型】

Thank you for waiting, John speaking.

此处用Thank you for waiting. 表示歉意，而不用Sorry for waiting.

或用：I am sorry you had to wait, John speaking. 久等了，我是约翰。

【知识点】（3）热情问候并报出公司或部门名称。如果对方打错电话，不要责备对方，知情时还应告诉对方正确的号码。

【技能训练句型】

A: QC Department, speaking please. 质检部，请讲。

B: Sorry, I must have dialed the wrong number. I wanted to reach the Sales Department. 对不起，我拨错号码了。我本想拨销售部的。

A: Take easy. Their extension is 9143. 没关系。销售部的分机是9143。

【知识点】（4）打电话前应准备好电话号码，考虑好说话内容、措辞和语气语调。如有必要，可以做一个书面的提纲，让谈话的内容更全面、更有条理。

【知识点】（5）如果对方不在，可请代接电话者转告。或向代接电话者询问对方的去处和联系方式，或把自己的联系方式留下，让对方回来后回电话。

【技能训练句型】

I'm anxious to talk to him, could you give me his home number?

我有急事找他，您能告诉我他家的电话么？

Could you have him call me back? My name is Chen Ji. My phone number is 87546203.

您能让他给我回个电话么？我叫陈济。我的电话是87546203。

【知识点】（6）如果来电找的同事正在接电话，就告诉对方他所找的人正在接电话，并主动询问对方是留言还是等一会儿。如果留言，则记录对方的留言、单位、姓名和联系方式；如果只是等一会儿，则将电话筒轻轻放下，通知被找的人接电话；如果被叫人正在接一个重要电话，一时难以结束，则请对方过一会儿再来电话，或是留下回电号码。切忌让对方莫名久等。

【技能训练句型】

He is on the phone. Would you like to hold on for a moment or can I take a message?

他在打电话。您能稍候么？要不有事我帮您转告一下。

Hold on please, he will be available in a few seconds.

请稍等，他马上就来。

He is busy with another call. Would you like to try again later?

他忙着讲电话。您稍后打来好么？

【知识点】3. 在商业投诉中，不能及时回电话最为常见。为了不丧失每一次成交的机会，有的公司甚至做出对电话留言须在一小时之内答复的规定。一般应在24小时之内对电话留言给予答复，如果回电话时恰遇对方不在，也要留言，表明你已经回过电话了。如果自己确实无法亲自回电，应托付他人代办。

【知识点】4. 拨打国际商务电话时应注意时差。打电话前要弄清楚地区时差以及各国工作时间的差异，不要在休息日打电话谈生意，以免影响他人休息，除非你了解对方的生活习惯。一般不要在早上8时以前或晚上9时以后给人打电话，中午也要注意对方的休息。即使客户已将家中的电话号码告诉你，也尽量不要往家中打电话。

【知识点】5. 恰当地使用电话。在美国你可以通过电话向一个素不相识的人推销商品，而在欧洲、拉美和亚洲国家，电话促销或在电话中长时间地谈生意就难以让人接受。发展良好商务关系的最佳途径是与客户面对面地商谈，而电话主要用来安排会见。当然一旦双方见过面，再用电话往来就方便多了。

【知识点】6. 打国际长途电话，特别是价格昂贵的地区，不要随便要求对方主动打过来，可以问清时间后打过去。

【知识点】7. 如果使用手机，应该注意，手机只能在合适的场所才能打开。在会场、医院、剧院、电影院等场所，均不宜使用手机；在飞机上禁止使用手机，在公共汽车、电车上使用手机也不合适；在餐厅用餐，必须离开桌子到餐厅一角去使用手机；在双向收费的情况下，说话更要简洁明了，以节约话费；优先拨打客户的固定电话，找不到时再拨打其手机；在嘈杂环境中，若听不清楚对方声音时要说明，并让对方过一会儿再打过来，或你打过去；在公共场合打手机，说话声不要太大，以免影响他人。

Part D Practice

I. Complete the Following Dialogues

(1)

Secretary: Good morning, Brain Time.

    Ling: Good morning. May I ___1___ to Ms. Jones?

Secretary: ___2___ Ms. Jones is that? We have several.

    Ling: Edna Jones.

Secretary: I'm ___3___ she isn't ___4___. May I take a ___5___ for you?

    Ling: Yes. I wanted to talk to her ___6___ ordering some computers. My name is Ling Lihua.

Secretary: ___7___ is your number?

    Ling: 2245109.

Secretary: OK, I'll tell her as soon ___8___ she comes in.

    Ling: Thank you. Good-bye.

Secretary: Good-bye.

(2)

Operator: May I ___1___ you?

    Cao: I'd like to ___2___ a collect, person-to-person call to Mr. Huang Hungwei please.

Operator: What's the name of the ___3___ calling?

    Cao: That's Cao Yong.

Operator: ___4___ a moment please.

(Cao hears the operator say: "I have a ___5___, person-to-person call for Mr. Huang Hungwei from Mr. Cao Yong. Will you accept the ___6___?" He hears someone at the other end say: "Just a moment, please. I'll ___7___ you with his ___8___." He hears the phone ring.)

    Huang: Hello.

Operator: Is this Mr. Huang Hungwei?

 Huang: Yes.

Operator: Will you ___9___ a collect call from Mr. Cao Yong in New York City?

 Huang: Yes, I will.

Operator: (*To Cao*) Go ___10___, please.

  (*Huang and Cao begin to talk.*)

II. Role-plays

Task 1

Students work in groups. Each student makes a business phone call to anther student. Design the situation by yourself and moves to another student when you finish. Try to talk to as many people as possible.

Task 2

Work in pairs.

Make up your own dialogue according to the given situation.

This evening, you made a supper date with your girlfriend, Nicole Kidman. However, your boss asked you to make a counter-offer to the trade company and to work late, so you telephoned Nicole to make the date on another day. You called two times, yet she was either on a conference or out. You had to leave a message to her.

Here are some useful expressions:

(1) Hello, this is ... speaking.

(2) Hello, I'd like to speak to ...

(3) I'm afraid ... is not available right now.

(4) May I know who is calling?

(5) Can I leave a message?

(6) Would you like to leave a message?

(7) Please tell her ...

(8) Hold on ...

III. Guided Talking

Student A is the receptionist at a large record company. She answers the phone for three busy executives. Below are their schedules for this afternoon.

NAME	1:00 PM	2:00 PM	3:00 PM	4:00 PM
Liu Yifei	lunch with the music fans	on a long-distance call to Paris	audition new bands	party at Shangrila Hotel
Wang An	out to lunch	visit the recording studio	in a press conference	her line is busy
Zhao Mingmin	lunch with Luther Martin	back at 2:30	meetings with lawyers	out of the office

(1)

Student B is a clerk in City Bank. She calls and wants to speak to Wang An. The message is that since the overdraft of his credit card has exceeded the permitted amount, he had better pay the due money, and he'd better go there as soon as possible. Use your own name and phone number.

The time of her call is 3:20 PM.

(2)

Student C is an accountant. He calls to speak to Liu Yifei. The message is that he has to cancel his appointment on Friday. He would like Liu Yifei to call him so that he can arrange a new time. Use your own name and phone number.

The time of his call is 2:00 PM.

(3)

Student D is an executive of another record company. He calls and wants to speak to Zhao Mingmin. The message is that he wants to ask about a new band.

The time of his call is 4:00 PM.

IV. Creative Discussion

The teacher divides the class into groups and asks them to discuss, then chooses the representatives of each group after discussion. The student who expresses well will be the winner.

Topic:

Imagine that the telephones everywhere suddenly stopped working. What would it affect on the daily life of people? Could you get along well without telephone?

Chapter 12 Terms of Payment

Learning Objectives
Upon completion of this chapter, you will be able to

- get used to different terms of payment.
- learn how to use different kinds of payment.
- learn how to open and arrange payment by L/C.
- perform the functions of skills of communication.
- conduct the activities to the theme of payment.

课文范读

Part A Situational Dialogue

 Communicative Scene 1

Demanding Payment by L/C

(*Mr. Smith, a businessman from Canada, is talking about the terms of payment with Miss Chen, who is working at Fujian Hope Import & Export Corporation. Finally, both of them agree the goods are paid by L/C and then arrange the details of payment.*)

Smith: We've settled a lot of things such as price, packing and shipment. Now, there's one question left to discuss, that is, terms of payment. <u>We recommend the goods be paid by D/A.</u>[1] What do you think of the terms of payment?

Chen: To tell you the truth, D/A is impossible. Because you're our new customer, our company would take a great risk if we accepted your terms. Perhaps after more business between us, we would consider payment made by collection. <u>Now, to be on the safe side, we only accept payment by irrevocable letter of credit payable against shipping documents.</u>[2]

Smith: Well, you know our order this time is very large. When I open the letter of credit with the bank, I have to pay a deposit and the bank charges. <u>To open an L/C for such a large amount is costly, which will add to the cost of our imports.</u>[3]

Chen: You can consult your bank and see if they can reduce some deposit and charges.

Smith: However, it also usually takes a couple of months from the time we open the credit until our buyers pay us, <u>our funds will be tied up.</u>[4] It may cause us a great deal of troubles in view of the current difficult economic climate. Could you be a little more flexible and make some changes? I wonder if you could accept other kinds of payment such as D/P?

Chen: I'm afraid not. We regret to say that we cannot accept your proposal for changing in payment. Our usual practice is to accept payment by L/C only. An irrevocable L/C gives our exports the protection of a banker's guarantee and we'll get the right amount of money.

Smith: <u>I'm sorry that you adhere to payment by L/C. For you, payment by L/C is the safest method, but for us, the point is that to open an L/C with a bank does mean additional expense.</u>[5]

Chen: In fact, L/C is fair and beneficial to both the seller and the buyer. However, to help you get rid of difficulty, I would like to suggest that you reduce the order by half. Then you can go on placing the rest of the order.

Smith: Well, I'll consider it. (*After calculating on the computer and thinking about for some time*) All right, I'll reduce the order by half. <u>However, let's make a compromise about the terms of payment.</u>[6] Do you think you could accept a time L/C and allow us to delay payment, say, 60 days after sight?

Chen: We usually demand payment by L/C available by draft at sight. Payment by sight L/C is quite usual in international trade. But to make a successful deal for this time and encourage more orders for the future, we'll consider your request.

Smith: Thank you. You are of great help.

Chen: Then let's arrange the details of payment. Could you send the L/C 30 days before shipment?

Smith: No problem. I'll arrange for the L/C to be opened in your favor as soon as I return. When will the goods be ready and the shipment made?

Chen: According to the manufacturer, the goods will be ready by the end of May.

Smith: <u>Since we are in urgent need of the goods and have to give our clients a specific delivery date, is it possible to persuade your manufacturer for an earlier delivery, say, at the beginning of May?</u>[7]

Chen: We wish to satisfy every request of our customers, especially a new one like you. <u>But our manufacturer has a heavy backlog on hand.</u>[8]

Smith: Well, then I hope that the goods can be dispatched promptly after you receive my L/C. The time between May and June is our busy season, therefore, we would very appreciate it if you'd ship the goods as soon as possible.

Chen: <u>You can rest assured of that.</u>[9] We'll make the necessary preparations and effect the shipment in the prescribed time after we get the L/C.

Smith: That'll be great. By the way, what about the term of validity?

Chen: The L/C should be valid for 15 days after the date of shipment.

Smith: Could you tell me what other documents will be provided?

Chen: Besides the draft, we'll send you a full set of bills of lading, an invoice, an insurance policy, a certificate of origin and a certificate of inspection.

Smith: Thanks. I appreciate your cooperation.

 Communicative Scene 2

L/C Amendment

(Miss Chen has received the relevant L/C, but she finds there are some differences between the L/C and Sales Contract No. 2345. So she calls Mr. Smith for the L/C amendment.)

Chen: Hello, Mr. Smith. This is Chen from Fujian Hope Import & Export Corporation.

Smith: Hi, Miss Chen.

Chen: I received your letter of credit on 8th of April. I'm afraid there are some differences between your L/C and Sales Contract No. 2345.

Smith: Go ahead.

Chen: First, goods should be insured for 110% of the invoice value, not 150%. Since all the terms in the L/C should be in full agreement with the contract, you should open the credit according to the clauses in the contract.

Smith: Really? It may be an oversight on my part. I'll check it up and inform you. Anything else?

Chen: Please insert the word "about" between "quantity" and "150M/T". What's more, the expiry date should be the 15th of June rather than the 5th of June.

Smith: I'm sorry for these mistakes caused by our carelessness. I'll approach the opening bank to amend the L/C immediately and I'll adopt some measures to avoid similar mistakes in the future.

Chen: Thank you for your cooperation. There is another thing I'd like to talk over with you. For some reason, there is only two vessels sailing for your port during May / June and it leaves here in the second half of a month. Shipping space for May is not available now. So we have to face two alternatives. It depends on you to extend the credit or allow transshipment.

Smith: Extension of credit will cause us a lot of troubles. I'll delete the clause "by direct steamer" and amend the credit to allow transshipment.

Chen: Thank you for understanding our situation and let us have your amendment notice as soon as possible so that we can effect shipment of the goods.

 Communicative Scene 3

Demanding Other Modes of Payment

(Mr. Smith and Miss. Chen are discussing about terms of payment of another order.)

Smith: Miss. Chen, I'm glad that we have concluded a successful transaction, although your prices are on the slightly high sides compared with those in Malaysia. Considering the superior quality and attractive design of your products, I would like to make another order, but the quantity depends on the terms of payment. If you could offer us easier terms of payment, it would possibly lead to an increase in business. Could you give more favorable terms?

Chen: Thank you for another order. Our regular practice concerning terms of payment is by L/C. What about your proposal?

Smith: As everyone knows, L/C involves many additional expenses for us, which leaves us few profit margins. Could you please accept payment by D/A?

Chen: I'm afraid that it's very difficult for us to accept your suggestion. This mode of payment might cause sellers some troubles. As you know, the international monetary market is very unstable, and the devaluation of dollars and its impact on other currencies have raised serious uncertainties in the world market.

Smith: Then, I wonder if you will accept D/P?

Chen: Well, with an eye to future transactions and trust established through the last business, I think we can make an exception for you at this time. <u>To meet you half way, what do you say 50% by D/P and the rest by L/C?</u>[10]

Smith: All right, thanks for your accommodation,[11] I'll increase my order.

Chen: Thank you for your order again. I should mention that we can't regard it as setting a precedent for all our future transactions. You'd better establish the relative L/C in the prescribed time. When the goods are dispatched, we'll issue a sight draft against you. We trust you will honor it on presentation.

Smith: Certainly we'll follow the usual procedure. Our negotiation has been very pleasant and fruitful. I sincerely hope that the trade between us will grow in the future.

Words and Expressions

1.	collection	n.	托收
2.	deposit	n.	保证金，押金；存款
3.	costly	adj.	昂贵的
4.	be tied up		占压（资金）
5.	compromise	v.	妥协
6.	draft	n.	汇票
	available by draft at sight		见票即付
7.	backlog	n.	（一般用单数）积压未办之事
8.	on hand		手头，现有
9.	rest assure of		尽管放心
10.	validity	n.	有效
11.	bill of lading (B/L)		提单
12.	an insurance policy		保险单
13.	Certificate of Origin		产地证书
14.	Certificate of Inspection		检验证书
15.	regular practice		惯常做法，惯例
16.	profit margin	n.	利润率，盈利率
17.	devaluation	n.	贬值
18.	uncertainty	n.	不稳定；不确定
19.	accommodation	n.	通融
20.	prescribed	adj.	规定的
21.	honor the draft on presentation		见票即付
22.	make exception		例外
23.	precedent	n.	先例
24.	procedure	n.	（正确的或通常做事的）步骤；手续

Notes

1. We recommend the goods be paid by D/A.
   我们建议用承兑交单的付款方式。

① recommend *v.* 建议，推荐，后可跟名词、动名词或从句，跟从句时须用虚拟语气。
The manager recommended that he (should) investigate the local market.
经理建议他调查当地市场。
Your firm has been recommended to us by the Chamber of Commerce in Beijing.
北京商会把贵公司推荐给我们。
② recommendation *n.*
We made a recommendation to the board.
我们向董事会提出建议。

2. Now, to be on the safe side, we only accept payment by irrevocable letter of credit payable against shipping documents.
目前为保险起见，通常我们采用不可撤销的信用证，凭装船单据付款。
① payable *adj.* 应付的，常用作后置定语。
注意以下词组：
bills payable 应付票据
amount payable 应付金额
account payable 应付账款
a check payable at sight 见票即付的支票
② shipping 装运，运输
注意和shipping有关的术语：
shipping documents 装运单据
shipping mark 装运标志
shipping agent 货运代理人
shipping instruction 装运须知
shipping advice 装运通知
shipping container 船运集装箱
shipping order 装货单
shipping space 舱位
shipping date 装船日期

3. To open an L/C for such a large amount is costly, which will add to the cost of our imports.
开立这么大金额的信用证费用太大，会增加我们的进口成本。
① open an L/C开立信用证
类似词组：
establish an L/C
issue an L/C
② amount *n.& v.* 数额，金额，总额；（金额）合计，达到
注意与amount有关的词组：
the amount of 金额计
to the amount of 金额计
for the amount of 金额计

to amount to ... 金额达到……

to come to an amount of 金额达到……

4. Our funds will be tied up.

我们的资金就要被占用。

tie up

（1）（资金）被占用，不能动用

My money is all tied up in shares.

我的钱全套在股票上了。

（2）（交通）阻塞，塞车

The accident tied up the traffic for many hours.

那起事故使交通阻塞好几个小时。

（3）忙得脱不开身

I'm tied up at the draft contract all day.

我一整天忙着做合同草案，脱不开身。

5. I'm sorry that you adhere to payment by L/C. For you, payment by L/C is the safest method, but for us, the point is that to open an L/C with a bank does mean additional expense.

真遗憾，你们坚持用信用证支付方式。对于你们而言，信用证付款是最保险的办法；而对我们而言，问题在于找银行开信用证就意味着额外的费用。

① adhere to 坚持，信守，后接介词 to

We should strictly adhere to the terms in the contract.

我们应该严格遵守合同条款。

We always adhere to the principle of equality, mutual benefit and exchange of needed goods.

我们一贯坚持平等互利、互通有无的原则。

② do在此为强调语气的助动词。例如：

They did tell him to take care of traps in commercial activities.

他们确实告诉过他要小心商务活动中的陷阱。

6. However, let's make a compromise about the terms of payment.

然而，我们还是应该在付款方式上折中一下。

make a compromise 妥协，让步

We managed to make a compromise on a price for the machine.

我们终于就机器的价格达成妥协。

7. Since we are in urgent need of the goods and have to give our clients a specific delivery date, is it possible to persuade your manufacturer for an earlier delivery, say, at the beginning of May?

因为我方急需这批货，并且要给客户一个明确的交货期，能否说服厂家提前一点交货？比如五月初？

be in urgent need of sth. 急需

类似表达：

be in great need of sth.

need sth. urgently

  need sth. badly

8. But our manufacturer has a heavy backlog on hand.

  但我们的厂家手头未完成的订单很多。

  ① backlog *n.* （一般用单数）积压未办之事

  a backlog of letters 很多未处理的信

  ② on hand 手头，现有

  We had no cash on hand to pay for the house.

  我们手头没有现金付房款。

9. You can rest assured of that.

  你尽管放心。

  ① rest assured of/rest assured that 尽管放心

  You can rest assured of our sincerity.

  你尽管相信我们的诚意。

  You can rest assured that I will not tell anyone.

  你尽管放心，我不会告诉任何人。

  ② assure sb. of sth./assure sb. 向某人保证……

  We assure you of our close cooperation.

  我们保证与你方密切合作。

  We assure you that we will cooperate with you closely.

  我们保证与你方密切合作。

10. To meet you half way, what do you say 50% by D/P and the rest by L/C?

  我们就做出让步，50% 用付款交单，余款用信用证支付好吗？

  meet sb. half way 与某人妥协，迁就某人

  To meet you half way, we'll give you a commission of 3%.

  我们愿做出让步，就付给你百分之三的佣金。

  If you can pay some amount of the bill, I'll meet you half way.

  如果你能支付账单的一部分，我也支付一部分。

11. All right, thanks for your accommodation.

  好吧，谢谢你方的通融。

  accommodation *n.*   accommodate *v.*

  accommodating *adj.* unaccommodating *adj.*

  accommodation 的几种用法：

  （1）通融，和解

  As a special accommodation, we will accept this mode of payment terms.

  作为特殊的通融，我们将接受这种付款方式。

  They have come to an accommodation over this issue.

  他们已就这个问题达成和解。

  （2）（酒店、火车、轮船等提供）的住宿膳食服务

The travel agency has arranged our accommodation.
旅行社已为我们安排好食宿。

*12. When the goods are ready for shipment and the freight space is booked, you can inform us and we will remit by telegraphic transfer.
当你方的货物备妥待运且舱位订好后,请通知我方,我们即电汇货款。

① book freight space 预订舱位
类似词组:
book shipping space
reserve shipping space
② remit *v.* 汇(款)
③ remittance *n.* 汇款,汇款额
Please remit payment by check immediately.
请速用支票汇出付款。
We have received your remittance.
我们已收到你方的汇款。

Part B Practical Key Sentences

1. introduce the topic on terms of payment
Now, there's one question left to discuss, that is, the terms of payment.
现在只剩下一件事需要讨论,那就是付款方式。
替换表达:
There's one other thing we need to discuss. That is, payment by D/P.
Would you like to have a talk with us about terms of payment now?
Shall we have a talk about terms of payment today?
What is your regular practice concerning terms of payment?
Let's come to the terms of payment.
I'd like to have a discussion with you about the modes of payment.

2. discuss the possibility of other terms of payment
I wonder if you could accept other kinds of payment such as D/A or D/P?
我想你们是否能接受其他付款方式,例如付款交单或承兑交单?
替换表达:
I wonder if you could be more flexible and accept other kinds of payment such as T/T or D/P?
Is it possible to find alternative terms of payment for this transaction, say, D/A or D/P?
Could you make an exception and accept D/A or D/P for this transaction?
In view of the unusually big size of the order, we hope you will offer us more favorable terms of

payment, what about D/P or D/A?

It would help us greatly if you would accept D/P or D/A.

3. insist on payment by L/C

Our usual practice is to accept payment by L/C only.

我们通常的做法就是只接受信用证的付款方式。

替换表达：

I'm afraid we've got to insist on payment by L/C, which is our usual practice.

We insist on payment by L/C, which is quite usual in international trade.

We regret to say that we must adhere to payment by L/C, which is customary in foreign trade.

4. promise to open the L/C

I'll arrange for the L/C to be opened in your favor as soon as I return.

我一回去就着手办理以你方为受益人的信用证。

替换表达：

I'll arrange for the L/C to be established in your favor as soon as I return.

I'll apply to the bank for the establishment of L/C in your favor as soon as I return.

I'll arrange with the bankers to issue an L/C in your favor as soon as I return.

I'll see about opening an L/C as soon as I arrive home.

5. make a compromise

To meet you half way, what do you say 50% by D/P and the rest by L/C?

我们迁就你们吧，50%用付款交单，余款用信用证支付好吗？

替换表达：

Let's make a compromise, how about 50% by D/P and the rest by L/C?

To avoid having our transaction tied up, how about 50% by D/P and the rest by L/C?

In order to close the deal, could you bend the rules a little, that is, 50% by D/P and the rest by L/C?

Part C Integration of Theory and Practice

1. terms of payment 付款方式

【知识点】在出口贸易中，卖方收取货款是交易的最终目的，那么付款方式就是合同中很重要的条款，由支付时间、地点和途径等组成。我国在进出口贸易中常用的付款方式有汇付、信用证和托收。汇付（Remittance）有信汇、电汇、票汇三种主要方式，现行的主要方式是电汇T/T（Telegraphic Transfer），即汇出行应汇款人的申请，用电报通知汇入行，指示汇入行对收款人支付一定金额的一种汇款方式，货运单据由出口方自行寄给进口方。一般来说，采用电汇有一定的风险，交易量和涉及的金额较小，但如果买方在卖方发货前已电汇预付货款，这对卖方则十分有利，出口方可以迅速收到货款。使用汇付时，应明确规定汇付的时间、具体的汇付方式和金额等。

【技能训练句型】
The buyer should pay 100% of the sales proceeds in advance by T/T to reach the sellers not later than April 15th.
买方应不迟于4月15日将100%的货款用电汇预付至卖方。

2. letter of credit（L/C） 信用证

【知识点】信用证是国际贸易中常见的付款方式，是一种银行开立的有条件承诺付款的书面文件，通常能保护出口方的利益。一般指开证银行根据进口方的请求和指示向出口方开立的一定金额的、并在一定期限内凭规定的装运单据承诺付款的书面文件。有关信用证的常见词组：

confirmed L/C 保兑的信用证
unconfirmed L/C 未保兑的信用证
revocable L/C 可撤销的信用证
irrevocable L/C 不可撤销的信用证
sight L/C (L/C at sight) 即期信用证
time L/C (L/C after sight) 远期信用证
transferable L/C 可转让的信用证
non-transferable L/C 不可转让的信用证
divisable L/C 可分割的信用证
indivisable L/C 不可分割的信用证
documentary L/C 跟单信用证

【技能训练句型】
（1）出口商要求用信用证付款，通常陈述的理由：
An L/C is quite common in the international trade.
信用证在国际贸易中相当普遍。
An L/C is a reliable and safe method of payment.
信用证是一种可靠而安全的付款方式。
An L/C gives the exporter the additional protection of the banker's guarantee.
信用证给出口商品增加了银行的额外担保。
An L/C can assure that the exporter get the right amount of money.
信用证可以保证出口商拿到该得的钱。
An L/C is fair and beneficial to both the seller and the buyer.
信用证是公平的，对买卖双方都有利。
An L/C protects the seller as well as the buyer.
信用证在保护卖主的同时，也保护了买主。

（2）进口商不愿意用信用证付款，通常陈述的理由：
An L/C would cause us a lot of difficulties.
信用证给我们造成许多困难。
An L/C would involve us some unnecessary inconvenience.
信用证给我们造成一些不必要的不便。
An L/C would cost us extra charges.
信用证需要我们另外多付一些费用。

An L/C would add to the cost of our imports.
信用证增加进口成本。
An L/C would need us to pay a deposit and the bank charges.
信用证让我们付订金和银行的费用。

3. collection 托收

【知识点】托收主要有D/P 和D/A 两种。使用托收方式时，应在买卖合同中明确规定交单条件、买方的付款或承兑责任以及付款期限等。D/P (documents against payment) 是指出口方装运货物出口后，备妥商业单据，委托银行托收时，指示银行等付款人付款后，才交付有关单证的方式。按时间不同又分为即期付款交单和远期付款交单。D/A (documents against acceptance)，承兑后交单，是指出口方在货物付运后，开具以进口方为付款人的远期汇票，连同各种货运单据一并交委托行寄往进口方代收行。出口方委托银行办理托收时，指示银行在进口方对汇票承兑后，才交付有关单证的方式。采用这种方式，进口方可先取单后付款，如果进口方在汇票到期日拒付，出口方有货款两空的风险，所以出口方要选择好的银行，并和对方有良好的贸易基础才敢采用此种方式。

Part D Practice

I. Complete the Following Dialogues

(1)

A: What do you think of ___1___ of payment?

B: I wonder if you can make payment ___2___ D/A or D/P?

A: No, I'm afraid not. It's very difficult for us to accept your ___3___.

B: Then what is your regular ___4___ considering the terms of payment?

A: We usually ___5___ payment by irrevocable L/C payable ___6___ shipping documents.

B: But an L/C will need us to pay a ___7___ and the bank charges.

A: Let's ___8___ a compromise, how about 50% by D/P and the ___9___ by L/C?

B: Thank you for your ___10___.

(2)

A: I find everything quite ___1___ except for the terms of payment.

B: Payment by L/C is quite ___2___ in international trade.

A: But to ___3___ an L/C will ___4___ to the cost of our ___5___.

B: I know. However, an irrevocable L/C can give the ___6___ the protection of a banker's ___7___?

A: Sorry you insist ___8___ payment by L/C. However, I'd very much ___9___ it if you could take our suggestion into further ___10___.

II. Interaction Activities

Task 1

Students work in pairs and make a dialogue based on the following situation:

Mr. John, a businessman from America, has ordered a total of USD 25000 worth of the sweaters. Mr. Lin is a salesman from China National Textiles Imp. & Exp. Corp., Fujian Branch. Now they have settled everything except the terms of payment. Mr. John suggests D/A or D/P terms. Mr. Lin tries to talk him into accepting payment by L/C, while Mr. John states his difficulties if demanded payment by L/C.

Task 2

Short conversation.

(1) Suppose you urge your client opening the L/C.

(2) State your reasons.

III. Actual Practice

Work in pairs.

Talk about the amendment to the L/C in details. The following information can be used for reference:

(1) The letter of credit is at sight instead of after sight.

(2) The amount of money should be USD 200000 instead of USD 20000.

(3) The expiry date should be the 5th of September rather than the 15th of September.

IV. Creative Discussion

The teacher divides the class into groups and asks them to discuss, then chooses the representatives of each group after discussion. The student who expresses well will be the winner.

Topic:

What are the main methods of payment? Say something about them.

Explain the payment terms of D/A and D/P.

Explain the payment terms of L/C.

Why is the exporter reluctant to accept D/A or D/P?

What benefit can the exporter receive by L/C?

Chapter 13 Business Negotiation

Learning Objectives
Upon completion of this chapter, you will be able to

- ☑ acquire knowledge of insurance and Form A.

- ☑ get to know exclusive agency and other business issues.

- ☑ learn the ways to reach the agreements with your clients through business negotiations.

- ☑ improve your skills of communication on the business negotiation.

- ☑ make yourself closer to be a successful businessman.

课文范读

Part A Situational Dialogue

Communicative Scene 1

Insurance and GSP Form A

(Mrs. Brown is talking insurance and Form A issues over with her supplier, Mr. Wang.)

Brown: Mr. Wang, since our price is based on CIF, let's classify what types of insurance clauses should be covered for our shipment.[1]

Wang: According to general practice, the insurance we cover for CIF price is All Risks for 110% of the invoice value.

Brown: Our requirements include not only All Risks, but also the insurance against Strikes Risk and War Risk.

Wang: I don't think we can provide the extensive coverage you mentioned, because there is only 0.3% room left for Insurance in our contract.[2]

Brown: The present world is not peaceful everywhere. Our vessel has to go through the sensitive areas and strikes are very common in our country. We have to make the insurance to avoid losses, just in case.

Wang: We understand your situation. As you know, it's the international trade practice that sellers insure the goods against the usual risks. If you insist on Special Additional Risks, the extra premium is borne by the buyer.

Brown: It makes sense but I'm wondering ...

Wang: Frankly speaking, our price is the most favorable you can get at present. We don't want to lose business, though the insurance only takes up a small percentage in the overall value.

Brown: What should we do then?

Wang: To make things easier, we suggest you cover Special Additional Risks yourself or accept CFR price.

Brown: Then I prefer a CFR basis.

Wang: Of course, we will deduct the cost for insurance from the original price and you can take care of the insurance yourself.

Brown: What is the difference?

Wang: It is different in some ways. First, we don't have to argue about what types of insurance should be covered. Second, if you make the insurance in your local insurance company, you can easily claim compensation in case something happens. Third, the L/C clauses will be simpler for both of us.

Brown: We can do it in this way.

Wang: The renewed contract with CFR price will be made immediately. We promise that we'll inform you immediately after the shipment so that you'll have enough time to carry out your insurance.

Brown: We wish to draw your attention to the GSP Form A. It should be issued as one of the documents for the L/C negotiation. It is vital important for us, because it will exempt us from higher tariffs.³

Wang: We have noticed that in our contract, to apply for Form A, we need to know some information, such as place of origin, consignee, notify party, port of destination, shipping mark, the country of consumption, and so on.

Brown: Our company will be the consignee and we will let you know the notify party and other information after we make the arrangement with our forwarder.

Wang: You bet.

 Communicative Scene 2

Exclusive Agency

(*Mr. Baker pays a visit to Ms. Liu's company. He is in negotiations with Ms. Liu over exclusive agency.*⁴)

Liu: Hello, Mr. Baker. It's a pleasure to see you in our company. You have been one of our best clients since our first meeting in Poland two years ago.

Baker: How time flies! I clearly remember that we started our business from women's garments. Under your encouragement, we have opened up a new market in this line. I appreciate it very much.

Liu: Thank you for saying so. From your email message, we learned that the main purpose of your visit this time is to discuss exclusive agency. Is that right?

Baker: Correct. To secure our ready set-up market, our company hopes to obtain exclusive agency for women's garments.

Liu: That is a very practical and an important matter.

Baker: As you may be aware, we have well-established wide business connections and reputation in the line of clothes in Europe. We know the European markets like the palm of our hand.⁵

Liu: Well-done.

Baker: Our company is the right one to act as your sole agent. If you do so, it will be beneficial for your trade by reducing rivals.

Liu: I appreciate your efforts in pushing sales of our new products. Do you mean your company is requesting exclusive rights of sales in your country?

Baker: Not exactly. As you know, our country is a small European country. The market is quite limited because the population of our country is only above 15 million, even less than that in your province.

Liu: Um. I see.

Baker: Nowadays inside the European Union, all the individual European countries are considered as a whole, especially from the view of economy and business. There is no border line at all between countries for commodity flow. For this reason, exclusive sales in a single European country by no means should be required.[6]

Liu: Well, in this case, what is the "Border Line" you'd like to have?

Baker: We prefer the whole of Europe.

Liu: I'm afraid that is impossible, much as we'd like to. We are selling our products in some of the East European countries already, such as Russia, Ukraine, etc. It is unfair to delete these countries from our customer list. What we can do is that we give you exclusive rights inside the European Union.[7]

Baker: Sounds reasonable. We agree to define our "Border Line" inside European Union.[8] Here is a draft agreement on the exclusive agency. Please take a look and we'll discuss it this afternoon.

Liu: OK.

 Communicative Scene 3

The Volume of Sales and Penalty

(A further discussion about sales volume and penalty is going on in the afternoon.)

Liu: Mr. Baker, we have had a careful look at your proposal. Besides the territory we discussed this morning, we basically agree on the starting time, product range of exclusive agency and other issues.

Baker: Fine.

Liu: Here we'd like to discuss some more about the volume of sales and penalty. Compared with other tool kits we sold, the annual value for women's garment is still much smaller though the business between us is growing fast. We really want the market to be much, much bigger than the present one.

Baker: This is why we are asking for the exclusive right. We have the same goal to make the business big enough so that we can both make more money.

Liu: Well, Mr. Baker, we'd like to talk about the annual quantity you will propose to sell.

Baker: We don't think it practical to make the volume of sales too high in the initial stage. We may encounter strong resistance.[9]

Liu: To solve this problem and reach our common goal, why don't we set a progressive limit for the volume of sales?

Baker: That's marvelous! Half a million sets per year for the first two years and a quarter million sets increase each year in every following two years. We expect to get 6% commission on the net value for sales.

Liu: Sounds good. The next point is the article of penalty, which seems unfair for our side.

Baker: Why do you say so?

Liu: The article specifies that we will be punished if we sell our products to other companies in the European Community.[10] We did not see any corresponding article of punishment if you buy the same or similar products from other companies or manufacturers. We'd like to have this portion added to the Agreement.

Baker: OK. I know "No victory comes out without price".[11]

Liu: In the interests of both companies, we agree to appoint you as our exclusive agency for a period of 4 years.

Baker: I am very pleased to get everything settled so quickly. I'm very grateful for your kindness and efficient work. I believe our cooperation in the future will be more fruitful and successful.

Liu: I'm very delighted to see the business between our two companies growing so smoothly and healthily.

Words and Expressions

1. GSP Form A (Generalized System of Preferences Certificate of Origin)		普惠制原产地证
2. All Risks		综合险
3. Strikes Risk		罢工险
4. sensitive	adj.	敏感的；灵敏的
5. Special Additional Risks		特别附加险
6. premium	n.	保险费
7. overall value		总值
8. renew	vt.	使更新；修补；重做
9. classify	vt.	分类；归纳
10. exempt	vt.	免除，豁免
	adj.	被免除的，被豁免的
11. tariff	n.	关税
12. consignee	n.	收货人；受托人
13. notify party		通知方
14. shipping mark		唛头
15. forwarder	n.	运输人，运输商
16. exclusive agency (sole agency)		独家代理
17. encouragement	n.	鼓励；赞助
18. territory	n.	地域；领土
19. Border Line		边界
20. Ukraine	n.	乌克兰
21. define	vt.	定义；详细说明
22. consumption	n.	消费，消耗

23. the volume of sales		销售量
24. encounter	v.	遇到；遭受
25. specify	vt.	规定；指定
26. progressive	adj.	累进的；逐渐的；进步的
27. marvelous	adj.	妙极的；了不起的
28. corresponding	adj.	相应的，对应的；符合的

1. Since our price is based on CIF, let's classify what types of insurance clauses should be covered for our shipment.

   既然我们的价格条款是成本加保险费、运费价，那么来确定一下我们的货物该上什么保险。

   ① classify v. 分类，归纳

   The insurance is classified as 3 basic types of coverage, General Additional Risk and Special Additional Risk.

   保险分为三种，基本险、一般附加险和特殊附加险。

   ② cover v. 给（货物等）保险，包含

   All the expenses, including room and board, round-way tickets, will be covered by ourselves.

   所有费用，包括食宿和往返机票，均由我方自己承担。

   We will have to cover the porcelain against Risk of Breakage to avoid losses in transit.

   我们将只好对陶瓷投保破碎险以避免运输中的损失。

2. There is only 0.3% room left for Insurance in our contract.

   我们合同中的"保险"仅有0.3%的余地。

   ① room n. 空间，余地（常指抽象事物）

   We could not load all the goods into the container. The room was fully occupied.

   我们无法把全部货物装进集装箱。空间被占满了。

   There is no room for improvement due to our limited working conditions.

   由于我们工作条件的限制，无法再改进了。

3. It is vital important for us, because it will exempt us from higher tariffs.

   它对我们很重要，可使我们免交高额关税。

   ① exempt from 免除，豁免（常与from连用）

   The new law exempts low-income families from taxation.

   新法律使低收入的家庭免除税收。

   The farm products from Taiwan are on the list of goods exempt from import taxes.

   台湾的农产品列在免税货物的清单上。

4. be in negotiations with sb. over sth.

与某人洽谈某事

The exporter is in negotiations with the representative of Technical Import & Export Corporation over compensation trade.

出口方与技术进出口公司的代表在洽谈补偿贸易。

5. We know the European markets like the palm of our hand.

    我们对欧洲市场的情况了如指掌。

    ① know sth. like the palm of one's hand 对……了如指掌

    Our exclusive agent knows the local custom of the buying country like the palm of his hand.

    我们的独家代理对购买地国家的风俗习惯了如指掌。

6. There is no boarder line at all between countries for commodity flow. For this reason, exclusive sales in a single European country by no means should be required.

    商品流通根本没有什么国界。因此要求一个欧洲国家的独家经营权毫无意义。

    ① by no means 决不

    The special compromise we made by no means should be taken as usual practice.

    决不能把我们这次所做的退让视为惯例。

7. It is unfair to delete these countries from our customer list. What we can do is that we give you exclusive right inside the European Union.

    我们不宜把他们从客户名单上划掉，我们只能给您欧盟内的独家经营权。

    ① It is unfair to ... 不公平的，不合适的

    It is unfair to insist on the shipment on time because of your delay opening L/C.

    由于你方延误开立信用证，坚持要求我方准时发货是不合适的。

    ② What we can do is that ... 我们所能做的是……

    What we can do is that you take measures to avoid such inferior goods reoccurring.

    我们所能做的是要求你方采取措施避免再出现劣质产品。

8. We agree to define our "Border Line" inside European Union.

    我们同意将"边界"限定在欧盟内。

    ① define vt. 下定义，阐释，详细说明

    I wonder if you can define "With Particular Average" more clearly? (I wonder if you can give a more clear definition of "With Particular Average"?)

    你能就水渍险给出更清晰的定义吗？

9. We don't think it practical to make the volume of sales too high in the initial stage. We may encounter strong resistance.

    我们认为在初期把销售额定得太高是不现实的，我们可能面临强大的阻力。

    ① We don't think it practical to ... 我们认为……是不可行的

    We don't think it practical to submit the disputes for arbitration before friendly negotiation.

    我们认为在友好协商之前就把争端提交仲裁是不可取的。

10. The article specifies that we will be punished if we sell our products to other companies in the European Community.

条款规定如果我们的产品销往欧盟的其他公司，将受到处罚。

① specify *vt.* 规定，确定，具体说明

Please specify the name of commodity, specification and quantity you require.

请具体说明所需的商品名称、规格和数量。

11. No victory comes out without price.

没人能随随便便成功。（美国著名电视剧《绝望主妇》的名言）

*12. make sense 有道理，（讲话等）有意义

His definition of Exclusive Agency doesn't make sense.

他对独家代理的定义没有解释清楚。

① make sense of 了解……的意义，明白

Through trade training, they make sense of *INCOTERMS* 2000.

通过贸易培训，他们了解了《国际贸易术语解释通则2000》的含义。

Part B Practical Key Sentences

1. **insurance**

   insurance on 表示所投保货物

   insurance against 表示保险种类

   insurance with ... 表示向……保险公司投保

   insurance for 表示保额

   We effect insurance on the 1200 cartons of sea food for 110% of invoice value against All Risks.

   我们按发票金额的110%对1200箱海产品投保了一切险。

   Insurance is to be covered by the seller on behalf of the buyer for 110% of invoice value against Overland Transportation with the People's Insurance Company of China.

   卖方代买方按发票金额的110%向中国人民保险公司投保陆上运输险。

   替换表达：

   I wonder what exactly insurance takes out according to your usual CIF terms.

   Free from Particular Average is too narrow for the shipment of this goods, please extend the coverage to include All Risks.

2. **premium**

   The insurance rate for such kind of risk will vary in accordance with the nature of the cargo.

   这类险别的保险费率将取决于货物的种类。

   As our general practice, insurance effects basic risks only, the extra premium involved would be for the buyer's account.

   按照我们的惯例，只保基本险，而额外的保险费则由买方负担。

替换表达：

The buyer requires the insurance against Special Additional Risks and agrees to pay the additional premium.

We have found out this risk is coverable at the premium rate of 0.3%.

3. **the trade practice**

We can't break international practice to allow Extraneous Risks by the seller.

我方不能违背国际惯例，让卖方投保附加险。

According to the regular trade practice, the L/C should be opened by the buyer 30 days before the date of shipment.

根据贸易惯例，信用证应在装船前30天由买方开出。

替换表达：

It's the international trade practice that the agent is given the authority to represent the principle in dealing with buyers.

As for terms of payment , our company mainly adopted some usual international practices.

4. **we wish to draw your attention**

本句型适用于提醒谈判对手可能忽视的重要事情。

We wish to draw your attention that the seller should send shipping advise to buyer before shipment on CFR basis.

我想提醒你注意，在CFR价格条件下，装运前卖方必须向买方发出装船通知。

替换表达：

We'd like to remind you that you must take delivery date into consideration because we need the goods urgently.

May I invite your attention to the fact that the GSP Form A should be issued as one of the documents for the L/C negotiation?

5. **it is impossible, much as we'd like to**

I'm afraid that it is impossible, much as we'd like to give you further discount.

尽管我们很想给你更低的折扣，但恐怕不行。

替换表达：

I'm afraid that it won't be possible, much as we want to.

I don't think it is workable, much as we'd like to.

I really don't like to say no, but I have to.

6. **as you may be aware**

As you may be aware, we are interested in setting up a joint venture company with you in Canada.

正如你所知，我们有兴趣与贵公司在加拿大建立合资企业。

替换表达：

As we may be aware that the purpose of my visiting is seeking for a possibility of general agency.

As you know, we have extensive business connections and reputation in the field of aquatic products.

7. **in the interests of**

In the interests of our long-term cooperation, we are glad to sign an agency agreement with you.
为了双方长期合作的利益，我们很高兴与贵公司签署代理协议。
替换表达：
For the sake of the development of business, a 10% commission will be granted for you to push the sales.
To the advantage of our trade, we are ready to give you a 10% discount.

Part C　Integration of Theory and Practice

1. cover insurance on the goods　货物投保

【知识点】按CIF和CIP条件成交的出口商品，卖方在确定装运期和运输工具后，按约定的保险金额和险别，向保险公司办理投保。

其他交易条件的投保，卖方务必及时发出装船通知，以便买方决定是否投保。延误发出装船通知，若造成损失由卖方承担。

【技能训练句型】

We promise that we will inform you immediately after the shipment so that you will have enough time to carry out your insurance.
我们保证在货物装运后会立即通知贵方，以便贵方有足够的时间投保。

三种基本险别：

（1）平安险 Free from Particular Average，简称FPA
平安险的保障范围一般只赔全部损失。

（2）水渍险 With Particular Average，简称WPA
水渍险的责任范围除包括"平安险"的各项责任外，还负责被保险货物由于恶劣气候、自然灾害所造成的部分损失。

（3）综合险（一切险）All Risks
综合险的责任范围除包括"平安险"和"水渍险"的责任外，还包括保险货物在运输过程中，因各种外因造成不论全部或部分的损失。一般附加险别包括其中。

只能在投保三种基本险中的某一种后，才能投保附加险。特别附加险，例如战争险（War Risk）和罢工险（Strikes Risk）等，不属于综合险的范围之内，按国际惯例应由买方投保。

【技能训练句型】

As you know, it's the international trade practice that sellers insure the goods against the usual risks. If you insist on Special Additional Risks, the extra premium is borne by the buyer.
但你知道，按国际惯例，卖方对货物只投保惯常险别。如贵方坚持保特殊险，则额外的保险费由贵方承担。

2. GSP Form A　普惠制原产地证

【知识点】普惠制是发达国家给予发展中国家出口产品普遍的、非歧视的、非互惠的一种关税优惠制度，是一项有利于发展中国家和地区扩大出口的关税优惠制度。普惠制产地证（Generalized System of Preferences Certificate of Origin，简称Form A）是依据给惠国要求而出具的能证明出口货物原产自受惠国的证明文件，并能使货物在给惠国享受普遍优惠关税待遇。国家出入境检验检疫局是中国签发普惠制产地证的官方机构。

如需办理普惠制产地证，买方会在合同和信用证中作出规定。

【技能训练句型】

We have noticed that the GSP Form A is written down in our contract. To apply for the Form A, we need to know some information, such as place of origin, consignee, notify party, port of destination, shipping mark, the country of consumption, and so on.

我们注意到此事已写在合同中。为了申请普惠制原产地证，我们还需要一些信息，比如原产地、收货人、通知方、目的港、唛头和消费国等。

【知识点】正确运用该优惠政策，有助于企业在欧盟等进口国享受到大幅关税减免，扩大外贸出口。普惠制产地证由受惠国出品商填制申报，受惠国签证机构审核、证明及签发。

3. certificate of origin　原产地证

【知识点】原产地证（Certificate of Origin）简称C/O，证明货物原产自某一特定国家或地区，是享受进口国正常关税（最惠国）待遇的证明文件。中国原产地证是证明我国出口货物生产和制造于中国的证明文件，是出口产品进入国际市场的护照。

Form A不同于一般产地证书C/O，一般产地证是享受最惠国待遇的有效证件，普惠制产地证，则是享受普惠制减、免税待遇的有效证件。

4. exclusive agency　独家代理

【知识点】独家代理是外贸的一种重要形式。出口方与代理商达成协议，利用代理商熟悉销售地市场和广泛的销售渠道的优势，代表出口方推销商品、签订合同，开拓出口市场。代理人在委托人授权的范围内经营，不承担销售风险和费用，通常按达成交易的金额提取约定比例的佣金。

谈判独家代理时应注意：

（1）了解代理商是否确实具有优势，选择好代理商，充分借助代理公司的销售渠道优势和良好信誉去开拓市场。

（2）独家代理通常要承诺最低成交数量或销售金额。若未能达标，委托人有权中止协议或按协议规定调整佣金。

（3）独家代理必须明确代理业务的地理范围，并约定代理协议有效期。

（4）确定代理商品的种类，规定委托人和代理的职责和义务。

（5）规定佣金率、支付佣金的时间和方法。独家代理具有专营权，若委托人与其他买主直接发生交易，仍应按交易金额向独家代理支付佣金。这是独家代理与一般代理的主要区别。

5. win-win negotiation　双赢的谈判

【知识点】成功的商务谈判要争取达成双赢的效果。谈判结果应使双方都得到商务发展的机会，让双方共赢。

在当今的外贸谈判中如坚持传统的谈判方式，斤斤计较，寸土必争，捞尽所有好处是不明智的。这样的战胜对方，必然使谈判各方不欢而散，生意不成，自己也无胜利可言，甚至还破坏了今后双方进一步贸易的机会。

争取双赢的技巧：

（1）做好谈判前的准备，制订详细的谈判计划。

（2）在谈判中寻找双方的共同点，互作让步。不光考虑自己，要替对方着想，留点好处给对方，让对方有谈判赢了的感觉。

（3）具有灵活的谈判策略，高效的谈判方式。

（4）相互信任，相互协调，相互合作。所提的方案，让对方觉得有道理。

（5）达成明智的双赢协议，使双方在贸易中都有利可图。

【技能训练句型】

A: We prefer to get the exclusive rights in the whole Europe.
我想要整个欧洲的独家经营权。

B: I'm afraid that it's impossible, much as we'd like to. It is unfair to delete our existing Eastern European countries from our customer list. What we can do is to give you exclusive rights inside the European Union.
我们很想满足您的要求，但恐怕不行。我们不宜把他们从我们的客户名单上划掉，我们只能给您欧盟内的独家经营权。

A: Sounds reasonable. You win.
很合理。你赢了。

I am very pleased to get everything settled so quickly. I'm very grateful for your kindness and efficient work. I believe our cooperation in the future will be more fruitful and successful.
非常高兴所有问题这么快就解决了。非常感谢您的友好态度和高效工作。我相信我们之间将来的合作会更有成效。

Part D Practice

I. Complete the Following Dialogues

Fill in the blanks with the proper words.

(1)

A: Peter, I quote the price on CIF basis. If you prefer to effect ___1___ at your end, please don't hesitate to tell us.

B: Well, we'd like to ___2___ what types of insurance we should take ___3___ according to your usual CIF terms.

A: Insurance to be covered ___4___ the 3000 pieces of sculptures for 110% of invoice value ___5___ All Risks.

B: I'd like to draw your ___6___ to the fact that the sculptures are valuable. We have to request for 130% of the invoice ___7___ .

A: As the regular trade ___8___, we regret to tell you that you have to bear the cost of the additional part since the amounts of value exceed the stipulated limit.

B: I guest there must be some ___9___ for discussion.

A: I don't think it ___10___, much as we'd like to.

(2)

A: Our business is concluded ___1___ a CFR basis. May I draw your attention to ___2___ insurance as soon as we send you the ___3___ advise?

B: Sure. Thank you for reminding me. To be ___4___, I'd like you to cover the insurance for us. The premium will be for our ___5___.

A: No problem. We'll arrange for the goods ___6___ All Risks for 110% of the invoice value ___7___ the People's Insurance Company of China.

B: Good. We wish to draw your attention to the GSP Form A. It should be issued as one of the documents for the L/C ___8___. It is important for us because it will ___9___ us from higher tariff.

A: OK. We'll make it according to the contract. I need more ___10___ to complete the GSP Form A. Could you send it to me soon?

B: All right. I'll check it and send it to you at once.

II. Interaction Activities

Task 1

A foreign importer asks the seller to insure the domestic glassware against Risk of Breakage, War Risk and WPA. Suppose you are the seller. You agree to accept the request on the condition that the extra premium should be born on the buyer.

The teacher divides students into pairs. Students make short dialogues and role-play them. The following expressions should be included in the dialogue:

(1) invite your attention to
(2) What types of insurance be covered
(3) be too narrow for
(4) extend the coverage to
(5) As you may be aware
(6) the trade practice
(7) the extra premium is borne
(8) I'm afraid that it is impossible
(9) Can't break practice to
(10) It makes sense
(11) have to pay Extraneous Risks

Task 2

The representative of Machinery and Equipment Corporation is in negotiations with the exporter over the commission rate for sole agency. Compose a conversation with your partner. Your conversation should cover the expressions below:

(1) As you may be aware

(2) well-established marketing channels

(3) talk over the possibility

(4) be experienced in

(5) appreciate the efforts

(6) invite your attention to commission

(7) As our general practice

(8) don't think it practical to

(9) push sales

(10) I'm afraid that

(11) In the interests of both sides

(12) be ready to

(13) appoint you as

III. Actual Practice

Mr. Victor is having a negotiation with Mr. Hong on sole agency. He praises that the silk products of Mr. Hong's company are popular in Indian market. He states the advantages of his company to deal with the silk products and expresses his intention to be a sole agency.

Mr. Hong points out the trade turnover of Mr. Victor's company is still too low to be an agent. In view of low volume of sales, Mr. Hong suggests that Mr. Victor try to sell more of silk products at an initial stage. When time is ripe, they will discuss sole agency again.

Students work in pairs and role-play the conversation.

IV. Creative Discussion

From Communicative Scene 2 and 3, you learn Mr. Backer is in negotiations with Ms. Liu over exclusive agency.

The teacher divides class into groups and asks students to discuss the topics with their partners and then share their opinions with other pairs.

Topics:

1. Why does Mr. Baker request the sole agency not only in single European country?

2. What's the reason Ms. Liu doesn't agree to give exclusive right in the whole Europe? Does it do something good if Ms. Liu approves Mr. Baker's requests for exclusive right in the whole Europe?

3. What consideration do we need to appoint an agent?

4. How to improve trade by means of sole agency?

Chapter 14 Sign a Contract

Learning Objectives
Upon completion of this chapter, you will be able to

- get used to the process of negotiating the terms of contract.
- check the contract carefully.
- learn how to sign a contract.
- conduct the activities related to the theme of signing a contract.

课文范读

Part A Situational Dialogue

 Communicative Scene 1

Going over a Draft Contract

(*Mr. Smith, a businessman from Britain, is talking about a draft contract with Miss Chen working at Fujian Wonderful Import & Export Corporation.*)

Smith: Miss Chen. I read very carefully the draft contract last night. <u>It seems to me we've come quite a long way. However, there are still some points which I'd like to bring up.</u>[1]

Chen: Please go ahead. I also think it is necessary for us to clarify some important terms before they are finally included in the formal contract.

Smith: First, about the packing. <u>I'm afraid the cardboard boxes are not strong enough for transport by sea.</u>[2] Would you please use wooden cases instead?

Chen: I'm sorry. <u>It's stipulated in the contract that the products are packed in cardboard boxes.</u>[3] And, what's more, they are easier to handle and cheaper in cost.

Smith: Well, carton is all right. But the packing must be strong enough to withstand rough handling. <u>So could you please take some measures to reinforce them?</u>[4]

Chen: OK. We can strengthen the cartons with double straps.

Smith: Thank you. Second, about the terms of payment. I wonder whether the payment is to be made by D/A or D/P?

Chen: I'm afraid not. As we all know, that might cause great trouble to the sellers. We want payment to be made by confirmed, irrevocable letter of credit, payable against shipping documents. That's our usual practice.

Smith: I see, but opening an L/C with a bank means additional expense.

Chen: I'm sorry, that can't be helped.

Smith: Then payment by L/C. But I must stress again that shipment should be effected and completed by the end of July. We can't accept any delay.

Chen: Of course not, as long as you open the covering L/C in due time.

Smith: I'll arrange for the establishment of the relative letter of credit with Bank of China, London as soon as I return, and let you know by fax at the moment it is opened.

Chen: Fine. Is there anything else?

Smith: What about the quality standard?

Chen: It is clearly stipulated in the contract that <u>"quality as per sample 23 and technical feature indicated in the illustrations submitted by seller"</u>.[5] Have you any questions about this stipulation?

Smith: No, it's all right. Next, I'd like to talk about arbitration. It is stipulated that arbitration shall take place in China. Is it possible to have it carried out in a third country?

Chen: No problem, since arbitration is very rarely resorted to. I hope all disputes can be settled through friendly consultations.⁶

Smith: Certainly. Well, it seems we have talked about the disputes in the draft contract. However, would you please check all the terms listed in the contract and see if there is anything not in conformity with the terms we agree on? ⁷

Chen: Fine. I'll get it ready and send it to your hotel tomorrow morning. Is that alright?

Smith: That's fine. Thank you.

 Communicative Scene 2

Checking the Contract One More Time

(*Miss Chen is checking the draft contract with Mr. Smith one more time to make sure that everything is all right.*)

Chen: Now, Mr. Smith, the contract is ready. Shall we check the contract one more time to make sure we have reached an agreement on all the terms?

Smith: OK. I think that's a good idea and will help avoid disputes and claims in the future. ⁸(*After checking*) Well, everything seems all right except some minor points. First of all, don't you think we should add this sentence here? "If one side fails to carry out the contract, the other side is entitled to cancel the contract." ⁹

Chen: Yes, I'll add it to the contract.

Smith: Second, what insurance will you take out for the goods, if we conclude the business on CIF basis?

Chen: We'll only insure WPA.

Smith: Could you cover the Risk of Breakage?

Chen: Your request is acceptable on condition that the additional charge is for your account. But I should remind you that claims are payable only for that part of the loss, that is, over 5%. So I don't think it necessary.

Smith: What you said is reasonable. W.P.A. is enough.

Chen: Now that the insurance is decided on, shall we go on to other terms and conditions?

Smith: Go ahead.

Chen: Have you any further questions concerning the packing and shipping marks?

Smith: I agree to the terms. Then do you have any problems that need to be worked out?

Chen: Oh, I think the "force majeure" clause is missing. We often have typhoons and floods during the summer, production might be affected and the execution of the contract would be delayed. I hope that you won't object to adding such a clause in the contract.[10]

Smith: All right. If it's nothing we can do to protest the nature, we'll add it to the contract. In case of "force majeure", you should notify us as soon as possible.

Chen: I will. Thank you for your friendly cooperation. I hope everything will go smoothly and no disaster will happen.

Smith: Now, I think it is essential to include in this clause, that is, "Any modification or alteration to the contract shall only be made with the consent of both parties."

Chen: No problem, I'll do it. Then I think we have reached an agreement on all the terms and the contract contains basically all we have agreed upon during our negotiation. However, if there are any problems, you can contact me at any time before we sign the formal contract.

Smith: Great. When can the contract be ready for signature?

Chen: I hope it can be signed next Monday, will that work?

Smith: Yes. I'll see you then.

Chen: See you.

 Communicative Scene 3

Signing a Formal Contract

(*Mr. Smith and Miss Chen check the items in the contract one by one and sign a formal contract.*)

Chen: Well, I think there will be no misunderstandings between us. Here is our contract. Would you please read it carefully again?

Smith: Fine, let's check the items in the contract one by one, the name of the commodity, specifications, unit, quantity, unit price and the total amount ... (*After checking all the items*) I'm glad that we've finally come to an agreement after repeated negotiation. Things that should be there are there. Do you have an English copy of the contract?

Chen: Yes, here it is. Please have a look.

Smith: (*After reading the contract*) No problem.

Chen: Now since everything is settled, shall we sign the contract now?

Smith: OK.

Chen: Please sign here. (*After all signatures*) Each has two formal copies of the contract. These two copies are for you. One is in English and the other is in Chinese. They are all in agreement with each other.

Smith: Thank you. Let's congratulate ourselves that this transaction has been brought to a successful conclusion.[11] The next step is to carry out this contract well. As we all know, once a contract is signed, it has legal effect.

Chen: I am sure both of our parties will value our commercial reputation highly and the contract will be executed smoothly. This deal will promote further expansion of the trade between us.

Sign a Contract

Words and Expressions

1. draft contract	n.	合同草案，草约
2. bring up		提出
3. clarify	v.	澄清，阐明
4. reinforce	v.	加固；加强
5. as per		根据，按照
6. indicate	v.	表示，标示
7. submit	v.	提交，呈递
8. arbitration	n.	仲裁
9. resort to		诉诸
10. consultation	n.	协商
11. conformity	n.	一致
12. be entitled to		给予（某人获得某物或做某事）的权利
13. force majeure		不可抗力
14. typhoon	n.	台风
15. execution	n.	执行
16. object to		反对
17. modification	n.	修改
18. alteration	n.	变化
19. consent	n.	同意
20. withstand	v.	经受住，抵挡
21. misunderstanding	n.	误解
22. original	n.	原件
23. legal effect		法律效力

Notes

1. It seems to me we've come quite a long way. However, there are still some points which I'd like to bring up.

   我认为我们已有很大进展，但仍有一些问题需要磋商。

   ① come a long way 有很大进展

   They have come a long way in the research.

   他们的研究取得很大进展。

   ② bring up

   a. 提出（供讨论）

   He brought up the subject of money at the meeting.

   他在会上提出钱的问题。

   b. 养育（孩子）

She brought up three children alone.
  她独自养育三个孩子。

2. I'm afraid the cardboard boxes are not strong enough for transport by sea.
   这种纸箱用于远洋运输，恐怕不够结实。

   ① enough 用做后置定语，在形容词或副词之后，而不是之前，后面可接to do sth.或for sth.

   The quality of the product is good enough for me to make a decision.
   产品的质量让我有足够的信心做出决定。

3. It's stipulated in the contract that the products are packed in cardboard boxes.
   合同规定产品用纸箱包装。

   ① stipulate *v.* 规定

   The contract stipulates that you should pay in advance.
   合同规定你方应预付款。

   ② stipulation *n.* 规定，规定（约定）的条件

   She agreed to the clauses, but with the stipulation that she would take 2% commission.
   她同意了这些条款，条件是她要得到2%的佣金。

4. So could you please take some measures to reinforce them?
   那么，你们可以采取一些加固措施吗？

   ① take measures 采取措施

   The government has taken stronger measures to combat smuggling.
   政府已采取更强有力的措施与走私作斗争。

5. ..."quality as per sample 23 and technical feature indicated in the illustrations submitted by seller"
   "品质以卖方提供的第23号样品和说明书的技术标准为准"

   ① as per 根据，按照

   We carried out the market research as per your instructions.
   我们根据你的指示开展市场调研工作。

   ② submitted by seller 修饰sample 23 和technical feature，indicated in the illustrations 又修饰technical feature。

   ③ submit to

   a. 提交，呈递

   He submitted the application to the committee for approval.
   他向委员会递交申请以求批准。

   b. 同意服从 (正式用语)

   We are willing to submit to arbitration.
   我们愿意接受仲裁。

6. No problem, since arbitration is very rarely resorted to. I hope all disputes will be settled through friendly consultations.
   没问题，因为很少进行仲裁。我希望所有的争议均通过友好协商解决。

   ① resort to 正式用语，（不得已时）诉诸（坏的或极端的办法）

   If other means fail, it is necessary for us to resort to force.

如果其他手段失败，我们有必要诉诸武力。

7. However, would you please check all the terms listed in the contract and see if there is anything not in conformity with the terms we agree on?
   然而，您是否能逐项检查一下合同的所有条款，看看还有什么意见不一致的地方？
   ① listed in the contract 修饰 all the terms
   ② in conformity with (正式用语) 与（规定、习俗等）一致，符合
   We must act in conformity with the commercial law.
   我们必须遵守商法。

8. I think that's a good idea and will help avoid disputes and claims in the future.
   我想这是个好主意，这样能避免今后的纠纷和索赔。
   ① claim 既可以当名词也可以当动词，在国际贸易中表示"索赔"时，注意以下词组：
   lodge a claim 提出索赔
   claim for 因……提出索赔
   claim on / against sb. 向……提出索赔
   accept a claim 接受索赔
   dismiss a claim 驳回索赔
   reject a claim 拒绝索赔
   withdraw a claim 撤回索赔
   claim a compensation of the shipment from sb. for sth. 因为……向某人要求赔偿
   asking for amends for the losses by replacing the inferior goods 要求更换劣质产品

9. If one side fails to carry out the contract, the other side is entitled to cancel the contract.
   如果一方未按本合同条款执行，另一方有权中止本合同。
   ① fail to do sth. 未做应做的事
   He failed to keep his promises.
   他没有履行诺言。
   ② be entitled to do sth. 给予（某人获得某物或做某事）的权力
   We are entitled to ask for compensation according to the contract.
   根据合同，我们有权要求赔偿。

10. I hope that you won't object to adding such a clause in the contract.
    我希望你方不会反对在合同中加入这一条款。
    ① object to 反对，to是介词，后面跟动词时要加 ing
    He strongly objects to accepting the clause.
    他强烈反对接受此条款。

11. Let's congratulate ourselves that this transaction has been brought to a successful conclusion.
    祝贺我们圆满达成交易。
    ① bring to a successful conclusion 达成交易
    相似表达法：
    come to terms
    come to a transaction

conclude a transaction
close a deal
put through the deal

Part B Practical Key Sentences

1. **discussing changing some points**

    There are still some points which I'd like to bring up.

    我想仍有一些问题需要磋商。

    替换表达：

    Don't you think we should add this sentence here?

    I want to point out that...

    I wonder if we can add this sentence here?

2. **confirm the terms in the contract**

    Would you please check all the terms listed in the contract and see if there is anything not in conformity with the terms we agree on?

    您是否能逐项检查一下合同的所有条款，看看还有什么意见不一致的地方？

    替换表达：

    Shall we check the contract one more time to make sure we have reached an agreement on all the terms?

    Would you please go through it to see if everything is all right?

    Would you please go over it and see whether there is anything wrong with it?

    Would you check all the details and make sure that everything conforms with what we have agreed on?

3. **confirm the time for signature**

    I hope to be able to sign the contract next Monday, is that alright?

    我希望在下星期一签字，可以吗？

    替换表达：

    The contract will be ready next Monday, will you come to sign it?

    I'll send the contract to you for your signature next Monday, will that work?

    Now everything is settled and I expect to have the contract ready for signature next Monday.

4. **reach an agreement**

    I'm glad that we've finally come to an agreement after repeated negotiation.

    我很高兴我们在反复协商之后最终达成协议。

    替换表达：

    I'm glad we have reached an agreement on all the terms.

    I'm very glad we have no questions about all the terms.

I'm glad the contract contains all we have agreed upon during our negotiation.

I'm glad our discussion has come to a successful conclusion.

I'm glad our discussion has successfully concluded.

I'm glad our negotiation has reached a successful result.

Part C Integration of Theory and Practice

【知识点】在商务活动中,交易双方通常对合同草案的条款进行逐一确认,然后由一方制定书面合同,经双方核对无误后签字。双方各持正本一份(国际贸易中含中英文文本),据此履行合同条款。合同的形式一般包括三个部分。

1. the first part of the contract   合同的第一部分

第一部分包括合同的标题及编号、签约的日期和地点、签约双方的名称和地址等。标题在合同第一页顶端的正中位置,如由卖方草拟并提出的合同称"销货合同"(Sales Contract),由买方草拟并提出的合同称"购货合同"(Purchase Contract)。接着是合同号码,然后是合同的日期,也就是说合同从这一天生效,通常是"date-month-year"或"effective date-month-year"。接下去是签约双方公司的全称和地址。合同的第一句话通常是"根据合同的规定条款,卖方同意出售,买方同意购买下述商品"。("Seller agrees to sell and buyer agrees to buy the under-mentioned goods subject to the terms and conditions.")

2. the second part of the contract   合同的第二部分

【知识点】第二部分是合同的主体,主要是具体的交易条款。合同的内容应尽可能全面,不仅要包括商品的名称(name of commodity)、规格(specifications)、单价(unit price)、装运港和目的港(port of shipment and port of destination),还要包含商品的品质(quality)、包装(packing)、运输标志(shipping mark)、交货期(delivery day)、付款方式(terms of payment)、保险(insurance)、商品检验(inspection),以及索赔(claims)、仲裁(arbitration)、不可抗力(force majeure)等条件。以下是签订合同时需要特别注意的事项。

(1)包装条款(Packing terms): 进出口双方应在合同中明确所要求的包装,因为不符合规定的包装会影响货物安全到达目的地或引起当地海关拒绝货物入境。

【技能训练句型】

在签订正式合同前,常用以下这些谈判用语:

We hope that you can make some improvements in the packing.

我方希望你方在包装上能稍作改进。

I'm afraid the cardboard boxes are not strong enough for transport by sea.

这种纸箱用于远洋运输,恐怕不够结实。

Could you please take some measures to reinforce them?

你们能采取一些加固措施吗?

When you pack, please put 3 different colors in each box.

装箱时,请每箱装三种颜色。

【知识点】（2）费用（Expenses）：对各种费用的考虑，包括价格、使用何种货币、利息、价格的递增和付款方式等，要注意价格可能不仅仅是货物的基本费用，还可能包含佣金和各种折扣的比率等。出口方应谨慎选择使用何种货币，不致因汇率变动而受损失，在我国，一般使用硬通货。利息条款应规定在何时、何地由买方支付，可以这样制定："在合同规定的信贷期内，利息按年率百分比收取。"（"Interest will be charged at the rate of ...% per annum on the credit period agreed in the contract."）如果签约日期与最后发货期间隔时间较长，出口方就需要在签订合同时，采取措施来防止一些变动可能带来的损失，例如确认合同价时就把可能上涨的幅度充分体现出来，在签合同时说明在一些情况下允许提高费用。采用何种付款方式，不仅取决于国际上行业的惯例，还取决于交易双方的关系及讨价还价的能力。

【技能训练句型】

在签订正式合同前，常用以下这些谈判用语：

I'd like to discuss the matter of discount with you.

我想跟你们谈谈折扣问题。

We have to adjust our price because the price of raw materials is constantly going up.

因为原材料不断涨价，所以价格也不得不调整。

We hope you can open a letter of credit in our favor as soon as possible, to be settled in US dollars.

我方希望你方能尽快开立以我方为受益人的信用证，以美元结算。

Could you make an exception this time and accept D/A or D/P?

你方这次能否破例一下，接受承兑交单或付款交单？

【知识点】（3）单证（Documents）：在合同中要明确说明所需的单据种类及份数，因为如果没有这些单据，出口方就不能从银行得到货款，进口方就提不到货。

【技能训练句型】

A: Could you tell me what documents you'll provide?

B: Besides the draft, we'll send you a full set of bills of lading, an invoice, an insurance policy, a certificate of origin and a certificate of inspection.

A: 请问你们将提供哪些单据？

B: 除了汇票外，我们还将给你们一整套提单、发票、保险单、产地证书和检验证书。

【知识点】（4）装运条件（Shipping terms）：合同应明确规定交货日期及谁来支付费用等，尽量避免"尽快装运"等含糊性词语。

【技能训练句型】

I must stress again that shipment should be effected and completed by the end of July. We can't accept any delay.

我必须再次强调你方要在七月底前完成装运，不得延误。

You should bear all the costs of transportation of the goods.

你方应该承担货物的一切运输费用。

【知识点】（5）仲裁条款（Arbitration clauses）：当国际贸易发生纠纷，交易双方无法以友好方式解决问题时，通常选择事先约定的仲裁机构来对当事人之间的纠纷予以公正合理地裁决。仲裁条款通常包含仲裁地点、机构、程序和仲裁的裁决力。仲裁地点通常由双方当事人协商决定。采用国际商会仲裁，合同可以包括类似的条款："与该合同有关的一切争议，将按国际仲裁调解规则，由一个或多个根据规定指定的仲裁员做出最终裁决。"（"All disputes arising in connection with the present contract shall be finally settled under the Rules of Conciliation and Arbitration of the International chamber of Commerce by one or more Arbitrators appointed in accordance with the rules."）

3. the last part of the contract　合同的第三部分

【知识点】第三部分包括合同的份数及双方的签字等。交易双方各保留一份经过会签的合同。合同在商务活动中起着重要的作用。它划分双方的责任和义务，约束双方的行为。在出现争议时，它也能保护双方的利益。只有正式的书面合同才具有法律效力。因此，在正式签字前，至少要做到以下三点：第一，与交易有关的任何条款都尽可能地商讨，特别注意容易被忽视的细节问题。第二，所有的条款都必须清楚明白，以避免产生歧义，损害双方的利益。第三，合同的格式要规范，必须由合适的人签字。

Part D　Practice

I. Complete the Following Dialogues

(1)

Fill in the blanks with the proper words.

A: Here's the ___1___ contract. Please ___2___ and see if there is anything else that should be ___3___?

B: (*After checking the contract*) Well, everything seems all right ___4___ for a minor point. This question is related ___5___ the packing. Would you please use wooden cases ___6___ of cartons? I'm afraid the cartons are not strong enough for transport by sea.

A: I'm sorry. It's ___7___ in the contract that the products are ___8___ in cartons.

B: Is it possible to be a little more ___9___? If not, could you please take some measures to ___10___ them?

(2)

Fill in the blanks with the proper words.

A: When the contract can be ready for ___1___?

B: If you have nothing else to bring ___2___, let us sign the ___3___ now. Well, would you please ___4___ your name here?

A: With ___5___. (*After signing his name*) Here you are.

B: Thanks.

A: Let's ___6___ ourselves that this ___7___ has been brought to a successful ___8___.

(3)

Fill in the blanks with the following useful expressions, and change the form if necessary.

be entitled to	come to a successful conclusion	to be signed
take some measures	in conformity with	be responsible for
on condition that	with the consent of	as per
resort to		

1. Will you _____ to reinforce the cardboard boxes?

2. Your request is acceptable _____ you pay for the extra charges.

3. Let's congratulate ourselves that this transaction _____.

4. You will _____ any delay in the shipment.

5. Any modification or alteration to the contract shall only be made _____ both parties.

6. If one side fails to honor the contract, the other side _____ cancel it.

7. If other means fail, it is necessary for us to _____ force.

8. Please check the contract carefully and see if there is anything not _____ the terms we agreed on.

9. The contract is ready _____, please check if there is anything wrong.

10. We carried out the research _____ your instructions.

II. Interaction Activities

The teacher divides students into pairs. Students make short dialogues and role-play them.

Task 1

Students work in pairs and make a dialogue based on the following situation:

Mr. Johnson, is going to import 1000 Olive Brand Sewing Machines. He negotiates with Mr. Chen, the Sales Manager of Oriental Machinery Imp. & Exp. Corp., about the terms of the draft contract. After they go over the packing, terms of payment, delivery and other general terms, the business is concluded. The following expressions might give you a hand:

(1) make a close study of, go over; check

(2) first, second, as for

(3) It's stipulated in the contract that ...

(4) any other questions?

(5) Let's congratulate ourselves that ...

Task 2

(1) Suppose you negotiate with your client about some minor points of the draft contract.

(2) Ask your client to check the draft contract again and discuss next time.

III. Actual Practice

Students work in pairs and role-play the conversation:

Talking about signing a formal contract. The following information can be used for reference:

(1) Take one more look before you sign.

(2) Things that should be there are there.

(3) Each has two formal copies of the contract: one in Chinese and one in English.

(4) congratulation

IV. Creative Discussion

The teacher divides the class into groups and asks them to discuss, then chooses the representatives of each group after discussion. The student who expresses well will be the winner.

Topics:

What should be negotiated before we sign a formal contract?

What skills can be adopted during the negotiation of the terms of the draft contract?

Chapter 15 Cargo Delivery

Learning Objectives
Upon completion of this chapter, you will be able to

- ☑ get used to the most important features of cargo delivery.
- ☑ resolve a variety of problems connected with cargo shipping.
- ☑ perform the functions of skills of communication.
- ☑ get the idea of international multimodal transport.

课文范读

Part A Situational Dialogue

 Communicative Scene 1

Interview: A Cargo Delivery Service

(*Li Hua is the Delivery Service Director of Fast Delivery Company. Mr. Wang, an interviewer from the local television station, interviews her about the typical features for the cargo delivery service in her company.*)

Wang: (*To audience*) Li Hua is the Delivery Service Director of Fast Delivery Company. Li Hua, could you tell us some typical features for the cargo delivery service in your company?

Li: Yes, you know, <u>delivery affects all the results of the trade and the reliability of the company.</u>[1] We have a good reputation in this area. We offer quality, reliability and scheduled delivery for all the cargos.

Wang: What kinds of cargo delivery services does your company offer?

Li: We have Express Plus service. <u>It is the fastest service for the most urgent cargos.</u>[2] It guarantees delivery within 2 days to all the cities in the world. You know, the service also includes telephone confirmation of delivery as soon as the goods are delivered.

Wang: OK. Do you have another service for cargo shipping?

Li: Of course, besides this, we have Express service; it is an ideal choice for most of the less urgent deliveries. For common cargos, we also have Expedited service.

Wang: <u>What about the shipping cost?</u>[3]

Li: There is no need to worry about it. Three models of cargo shipping can meet different requirements of the customers. Our charges are reasonable. The prices of Express service and Expedited service are certainly cheaper than that of Express Plus service.

Wang: Yes, which features do you think are the most important for the cargo delivery service?

Li: Well, I think punctuality and security are of the most important. The quality of service is also important as well as the length of time taken. As long as we can offer high quality service, our business will develop quickly.

Wang: Thank you. It's been nice talking with you.

 Communicative Scene 2

Choosing Air Transport

(*Bill comes from Bright Company. He talks about shipping to London with Dhana of Dispatch*

Department. Bill would like to choose air transport.)

Dhana: Dispatch Department. Dhana speaking.
Bill: Dhana, this is Bill from Bright Company.
Dhana: Hello, Bill. What can I do for you?
Bill: Please ship thirty cases of flowers from Hong Kong to London, which is to be delivered within 2 days.
Dhana: It's a long way to reach London, isn't it? Anyway, I think we can meet your requirement. We can assure you that it will be on time.
Bill: You know that it is very urgent, so please consider air transport. I hope you can give our request your special consideration. I would like to know the shipping cost.
Dhana: It depends on the goods. <u>Usually we should calculate charges according to the size, weight or value of the goods and sometimes risks.</u>[4]
Bill: OK. We have 30 cases of flowers. Every case weighs 20 kilograms, and the volume is 0.5 cubic meters.
Dhana: Um, 30 cases, 20 kilograms, 0.5 cubic meters. OK. The weight and size are all available. Please wait a moment. Don't worry. There's enough time. Um, they will arrive in London the day after tomorrow if there is no surprise.
Bill: Thank you.
Dhana: <u>The freight charges are £4.00 for each kilogram, plus £2.00 for Airway bill of loading and £21.00 for customs clearance.</u>[5] Um, I believe that the flowers will reach you in time and in good order. Hope they will give you complete satisfaction.
Bill: Great. Thanks a lot.
Dhana: You're welcome. If you have any problems, you can contact me at any time.
Bill: OK. Bye.
Dhana: Bye.

 Communicative Scene 3

International Multimodal Transport

(Barry and Eileen are talking about the delivery of the furniture. They would like to choose international multimodal transport.)

Barry: Jupiter Products. Barry speaking.
Eileen: Hello, this is Eileen.
Barry: Hello, Eileen.
Eileen: I'm phoning about the delivery of these 30 sets of furniture from Tianjin to Chicago this month.

Barry: I see. I believe it will be better to transport the furniture by multimodal transport.
Eileen: So do I. <u>Containers are safe, and the goods don't need to be conveyed many times.</u>6/7
Barry: Yes, we can unload at the port and then we deliver the furniture to the customers by trucks.
Eileen: Could the expenses be very high?
Barry: International multimodal transport is a very effective way of transportation. The combined transport operator is responsible for the whole process of different ways of transportation. It's a safe and competitive way of transportation. It saves the transportation cost and time so the freight is reasonable.
Eileen: That's good. <u>What about the Bill of Lading?</u>8
Barry: <u>We supply Combined Transport Bill of Lading.</u>9
Eileen: <u>So we should advise our bank to accept it during establishment of L/C instead of the usual B/L.</u>10
Barry: OK. When do you want the delivery made?
Eileen: We are going to book shipping space before this weekend.
Barry: No problem. Is your furniture ready?
Eileen: Yes. Could the container reach our warehouse?
Barry: It will be to your warehouse this Thursday.
Eileen: Great!

Words and Expressions

1. Delivery Service Director		递送服务部主管
2. cargo delivery service		货物递送服务
3. reliability	*n.*	信度
4. Express Plus service		加急快递服务
5. Express service		特快服务
6. Expedited service		快件服务
7. scheduled	*adj.*	准时的，准点的
8. punctuality	*n.*	准时，守时
9. security	*n.*	安全；抵押品
10. dispatch department		配送部
11. air transport		空运
12. shipping cost		运费
13. delivery charge		送货费用（指将货物运送到指定地点交给指定人过程中所产生的费用，如运费、装卸费等）
14. cubic meter		立方米
15. freight charges		运费
16. Airway bill of loading		空运单
17. customs clearance		结关；海关出口放行；海关出口许可证
18. container	*n.*	集装箱

19. International multimodal transport	国际多式联运
20. Combined Transport Bill of Lading	联运提货单

1. Delivery affects all the results of the trade and the reliability of the company.

    配送服务影响着公司贸易的最终结果。

    ① delivery *n.* 交货，指卖方将货物转交给买方。交货的概念主要包括3个方面，即交货地点、交货方式和交货时间。国际贸易中有实际交货和象征交货两种。在实际操作中，多用象征交货，即卖方将货物交付给运送人之后，取得足以证明交运货物所有权的文件，把文件提供给买方或银行，即已履行交货义务。

    ② reliability *n.* 信度

    Letter of credit is characterized by its reliability.

    ③ 信用证以可靠性著称。

    reliable *adj.* 可靠的

    We can give you a loan if you can provide us with reliable guarantee.

    如果贵方能够提供可靠的担保，我方可以向你方提供贷款。

2. It is the fastest service for the most urgent cargos.

    （加急快递服务）适合于紧急货物的最快速的递送。

    ① express *v.* 快递，快运

    ② express consignment 快件，快达货物

    ③ express fee 快递费

    ④ express goods 快运货物

    ⑤ express mail 快信（邮）

3. what about the shipping cost?

    装运费是怎么样的?

    ① shipping cost 相当于 shipping charges，shipping expenses。

    ② shipping container 海运集装箱

    ③ shipping invoice 装运发票

    ④ shipping list 发货清单

    ⑤ shipping permit 装运许可证

4. Usually we should calculate charges according to the size, weight or value of the goods and sometimes risks.

    我们通常按货物的规格、重量、价值来计算运费，有时还要考虑风险。

    ① calculate *v.* 计算，考虑，计划

    calculate the output 计算产量

② calculated *adj.* 计算出的

calculated risk 计算风险

③ calculation *n.* 计算，考虑

calculation center 计算中心

5. The freight charges are ￡4.00 for each kilogram, plus ￡2.00 for Airway bill of loading and ￡21.00 for customs clearance.

运费是每千克4.00英镑，外加2.00英镑空运单和21.00英镑结关。

① clearance (cl.) 结关，通关

相关词汇：

clearance fee 结关手续费

clearance papers 报关许可证

6. Containers are safe.

集装箱运输安全可靠。

相关词汇：

① container vessels 集装箱船

② container rate 集装箱运价

③ container terminal 集装箱码头，集装箱装卸区

④ Container Transport International 国际集装箱运输公司

7. The goods don't need to be conveyed many times.

货物不必转运好几次。

① convey *v.* 运输，运送

This train conveys both passengers and goods from Beijing to Russia.

这趟火车装载乘客和货物从北京到俄罗斯。

② conveyance *n.* 运输，运输工具

8. What about the Bill of Lading?

提货单的情况怎么样？

Bill of Lading 提货单，有3种功能：（1）承运货物的收据；（2）承运人和托运人之间运输合同的证明；（3）货物所有权的凭证。

9. We supply Combined Transport Bill of Lading.

我们这一次用的是联运提货单。

① combined transport 联运，联合运输（指用水路、铁路、公路、航空中至少两种以上方式的运输）

② Combined Transport Bill of Lading (C.T.B/L) 联运提单

③ Combined Transport Document (CTD) 联运单据，由联运运货人签发的运货凭证

④ Combined Transport Operator (CTO) 联运经营者，联运承运人

10. So we should advise our bank to accept it during establishment of L/C instead of the usual B/L.

那我们开立信用证时会建议银行接受联运提单而不是通常所用的普通提单。

① advise *v.* 通知，建议

advise somebody of something 通知某人某事

② advice *n.* 通知，通知单，通知书
Shipping Advice 装船通知书

Part B Practical Key Sentences

1. time of delivery

（1）根据实际情况对于发货时间的询问，买方可以说：

When at the earliest can we expect the shipment?

最早能在什么时候发货？

替换表达：

What time is the earliest you can make delivery?

What is the earliest time you can make delivery?

When will you deliver the goods to us?

When will the products reach our port?

还可以说：

How long does it take you to make delivery?

多长时间可以交货呢？

When do you want the delivery made?

你想何时发货？

替换表达：

When will the goods be delivered?

How long does it probably take for delivery?

When is the delivery time?

（2）卖方对于发货时间询问的回答，可以说：

I think we can meet your requirement.

我想，我们可以满足您的要求。

替换表达：

I'm sure the shipment will be made on time.

We will get the goods dispatched within two weeks.

2. an early shipment

（1）买方要求提前装运时，可以开门见山地问：

Is it possible to make an early shipment?

有可能提前装运吗？

替换表达：

You may know that time of delivery is a matter of great importantce. Is it possible to deliver the goods two weeks ahead of time?

Could we expect an earlier shipment within three weeks?

Will it be possible for you to ship the goods before early May?

Is there any way to make an early shipment?

Could you make shipment 7 days earlier?

Can't it be delivered in early April?

We hope the delivery can be pushed to mid-May.

（2）卖方可以这样回答：

The earliest time we can make is mid-May.

我们最快只能在五月中旬发货。

Sorry, we cannot advance the time of delivery.

对不起，我们不能提前发货。

替换表达：

I'm afraid it won't be ready until mid-May.

Early May is unlikely, the earliest would be mid-May.

Sorry, we cannot advance the time of delivery.

We cannot make the delivery earlier.

Part C Integration of Theory and Practice

1. background information 运输背景知识

【知识点】随着时代的发展，传统的运输方式已远远不能满足企业的需要。货物运输主要可分为航空货物运输、铁路运输、公路运输、海上运输、集装箱运输及国际多式联运等。运输公司同样也有包裹递送服务的各项业务，主要包括加急快递服务、特快专递服务和递送服务。

航空货运速度快，安全性高，但运量小，运价高。铁路运输受天气等不可抗力因素的影响较小，准确性较高，运输安全，且速度快、运量大，成本也较航空货运低。海上运输是指船舶在不同地区和港口运送货物，具有运量大、运费低、速度慢的特点。据统计，我国进出口货运90%都是由海上运输承担的。

集装箱运输能很好地保护货物的安全，货物的交接地点可以在目的港，也可以通过其他运输方式有机结合的多式联合运输延伸到内陆地区，最终完成货物运输。

2. transportation terms and sentences 运输专有词汇及常用句式

【知识点】在国际商务口语的学习中，光有国际商务理论知识是远远不够的，学习者必须努力拓宽国际商务专业词汇，举一反三，做到多听、多说、多记，尽量缩小母语与目的语的差别。例如：

Bill of Lading（B/L）提货单（指承运人在收到货物时签发给托运人的货物收据，也是持有者在目的地的提货凭证）

Delivery Advice 交货单，交货通知（指以出口国指定地点交货成交条件下，卖方将货物运

送到指定地点或装上指定运输工具时向买方发出的已交货通知书）

  immediate shipment / prompt shipment　立即装运
  initial shipment　第一批船货
  monthly shipment　每月装运量
  partial shipment　分批装运
  port of shipment　装运港
  total shipment　总发货量，总装运量

  除词汇、短语外，国际商务交流中句子的表达也要力求地道，言简意赅，准确达意，要尽力避免语用失误造成的损失。

  （1）要求采取某种运输方式时，常用的表达方式有：

【技能训练句型】

Please use direct shipping instead of installment.
请用直运而不是分批装运。
Is it possible to use container for shipping?
可以用集装箱进行货运吗？
We deliver our goods by lorries.
我们用卡车运送货物。
We advise the cargos to be sent by express trains.
我们建议用特快火车发货。
I propose multimodal combined transport by air and sea.
我提议用海空联运。
We'd like to ship them by air.
我们决定空运这批货物。
It is very urgent, so please consider air transport.
这批货急用，能否考虑空运？
It is better to use container for freight.
最好用集装箱来运输。
We will be more careful with shipping.
我们在装运时会更加小心。

【知识点】（2）当无法确认是否能满足对方的运输要求时，稳住客户尤为重要，我们应该有礼有节，提出尽力提前发货的措施。

【技能训练句型】

We will speed up the production in order to ship your order in time.
我们一定加速生产以确保准时发货。
相关表达：
If you desire earlier delivery, we can only make a partial shipment.
如果你方要想提前发货，我们只能分批装运。
The earliest delivery we can make is in May, but I can assure you that we'll do our best to advance the shipment.

我方最快在五月发货,我保证我方会尽力将发货时间提前。

Thank you very much for your cooperation. I'll find out with our home office. We'll do our best to advance the time of delivery.

非常感谢您的合作。我必须和总部联系。我们将会尽力将发货时间提前。

I believe that the products will reach you in time and in good order and hope they will give you complete satisfaction.

我相信货物会准时完好地到达贵方。希望您能满意。

3. freight calculation 运费的计算

【知识点】运费的计算要考虑到双方的协议,根据货物的重量、体积、商品的价值等进行合理支付。航空公司规定,当货物体积小、重量大时,按实际重量计算;当货物体积大、重量小时,按体积计算。在集中托运时,一批货物由几件不同的货物组成,有轻货也有重货。其计费重量则采用整批货物的毛重或总的体积重量,按两者之中较高的一个计算。

总之,相关工作人员对货物运输的策划、海关申报、运费、风险规避到货物抵达装卸等每一个环节都要十分熟悉,包括其流程及规章制度并在此基础上有效地运用国际商务英语进行交际,力求做到清晰达意,不失礼节。

4. international multimodal transport 国际多式联运

【知识点】国际多式联运是一种以方便托运人和货主为目的的先进的货物运输组织形式。它是一种重要的国际集装箱运输方式,也是现在国际运输发展的主要趋势。

国际多式联运是指按照多式联运合同,以至少两种不同的运输方式,由多式联运经营人将货物从一个国家的国境内接管货物的地点运至另一个国家的国境内指定地点交付的货物运输。

国际多式联运是一种利用集装箱进行联运的新的运输组织方式。它通过采用海、陆、空等两种以上的运输手段,完成国际间的连贯货物运输,从而打破了过去海运、铁路、公路、空运等单一运输方式互不连贯的传统做法。提供优质的国际多式联运服务已成为当今集装箱运输公司提高竞争力的强有力方式。

国际多式联运是一种以实现货物整体运输的最优化效益为目标的联运组织形式。其主要特点是,由多式联运经营人对托运人签订一个运输合同统一组织全程运输,实行运输全程一次托运、一单到底、一次收费、统一理赔和全程负责。

【技能训练句型】

International multimodal transport is a very effective way of transportation. The combined transport operator is responsible for the whole process of different ways of transportation. It's a safe and competitive way of transportation. It saves the transportation cost and time so the freight is reasonable.

国际多式联运是一种货物整体运输最有效的运输方式。多式联运经营人负责不同方式的运输全程。它是一种安全和富有竞争性的运输方式。能节省运输费用和时间。因此,运费十分合理。

Part D Practice

I. Complete the Following Dialogues

(1)

Li: Dispatch Department. Li Ming speaking.
Bill: Hello, Li Ming. This is Bill from LTT Company.
Li: Hello, Bill. What can I do for you?
Bill: When will you ___1___ the products to us?
Li: The earliest delivery we can ___2___ is at the end of October.
Bill: Will it be ___3___ for you to ship the goods before early September?
Li: I'm sorry. We can't ___4___ the time of delivery.
Bill: You know that ___5___ of delivery is very important to us. I sincerely hope you can give our ___6___ your special consideration.
Li: We'll try our best to speed up the production in order to ___7___ your requirement.
Bill: Thank you very much.

(2)

A: Excuse me. What's the ___1___ on this parcel to Australia, please?
B: That's USD 72 cents per ounce for overseas mail. Please wait a moment. I have to weigh it first. Um, it's a little overweight. You have to pay 23 cents ___2___ .
A: OK. Anything else?
B: The insurance is ten cents.
A: When will the post be ___3___ ?
B: The first ___4___ is at 8 a.m.
A: Thank you. Please ___5___ this parcel off by special delivery.
B: Be sure to put down the address of the ___6___ clearly.
A: Thank you.

II. Interaction Activities

Task 1

The teacher divides students into several groups to make discussion. Each group is suggested to be 5 students.

Topics:

Which features do you think are the most importace for dispatch department?

There are some useful expressions for you to complete this task.

(1) I believe that ... is of the most importance for dispatch department.

(2) high quality of service

(3) shipping charges

(4) lower cost

(5) reputation and reliability

(6) security

Task 2

Students work in pairs.

One of your customers has sent you e-mail and wants to know why 30 high definition televisions he ordered have been delayed.

There are some useful expressions for you to complete this task.

(1) I'll check it out immediately.

(2) What's your number of your bill of lading?

(3) I would like to know why the ship has been delayed?

(4) The ship was delayed by ...

(5) We apologize for the delay.

(6) contact sb. at any time

III. Actual Practice

Task 1

Students work in pairs.

Suppose you work in the ABC Company. Last month you placed an order with Bright Future Inc. for 1,000 pairs of shoes. The goods were delivered on Monday. But you find out that 50 pairs of shoes didn't meet your requirement. Decide what you are going to do?

There are some useful expressions for you to complete this task:

(1) I'm sorry to let you know that ...

(2) I'm sorry to have to say this but ...

(3) I bought ... and I've got a bit of problem here, you see ...

(4) There seems to be a mistake.

(5) We ordered ... but we received ... instead.

(6) There has been a slip-up in our... dept.

(7) We are very sorry about the mistakes ...

(8) I'm extremely sorry to hear about your complaints. I can assure that ...

(9) It's perfectly all right.

Task 2

Students work in pairs.

Suppose you work in dispatch department of the ABC Company. Your partner calls for the early delivery of 1,000 packages of the LTT fans his company has ordered. Try to give his request your special consideration.

There are some useful expressions for you to complete this task:

(1) What is the earliest time when you can make delivery?

(2) We can assure you that the shipment will be made not later than ...

(3) I hope you can give our request your special consideration.

(4) We'll do our best to advance the time of delivery.

(5) Please let me know whether it is available or not.

(6) I believe that the products will reach you in time and in good order and hope they will give you complete satisfaction.

IV. Creative Discussion

The teacher divides the class into groups, and the students make a discussion with their partners and share their opinions with other pairs.

Topic:

Suppose you work in a dispatch department. One of your customers would like to know how to decide the best way to send the goods to its destination.

There are many ways of delivery. Discuss which one you prefer and show the reasons. If possible, discuss the advantages and disadvantages of each way.

There are some useful expressions for you to complete this task:

(1) It just depends on ...

(2) We need to consider that ...

(3) We choose different delivery methods according to ...

(4) It's suitable for / ideal for ...

(5) There are some advantages of ...

Chapter 16 Business Conference

Learning Objectives
Upon completion of this chapter, you will be able to

- get used to the process of business conference.
- make good preparation for business conference.
- learn how to express one's opinions and ask for others' opinions.
- take an active participation in business conference.

课文范读

Part A Situational Dialogue

 Communicative Scene 1

Conference Arrangement

(*Mr. Brown is discussing about the arrangement of the sales conference with Miss Li, the secretary.*)

Brown: Miss Li, could we have a quick discussion about the sales conference?
Li: Yes, <u>I'm glad to go through it now.</u>¹
Brown: You know, the meeting is scheduled at 2:00 p.m. this Friday afternoon, which will last for 3 hours. <u>And there will be 150 top managers from 10 countries to participate in this conference.</u>² Will you please arrange it for me?
Li: Of course, Mr. Brown, but could I have your plan?
Brown: Please send formal invitations first. Oh, all things to be done are written here.
Li: May I keep it? <u>I need it when I draw up the notice of the meeting and the agenda.</u>³
Brown: Go ahead, it's for your reference. By the way, please make a special agenda for me.
Li: You mean you need a more detailed agenda for yourself?
Brown: That's right. I'm going to chair the meeting.
Li: OK, I see. <u>I will prepare it carefully and distribute all the agendas in advance so that the participants will have time to think about all the agenda items before the meeting.</u>⁴
Brown: Good. And I wonder if you have any good place for the meeting in your mind.
Li: Yes, it can be in West Lake Hotel. The conference room there is of adequate size. In addition to size, the facilities offered there are sufficient and the cost of hiring is reasonable.
Brown: Could you tell me what the budget is?
Li: 20,000 yuan maximum.
Brown: That'll be fine. <u>But you'd better check if the lighting, air-conditioning and the video projector are OK, and if water, glasses, ashtrays, pens and papers are available before the conference.</u>⁵
Li: You're right.
Brown: By the way, we'll have several foreign guests attend the meeting. What have you got then?
Li: I'll arrange for an interpreter to be present.
Brown: There are simultaneous translation facilities in the auditorium, aren't there?
Li: Yes. I'm not familiar with every participant.
Brown: That's OK. Another thing, how would you seat our guests?
Li: <u>I'm not familiar with every participant.</u>⁶
Brown: Oh, that's easy. I'll write you a list of the names.

Li: Very good. So I can make a seating plan with the names and I'll prepare name cards to be put on the conference table for guests to sit by. Well, what time would you like the refreshments served?

Brown: After Mr. White's report there'll be an interval for rest and refreshments.

Li: And then what are we doing for refreshments?

Brown: Why not have a buffet?

Li: OK, I'll arrange it. If you don't mind, I'll withdraw and get down to it.[7]

 Communicative Scene 2

At the Conference

(Mr. Brown, Mr. Heine, Mr. Glover, Mr. Jobe, Mr. Boiler and Mr. Graber are at the conference. They are discussing about whether to carry out a new plan.)

Brown: Ladies and gentlemen, may I have your attention? Please take a seat. We are about to start our meeting.

Heine: Where's Mr. Glover? He's supposed to join us.[8]

Brown: Oh, here he comes. Speak of the devil ...[9]

Glover: I'm sorry to keep you waiting.

Brown: OK, everyone's here. Let's begin. We all know what we're here for. The client's meeting is tomorrow and between now and then we've got to come up with some original ideas.[10] So everyone just speak your minds, because there's no such thing as stupid idea in the brain-storming session. Now we'd like to hear your ideas about the whole issue, Mr. Glover?

Glover: Well, I must admit I still somehow doubt this business. Here is the chart showing our company's latest financial status. From the chart, we can see clearly that our profits have dropped recently because of the high rate of inflation. The Purchasing Department is now having to pay double for supplies of raw materials.

Brown: What have you got to say about this matter, Mr. Jobe?[11]

Jobe: I have no strong feelings about the ideas. I am just wondering if Mr. Heine has got any ideas for us.

Brown: Mr. Heine?

Heine: Can we cut down any of our costs?

Jobe: Transport costs seem very high, too.

Boiler: This is due to the increasing charges for air-freighting goods.

Jobe: Why don't we ship our goods down the Yellow River from Hankou? That would reduce costs considerably.

Graber: I'm afraid I have different views on this.

Brown: Could you be more specific on this point?

Graber: <u>If we do that, we'll have to revise all our schedules to allow for the longer time it would take.</u>[12]

Boiler: Yes, we would have to dispatch goods well in advance to make sure the customers got them on time.

Heine: Isn't there a risk of delays? The volume of traffic on the Yellow River is very heavy.

Jobe: Delays certainly would be very bad for public relations. We can't afford to lose customers through delayed deliveries.

Glover: It seems to me that our first job is to find out what it's likely to cost us to get started, and what kind of return we can expect over the next two or three years.

Heine: You see, costs are not our only concern. We've been waiting for an opportunity like this for years. <u>I suggest we carry out this plan right now.</u>[13] It's a chance of a lifetime.

Glover: I'm not saying that I'm against this plan, but we'll need some verification before we can rush into any decision.

Jobe: You said it. We need to be more cautious regarding the present market situation.

Brown: Well, we seem to agree with the project, but let me just clarify one thing before we go. If this plan is to be carried out successfully, it needs everyone to work together. <u>The financial support is going to be available if we can convince our sponsor that the plan will finally benefit all investors.</u>[14] So, to sum up, it's vitally important that all departments cooperate with each other and make sure it goes smoothly. <u>OK, let's call it a day.</u>[15]

 Communicative Scene 3

Taking Notes in Meetings

(The new secretary, Miss Fang, is asking Miss Li, an experienced secretary, some questions about how to take minutes at the meeting.)

Fang: Miss Li, shall I take minutes in the conference?

Li: Yes, of course. The minutes should be taken carefully.

Fang: So could you explain how to do it?

Li: OK. Oh, I have my notebook here ready for the meeting. You can read it.

Fang: Thank you. Err... what's this?

Li: This is the heading... the Star Machinery Import & Export Corporation. Then underneath that... Minutes of Meeting of Branch Managers at 2:00 p.m. on Thursday, 8th, March, 2006, then underneath that... Present: Mr. Brown, CEO, in the chair.

Fang: And you've left a space underneath to fill in the name of the managers, haven't you?

Li: Yes, that's right. Then the first item is always ... apologies for absence.

Fang: What comes next?

Li: The next item is always ... Minutes of Last Meeting. As soon as the minutes of the last meeting have been read, you can write "The minutes of the last meeting were read, confirmed and signed."

Fang: Signed?

Li: Yes, when the minutes have been confirmed, the chairman will sign them.

Fang: Do I have to write down every word that everyone says?

Li: Oh, no. It's very difficult and hardly necessary. You just need to make a note of the topics that are discussed and the result of the discussion.

Fang: The result of the discussion?

Li: When a topic has been discussed for some time, someone usually proposes that some action should be taken.

Fang: Then what happens?

Li: Then the chairman asks whether the members agree to the proposal. And if they do agree, you can write down "It was agreed that ..." or "It was resolved that ...".

Fang: Is there a difference?

Li: Not really. "Resolved" is a special committee word. When a proposal has been agreed by the committee, it is called a "resolution". Look, here is a copy of the minutes of the last meeting and here are my notes.

Fang: Oh, that's wonderful. I'm interested in what you wrote in your notes: It was resolved that the office would be closed on 15 March.

Words and Expressions

1.	chair	n.	（主持会议的）主席的职位
		v.	主持（会议）
2.	distribute	v.	分配，分送
3.	facilities	n.	设备
4.	sufficient	adj.	足够的
5.	budget	n.	预算
6.	projector	n.	投影仪
7.	interpreter	n.	口译员
8.	simultaneous	adj.	同时的
9.	auditorium	n.	会堂；礼堂
10.	interval	n.	（戏剧、音乐会各段落间的）间隔时间
11.	refreshments	n.	点心
12.	buffet	n.	自助餐
13.	the brain-storming session		头脑风暴环节
14.	inflation	n.	通货膨胀
15.	air-freighting	adj.	空中货运的
16.	verification	n.	鉴定，证实
17.	resolve	v.	投票表决，决议

18. resolution	n.	决议
*19. definitely	adv.	明确地
*20. take minutes		会议记录
the minute book		会议记录本

1. I'm glad to go through it now.
   我很高兴现在谈论这个问题。
   go through
   ① 详细讨论
   Let's go through the data again.
   让我们将这些数据再详细讨论一遍。
   ② 履行，参加
   She made him go through a religious wedding.
   她让他举行了宗教仪式的婚礼。
   He went through the degree ceremony without getting too nervous.
   他自如地参加了学位授予仪式。

2. And there will be 150 top managers from 10 countries to participate in this conference.
   而且将会有来自10个国家150名高级经理参加这次会议。
   ① participate in 分享，参与
   In a modern democracy, people want to participate more fully.
   在现代民主政体中，人们要求更多地参与。
   ② participate with sb. in one's sufferings 与某人共患难
   ③ participant n. 分享者，参与者

3. I need it when I draw up the notice of the meeting and the agenda.
   我草拟会议通知和会议日程时需要它。
   draw up
   ① 草拟
   draw up a memorandum 起草一份备忘录
   ② 使停住
   A freight car drew up outside their house.
   一辆运货车在他们房子外面停下。

4. I will prepare it carefully and distribute all the agendas in advance so that the will have time to think about all the agenda items before the meeting.
   我会认真准备并且在会议开始前送出日程表，以便与会者有时间在会议开始前考虑日程表上的议程。

① in advance 事前，预先，该词组常与介词 of 搭配

It's unwise to spend your income in advance.

把你的收入预先花掉是不明智的。

② in advame of 超过

Galileo's ideas were in advance of the age in which he lived.

伽利略的思想超越了他生活的时代。

5. Then you have to check if the lighting, air-conditioning and the video projector are OK, and if water, glasses, ashtrays, pens and papers are available.

那么你还得检查一下灯、空调和投影仪是否都很正常，还有水、玻璃杯、烟灰缸、钢笔和纸是否都已备好。

6. The participants can also count on them.[6]

开会时，与会者也可以依靠同声传译设备

① count on 指望，依赖

You had better not count on an increase in your salary this year.

你今年最好不要指望加薪。

7. If you don't mind, I'll withdraw and get down to it.

如果你不介意，我站着手办了。

① get down to 开始认真对待（工作等）；开始认真注意（细节等）

The company really gets down to improving working conditions.

公司确实开始改善工作条件。

I get down to discussing my workload.

我开始讨论我的工作量。

8. He's supposed to join us.

他是要出席会议的。

① be supposed to do sth. 认为必须，认为应该

When is the cargo ship supposed to leave?

货船应该在什么时候开？

We are supposed to be there at six.

我们得在6点钟到达那里。

9. speak of the devil ...

这句话完整的表达是：Speak of the devil and he will appear.

说曹操，曹操到。

10. The client's meeting is tomorrow and between now and then we've got to come up with some original ideas.

明天就要见客户了，从今天到明天的这段时间里，我们一定要想出些有创意的点子。

① come up with（针对问题、挑战等）提出，想出

He could always come up with a reason for them to linger another month.

他总能想出个理由来让他们再延迟一个月。

11. What have you got to say about this matter, Mr. Jobe?

那你是怎么看的呢，朱比先生？

12. If we do that, we'll have to revise all our schedules to allow for the longer time it would take.
    如果那样的话会花更长的时间,我们将不得不提早发货。
    ① allow for 考虑到,顾及
    Allowing for inflation, the cost of the project is MYM 2 million.
    考虑到通货膨胀因素,这个项目的费用为200万美元。

13. I suggest we carry out this plan right now.
    我提议我们马上实施这个计划。
    文中另外两句话:So, to sum up, it's vitally important that all departments cooperate with each other and make sure it goes smoothly.
    总之,至关重要的是,所有的部门能够通力合作,确保计划的顺利进行。
    When a topic has been discussed for some time, someone usually proposes that some action should be taken.
    一个话题经过一段时间讨论后,通常就有人建议实施。
    这三句话中都使用了虚拟语气。一般在动词suggest、propose或it's important等后面的从句谓语动词常使用虚拟语气,结构为should + v.,其中should可以省略,例如:
    He proposes that we should talk to each other in teleconference.
    他建议我们通过电话交谈。
    It is essential that this mission not fail.
    这项任务不失败至关重要。
    至关重要的是这项任务没有失败。
    He suggested that a contract be signed.
    他建议签订契约。

14. The financial support is going to be available if we can convince our sponsor that the plan will finally benefit all investors.
    如果我们能使赞助商相信这个项目最终可以让所有的投资人受益的话,那么资金就一定会到位。
    ① convince sb. of sth. 使某人确信
    I am convinced of his honesty.
    我深信他的诚实。

15. OK,let's call it a day.
    好的,今天就到这儿吧。

Part B Practical Key Sentences

1. **asking for somebody's opinion**
   What have you got to say about this matter, Mr. Jobe?

你对这个问题有什么看法，朱比先生？

替换表达：

Do you have any views on this matter, Mr. Jobe?

How do you feel about this matter, Mr. Jobe?

What do you think of this matter, Mr. Jobe?

Do you have any points on this matter, Mr. Jobe?

What's your opinion of this matter, Mr. Jobe?

What's your view on this matter, Mr. Jobe?

What do you reckon to this matter, Mr. Jobe?

What are your feelings about this matter, Mr. Jobe?

What do you make of this matter, Mr. Jobe?

2. **expressing your opinion**

It seems to me that our first job is to find out what it's likely to cost us to get started, and what kind of return we can expect over the next two or three years.

我觉得我们首先要弄清楚启动这项计划要花费多少，以及在接下来的两三年里我们会有什么样的回报。

相似表达：

I think the quality is fine.

I believe the payment term is rather reasonable.

As I see it, extending L/C is a common thing.

As far as I'm concerned, I think the price is rather reasonable.

In my opinion, the business talk is very successful.

I reckon that the customer isn't likely to come.

From my point of view, the shipping date is too late.

3. **stating you have no opinion**

I've no strong feelings about this ideas.

我对这个计划没有什么看法。

替换表达：

I have nothing to say about this plan.

I really don't know what to say.

I don't have any ideas yet.

I really don't have any opinion about this plan.

4. **stating you have different opinion**

I'm afraid I have different views on this.

恐怕在这方面我的意见与你有所不同。

替换表达：

You approach it in a different way than I do.

I'm afraid I can't agree with you there.

5. **asking for further explanation**

Could you be more specific on this point?

你能把这点说得再具体一些吗？

替换表达：
Can you further explain what you mean by that?
Could you elaborate on it?

Part C Integration of Theory and Practice

meeting 会议

【知识点】1. 会议是商务活动中常常被采用的一种手段。通过会议人们可以互通信息、讨论问题，各部门对现有问题或下一步计划进行磋商。在会议前，会议组织者必须做好充分的准备。首先，会议组织者必须确定会议日期和地点并提前通知与会者。

【技能训练句型】

You know, the meeting is scheduled from 2:00 p.m. this afternoon. And I've chosen a good place for it. It's in West Lake Hotel.
会议定在下午两点钟举行。我已挑好地点，在西湖酒店。

【知识点】2. 在会议要开始时，会议主持人常常会提高自己的声音，与会者就会停止交谈，准备开会。

【技能训练句型】

宣布会议开始的表达方式有：
Ladies and gentlemen, shall we get started?
先生们，女士们，我们开始吧？
Please take a seat. The meeting is about to start.
请就座。会议马上就要开始了。
May I have your attention, please?
请大家注意一下，好吗？
Attention, please!
请注意！

【知识点】3. 如果会议当中没有女士，会议主持人就只用gentlemen，如果会议主持人不清楚是否有女士在场，直接用everyone或者everybody也就是我们通常说的"所有人"！

【技能训练句型】

OK, everyone!
好了，所有人（注意）！
The meeting is about to start.
会议马上就要开始了。
Please be seated.
请就座。

【知识点】4. 一个成功的会议，一般都要设定一个议程。

【技能训练句型】

会议主持人可以这样表达：
As you can see from our agenda, we need to look at 3 items today, and they are ...

从我们的议程安排可以看出，今天要讨论三个问题，它们是……
I suggest we take a look at them one by one.
我建议一个个来讨论。

当然，与会者可以根据议程的重要性来决定会议讨论的顺序。

【技能训练句型】

I suggest we take the items in this order.
我建议按这样的程序进行。
Could we take the third item first?
我们可以先从第三项开始吗？
I think it's very important for us to look at the last one first.
我认为先看最后一项是很重要的。

【知识点】5. 往往一次会议的终结意味着另一个会议的开始，一个问题的深入会导致多个问题的出现，这些都有可能使我们进入一个无休止的会议的循环往复。会议主持人会询问记录人员上次会议谈到哪里。这时会议主持人会说："Where were we last time"

【知识点】6. 开会时经常会遇到跑题的情况，所以会议的主持人最好能在会议一开始就确定会议的目标和最终要达到的效果，否则，会议就会失去原本的意义，会议主持人一定要时刻提醒与会者。

【技能训练句型】

表示会议目的可以这样表达：
The goal for our meeting is to ...
今天会议的目的是……
Our aim is to ...
我们的目的是……
I've called this meeting in order to ...
会议的主题是……
会议主持人要提醒与会者可以这样表达：We have to get down to business.

【知识点】7. 在会议中征询会议主持人他人的意见是很常见的，也是使与会者各抒己见、避免冷场的一种好办法。

【技能训练句型】

How do you find things over the bargain?
你觉得这笔买卖怎么样？
How do you see things like this?
你对这类事怎么看？
What do you reckon, Tom?
你是怎么考虑的，汤姆？
Have you got any comments on this new plan?
你对这个新计划有何评论？
Do you have any particular view on the present market?
你对目前的市场有什么特殊的见解？

【知识点】8. 召开会议就是要集思广益，找到最佳方案，从而做出最有利的决定。所以，在会议中，与会者在发言时必须要做到观点明确、简洁和具体。

【技能训练句型】

In my view, the business talk is very successful.
在我看来，这次业务洽谈非常成功。

Don't you think this design is rather beautiful?
你不觉得这个设计很漂亮吗？

Personally, I believe quality is still a great problem.
我个人认为质量依然存在很大问题。

I'd just like to say your arrangement is satisfactory.
我想说您的安排令人满意。

Well, I must say it would be better to pack the goods in wooden cases.
我认为用木箱子包装更好。

The way I see it, goods at lower prices are not certainly popular items.
在我看来，低价格的产品并非畅销。

【知识点】9. 若与会者对某项计划还没有什么看法时，也必须清楚地表明。

【技能训练句型】

I have nothing to say about this plan.
我对这个计划没有什么可说的。

I really don't know what to think about this transaction.
我确实不知道怎么考虑这笔生意。

【知识点】10. 当然，有时与会者会对某项计划持截然不同的观点。为避免言语冲突，在表达自己的看法时可以避免直抒己见。

【技能训练句型】

I'd prefer not to say anything about the issue.
对这件事我宁愿不发表任何意见。

I'd rather not say anything about the new plan.
对新计划我宁愿不发表任何意见。

That's an interesting idea, but it's not for me to say.
这是个有趣的想法，不过这不是我说了算。

I'd rather not commit myself on that, if you don't mind.
如果你不介意，我倒希望不对此发表意见。

【知识点】11. 会议总是冗长的，与会者各抒己见，但往往会花去大量时间。在商务活动中，时间就是金钱，因此要讲求工作效率。所以，会议主持人在确认会议已取得原定效果的前提下，应该及时得体地结束会议。

【技能训练句型】

Let's leave the details to our next meeting.
我们可以把细节问题留到下一个会议。

I'm afraid we have to finish here.
恐怕今天就到此为止。

Let's call it a day.
今天就到这儿吧。

OK, time to wrap it up.
该结束了。

Part D Practice

I. Complete the Following Dialogues

(1)

A: Is the room ready for the meeting?

B: Yes. I've put the ___1___ book and some spare copies of the ___2___ on the table including pens and papers.

A: Well, everyone is going to Mr. Brown's speech. Have you ___3___ the microphone?

B: Yes. It's OK.

A: Good. We'll have some foreign guests to attend the meeting. What have you got then?

B: I've ___4___ for an ___5___ to be present.

A: Then how would you ___6___ our guests?

B: I've prepared name cards to be ___7___ on the conference table for guests to sit by.

A: Nice work. I hope our organization of the meeting will be ___8___.

(2)

A: Do you have any points, Tom?

B: Well, I must ___1___ I'm still a bit ___2___ about this plan. Electronic products trade is always a ___3___ affair.

A: I think electronic products trade is ___4___ to be a booming business soon. What do you ___5___, Bill?

C: It seems to me that our first job is to find out what it's ___6___ to cost us to get started, and what kind of return we can ___7___ over the next four years.

D: You are right.

A: Good. Now let's put it to the ___8___.

II. Role-plays

Task 1

The teacher divides students into groups. Each group is suggested to be 5 students. Make dialogues and role-play them.

Hold a business conference according to the following hints: Student A is the manager of a company. Now you are presiding over a conference at which a discussion is held about whether to carry out a proposed plan or not; Student B, Student C are for the plan; Student D and Student E are against the plan.

Task 2

Short conversations.

Suppose you are a secretary of a company. You are asked to prepare for the coming conference. Now you report your work to the boss and answer the boss's questions.

III. Guided Talking

Work in pairs.

Use the minutes of the meetings below to practice with your partner.

HENG XING SILK TRDING CO.

Minutes of Meeting of Branch Managers

Dec. 8, 2006

Presiding: Mr. White, President

　Present: Mr. Wang, Personnel Manager

　　　　　Mr. Wu, Sales Manager

　　　　　Mr. Li, Technical Manager

Minutes:

After calling the meeting to order at 3:00 p.m., the President asked Mr. Wu for a brief report. Mr. Wu explained that profits had dropped recently owing to the high rate of inflation. He pointed out that the Purchasing Department was now having to pay double for supplies of raw materials.

The President asked Mr. Wang to comment. Mr. Wang suggested that they ship their goods down the Yang tze River from Wuhan. He felt that would reduce costs considerably.

Mr. Li pointed out that if they did that, they would have to revise their schedules to allow for the longer time it would take.

Mr. Wu wondered if there wasn't a risk of delays. He felt the volume of traffic on the Yangstz River was very heavy.

Mr. Wang believed that delays would certainly be very bad for public relations. He felt they couldn't afford to lose customers through delayed deliveries.

There was no agreement on this issue.

The meeting was adjourned at 4:30 p.m.

　　　　　　　　　　　　　　　　　　　　　　　　　Respectfully submitted

　　　　　　　　　　　　　　　　　　　　　　　　　Janet Olliphant, Secretary

　　1. Asking how to take notes at the conference.

　　2. Explaining how to take steps.

IV. Creative Discussion

The teacher divides the class into groups. Think first and then discuss in the group. Choose the representatives of each group after discussion. The student who expresses well will be the winner.

Topic:

Sometimes you are asked to make a speech at the conference. Will you feel nervous to speak in front of the crowd?

Please discuss with your partner about how to overcome nervousness to make a good speech at the conference.

Chapter 17 Sales Promotion

Learning Objectives
Upon completion of this chapter, you will be able to

- acquaint yourselves with the process of sales promotion.
- learn how to persuade others and talk about one's intention.
- conduct the activities related to the theme of sales promotion.
- make yourself more knowledgeable in more fields.

课文范读

Part A Situational Dialogue

 Communicative Scene 1

Sales Call

(*Rose, from Sales Department of Sunrise Health Products Company, calls at a toy factory and is talking with Jack to push the sale of their products.*)

Rose: Good morning. I'm from Sunrise Health Products Company. We are a major manufacturer of massage chairs. <u>I wonder if you could spare me a few minutes to listen to my brief introduction of our product.</u>[1]

Jack: I'm sorry, but this is a toy factory. Do our staff have to make the lovely toys on your chairs?

Rose: Are you joking?

Jack: <u>So could you tell me what on earth your massage chairs have to do with us?</u>[2]

Rose: Certainly, quite a lot. Recently many workers have suffered from neck pain and back pain, haven't they?

Jack: Yes, they have.

Rose: <u>Your staff are stressed out and they have to work on the assembly line for a long time.</u>[3] <u>No wonder they are not very well.</u>[4] By the way, what do they usually do with their pains?

Jack: Go to the massage hospital after work.

Rose: Your factory is located in the suburbs, <u>so you are a long way from the town, aren't you?</u>[5]

Jack: Er, yes. It's about seven kilometers away from downtown.

Rose: So it's not convenient for your workers to cure their disease, is it?

Jack: You said it.

Rose: I'm sure that the pains will have a great effect on your staff's working efficiency if that's the case. So why not try our massage chairs?

Jack: Yes?

Rose: They are designed to stimulate the circulation of blood and relax muscles.

Jack: Then?

Rose: It can rub their necks and upper backs. At the same time, your workers don't need to travel a long way to cure their pains.

Jack: Sounds good. May I have a try?

Rose: Of course. (*Let the manager sit in the chair.*)

Jack: (*After a while*) Wow, it feels so good.

Rose: Your staff will save much money paid for a chiropractor if you buy some of our massage chairs.

Jack: Could you show me how to operate it?

Rose: No problem. First you have to plug it in. There is a control panel on this armrest.

Jack: A control panel?

Rose: Yes, press the "Power" button to turn it on and off. Next you can press the "Mode" button to choose a mode. In this model, we have different modes including "Rub" and "Pound".

Jack: "Rub" and "Pound"? Oh, now I do feel as if someone is rubbing my back with his hand. So it must be in "Rub" mode.

Rose: That's true. (*Press the "Pound" button*.) You will feel as if someone is pounding you with a hammer lightly if you choose "Pound" mode.

Jack: Wonderful!

Rose: If your staff is free from pains, they will be happy and work more efficiently.

Jack: It sounds great!

Rose: Are you in favor of what I said? And do you have any interest in our massage chairs and intend to place some orders?

Jack: What you said is really attractive. But I'd like to think it over before I make the final decision.

Rose: Well, I'll call again in a day or two. Here is my card. Could you give me a ring whenever you need me?

Jack: Thank you. I will.

Communicative Scene 2

Describing the New Product to the Customer

(*Juliet, specializing in women's clothes in America, comes to trade with Mr. Wang, the sales manager. She is talking with him about the features of new product.*)

Wang: Welcome to China, Juliet.

Juliet: It's my pleasure to visit your company. I hope we can do business together.

Wang: So do I. Have you seen our catalogue?

Juliet: Oh, yes. I've gone over the catalogue and the pamphlets enclosed in your last letter.

Wang: What do you think of our latest product?

Juliet: I'm very favorably impressed.

Wang: So happy to hear that. In fact, it's a revolutionary new product we've just developed. The yarn is carefully selected for quality and woven very tightly in this fabric. So far it has been sold in a number of areas abroad. They sell like hot cakes.

Juliet: Sounds good. How many colors are available for this item?

Wang: We have two standard colors. What's your favorite color?

Juliet: The darker one as it will cater more to the elders.

Wang: I agree with you. If the quantity is 5,000 sets or more, you may choose any color you like.

Juliet: Do you have any samples here?

Wang: Yes, they're in the showroom. Would you like to have a look?

Juliet: I'd love to.

Wang: Let me take you to the showroom.

Juliet: That's very kind of you.

Wang: It's my pleasure. This way, please. (*A few minutes later*) Here is our showroom. Almost all of our company's products can be seen here.

Juliet: Oh, you have a large collection of samples. Do you get many overseas buyers here?

Wang: Yes, quite a lot. They like to keep up-to-date, so we change our display pieces every month.

Juliet: What's the percentage of overseas markets in proportion to domestic markets for your products?

Wang: The ratio is about 7 overseas to 3 domestic.

Juliet: I see.

Wang: Juliet, please step this way. Our latest models are over there.

Juliet: Oh, look at this one. I like this rose pattern. It makes us feel warm and romantic.

Wang: That's true. And also this kind of material is very easy to wash.

Juliet: Really?

Wang: Yes. Just put it in your washing machine and then dry it. It doesn't need any extra care.

Juliet: That'll be very convenient. How much is a yard?

Wang: 50 yuan per yard. But it depends on quantity.

Juliet: Are these available now?

Wang: We have available stocks for some of the items displayed because they are now in great demand. You'll have to wait a week before we can supply you with the rest. Before you leave, would you place some orders?

Juliet: Mmm...I think your price is higher than that of other companies. And your latest product is new to the consumers of our country. You know, it is not easy to open up a new market.

Wang: That's true, but when we compare prices, we'd better take quality into consideration first. Everyone in the trade knows that our product is of superior quality to those from other companies.[6] I can assure you that our price is practical and reasonable. So we are sure that our product will stand a good chance with your clients.[7]

Juliet: Well, if you can make a discount, I intend to consider the order.

Wang: We can offer a 10% discount for orders over 1,000 pieces.

Juliet: OK, I'm willing to give your latest model a try. When is the earliest we can expect delivery?

Wang: By the end of the month.

Juliet: All right. But delivery dates must be kept.

Wang: Yes, of course. We always give priority to export orders.[8] No need to worry.

Juliet: Then when can we work out a deal?

Wang: Would tomorrow morning be convenient?

Juliet: Yes, that'll be fine.

Sales Promotion

 Communicative Scene 3

Talk about the Advertising Campaign

(Juliet likes to do business with Mr. Wang's company. Now she is talking with Mr. Wang about the advertising campaign.)

Juliet: Mr. Wang, I'm deeply impressed by your new product and I'd like to do business with you. But now my main concern is business promotion. You know, there are a lot of ways to push sales. So I'm wondering if you could tell me something about your company's advertising campaign for the new product.

Wang: Sure. Our product enjoys a good reputation here, but it is quite new in your country. So market positioning must be considered first. We must carry out market research, then decide who are the most probable buyers.

Juliet: You're quite right. We should set the target customer before publicizing the product.

Wang: And we think advertising, price and free samples are the most important when we introduce a new product. First we need to advertise the product. We must make the new product known to the consumers.

Juliet: I couldn't agree with you more.

Wang: We think the next thing is what media we should use and when we should place advertising in the media.

Juliet: Media? Only by showing the goods in an attractive way can the consumers pay for them.[9]

Wang: Yes, media. Very often in a campaign, two or more media are used together. The purpose of our advertising is to draw the local customers' interest and keep hold of their attention, so that they may do something in return.

Juliet: What media would you like to choose?

Wang: We think television advertising has a bigger impact on the choice the customers make in buying products. For example, the advertisers often use famous people to make the customers believe the product is worth buying.

Juliet: Truly.

Wang: And also the television covers a large number of audiences, so advertising on television can reach a lot of people.

Juliet: But advertisement on TV will cost a lot of money.

Wang: I suppose it's worth doing so long as the result is satisfactory.

Juliet: That sounds reasonable. And when shall we make this advertisement?

Wang: How about the beginning of this summer?

Juliet: All right. I suggest that besides television, we use other channels to advertise the product at the same time.

Wang: What are they?

Juliet: How about advertising the product in newspapers, magazines, direct mail, Internet and radio?

Wang: That's great. Through advertisements on various media, we can point out the different characteristics about our new product and get more people to learn about the product and change their views. We are also trying our best to sell on line.

Juliet: Nowadays, online sales are becoming a popular way to push sales.[10]

Wang: We'll try to find the most effective way to let customers know our site and new products.

Juliet: Good. By the way, as a new foreign product, we cannot set a very low price. Or it will cut the value of the product in our customers' mind.

Wang: Absolutely. And because we are facing fierce competition from the existing similar product in your market, we may well need to hold a news conference to introduce our product.

Juliet: Don't worry. I'll contact the journalists from some important media, potential clients and salespersons later on to join the news conference.

Wang: Great! We had better get down to business.

Words and Expressions

1.	massage	n.	按摩
2.	efficiency	n.	效率
3.	stimulate	v.	刺激，激励
4.	circulation	n.	循环
5.	rub	v.	摩擦
6.	chiropractor	n.	按摩关节（尤指脊椎）以治病者
7.	panel	n.	仪表板
8.	armrest	n.	扶手
9.	pound	v.	连续重击
10.	feature	n.	特点
11.	yarn	n.	纱，线
12.	fabric	n.	织物
13.	weave	v.	织（纱、线）成布等
14.	ratio	n.	比例
15.	campaign	n.	（为达到某一特殊目标所做的一连串有计划的）活动
16.	business promotion	n.	促销
17.	market positioning		市场定位
18.	publicize	v.	宣传
19.	fierce	adj.	强烈的，剧烈的

Notes

1. I wonder if you could spare me a few minutes to listen to my brief introduction of our products.

   我想占用你几分钟的时间,简单介绍一下我们的产品。

   ① spare 提供(时间、金钱等)给某人或为某种目的匀出,分出

   Can you spare me a few litres of petrol?

   你能分给我几公升汽油吗?

   I can't spare the time for market research.

   目前我抽不出时间做市场调查。

2. So could you tell me what on earth your massage chairs have to do with us?

   那么,你能跟我说说到底按摩椅与我们公司有什么关系?

   ① have sth. / nothing / not much / a great deal, etc. to do with 与……有(无、没多少、有很大等)关系

   His instruction had something to do with my decision to do business.

   他与我决定从商有关系。

3. Your staff are stressed out and they have to work on the assembly line for a long time.

   你们公司的员工工作压力大,而且他们得在流水线旁工作很长时间。

   ① stress out 使紧张,使感到压力

   Interviews always stress me out.

   面试总让我感到紧张。

4. No wonder they are not very well.

   难怪他们的身体状况不太好。

   ① no wonder 难怪

   No wonder your trial order was so late.

   难怪你的试订单来得那么迟。

5. So you are a long way from the town, aren't you?

   那么你们离市里有很长一段距离,是不是?

   ① be free from 无……的;摆脱了……的

   You are free from blame.

   你没有过错。

6. Everyone in the trade knows that our product is of superior quality to those from other companies.

   同行都知道我们产品的质量优于其他公司。

   ① superior *adj.* 优越的

   ② be superior to 比……更好,比……更优越

   ③ be inferior to 比……劣、差

   He thinks he's superior to us because his father is CEO.

他认为父亲是CEO，他就高人一等。

7. So we are sure that our product will stand a good chance with your clients.

所以我们确信我们的产品很有希望获得你们客户的欢迎。

① stand a chance 有希望，有可能

She stands a good chance of getting promotion.

她很有希望晋升。

8. We always give priority to export orders.

我们一直对出口订单给予优先。

① give priority to 最优先考虑

类似的短语还有：

place / put high / top priority on

attach high priority to

give first priority to

9. Only by showing the goods in an attractive way can the consumers pay for them.

只有吸引消费者，他们才可能购买。

副词only置于句首，强调方式状语、条件状语、地点状语、时间状语等状语时，主句要进行部分倒装。如果被only所强调的状语为状语从句，该状语从句不倒装，只对主句进行倒装。

10. Nowadays, online sales are becoming a popular way to push sales.

当今，网上交易正在成为推销产品的十分流行方式。

① online sales 网上交易 push sales 促销

You must push your wares if you want better sales.

如果你想要有好的销路，必须推销你的商品。

*11. enclose 把……装入信封（或包裹等），附入

A cheque is enclosed herewith.

随信附上支票一张。

*12. cater to 满足某种需要或要求

Some tabloid newspapers cater to low taste.

有些小型报纸迎合低级趣味。

*13. cater for 提供，迎合

TV programs usually cater for all tastes.

电视通常提供各种不同趣味的娱乐节目。

Part B Practical Key Sentences

1. **selling**

（1）Expressing something sells well 表达某物卖得好

The feedback shows these handicrafts have a ready market in Asia.

反馈显示这些手工艺品在亚洲很畅销。

替换表达：

Our bikes are very popular in Asia on account of their superior quality and competitive price.

This product is one of the best sellers in Asia.

（2）When expressing something doesn't sell well, we can say 当表达某物卖得不好，我们可以说

Promoting the sale of your cars has proved unsuccessful.

推销你方的汽车证明不成功。

替换表达：

There is a poor market for your razors.

We've spared no effort and spent money in pushing the sales but the result is disappointing.

2. **reason**

And because we are facing fierce competition from the existing similar product in your market, we may well need to hold a news conference to introduce our product.

因为面对在你们国家市场上现已存在的类似产品的激烈竞争，我们也需要召开一个新闻发布会来介绍我们的产品。

替换表达：

Our bikes are very popular in Asia on account of their superior quality and competitive price.

One possible cause of the decline seems to be their large and increasing trade deficit, which means that all foreign imports have been reduced.

I'll buy the endowment policy, for it enables me to save money for my old age.

Since there is a growing demand for this product, please ensure the supply is sufficient.

3. **persuasion**

That's true, but ... 不错，但是……

That's true, but when we compare prices, we'd better take quality into consideration first.

不错，但是当我们比较价格时，最好先考虑产品的质量，不是吗？

替换表达：

But surely you can see when we compare prices, we'd better take quality into consideration first.

Yes, but you must admit when we compare prices, we'd better take quality into consideration first.

That might be right, but you didn't get the main point when we compare prices, we'd better take quality into consideration first.

4. **suggestion**

How about advertising the product in newspapers, magazines, direct mail, Internet and radio?

在报纸上、杂志上、通过直接邮购和通过广播来宣传我们的产品怎么样？

替换表达：

What about making yourselves known by TV ads?

I suggest that besides television, we use other channels to advertise the product at the same time.

We would like to recommend here a few popular items available for immediate shipment.

A transaction at this price is recommended.

5. intention

（1）Asking about somebody's intention 询问某人的打算

Do you have any interest in our massage chairs and intend to place some orders?

你对我们的按摩椅感兴趣吗？有没有想订几台我们的按摩椅？

替换表达：

Your intention is to help advertise the products, isn't it?

Do you have any intention of carrying out a market survey?

Does this sales representative plan to pay regular visits to these customers?

Are you thinking of making all efforts to promote the sale of your products?

（2）Stating your intention 说明你的打算

If you can make a discount, I intend to consider the order.

如果你们给予打折，我会考虑试着下订单的。

替换表达：

I would like to buy a large quantity of your goods if your price is competitive.

We have every intention to establish business relations with your company if you can spend a sum of money on advertisement on TV.

6. liking

I like this rose pattern.

我喜欢这种玫瑰花的图案。

替换表达：

I love advertisements with catchphrases in them.

I really enjoy attending business talk.

I have a fancy for this sales drive.

I'm keen on the new formulas you are advertising.

I'm crazy about the work of samples and propaganda.

Part C Integration of Theory and Practice

1. sales promotion 促销

【知识点】促销的关键目标是提供信息、刺激需求和突出价值。促销必须向市场提供有什么产品、产品的特色以及如何使用等信息。专业的推销人员具备对推销过程的全面知识。这个过程包括开发潜在客户、接近客户、介绍和演示产品、处理用户的反对意见、完成交易,即锲而不舍地跟踪一笔交易。

2. prosperous customer 潜在的客户

【知识点】在接近客户之前,推销人员要先开发潜在客户,即辨认出哪些是最有购买意向的企业和人群。在企业间的交易中,选定可能的用户之后,推销人员就要接触该企业的决策者。接下来是产品介绍和演示、推销人员调试和操作设备、回答问题以及承接订货。产品介绍并没有定规。它也许更接近于一个非正式的谈话,在谈话间推销人员介绍产品的特色和用途,潜在客户或许对此感兴趣。

【技能训练句型】

A: You can now do all your cooking in beautiful Ceramic Ware—cook and serve food in the same lovely dishes! Boil, fry, roast, bake—do it all in Ceramic Ware. Freeze food in the same dishes, if you wish. These beautiful utensils, made of the same amazing ceramic used in missile cones, can go from freezer to stove to table. You then slip them into the dishwasher or the sink with the other dishes. Never slave at scouring pans again.

B: Sounds good.

3. salesperson 推销员

【知识点】专业的推销人员应该具有良好的品性,应当了解或熟悉广博的知识,应当很好地支配自己的时间,应当对自己的工作和产品充满激情。他们的推销宣传应该以产品的实用性和会带给客户何种益处为根本,而不是仅仅介绍产品本身或产品的外在形式。在面对客户时,要事先想好客户可能会感兴趣的话题。只要能使气氛活跃起来,随便谈什么都可以,但是言语上不能过火或者过于刻板。在轻松的谈话中,你可以开始向对方询问一些生活上的问题,这样就灵活自然地过渡到推销的正题上。

优秀的推销员除了要有说服力、自信心和洞悉顾客心理的能力外,还要能经常介绍公司的最新或最畅销的产品。可以说"This is our newest product." 或 "This is our most recently developed product."(这是我公司最新产品),甚至还可以强调 "They are of the newest patterns that can be obtained in town."(这个款式目前在市面上绝无仅有)。面对令人眼花缭乱的产品,特色是顾客考虑的要素之一。所以,把 "Its durability will be an agreeable surprise to you."(它的耐久性将让您吃惊)常挂嘴边是必要的。

4. showroom 展室

【知识点】多数客户都秉持"眼见为实"的审慎做法,所以带客户参观样品展览室,可以帮助客户建立对公司产品的信心。你不妨主动提出带客户参观样品展览室。在样品展览室是你向客户大力推销公司产品的大好时机。你必须针对参观时客户感兴趣的产品重点解说。当客户对某个环节有疑问或心存疑虑时,推销员要充满信心,措辞有力,详细说明自己产品的优点,这样才能吸引客户,促成交易。

【技能训练句型】

A: Would you like to have a look at our showroom?
B: I'd love to.
A: This way, please.

B: Oh, you have got a large collection of sample medicines.

A: We make two kinds of things: medicines to fight disease and products for health care. Look, that's a new product we've just developed.

B: What's it about?

A: It is manufactured with traditional Chinese medicinal herbs. It can cure sporadic hair loss and baldness. This series of drugs has been exported to many countries. And the demand is getting greater and greater.

5. advertisement 广告

【知识点】广告是一种很好的推销宣传公司产品的方式，但是每一个公司都必须决定哪一种广告媒介对自己的产品最合适。做出这种选择的影响因素，一是媒介体的费用，二是目标对象是否可接触到该媒介体。

【技能训练句型】

A: What kind of advertising will you do for us?

B: Many kinds. We can announce your superior quality through mass media including radio, TV, or newspaper. We can print it on posters and send them to citizens by direct mail. We can imprint it on thousands and thousands of ceramic mugs and caps. All these will create a large market for your products.

6. online sales 网上交易

【知识点】网上交易主要是利用网络为载体或传播媒介，对产品和服务进行宣传推销，利用电子商务的各种手段，达成买卖的虚拟交易过程。网上交易的市场范围超越了传统意义上的市场范围。能跨越国界进行交易，使得国际贸易进一步多样化。互联网为企业提供了全球范围的商务空间。能跨越时空，组织世界各地商务人士参与同一项目的运作，或者利用跨境电子商务平台向全球的消费者展示并销售新上市的产品。

【技能训练句型】

Nowadays, online sales are becoming a popular way to push sales.
当今，网上交易正在成为十分流行的推销产品的方式。

Part D Practice

I. Complete the Following Dialogues

(1)

A: Our new products have been sold in a number of areas abroad. They sell like ___1___ cakes.

B: The exhibits in the showroom certainly look ___2___.

A: I'm sure they will sell well in your market, too.

B: I'm willing to ___3___ your products a try, but your delivery must be ___4___ to sample.

A: Certainly. Our ___5___ in business is to -Honor the contract and keep our promise-. Here is some technical data. We also have a video which ___6___ the operation of our latest products.

B: That'll be ___7___ great help.

A: If you like, I can ___8___ a meeting with our technician, who can give you an ___9___ understanding of our products.

B: Good. I'm looking forward ___10___ meeting him.

(2)

A: Did you see our catalogues?

B: Yes.

A: How do feel about our new product?

B: I'm favorably ___1___. Your catalogues say that you have more than 20 ___2___ with over 100 designs, right?

A: Yes. I hope this is a big enough collection for you to ___3___ from.

B: Well, we think the Christmas teddy bears are cute. You know teddy bears are very ___4___ here, and the holiday season is coming.

A: Yes, I know. And I'm sure our well-made teddy bears will ___5___ your satisfaction.

B: What materials are they made of?

A: We have a variety of ___6___ such as cloth, velvet, linen, flannel, etc. You can order whichever you like.

B: Great. What ___7___ do you have?

A: Usually we have 5 sizes, mini, small, ___8___, large and extra large. We can also have the toys made to customers' ___9___. So if you have your own designs and ask for special sizes, please ___10___ us know.

II. Role-plays

Task 1

The teacher divides students into groups. Students make dialogues and roleplay them:

Discussion is held between the host and the visitor about the samples of products according to the following hints.

Student A plays the host, Mr. Fang, the sales manager of a carpet company, student B is Jack, a businessperson from Austria. Student A's role: As a sales manager of a carpet company, you are now having a talk with a businessman from Austria about your products, trying to persuade her to buy your products. Student B's role: You are a businessperson from Austria. This is your first visit to China. You are not sure whether you can close a deal or not. After visiting the showroom, you find some items very attractive. So you ask a few questions.

Task 2

Short conversations.

Suppose you meet an old customer, Mr. Brown, who comes to your company. Mr. Brown likes to do business with your company again, so you discuss about how to push sales with him.

III. Guided Talking

Work in pairs.

Zhang Hua from ABC Company comes to the MIG Health Products Company which his own company hasn't established business contact with before. First he persuades Mr. White, the manager in MIG Health Products Company to listen to his promotion. Then he tries his best to describe the strong points of his company's new product. For example, it has fine quality and reasonable price. Finally the manager agrees to give ABC Company's new product a try.

IV. Creative Discussion

The teacher divides the class into groups and asks them to discuss, then choose the representatives of each group after discussion. The student who expresses well will be the winner.

Topics:

1. Promotion is very important in our daily life, especially in sales promotion. What tips have you got?

Please discuss with your partner about how to make promotion effectively.

2. Discuss your experience in online sales.

Chapter 18 Interview

Learning Objectives
Upon completion of this chapter, you will be able to

- ☑ talk about job applications and interviews.
- ☑ get familiarized in an interview.
- ☑ learn some etiquettes of attending an interview.
- ☑ know how to perform at the interview.

课文范读

Part A Situational Dialogue

 Communicative Scene 1

At the Reception Desk

(Mr. Liu has just graduated from the university. Looking for a job, today he will take part in an interview. He walks towards the receptionist, Miss Gao, who welcomes the applicants.)

Liu: Good morning.

Gao: Good morning, sir. What can I do for you?

Liu: I'm coming for an interview at nine o'clock this morning. I received a call the day before yesterday, informing me of my interview.

Gao: I see. So can I have your name, please?

Liu: Sure, my name is Liu Feng.

Gao: (*Taking a quick glimpse at the name list.*[1])

Oh, yes, your number is 6. Would you please sit there and wait a moment? I'll call your name when it is your turn.

Liu: OK, thank you.

(About twenty minutes later, Miss Gao gestures to Mr. Liu.)

Gao: Mr. Liu, it's your turn now. Our interviewers are waiting for you in Room 201. Please come this way!

Liu: OK! You are so kind, thank you!

Gao: Don't mention it. Good luck to you!

Liu: Thank you very much.

Gao: You're welcome.

 Communicative Scene 2

At the Interview

(When Mr. Liu enters the interviewing room, the personnel manager, Miss Lin and her colleagues are waiting for him.)

Liu: Good morning. My name is Liu Feng.

Lin: Good morning, Mr. Liu. Nice to meet you, I'm Lin Qing from Personnel Section. Just sit down, please.

Liu: Thank you, Mrs. Lin.

Lin: I see by your resume that you have just graduated from college. Please tell me something about yourself.

Liu: I've just graduated from Peking University, and <u>I studied Economics, with an emphasis on International Trade.</u> ²

Lin: How were your scores at university?

Liu: They were excellent. <u>I worked hard and I made fine records in almost every examination. I've got scholarship on merit.</u>³ You can see it from my resume.

Lin: And you know our company is a very large international trading company. It has offices in over 10 countries. You would be using mainly English on this job, so how do you describe your English ability?

Liu: <u>I think I have a good command of English.</u>⁴ <u>I'm proficient in both written and spoken English.</u>⁵ I have passed CET-6 and I got high scores in almost every exam.

Lin: Well, I can see it from your resume. <u>How do you think the education you've received will contribute to your work in this company?</u>⁶

Liu: <u>My specialization at the university is just in line with the areas your company deals with.</u>⁷ I'm sure I can apply what I have learned to the work in your company.

Lin: What kind of personality do you think you have?

Liu: I'm not sure what information you'd like to know about me. Well, I approach things very enthusiastically, I think, and I don't like to leave something half-done. It makes me nervous. <u>I can't concentrate on something else until the first thing is finished.</u>⁸ In all, I think I'm an ambitious, self-motivated person and <u>I always keep my promise.</u>⁹

Lin: Well, I really appreciate that. <u>Would you describe yourself as outgoing or more reserved?</u>¹⁰

Liu: Well, I'm not really sure, maybe partly both. Sometimes I want to be by myself, but most of the time I prefer being with a group of people. I was very active in my university club.

Lin: <u>Are you more of a follower or a leader?</u>¹¹

Liu: I don't try to get in front of people and lead them, particularly. I'd rather cooperate with everybody else, and get the job done by working together.

 Communicative Scene 3

The Interview Continued

(Miss Lin changes her opinions with her colleagues sitting beside her.)

Lin: Why did you choose our company? There are so many foreign trading companies in this city.

Liu: Because yours is one of the most effective and respectable companies in our city. You provide your employees with an open, team-based environment. I am also aware that you provide a mentor for all new employees, <u>I'll embrace any opportunity to work with a mentor and I think</u>

working in this company would provide me with more opportunities to use my knowledge.[12]

Lin: But you have no experience, why should I hire you?

Liu: Lack of experience doesn't mean inability. Theoretically, I have learned what international trade is and how it works. And I feel strongly that my enthusiasm, diligence and adaptability could compensate. I sincerely believe that I'm the best person for the job. Please give me a chance to prove my ability!

Lin: How about overtime work? You know, sometimes we are so busy, so you have to work overtime. Do you have any complaint if you have to work on the night shift?

Liu: Of course not. I think it's a natural thing.

Lin: Although you haven't asked anything about the salary, I think you'd like to know it. What salary are you expecting?

Liu: I would accept the starting salary in your company of my qualification. But I hope raises are given according to my ability. Your firm has a reputation of compensating employees fairly and I trust you would do the same in my case.[13]

Lin: OK! Is there anything else you'd like to ask me before we terminate the interview?

Liu: When can I know whether I'm accepted or not?

Lin: We'll notify you of our decision by early next week if you're wanted.[14] But we'll have to take you on three months' probation first. That's our usual practice.

Liu: I understand.

Lin: All right. Thank you for coming today, Mr. Liu.

Liu: Thank you for giving me the opportunity, Mrs. Lin. I hope to see you again.

Lin: Good luck to you.

Liu: Thank you, Mrs. Lin. Goodbye.

Words and Expressions

1. glimpse	n.	一瞥，一看
2. Personnel Section		人事部
3. scholarship on merit		学业成绩优良奖学金
4. proficient	adj.	精通的，熟练的
5. specialization	n.	专业
6. enthusiastically	adv.	热心地，热情地
7. ambitious	adj.	有雄心壮志的
8. self-motivated		自我约束
9. mentor	n.	导师
10. embrace	v.	接受、拥抱
11. theoretically	adv.	理论地，从理论上来讲
12. diligence	n.	勤奋，勤勉
13. adaptability	n.	适应性

14. compensate	v.	补偿
15. overtime work		加班
16. night shift		夜班
17. qualification	n.	资格
18. probation	n.	试用期

1. Taking a quick glimpse at the name list.
   快速地看了一下名单。
   ① glimpse at 匆匆看一下，瞥一下
   He took a glimpse at himself in the mirror.
   他瞥了一眼镜子中的自己。

2. I studied Economics, with an emphasis on International Trade.
   我学经济，主修国际贸易。
   ① emphasis on (upon) 强调，重点
   This is a new economic policy, with a greater emphasis on reducing inflation.
   这是一项更加强调降低通货膨胀的新经济政策。

3. I worked hard and I made fine records in almost every examination. I've got scholarship on merit.
   我很努力学习并几乎在每一场考试里都取得了好成绩。我是奖学金的获得者。
   ① make fine records 得高分
   ② prize fellow 奖学金获得者

4. I think I have a good command of English.
   我觉得我英语学得很好。
   ① have a good command of 在……方面很在行，精通
   He has a good command of French.
   他精通法语。

5. I'm proficient in both written and spoken English.
   我英语口语和书面能力都很强。
   ① be proficient in (at) 精通……
   She is proficient in / at operating the computer.
   她精通计算机操作。

6. How do you think the education you've received will contribute to your work in this company?
   你觉得你在学校里受到的教育能够应用到我们公司的工作当中去吗?
   ① contribute to 起促成作用
   The new policy contributes greatly to the commercial growth to the country.

新政策大大地促进了这个国家商业的发展。

7. My specialization at the university is just in line with the areas your company deals with.

我在学校里学的专业和你们公司所处的领域是对口的。

① in line with 和……在一条直线（水平线）上的，和……一致的

The wheel at the back isn't in line with the one at the front.

后轮和前轮没有保持在一条直线上。

8. I can't concentrate on something else until the first thing is finished.

除非一件事做完，否则我无法专心做其他事情。

① concentrate on (upon) 集中（思想、精力、注意力等）

This year the company has concentrated on improving its efficiency.

这家公司今年致力于提高效率。

9. I always keep my promise.

我总是信守诺言。

① keep promise 信守诺言

If you make a promise you should keep it.

假如你做了承诺，就要守信。

10. Would you describe yourself as outgoing or more reserved?

你说自己性格是外向型还是内向型的？

① outgoing *adj.* 好交际的，外向的

We need an outgoing person to receive our foreign visitors.

我们需要一个善于交际的人来接待我们的外国客人。

② reserved *adj.* 沉默寡言的，含蓄的，内向的

Bob is very reserved—you never know what he's thinking.

鲍伯相当沉默寡言——你决不会知道他在想什么。

11. Are you more of a follower or a leader?

你是一个从众者，还是一个领导者？

① follower和leader 在这里分别指"跟随者，被领导者"和"领导者"。

② more of 更多的……

Can I have some more of that apple pie this time?

我可以再来一些苹果派吗？

12. I'll embrace any opportunity to work with a mentor and I think working in this company would provide me with more opportunities to use my knowledge.

我会珍惜每一个和前辈工作的机会，而且我相信在贵公司工作会给我提供更多的机会学以致用。

① embrace *v.* 接受

to embrace an opportunity 很高兴有机会……

② to provide sb. with sth. 为提供……

These letters should provide us with all the information we need.

这些信函为我们提供所需要的全部信息。

13. I trust you would do the same in my case.

    我相信你们也会对我一视同仁。

    ① in one's case 就……情况而言

    Jane's bad results were partly due to illness, but in John's case / in the case of John, no such excuse is possible.

    简的成绩不好，部分原因是由于她生病，但就约翰的情况而言，这样的理由却站不住脚。

14. We'll notify you of our decision by early next week if you're wanted.

    如果你被录用，我们会在下周初通知你的。

    ① notify sb. of sth. 通知某人某事

    You will be notified of any changes in the system.

    系统有任何变化你都会接到通知。

Part B Practical Key Sentences

1. Please tell me ...

Please tell me something about yourself.

请谈谈你个人的一些情况。

替换表达：

Would you mind answering a few personal questions?

Would you begin by telling me something about yourself?

Can you tell me something about yourself?

Would you please say something about yourself?

2. How are your scores ...

How were your scores at university?

你在大学里成绩如何？

替换表达：

How were your grades in college?

What grades did you get at university?

3. What kind of personality ...

What kind of personality do you think you have?

你认为你是什么样的人？

替换表达：

How would you describe yourself?

How do you feel about yourself?

面试中询问个性的表达方式还有：

Would you describe yourself as outgoing or more reserved?

你性格外向还是内向?

替换表达:

Do you think you are more outward-looking or more inward-looking?

Are you more of a follower or a leader?

Are you a team player?

4. **Why do you choose ...**

Why did you choose our company?

你为什么选择我们公司?

替换表达:

Why you are interested in working at our company?

What made you decide on choosing our company?

Why do you want to work for our company?

5. **Why should we hire ...**

Why should I hire you?

我为什么要录用你呢?

替换表达:

Why should we offer you the job?

Why are you the best person for the job?

6. **What salary ...**

What salary are you expecting?

你期望拿到多少薪水?

替换表达:

What is your expected salary?

What are your salary expectations?

If you are accepted, how much salary would you expect?

How much do you wish to have for your salary?

What kind of salary are you seeking/looking for?

Part C　Integration of Theory and Practice

1. **dress for interview success　面试时的衣着**

【知识点】职业面试时对着装有一定的讲究,以下是获得面试成功的衣着建议。

Men's wear:

（1） Conservative two-piece suit.

（2） Necktie should be silk with a conservative pattern.

（3） Short hair

(4) Dark shoes

(5) Dark socks

(6) No beards

(7) No rings other than wedding ring

(8) No earrings

Lady's garment:

(1) Conservative suit

(2) Shoes with conservative heels

(3) Conservative socks at or near skin color

(4) Carry a briefcase, not a purse

(5) You'd better have no nail polish

(6) Minimal use of makeup (it should not be too noticeable)

(7) No more than one ring on each hand

(8) One set of earrings only

2. some standard interview questions   面试时考官常问的问题

【知识点】面试的问题常涉及个人信息、教育背景、工作经验、申请理由、工作要求、兴趣爱好和与工作相关的问题。

(1) Personal information(个人信息):

① Where is your birthplace?

② Are you a resident of Shanghai now?

③ What is your nationality?

④ How large is your family?

⑤ Would you talk about your merits?

⑥ What kind of personality do you think you have?

⑦ You a team player?

⑧ You handle pressure well?

⑨ What are your greatest strength and your greatest weakness?

(2) Educational background (教育背景):

① Can you talk about your educational background?

② What department did you study in?

③ What subjects were you doing?

④ How about your scores at college?

⑤ Have you received any honors or rewards at college?

(3) Working experience(工作经验):

① Have you worked as a secretary?

② Could you tell me what was your last job?

③ Did you make any notable achievements or receive any honors in the company?

(4) Reasons for applying(申请理由):

① Why should I hire you?

② Why did you choose this career?

③ When did you decide on this career?

④ What do you know about our company?

⑤ Why are you interested in our company?

（5）Hobbies and interests(兴趣爱好):

① Do you have any hobbies? What is it or what are they?

② How do you spend your spare time?

③ What kind of books are you interested in?

④ What do you usually do when you are free?

（6）Salary(工资):

① How much are you looking for?

② How much do you expect, if we offer this position to you?

③ What kind of salary are you worth?

3. how to write a resume　　如何写简历

【知识点】（1）The Content of Your Resume:

① Full name (pinyin and Chinese Characters)

姓名（拼音及汉字）

Former name(s) (Maiden, Religious, Professional, Aliases)

曾用名（婚前姓名、教名、职业名、别名）

② Present address (postal zone)

现在住址（邮政编码）

Telephone number

电话号码

③ Date of birth (day, month, year)

出生日期（日、月、年）

④ Place of birth (city, province, country)

出生地点（市、省、国）

Nationality or citizenship

国籍

⑤ Sex (female, male)

性别（女、男）

Marital status (married, single, widowed, divorced)

婚姻状况（已婚、未婚、鳏寡、离婚）

⑥ Height and weight and health

身高、体重与健康状况

⑦ What is your present job/occupation?

现有的工作、职业

Post of rank held at present

现在的职位

⑧ Employment record/Experience

经历

Names and addresses of firms or organizations to which you belonged

曾供职过的公司或机关名称和地址

Principal former positions

曾任职过的主要职位

Reasons for leaving

离职原因

⑨ Education (Qualification)

学历

Schools attended (including middle school, technical school, college, etc.)

曾就读过的学校名称（包括中学、技校、大学等）；注明何时毕业

School transcripts

学习成绩单

⑩ Professional experience and skills

专业技能

除了上述十项内容外，如果应聘者曾有著作、论文出版、发表等也要一并附上。

【知识点】（2）一份好的简历，应做到以下几点：

① 简明扼要、完整无缺。

要做一份好的简历，首要的一条就是要简明，同时也要注意完整。简历表上的学历和工作经历包含了求职者的大半生，每一年都要包括在内。

写简历时，因为用表格形式，就不必用完整的文句来述说经历，应尽量写得简要。但对一些学校、单位、公司等的名称，却不可用缩略语，而要写出全称，以免造成不必要的误会。

② 工作经历和资历要详而全。

为了让主试人员对你的工作能力和成绩有一个充分全面的了解，你必须将所任的工作和职务、取得过何种评语和嘉奖，尽量在主试人员面前展示出来。

③ 语言要规范，用词要得当。

所谓语言规范，指的是从语法、拼写、标点各个方面都要正确，符合习惯；同时，在填写简历时要注意实事求是，不可言过其实，但也不要妄自菲薄。

④ 简历表要用打印。

个人简历表要打印在16开大小的全白纸上。

【技能训练】（3）Sample Resume

Name: Lin Hao

Address: No. 128 Lianghua Road. Gulou District. Fuzhou

Postal: 350001

Telephone Number: 13509372951

Birth Date and Birth place: October 13, 1982

Sex: Female
Marital Status: Single
Height: 162cm
Weight: 45kg
Health Condition: Excellent
Education:
    2004.9-2006.6 Dept. of Automation, Graduate School of Tsinghua University
    2000.9-2004.7 Dept. of Automation, Beijing Institute of Technology
English Skills
    Have a good command of both spoken and written English. Past CET-6,
    TOEFL: 619; GRE: 2193
Scholarships and Awards
    2005.3   Guanghua First-class Scholarship for graduate
    2003.3   second-class scholarship
    2002.3   first-class scholarship
Qualifications
    General business knowledge relating to financial, healthcare
    Have a passion for the Internet, and an abundance of common sense

Part D Practice

I. Complete the Following Dialogue

(*A is an applicant, and B is the personnel manager.*)

A: Good morning. Mr. Smith.

B: Good morning, Mr. Liu. Please ___1___.

A: Thank you.

B: I've learnt from your ___2___ that you have just graduated from the college. Please ___3___.

A: I've just graduated from Xiamen University, and I studied commerce, with an ___4___ on foreign trade.

B: How's your ___5___ at university?

A: I got high scores in almost every examination. You can see it from my resume.

B: Do you think your English is quite good? Tell me something about your English education.

A: I think I have a good ___6___ of English. My English teacher has said that my English is quite good, and I scored high in a TOEFL test last year. I am ___7___ in both written and spoken English.

B: Very well. Can I ask you what made you ___8___ our company?

A: A friend of mine works here. And he told me about your company.

B: I see. It's been pleasant talking with you, Mr. Liu. We'll ___9___ you of our decision by next Monday. If you're accepted, we'll put you on six months' ___10___ first. Good luck!

A: Thank you. Mr. Smith. Good bye.

II. Oral Translation

A：你好，我是人事处经理彼得。

B：很高兴见到你。

A：请先谈谈你的学历情况吧。

B：一年前我从汕头大学毕业。我的专业是英语语言和文学。

A：你认为你的英语好吗？

B：是的，我的英语很好。在学校几乎每一次考试我都得高分。在英语专业八级的考试中我也取得了很好的成绩。我还是学生时，就有好几家公司请我去当翻译。

A：很好。什么原因使你选择我们公司呢？

B：贵公司有很好的名誉。我想在贵公司工作将会给我提供很多的机会，使我学有所用。

A：我知道了，和你交谈很愉快。下星期前我们就会通知你结果的。

B：谢谢。

III. Situational Talks

Task 1

Suppose you are a manager of a company and a job applicant is coming for an interview. You'll ask about his educational background, foreign language abilities and working experience, reasons for applying.

Task 2

You apply for the sales marketing position, but it is very competitive. Please try your best to convince the personnel manager that you are well qualified for the position.

IV. Practical Questions and Answers

Discuss the following questions with your classmates.

1. You are a manager of a certain company. In an interview, you want to know whether the applicant can speak English well or not. How do you ask?

2. You are an applicant for a job in a company. When you are asked why you pick their company, what would you answer?

3. You are working in a small company and the salary is low. When you are asked why you want to change your job, what would you answer?

V. Writing

Students try to write a resume according to their own situation.

Students work in pairs and write the applicant's letter of application.

VI. Creative Discussion

1. The teacher divides the class into groups and asks them to discuss, then chooses the representatives of each group after discussion. The student who expresses well will be the winner.

Topics:

(1) What is the most important thing in choosing a job?

(2) Do you design the presentations yourself?

2. Mock interview.

The teacher and some students will act as interviewers and the students will practice in turn as an interviewee.

Chapter 19 Complaints

Learning Objectives
Upon completion of this chapter, you will be able to

- learn how to make complaints to the seller.
- learn how to settle a claim.
- perform the functions of skills of communication.
- conduct the activities related to the theme of complaints.

课文范读

Part A Situational Dialogue

 Communicative Scene 1

No Spam Please!

(Jenny logged in a website and signed up, yet never expected the endless spam. She pours out her experience to her friend.)

Jenny: This almost drives me mad!
Shelley: What's up?
Jenny: My mailbox is stuffed with Spam.
Shelley: What for?
Jenny: <u>I browsed the eBay</u>[1] and was interested in an article of a cyber store, so <u>I signed up for more information about their commodity.</u>[2]
Shelley: So they served you information as you wished...
Jenny: OK, but later I didn't like their solicitation, and have requested numerous times to be taken off the mailing list, and they have promised to do it each time but I still get mail...
Shelley: Understandable, so you got hooked by them.
Jenny: Yes, but now after hundreds of requests via fax and phone, they act like I'm the one harassing them...
Shelley: <u>I think you can get yourself removed out of the Spam list with certain instructions given on the Internet.</u>[3] When a consumer no longer wishes to get mail, the company has an obligation to stop sending the mail.
Jenny: I tried, thousands of times...they are just liars. These people are basically refusing to do that. One guy told me "I removed your name myself the day you called". Everything remains. I got mail again yesterday!
Shelley: Gosh... so frustrating...so what are you going to do?
Jenny: Nothing but tit for tat. They continue to lie and I keep getting mail so I will continue to call, fax and email until they stop. If they don't want calls in the middle of the night, they shouldn't send me mail with their cell phone numbers on it, right?

 Communicative Scene 2

Commercial Fraud

(<u>A women made a call to Complaints Center to expose a commercial fraud.</u>[4])

Clerk: Complaints Center. Can I help you?

Madame: Ah... afternoon, it's terrific for me to have somewhere to complain.

Clerk: Glad to serve you, Madame, what is it?

Madame: Well, Horizon Travel Company duped us. Two years ago, <u>my husband and I attended their presentation on timeshares.</u> [5]

Clerk: Didn't you refuse to buy anything?

Madame: How couldn't we buy? <u>The sales men persisted for several hours sweetening with all manners of inducements</u>[6] and they promised us free trips to Vegas. At last I bought their timeshare points.

Clerk: So you got the free trips?

Madame: No, the free trip is fixed on certain days. <u>Unforeseen problems came up with our child,</u>[7] so we gave it up. But the nuisance is that recently I called to book a trip and found I have no points left at all.

Clerk: How come?

Madame: I don't know, I thought I had accumulated points since I had never used it, but I was told I actually lost them for paying to be in the club. Their representatives had never mentioned the surprise maintenance fees on a membership. <u>If all that had been stated up front that I would not have signed anything.</u>[8]

Clerk: OK, I have noted down your complaint. We will accept your complaint and transfer the case to relative administrations as soon as possible.

Madame: Thank you. I will never again attend one of these fiascos. I knew it sounded too good to be true!

 Communicative Scene 3

Wrong Shipment

(Stevenson complains about the wrong shipment. The secretary of his business partner receives his complaints.)

Stevenson: Morning, I'd like to speak to Mr. Li, your manager of Sales department.

Secretary: Sorry. He is on vacation now. I'm his secretary responsible for his work during his absence. Can I help you?

Stevenson: I'm Stevenson from Holland. I have a complaint to make.

Secretary: What is it?

Stevenson: OK, I'll explain the problem briefly. It's about our order No. 1326 placed 2 months ago. We have received the articles, yet when we opened the carton, we found 1/4 of them contained completely different articles. Obviously you packed the wrong articles and this troubles us a lot.

Secretary: I'm sorry to hear that. I'll go into this matter. If it's really our fault, we'll send you the replacement immediately.

Stevenson: For the time being, we'll hold these wrong articles at your disposal. So it's peak season for the ordered articles,⁹ we need the goods urgently. If we fail to receive the articles in two weeks, we have to cancel that part of the order and ask for refund.¹⁰

Secretary: Even if we made the mistake as you mentioned, it's impossible for us to ship it and let it arrive in 2 weeks.

Stevenson: In that case, you have to make the shipment by airfreight instead of original sea freight.¹¹ By the way, we'll not share the difference between the 2 freight charges.

Secretary: But before I'm clear about this matter, I have no way to talk about shipping the replacement. Please send us the inspection report and pictures by fax or e-mail, I'll let you know the result as soon as possible.

...

Secretary: I'm sorry, we indeed made a mistake in packing through a confusion of numbers. Since it's our fault, we'll dispatch the right goods by airfreight and pay the difference between freight charges as you will. You know, the freight charge cannot even be covered by the cost of the articles,¹² but we really need your support in that new market.

Stevenson: Business is business. We appreciate your cooperation very much.

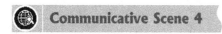

Communicative Scene 4

Product Defectiveness

(Mr. White files a complaint against the product defectiveness. Mr. Wang, the representative of the local producer, claims the responsibility and promises to improve QC.)

White: Mr. Wang, we have long been satisfied with the quality of your product, but I am shocked this time.

Wang: What for? Something is wrong with our product?

White: We just received the shipment of our order No. 3261. We discovered the defective percentage is nearly 5%, far beyond the stated 2%. What's wrong?

Wang: How can that be? Every batch is produced to identical standards in design and performance¹³ and was inspected by QC department before being sent out.

White: Seeing is believing. Here are the inspection reports.

Wang: (*Embarrassed*) OK, as your agent here, we're really sorry for that. The Spring Festival is coming and the manufacturer has to run up the order in only one month.¹⁴ Haste makes waste. Maybe this batch of product slipped through the normal examination.¹⁵

White: So what shall we do?

Wang: We'll send a team immediately to the manufacturer to notify them of the problems and take action to rectify the situation.

White: I mean about our loss...

Wang: We'll also try to negotiate with the suppliers on your behalf, and get the fair compensation from them within the shortest time.

White: I hope you can solve this problem as soon as possible. The defective rate must be kept within 2%.

Wang: I promise we'll improve the quality control. We'll send personnel to supervise on-site. To avoid the same problem, we assure you that we'll inspect the goods more thoroughly and strictly.

White: The most important is to have a qualified supplier. If the situation cannot be rectified, we suggest that you look for another supplier.

Wang: No problem.

Words and Expressions

1.	stuff	v.	塞满
2.	spam	n.	junk mail 垃圾邮件
3.	browse	v.	浏览
4.	cyber store		网上商铺
5.	sign up		签约，注册
6.	solicitation	n.	兜售
7.	harass	v.	烦恼
8.	obligation	n.	义务
9.	tit for tat		针锋相对
10.	fraud	n.	欺骗
11.	dupe	v.	欺骗，愚弄
12.	timeshare	n.	分时度假
13.	sweeten	v.	变甜，说好话
14.	inducement	n.	刺激物
15.	stated	adj.	规定的
16.	up front		预先
17.	membership	n.	会员
18.	fiasco	n.	惨败，大失败
19.	for the time being		暂时
20.	at one's disposal		由某人做主
21.	refund	n.	偿还额，退款
22.	defectiveness	n.	有缺陷，缺乏
23.	batch	n.	一批
24.	run up		赶制
25.	haste makes waste		欲速则不达
26.	rectify	vt.	矫正，调整
27.	compensation	n.	补偿，赔偿
28.	on-site		现场

1. I browsed the eBay.

   我在易趣网上购物中心闲逛。

   ① eBay *n.* 易趣，购物网

   ② browse through 浏览

   I was browsing through a newspaper when I spotted your name.

   我们通过报纸得知贵公司。

2. I signed up for more information about their commodity.

   我注册以希望得到更多的有关他们产品的信息。

   ① sign up (for) 经报名参加（课程学习）

   ② sign in / (out) 签到/签名登记离开

   Remember to sign in at the reception.

   记得到报到处登记。

3. I think you can get yourself removed out of the Spam list with certain instructions given on the Internet.

   我想按照网上的说明，你应该能够自己退出他们的联系人列表吧！

   ① removed from (a place) / (a job) 迁移/开除

   Our office has removed from Boston to New York.

   我们的办公地址从波士顿迁到了纽约。

   The merciless boss removed poor Tony from his beloved position.

   无情的老板开除了可怜的托尼，他离开了钟爱的岗位。

4. A women made a call to Complaints Center to expose a commercial fraud.

   一位女士致电投诉中心投诉一桩商业欺诈。

   ① Complaints Center

   投诉受理中心

5. My husband and I attended their presentation on timeshare.

   我和丈夫参加了他们分时度假项目的推介会。

   timeshare 分时度假（又称Vacation ownership或 Holiday ownership）。最初是指人们在度假地购买房产时，只购买部分时段的产权，几户人家共同拥有一处房产。共同维护、分时使用的度假形式，后来逐渐演变成每户人家在每年只拥有某一段的度假地房产使用权，并且可以通过交换系统对不同房产的使用权实行交换。

   国际上一度通行的惯例是：将一处住宿设施（如饭店、公寓、度假别墅等）的住宿单元每年的使用期分为52周，将52周中的51周分时销售给顾客。每个单位的分时度假产品，就是在约定的时期内（一般为20～40年）每年在这一住宿单元中住宿一周的权利。

6. The sales men persisted for several hours sweetening with all manner of inducements.

那些推销员缠了我们几小时，以各种各样的优惠来讨好我们。

① manners *n.* 礼貌，礼仪

She has good / no manners.

她很有/没有礼貌。

Where are your manners?

你的礼貌哪儿去了？（指某人，尤指孩子，不懂礼貌）

7. Unforeseen problems came up to our child.

   我们的孩子出了点意外。

   ① come up 出现或发生

   Your name came up in our conversation once or twice.

   你的名字在我们的谈话中被提到了一两次。

   ② come up to sth. 比得上，达到

   This doesn't come up to the standard of your usual work.

   这次你们的工作有失水准。

8. If all that had been stated up front that I would not have signed anything.

   要是预先说明（要交纳会员费）的话，我才不会签约呢！

   ① fiasco *n.* 彻底的惨败

   The first lecture I gave was a complete fiasco.

   我讲的第一次课彻底失败了。

9. So it's peak season for the ordered articles.

   所以，现在是我们所订货品的销售旺季。

   ① peak season 销售旺季

   ② reach your peak 达到巅峰时期

   Most athletes have reached their peak by the time they're 20.

   大多数运动员20岁时已达到巅峰时期。

10. We have to cancel that part of the order and ask for refund.

    我们不得不撤销这部分订单并要求退款。

    ① refund *n.* 退款

    ② allowed (make) no refund 不予退款

    ③ give (pay) a refund 给付退款

11. You have to make the shipment by airfreight instead of original sea freight.

    你们必须以空运代替原先的海运出货。

    ① airfreight *n.* 空运

    ② seafreight *n.* 海运

    ③ freight charge 运费

    We'll not share the difference between the two freight charges.

    我们不会分担两种运费的差价。

    ④ share *v.* 分担

    share responsibility 分担责任

share the cost 分担费用

12. The freight charge cannot even be covered by the cost of the articles.

    运费甚至不抵货款。

    ① cover for sb. 代替（某人的工作）

    Who's going to cover for you when you're on holiday?

    度假期间谁接替你的工作？

    ② cover sth. up 掩饰，隐瞒

    The whole thing was very well covered up and never reached the newspapers.

    整个事情都被巧妙地隐瞒起来，始终没有在报纸上曝光。

13. Every batch is produced to identical standards in design and performance.

    每一批货都是按照相同的设计和性能标准来生产的。

    ① performance *n.* （机器或汽车的）性能

    The car's performance on mountain roads was impressive.

    这辆汽车在山路上表现出的性能给人留下深刻的印象。

    ② performance *n.* （工作或活动中的）表现

    Jodie's performance in the exams was disappointing.

    乔迪的考试成绩令人失望。

14. The Spring Festival is coming and the manufacturer has to run up the order in only one month.

    春节就要来了，厂家不得不在一个月内赶完所有的订单。

    ① run up a bill 积欠账款

    She ran up an enormous phone bill.

    她积欠了很多电话费。

15. Maybe this batch of product slipped through the normal examination.

    也许这批货漏检了。

    ① slip through the net 漏网，未受到有关部门的处理

    Sales slip sharply last year.

    去年的销售量急剧下降。

Part B Practical Key Sentences

1. **I have a complaint to make**

   I want to file (make) a complaint.

   我要投诉。

   替换表达：

   I complain that…

   I complain about…

I'm not satisfied with…
Really, I'm fed up with your…
I've just about had enough of that.
For God's sake, could you keep silent for a while?

2. **submit a complaint**
You'd better settle down the mess before she lodges an official complaint.
最好在她没有正式起诉之前,就把乱子摆平。
The BBC received a stream of complaints against this program.
BBC广播公司源源不断地收到了对这个节目的投诉。
替换表达:
The buyer files a complaint against the poor quality of exercises machines.
Many consumers lodge complaints against the safety of the toys.

3. **grounds for complaint**
The loss we suffered in this business gives us the grounds for complaint.
这笔生意损失惨重,我们当然有理由投诉。
Our main complaint is the poor standard of the service.
我们投诉主要是因为服务质量差。
替换表达:
The reasons for complaint is that the products slipped through the normal examination.
The cause for complaint is due to the discovery of high percentage of defective products.

4. **going into the matter**
We'll study the letter of complaint and inquiry into the case.
我会关注投诉函并调查这件事情。
替换表达:
I'll examine this matter thoroughly and give a refund if necessary.
Let's investigate the complaints and solve the problem as soon as possible.

Part C Integration of Theory and Practice

在商务活动中,买卖双方来电抱怨的情形时有发生,抱怨的问题也多种多样。
1. 在接到货物之前,买方会抱怨出货速度太慢。
【技能训练句型】

George: We need to know if you shipped our order no. SW-012 by the end of July. Have you sent out the shipping advice?
我必须知道你们是否已于七月底装出我们的订单SW-012,何时可以给我们出货通知?

Lily: Sorry, this order will be delayed to August 15.
抱歉,这张订单要延迟到8月15日。

2. 买方抱怨出货速度太慢时，卖方要能提出适当理由，并和买方协商，否则买方可能会要求取消订单或者要求卖方改空运出货，并负担空运费。卖方发货延迟的理由有很多。

【技能训练句型】

（1）船期不对。There is no vessel available this week.

（2）生产荷载过大。The production line is over booked / due to too tight a schedule.

（3）生产期内公共假日过多。There are too many holidays this month.

（4）不良率太高。The defective rate is too high.

（5）进口原料慢到。The imported raw material has been delayed for two weeks.

【知识点】3. 如果是买方过失，例如信用证开出较慢，卖方就不需要负责任。

【技能训练句型】

George: How about the order now? Our customer needs the goods urgently.
我们的订单现在如何了？我们的顾客急需这批货。

Lily: We understand, but we can't make the shipment without receiving payment.
理解您的处境，但是我们要先收到货款才能出货。

【知识点】4. 如果是不可抗力事件，例如天灾、战争、罢工等，则双方都无责任，此状况下就由买卖双方共同负担所有损失。

【技能训练句型】

George: I'd like to know what's the reason causing the delay in the shipment of our order No. 2423.
我想知道什么原因造成了我方第2423号订单延迟出货。

Lily: As you know, our factory is in the middle of Taiwan and recently there was a serious earthquake that happened there. Our factory has been damaged and we need time to have the factory repaired first.
如您所知，我们工厂在台湾中部，最近那儿发生严重的地震，我们工厂被震坏，需要一些时间修复。

【技能训练】5. 接到货物后，买方可能会抱怨以下一些问题：

We found

（1）some parts are damaged.
一些零件坏损。

（2）the quantity is different from that shown on your packing list.
数量与包装表上显示的不符。

（3）the color is lighter than that of the sample.
颜色比样品浅。

（4）the size is too small to use.
尺寸太小，无法用。

（5）some parts are not what we ordered.
有些零件不是我们订购的。

（6）the defective rate is too high.
不良率太高。

【知识点】6. 针对买方收到货物后的赔偿要求，卖方可以先请客户退回不良样品。

【技能训练句型】

> Since we did 100% inspection before shipment, we are wondering why the problem happened. Anyway, please send back some defective samples for our evaluation.
>
> 由于我们出货前都做100%检验，我们奇怪为何会发生这种问题。无论如何，请先寄回一些不良样品以供评估。如果是我们的过失，我们将马上赔货给您。

7. 卖方收到不良样品后，先分析原因，再了解问题，之后再确定责任的归属，是买方、卖方、保险公司还是运输公司？如果是卖方责任，就应依照合同给予赔偿，并提送更正报告。

Part D Practice

I. Complete the Following Dialogues

(1)

A: I would like to know if you have shipped our order No. 443? When will we be able to get the ___1___（出货通知）?

B: Sorry, the shipment has to be put off, because of the shortage of the ___2___（原材料）, the high ___3___（缺陷率）on our production, and the delay on ___4___（模具）, and the serious ___5___（人力短缺）.

(2)

A: What about the ___1___（打样样品）we ordered from you?

B: I'm sorry. We're unable to make them according to your ___2___（规格）.

A: Oh! Why didn't you inform us earlier?

B: We had thought we could make it...Well, we'd like to suggest you use ___3___（替代品）. It's ___4___（相当）to you original sample in quality, function and efficiency, but has slightly different ___5___（外观）. Will that be acceptable to you?

(3)

A: What causes ___1___（延期发货）of our order No. 285. I've been ___2___（如坐针毡）for the last few weeks. How's everything going ___3___（你方）?

B: There was a typhoon ___4___（袭击）our city last week. Several container cranes at the harbor were damaged. This caused a severe jam ___5___（装载工作）.

(4)

A: I have a complaint to make about our order No. 443. We found that the quality is different from that of ___1___（确认样品）.

B: I'm sorry to hear that. Can you give us more details about the problem?

A: Yes, of course. We found that

(1) ___2___ （颜色较浅）than that of the sample.
(2) ___3___ （尺寸）is too small to use.
(3) the quantity is different from that shown on your ___4___ （装箱单）.
(4) ___5___ （一些零件）are not what we ordered.

II. Role-plays

Task 1

Carrying out a conversation about a complaint.

Student A refers to the paragraph A, and student B refers to the paragraph B.

Paragraph A: You placed an order with a company last month. Now you have received the shipment of that order, yet found that some cartons are broken and some parts are damaged. So, the quantity is not enough now. You make a call to that company to complain and ask for more replacement.

Paragraph B: You accepted an order last month. You have delivered the ordered articles to the buyer. Now you receive the complaints from the buyer on the shortage of quantity caused by the defectiveness. You tell the customer there is a carton of spare parts attached with the shipment and you can send more replacements if needed.

Here are some useful expressions:

(1) ABC company, can I help you?

(2) This is ...

(3) We received ..., we found ...

(4) Don't worry. There is ...

(5) What if ...

Task 2

Making up a conversation about a complaint.

Student A refers to the paragraph A, and student B refers to the paragraph B.

Paragraph A: You work in a "dot com" company and recently you have to work overtime frequently. You have grumbles about this, and complain to your colleague.

Paragraph B: You work in a IT company and recently you and your colleague have to work for more hours per day due to a new task. Your colleague complains about the overtime, you just initiate a talk with him.

Here are some useful expressions:

(1) What's the problem? You have a long face.

(2) I have to work overtime recently and I have no time to ...

(3) I can understand you ... but ...

III. Conversation Activity

Topic: Who is next?

Purpose: Practice Complaining and Persuading

Participants: Whole class

Procedures:

1. The whole class stands up and moves around.

2. Each student acts both as a customer and a shop assistant in turn.

3. The teacher (customer) sets the ball rolling by making a complaint and then asking one student (assistant) to offer the excuses and solutions. The student (assistant) can either accept or refuse the complaint, but he/she must make the customer feel satisfied.

4. After satisfying the customer, the assistant turns to be the customer and hunts for next assistant in the class.

5. Repeat the above process among the class.

IV. Actual Practice

1. Complain to the given people in the given situations.

(1) You want to return a pair of new pants because you found a hole in them.

(2) Ask a waitress to bring you water with ice because the water she gave you is warm.

(3) You are eating in a restaurant and someone begins to smoke next to you, ask him / her to stop.

2. Respond to these complaints in the restaurant.

(1) Miss, can you ask the cook to heat this food up? It's too cold.

(2) Excuse me, but do you mind if you speak a little softer? I can't speak with the people at my table.

(3) Waiter, there aren't enough chairs for us here.

V. Creative Discussion

The teacher divides the class into groups and asks them to discuss, then chooses the representatives of each group after discussion. The student who expresses well will be the winner.

Topic:

There is an expression in English that "The customer is always right." when a dispute appears between the customers and the sellers. There is also another expression that "Business is business", that is, no sellers would like to lose money in business. How do you keep the balance in between?

Chapter 20 Banquet and Parting

Learning Objectives
Upon completion of this chapter, you will be able to

- get used to the process of having a banquet.
- learn how to communicate with foreigners at the banquet.
- know how to make a toast at the banquet.
- conduct welcome and farewell speeches at the banquet.

课文范读

Part A Situational Dialogue

 Communicative Scene 1

At the Table

(*Mr. Smith and his colleagues are invited by Ms. Liu, board chairman of the enterprise corporation to a dinner at a restaurant.*)

Liu: Good evening, Mr. Smith! Welcome to our dinner party.

Smith: Good evening, Chairman! Thank you for inviting us to dinner.

Liu: You're welcome! First, please allow me to introduce my colleague to you. Mr. Smith, This is Wang Hong, the production manager of our company. And this is Mr. Smith, Vice General Manager of American Electronic Company.

Wang: Pleased to meet you, Mr. Smith.

Smith: It's my pleasure, too.

Liu: Now that everybody knows everybody else,[1] shall we sit and talk?

(*They all take seats.*)

Smith: I was told that they serve good food here in this restaurant.

Liu: Yes, the food here is excellent. And the service here is also beyond comparison.

Liu: Mr. Smith, I wonder if you have a particular preference?

Smith: Well, when in Rome, do as the Romans do.[2]

Liu: Then I hope that our selection of dishes this evening will be to your liking.[3]

Smith: We have heard a great deal about the famous Chinese dishes and we are looking forward to tasting them.

Liu: So you may also want to use chopsticks as we Chinese do? Of course, you may still use knife and fork if you don't feel confident with chopsticks.

Smith: I'll try chopsticks, but I'm afraid if I use them all the way through, I'll come back to the hotel with a half empty stomach. So, I'll also use knife and fork in case I have problems taming my chopsticks.

(*All laugh.*)

Liu: And what do you like to drink?

Smith: We'd like to have Chinese drinks. But we haven't got the faintest idea of the Chinese drinks. Would you please recommend me some?

Liu: Yes, of course. We have some famous brands of alcohol, such as Maotai, Wuliangye, Jiannanchun, Kongfu Jiajiu, and so on. And we also have some good red wine and white wine, such as Changyu Red Wine and Great Wall White Wine. Which do you prefer?

Smith: They say that Maotai tastes quite good.

Liu: Yes. It is one of the most famous liquors in China. It's good indeed. It never goes to the head.

Smith: OK! I'd like to try it.

(*Dinner is served.*)

Liu: Here are the Chinese cold dishes. <u>Please help yourself and make yourself at home.</u>[4]

Smith: Thank you. These dishes are all delicious.

Liu: I'm glad you like it. May I help you to some more?

Smith: Thank you, just a small helping.

Liu: Have some Beijing roast duck, this is one of Beijing's famous delicacies.

Smith: Yes, please. Oh, how delicious! It's tender and crisp. I've never tasted anything like that.

Liu: Really? So please have some more.

Smith: Thank you. From what I heard about your banquets, there are many more courses to come. So I think I'd better go easy at the beginning.

Liu: Mr. Smith, you seem to be quite an expert at chopsticks.

Smith: Thank you for encouraging me.

Liu: How about some prawns?

Smith: Yes, please. It's tasty too.

Liu: <u>You seem to have a good appetite.</u>[5] (Joking) <u>This calls for a drink.</u>[6] To your health, cheers!

All: Cheers!

Smith: By the way, what do you say in Chinese for "<u>Bottoms up</u>[7]"?

Liu: We say "Gan Bei".

Smith: <u>Well, I wish to propose a toast to our friendship and cooperation, Gan Bei!</u>[8]

Liu: You are learning fast, Mr. Smith. Gan Bei!

Smith: This one is really palatable. What is it?

Liu: I don't know its English name, but in Chinese we call it "suji", which literally means "vegetarian's chicken".

Smith: Suji? Er, incredibly tasty!

Liu: Let me help you to some seafood hot pot, the specialty of this restaurant.

Smith: Please. I'm fond of sea food. It's fresh and tasty. And it looks beautiful.

Liu: Yes, <u>Chinese cuisine places stress on color, aroma and flavor all at the same time.</u>[9] Oh, would you like to have some Jiaozi?

Smith: What is it?

Liu: It is a kind of boiled dumpling stuffed with minced meat and vegetable.

Smith: Sounds interesting. I'd like to have some.

Smith: <u>This Specially Flavored Chicken really works up my appetite.</u>[10]

Liu: <u>It seems we have the same taste.</u>[11] Help yourself to some more, please.

Smith: Thank you, but I have to watch my weight.

Communicative Scene 2

Make a Toast

(Almost an hour has passed since the dinner started. Chairman Liu clears her throat and stands up with a glass of wine in her hand. Everyone stops talking and turns towards her.)

Mr. Smith,

Ladies and gentlemen:

I don't want to spoil your enjoyment of this evening's festivities with a long and boring speech, but I would just like to say a few words.

<u>On behalf of our company, I would like to say how delighted to have Mr. Smith and his colleagues with us tonight.</u>[12] As the saying goes, <u>"What a joy it is to have friends coming from afar!"</u>[13] <u>Our distinguished guests come from the other side of the earth, so our joy tonight is beyond expression.</u>[14]

I'm glad to tell you that this trip of our American friends has been very fruitful—we've struck a deal worth 30 million dollars and reached an agreement for long-term cooperation, which has sown the seeds for a bright future of our business relations. The only regret is that your stay is too brief, so I look forward to another chance to receive you in China.

I'd like to take this opportunity to propose a toast to the friendship between our two companies, to the prosperity of our two companies, to a pleasant journey tomorrow. Cheers!

All: Bottoms up!

(All the people stand up and raise their glass, then take a sip of wine and clap.)

 Communicative Scene 3

A Reciprocal Reception

Chairman Liu,

Distinguished guest, ladies and gentlemen:

Thank you for your kind words, Chairman Liu. I'd like to take this opportunity to express our sincere thanks to your nice welcome and hospitality.

I believe we have accomplished a great deal during our brief stay. We have concluded a deal worth 30 million dollars and reached an agreement for long-term cooperation. More importantly, we have seen and talked with your people. We have dined with you, drunk with you, bargained, worried and laughed with you. In all this, our respect has grown, our friendship warmed. We have certainly achieved more than we hoped, and I'd like you all to know that we are most appreciative of your efforts in making this possible.

Tomorrow, my colleagues and I are leaving your beautiful city, but we will remember this pleasant visit all the time. And I hope that one day you can also visit our city so that we can reciprocate your warmness and hospitality.

Now, may I propose a toast? Here is to our hosts, to your good health, and, of course, to our friendship and our mutual cooperation. Cheers!

All: Cheers!

(*Warm flutters of applause. And the next course is served. The dinner goes on for another twenty minutes or so, as does the lively flow of conversation.*)

Words and Expressions

1. board chairman		董事长
2. preference	*n.*	偏爱，偏爱的东西
3. chopsticks	*n.*	筷子
4. knife and fork		刀叉
5. tame	*v.*	驯服
6. helping	*n.*	（食物的）一份
7. delicacy	*n.*	佳肴
8. tender and crisp		又脆又嫩
9. prawn	*n.*	对虾
10. tasty	*adj.*	美味的
11. cheers	*v.*	干杯（举杯敬酒之用语）
12. palatable	*adj.*	可口的，美味的
13. vegetarian	*n.*	素食（主义）者
14. incredibly	*adv.*	不可思议地
15. seafood hot pot		海鲜火锅
16. specialty	*n.*	特色菜
17. cuisine	*n.*	烹调
18. aroma	*n.*	芳香；香味
19. flavor	*n.*	味道
20. dumpling	*n.*	团子
21. stuffed with minced meat		肉馅的
22. Specially Flavored Chicken		怪味鸡
23. watch my weight		注意我的体重
24. clear her throat		清清喉咙
25. spoil	*v.*	损坏
26. festivity	*n.*	欢乐气氛

27. sip	v.	啜
28. reciprocate	v.	回报
29. hospitality	n.	好客
30. flutter	v.	拍打

1. Now that everybody knows everybody else.
   既然大家都互相认识了。
   ① now that 既然，由于
   Now that John's arrived, we can begin.
   约翰来了，我们可以开始。

2. When in Rome, do as the Romans do.
   入乡随俗（谚语）。
   亦可说：Do in Rome as the Romans do.
   英语中常用的含有Rome的谚语还有：
   All roads lead to Rome.
   条条大路通罗马。
   Rome was not built in a day.
   罗马非一日建成。

3. Then I hope that our selection of dishes this evening will be to your liking.
   那么我期望我们今晚选择的菜肴你们能够喜欢。
   ① to one's liking 对某人的胃口，合某人的意
   Was the meal to your liking, madam?
   太太，饭菜合您的意吗？

4. Please help yourself and make yourself at home.
   请自便，就像在自己家里一样。
   ① make oneself at home 随便（像在家里一样），不要拘礼
   Make yourself at home while I get some coffee.
   随便坐吧，我去倒杯咖啡。

5. You seem to have a good appetite.
   你看来胃口不错。
   在餐桌上一般不评论客人的胃口或体重，以免冒犯客人，但开玩笑可用。此处为开玩笑。
   ① have a good/healthy appetite 胃口好，食欲很好

6. This calls for a drink.
   这值得干一杯。
   ①call for 要求，提倡
   President Xi called for building together the Belt and Road Initiative, and push forward the building

of a community with a shared future for mankind.

习主席号召积极共建"一带一路",推动构建人类命运共同体。

② call for 需要,值得

Are you getting married? This calls for a celebration.

你要结婚了?这值得大大庆祝一番。

7. Bottoms up!

干杯!

中西方文化不同,中国人流行劝酒,西方一般不提倡一饮而尽的干杯 Bottoms up或Gan Bei! 敬酒时的用语,最好说Cheers!

8. Well, I wish to propose a toast to our friendship and cooperation.

那么,我想提议为了我们的友谊和合作,干杯!

① propose a toast to 提议为……干杯

I propose a toast to the health of all the guests.

我提议为所有来宾的健康干杯!

9. Chinese cuisine places stresses on color, aroma and flavor all at the same time.

中国菜肴强调色香味俱全。

① place stress on 强调

The teacher place particular stress on the need for accuracy.

教师特别强调准确的重要性。

10. This Specially Flavored Chicken really works up my appetite.

这怪味鸡使我胃口大开。

① work up my appetite 使我胃口大开

11. It seems we have the same taste.

看来咱俩的口味相同。

① to one's taste 合乎某人的口味

Oh, they look delicious, I'm sure they will be to my taste.

菜看起来味道很不错,一定会对我的口味。

12. on behalf of our company... 我代表本公司……

① on behalf on 代表,为了,因为

The president can't be here today, so I'm going to speak on his behalf.

今天总裁不能来,我将代表他发言。

13. What a joy it is to have friends coming from afar!

(谚语)有朋自远方来,不亦乐乎!

14. Our distinguished guests come from the other side of the earth, so our joy tonight is beyond expression.

我们尊贵的客人来自地球的另一边,所以我们今晚的欢喜是无法形容的。

① distinguished 尊贵的,杰出的

② a distinguished writer 一个杰出的作家

③ distinguished guests 贵宾

Part B Practical Key Sentences

1. **welcome to ...**

   Welcome to our dinner party.

   非常乐意邀请你加入我们酒会。

   be welcome to ... 可以随意

   You are welcome to attend the business conference.

   欢迎参加商务会议。

   替换表达:

   Welcome to China!

   Welcome to our country!

2. **take a seat**

   Shall we sit and talk?

   请坐下谈。

   这个句型用于邀请客人入席。

   替换表达:

   Will you take this seat, please?

   Be seated, please.

   Please sit here on my right.

   Shall we go into the dining-room?

   Shall we go this way to the dinner table?

   Come on. Let's go into the dining-hall.

3. **make yourself at home**

   Please help yourself and make yourself at home.

   别客气,请随便吃。

   这个句型用于用餐时让客人放轻松,可以使客人感到宾至如归。还可以用以下几种表达法:

   Please help yourself to whatever you like.

   Enjoy yourself!

   Don't stand on ceremony.

   别讲究客套,别客气。

   Take your jacket off, we don't stand on ceremony at our home.

   脱下你的夹克吧,我们家里不拘泥于礼节。

   Please don't stand on ceremony!

4. **Let me help you to ...**

   Let me help you to some seafood hot pot.

   我给您来点海鲜火锅。

这句型为餐桌上主人向客人让餐时常用的句型。

help sb. to sth. 给某人拿/取某物

Let me help you to the roast duck.

我给您夹块烤鸭。

help oneself to 自己亲自拿或取某物

Please help yourself to a steak.

请来一块牛排。

常用的让餐的表达法还有：

Would you like to have some more... (roast duck, beef, fish)

May I help you to some more...

5. this calls for a drink

This calls for a drink. To your health, cheers!

值得喝一杯。为您的健康，干杯！

这句话用于餐桌上敬酒。

替换表达：

Now, let's drink a toast to our guests.

I wish to propose a toast to... (our cooperation)

Let me propose a toast to... (our good relationship)

Let's drink to... (the success of our talks)

6. go to someone's head

（酒）上头，使某人醉

It never goes to the head.

不会使人醉。

The wine went straight to my head.

我很快感到酒力上头了。

这个句型常用于席间劝酒，还可以说：

A drop won't hurt.

喝一点酒没关系。

I've had a drop too much.

我有点醉意。

Part C Integration of Theory and Practice

1. the congratulatory words 祝语

【知识点】在演讲结束时，常用一些表示祝贺或祝福的话语，使气氛达到高潮。以下是一些常用的祝贺语：

【技能训练句型】

I hope this gathering will help keep our friendship till the end.

希望这次聚会能使我们的友谊地久天长。

Now, let us propose a toast on this happy occasion. Here's to our friendship!

现在,在这欢乐的时刻,让我们举杯庆贺,为我们的友谊干杯!

We take our hats off to you. Good luck and God bless you.

我们向您致敬!愿您福星高照,愿上帝保佑您。

We wish you the very best of luck in your future.

我们祝您一帆风顺、万事如意!

May the friendship between our two countries be further developed and consolidated.

愿我们两国之间的友谊进一步发展和巩固。

All our best wishes for you.

衷心祝你万事如意。

Best wishes to you.

祝你万事如意。

2. ordering the food 点菜

【知识点】点菜在中西方也有较大的不同。在中国讲究客随主便,通常是由主人点菜。而西方人则认为点菜是能否享受饮食的第一步,所以总是请客人点菜。接待国外的客人时,许多客人对当地的饮食可能并不熟悉,所以点菜的时候问客人喜欢吃什么菜是一种礼节。

【技能训练句型】

What kind of food do you like?

What drinks do you like?

Do you like Chinese food?

What would you like to have?

3. different eating habits 不同的饮食习惯

【知识点】东西方的饮食习惯也有极大的不同。比如西方人喜欢吃生菜,即使肉类、鱼类等食物也煮得很生。他们认为煮得太熟会破坏食物的营养价值,蔬菜也大多生吃。因此在吃西餐时,服务员一般都会询问客人所点的菜要做成什么样子。西方对食物的生熟程度一般分为5种: rare(半熟)、medium rare(中等偏生)、medium(中等熟)、medium well(中等偏熟)、well-done(熟透)。

【技能训练句型】

How would you like your steak?

Do you want your steak well-done, medium or rare?

Rare, please.

4. etiquette of eating western-style food 西餐礼仪

【知识点】(1)吃西餐时使用刀叉,一般是右手持刀,左手执叉。每道菜吃完后,将刀叉并拢平放在盘里,以示吃完。如未吃完,应摆成八字或交叉放着,刀口应向内。

(2)喝茶或咖啡时,应右手拿杯把,左手拿盛杯的小碟。

(3)在吃西餐时,应把餐巾铺在双膝上。中途离席时,应把餐巾放在椅子上,如放在桌上则意味着你不想吃了。餐巾应用来擦嘴，不能用来擦汗。

5. menu　菜谱

【知识点】中国人在请客时要准备很多菜，还要说"菜不多，请多包涵"之类的客气话。而英美人招待客人则一般只准备三、四道菜。

英美人请客比较正规的菜谱如下。

第一道：开胃食品（appetizer）——汤、果汁或色拉。

第二道：主食（main course）——往往是一种肉或鱼，配以土豆、蔬菜、调味品等。

第三道：甜食（dessert）——冰淇淋、水果馅饼或布丁等。

6. different kinds of wine　不同种类的酒

【知识点】酒在宴会中也是不可或缺的。英美人有饮酒的嗜好。英国人爱喝啤酒、葡萄酒和白兰地。美国人则爱喝白水、葡萄酒、啤酒、可乐等。美国人喝的葡萄酒（grape wine）带较重的酸味，所以又称这种酒为dry wine。有的英美人喝酒精含量较高的酒，如brandy、whisky，他们把这类酒称为liquor。

wine 通常分为以下四类：

（1）still wine 没有气体的酒　　例如：Dynasty 王朝葡萄酒

（2）sparkling wine 有气体的酒　　例如：champagne 香槟酒

（3）fortified wine 掺加烈酒的酒　　例如：sherry 雪梨酒

（4）distilled wine 经过蒸馏的酒　　例如：brandy 白兰地

Part D　Practice

I. Complete the Following Dialogues

A: I hope that the dishes tonight will be ___1___ your liking.

B: Thank you. These dishes are all delicious. They really work ___2___ my appetite.

A: Here are some cold dishes. Please help yourself and make yourself ___3___ home.

B: Thank you!

A: I'm glad that you have a good appetite. This calls ___4___ a drink. Cheers!

B: ___5___ our health, Gan Bei!

B: The wine also tastes quite good.

A: Yes, Maotai is one of the most famous liquors in China. It never goes ___6___ the head.

A: You seem to be quite an expert ___7___ chopsticks.

B: Thank you! I have practiced it for two months before I came to China.

A: Really? I'd like to propose a toast ___8___ your progress in using chopsticks. Cheers!

B: Cheers! Oh! This duck is not only tasty and fresh, but also beautiful!

A: Yes, Chinese cuisine places stress ___9___ color, aroma and flavor all at the same time.

B: I like it very much. Let's help ourselves ___10___ some more, please.

II. Oral Translation

Task 1

Translate the following sentences into English orally.

（1）我建议为我们的主人干杯。
（2）我代表所有在座的中国人说几句话。
（3）你们的特色菜是什么？
（4）我给您再夹些菜好么？
（5）为这，我们得喝一杯。为您的健康，干杯！
（6）这个火锅使我胃口大开。
（7）恐怕我得注意我的体重了。
（8）这种食物正合他的口味。
（9）谢谢你们的好客。
（10）那就入乡随俗吧。
（11）你有没有一些个人的喜好呢？
（12）希望今天的菜肴你能喜欢。
（13）请您自便吧。
（14）这种酒不会上头的。
（15）我对中国菜一点都不了解。

Task 2

Translate the following dialogue into English orally.

A: 谢谢你请我们赴宴。
B: 你们能出席我们的宴会，我们深感荣幸。我们入座吧。
A: 好的。听说这儿的菜很好吃，服务也无可比拟。
B: 是啊，你可以试一下。你有没有什么个人的喜好呢？
A: 没有，还是入乡随俗吧。
B: 我们再喝点酒吧？喝一点酒没关系的。
A: 够了，我有点醉意了。
B: 那再吃喝点汤吧，请不要客气。

III. Oral Practice

Task 1

Work in pairs.

You are hosting a dinner for your partner. Serve your partner with the following Chinese food:

(1) shredded pork with spicy sauce（鱼香肉丝）

(2) sour spicy soup（酸辣汤）

(3) sweet and sour spare-rib（糖醋排骨）

(4) prawn cooked with soy sauce（红烧明虾）

(5) specially flavored chicken（怪味鸡）

Task 2

Work in groups of two and practice proposing toasts and responding to toast to the following:

(1) friendship

(2) health

(3) family

(4) cooperation

(5) progress in speaking Chinese

IV. Situational Talks

Students work in pairs and make dialogues according to the following situation:

The hosts: Mr. Wang and his colleagues, Mr. Wang is the manager of Changyu Company.

The guests: Mr. Brown and his colleagues, come from Australia. Mr. Brown is the vice manager of Crane Company.

They are at a welcoming banquet. Mr. Brown and his colleagues have just arrived, their purpose of the journey this time is to investigate the cooperation possibility between the two companies.

(1) Dinner is ready. The host invites his guests to take a seat at the table and then make a toast to welcome them.

(2) Try to make a welcoming speech and thank you speech.

V. Creative Discussion

The teacher divides the class into several groups to discuss those questions below:

1. What are the common topics at the table? What kind of topics should be avoided?

2. List the table manners.

Appendix 1 Translation to Situational Dialogues

（情景对话参考译文）

第一章　迎接客户

第一部分　商务情景对话

交际精品1　办理海关手续费（出国经商）
（彭先生是中国机械进出口公司的经理，第一次出访美国。领取了行李后，他前往海关服务台。）
海关官员：下午好。请出示护照和报关申请表。
　　　彭：当然可以，给您。
海关官员：谢谢。还有健康申报表。
　　　彭：好，请稍候。哦，在这儿。
海关官员：您的国籍？
　　　彭：我是中国人。
海关官员：您不在意告知此行的目的吧？
　　　彭：一点也不，我们打算与机械公司进行洽谈，从贵国进口一些先进的设备。
海关官员：明白了，您打算逗留美国多长时间？
　　　彭：仅两周时间。
海关官员：这些是您的行李吗？
　　　彭：对。
海关官员：有什么特别的东西要申报纳税吗？
　　　彭：我想没有，除了一部数码相机、一些样品和个人用品。这些是免税的吗？
海关官员：样品和个人用品免税。
　　　彭：我随身携带2万美元，需要申报吗？
海关官员：是的，请填写货币申报单。
　　　彭：好，我就填写。
海关官员：谢谢。
　　　彭：通关手续办完了吗？
海关官员：是，您的通关手续办好了。请往前走，这边请。
　　　彭：谢谢。

交际精品2　机场迎宾
（谢莉是中国进出口公司的秘书，她在机场迎接来自巴西公司的琼斯先生。）
谢莉：请问，是从巴西公司来的琼斯先生吗？

琼斯：对，我就是。我想我们未曾见过面。
谢莉：是的，可以冒昧地自我介绍吗？我叫谢莉，是中国进出口公司的秘书。
琼斯：认识您真高兴！
谢莉：我也很高兴。欢迎到北京！
琼斯：谢谢。很荣幸有机会再次来贵国。
谢莉：我们公司的执行总裁本打算亲自到机场接您，但是很遗憾他今天因重要商务无法脱身。
琼斯：没关系。我知道他可是个大忙人。
谢莉：您完全有理由这么说。他的事业很成功，而且为人也踏实，确实是个容易合作的人。
琼斯：他对我们的业务进展帮助很大，我真想见到他。
谢莉：飞行旅程怎么样？长途旅行后您一定很累了。
琼斯：哦，不，旅行既舒服又愉快。但我无法在飞机上入睡，现在有些飞行时差反应。
谢莉：在我们洽谈前请您好好休息一下。
琼斯：那再好不过了。
谢莉：我们已在美丽的湖畔为您预订了住房。希望您在北京过得愉快。
琼斯：您考虑得十分周到。
谢莉：我们现在回酒店歇息好吗？
琼斯：好极了！

交际精品3　相互介绍

（郑东晓正在迎接一家跨国公司的总裁密尔顿·沃尔特。他想认识销售经理山姆·奥登先生。）

郑东晓：早上好！如果我没搞错的话，您一定是跨国公司的总裁沃尔特先生吧。请允许我自我介绍，我叫郑东晓。
沃尔特：您好！我是密尔顿·沃尔特。
郑东晓：您好！我常听到关于您的事情，很久以来一直期望与您相见。
沃尔特：请问，你的名字怎么拼写？我觉得中国人的名字很难记。
郑东晓：Z-h-e-n-g D-o-n-g-x-i-a-o。我的名片上有。这是我的名片。
沃尔特：好，我现在记住了。喏，这是我的。
郑东晓：谢谢。请替我引见那位营销部经理好吗？
沃尔特：你们还没见过面吗？
郑东晓：嗯，还没有。
沃尔特：我很乐意把他介绍给你。
郑东晓：好的。
沃尔特：山姆，来见见东晓。这位是山姆，我的同事。
郑东晓：您好，山姆·奥登先生！经过多次的电子邮件、电话和传真联系后，真高兴终于和您见面了。
奥登：是，终于见面了！见到您真好。
郑东晓：我来帮你们拿行李吧。
奥登：谢谢。
郑东晓：不客气！我们安排一下明天的行程吧。

沃尔特：我建议明天上午十点见。
郑东晓：这是我专为您和奥登先生制定的日程表，希望能符合你们的要求。
沃尔特：好，我回宾馆再看。
郑东晓：再见！
沃尔特：再见！

第二章　寻找贸易机会

第一部分　商务情景对话

交际精品1　寻找贸易机会技巧

（范欣小姐刚从大学毕业，就职于中国茶叶出口公司。她急于开拓业务，于是求教经验丰富的业务员刘涛。）

刘：范欣，你好像有心事，有什么想说吗？
范：哦，刘先生，我想问您几个问题。
刘：行，请讲。
范：您知道，我是新手，缺乏经验。您可否告诉我如何寻找贸易机会？
刘：当然可以，行行都有窍门。
范：我渴望着学会。
刘：进入21世纪，贸易方式发生了很大变化。我们可以通过许多渠道与相隔千万里外的公司建立起商务联系。
范：听起来很有趣。
刘：我想向你介绍一些主要的渠道。依我看来，当今寻找客户最有效的方法是通过网络查寻，优势在于既快捷又便宜。你可以在网络搜寻到预期的客户。
范：好主意。很遗憾我居然在课堂上没学多少。
刘：电子商务在现代商务中起重要作用，在网上寻找潜在的客户方便省时。我们不必到处奔波寻找客户，正所谓"秀才不出门，便知天下事"。
范：啊，真想马上就试试。
刘：还有商会是获得信息和联系商人的重要渠道。
范：商会是什么？
刘：商会是商人的组织机构，主要任务之一就是要帮助公司和成员提供商贸信息和寻找贸易机会。
范：我记住了，还有吗？
刘：查看工商名录也非常有用。
范：我该怎样查？
刘：你可以按具体的行业分类查找。你就会获得你期望的公司名称、地址和电话号码。
范：我从书本学到银行总是为商人提供公司名称地址。
刘：实际上这并不确切。银行帮助公司进行资信调查，但同时又要对客户的信息保密。实际上现在外贸活动中依赖银行帮助寻找客户不太靠得住。

范：哦，真的吗？
刘：过去出版的外贸书籍某些观点也许已过时了。你学习时要注意摒弃旧观念。
范：说得是！
刘：你可以从驻外使馆商务处、报纸杂志的广告获得必要的信息。参加交易会可能有与客户接触的好机会，但费用昂贵。
范：嗯，我明白。
刘：当你得到所需的姓名与地址后，就可通过发电子邮件、传真或打电话开展业务。
范：噢，是的。
刘：由于通信方式的改善，我们不再需要到邮局发电报或电传了。
范：是呀，现代化已使电报和电传过时了。
刘：目前通信最基本和最快速的途径是发电子邮件、传真或打电话。
范：我同意。
刘：我们可以通过国际互联网和电脑随时与任何人联系。
范：原来在办公室就有可能做成生意。我现在对开展贸易更是充满信心。

交际精品2　联系客户

（范欣小姐正在与一家国外的公司接触，寻找贸易机会。）

范：喂，我找进口部经理。
兰斯：我是进口部的兰斯，请问您是哪位？
范：我是中国茶叶出口公司的范欣。
兰斯：我能为您做些什么？
范：通过国际互联网，我得知贵公司是欧洲市场主要的茶业进口商之一。我很高兴地向您介绍本公司，我们是专业从事茶叶产品生产和出口的。
兰斯：哦，我很感兴趣。你能告诉我贵公司的经营范围吗？
范：当然可以。我们公司信誉卓越，出口红茶、白茶、绿茶、乌龙茶和茉莉花茶等各种各样的茶。公司在此行业已有50多年之久的经营历史。
兰斯：真不错。那茶叶的质量怎样？
范：您尽可放心。我们经营的茶叶以其优异的品质深受广大消费者的喜爱。公司拥有自己的加工厂和一批经验丰富的技术人员。我们的一级茉莉花茶荣获国际优质奖。
兰斯：太让人心动了。目前袋泡茶很适应现代消费的习惯。贵公司可否供货？
范：行，我们全力以赴开发新市场，不断推出新产品。为满足国际市场的需要，我们正在生产袋泡茶。
兰斯：真巧！我们求之不得。
范：我们还生产冰茶和乌龙浓缩液，该产品冲泡方便。
兰斯：好。若您能寄来产品目录或小册子，将有助于我们的进一步研究。
范：为了让贵方大体了解对我方的产品，我们将通过快递寄出我方最新附图目录，以供细阅。
兰斯：请寄一些袋泡茶和茶叶新产品的样品。
范：没问题。

兰斯：我们研究后就通知贵方结果。
范：好，期待着尽快收到贵方的好消息。

交际精品3　建立贸易关系
（兰斯先生正在与范欣小姐联系，建立贸易关系。）
兰斯：喂，范小姐，我是兰斯。
范：您好，兰斯先生。
兰斯：收到贵方邮寄来的小册子、袋泡茶和茶叶新产品的样品。
范：您认为我方的产品怎样？
兰斯：经过仔细检查，我们发现贵方的茶叶正如上回您所说的那样，品质上乘、包装精美。
范：确实如此。重合同、守信用是我们的经营原则。
兰斯：我方就贵方的袋泡茶和茶叶新产品做了市场调查，发现很受市场欢迎。
范：那太好了。
兰斯：鉴于贵方的茶叶产品与我方的经营范围一致，我们愿意同贵公司建立业务关系。
范：贵公司想同我方建立业务关系的愿望与我们是一致的。建立直接的业务关系，双方将互利互惠。
兰斯：毫无疑问，这将给我们双方带来更紧密的联系。
范：我方与国外的贸易总是建立在平等互利的基础上。
兰斯：我明白。我们正考虑与贵司扩大业务。
范：如能这样，我太高兴了。
兰斯：哦，是的。我方愿意在这行业与贵司开展业务。
范：好极了！
兰斯：我想用电子邮件与您探讨更具体的业务事宜。
范：行。我们之间的相互了解与合作必将促成今后的生意。
兰斯：再见。
范：再见。

第三章　询价

第一部分　商务情景对话

交际精品1　一般询价
（鲁宾逊纺织品进口公司经理汉纳太太正在对一家纺织品有限公司进行一般询价。）
汉纳：您好，是纺织品有限公司吗？
薛：是的，有事吗？
汉纳：我是鲁宾逊纺织品进口公司的安娜·汉纳。我们看到刊登在《中国日报》上的广告，贵公司的纺织品看起来真是好极了。
薛：哦，真的吗？
汉纳：我们是纺织品的进口商。近来我们做了市场调查，发现你方广告刊登的纺织品在我国市场前景广阔。因此，我们想把生意扩大到中国市场。
薛：嗯，好主意！请问您对什么产品感兴趣？
汉纳：我们对布匹和纺织成品很感兴趣。
薛：唔，我们是一家大型纺织品生产公司，生产高质量的色布、花布和全棉服装。我们生产多种男女服装和童装，例如：夹克衫、衬衫、裙装、裤子、牛仔服、睡衣和运动装。
汉纳：哇，真了不起！
薛：自从中国加入WTO后，我们的纺织品在国际市场变得越来越有竞争力。
汉纳：这就是我们与贵公司联系的原因。
薛：我们愿和贵公司建立业务关系。
汉纳：我也这么想。相信通过双方的共同努力，我们的贸易关系会得到持续扩展。
薛：完全赞成。
汉纳：能否寄给我们目录和必要的信息供我方参考？
薛：当然可以。我们打算快邮寄上附图目录和一些免费样品，以供你方考虑。
汉纳：若是您能附上这些服装的价格单，我们将不胜感激。
薛：好，我们乐意效劳。但由于近期原料价格不断上涨，这些价格应以我方最后确认为准。
汉纳：噢，天哪！我们希望价格应合理。
薛：当然了，汉纳太太。尽管原材料价格上涨，我方价格仍均有竞争力。
汉纳：请问你们一般采取什么出口条件？
薛：我们在价格单上通常报FOB价格。如果知道对方目的港，我方可根据客户要求报CIF 或 CFR价格。
汉纳：很好。能付给我们佣金吗？
薛：没问题。
汉纳：好，那就开始干吧。

交际精品2　具体询价

（来自加拿大进口公司的佩恩先生正在具体询价。）

佩恩：杨小姐，我想感谢你寄来活页说明和样品，我在周一就收到了。
杨：我很高兴。
佩恩：我们对外观漂亮的电熨斗特别感兴趣。
杨：很好。您更喜欢哪种型号？
佩恩：我们打算购买E013型和E016型的电熨斗。它的电器参数是AC 220V、1000W，但我对蒸汽发生方式还不清楚。
杨：是滴下式的。
佩恩：你现在有现货吗？
杨：有，可供现货出口。
佩恩：太好了！感恩节临近，我们急需这些产品，贵方何时可以装运？
杨：别担心，我们将根据您的请求立即装运。
佩恩：好。请报这两种型号的竞争性CIF温哥华价格，我们将不胜感激。
杨：很好，但能否告知贵方想要的数量，以便我们计算价格？

佩恩：我们打算订100,000台电熨斗，即两种型号各50,000台。
杨：明白，您总共需要100,000台电熨斗。
佩恩：完全正确。
杨：我想您一定注意到最近国际市场原材料的价格暴涨。
佩恩：天哪，我想您不会开玩笑吧。能保持原来具有竞争的价格吗？
杨：我不开玩笑。不过，考虑到我们新建立的友好关系，尽管原材料价格不断上涨，我方的价格仍然维持不变。
佩恩：很高兴听您这样说。顺便问一下，能否寄给我们电熨斗的形式发票？
杨：哦，贵方需要形式发票？
佩恩：是的，这有助于做好预先的进口安排。
杨：明白了。
佩恩：希望尽快收到对我方询价的答复。
杨：我会的。

交际精品3　首次询价

（哈特先生正在对他从未交易过的供应商作首次询价。）

秘书：下午好！家具实业公司。
哈特：您好！请找付先生。
秘书：请稍等。
付：您好！我姓付。
哈特：我是哈特。我国的商会把您的大名和公司介绍给我们。我们了解到贵公司专门经营新型家具。
付：是的。请问您需要哪一种家具？
哈特：我们对藤制家具很感兴趣。
付：太好了。我们从事此行业已有25年，现正在生产新款的木、藤、竹、柳家具。我们的藤制家具在国际市场很畅销。
哈特：是的。我相信贵方的藤制家具在我国市场也会旺销。
付：我有同感。
哈特：若您能报出有竞争性的藤制家具欧洲主要港口成本加运费价，我们将感到十分高兴。
付：谢谢您的询盘。
哈特：需要特别强调的是价格应具有竞争性，因为我方客户对价格特别敏感。
付：我们保证所报价格极具竞争性，足以吸引客户。
哈特：谢谢。若价格可行，我们准备首次向贵方下试订单。
付：明白。
哈特：我们的客户见到藤制家具后，就会下大订单。
付：希望如此。
哈特：能否帮忙寄上更多相关宣传小册子，以便我们分发给客户。
付：当然可以。
哈特：我们期待着贵方报盘。

付：我们计算后，就会尽快告知贵方。

第四章　商务约会与安排

第一部分　商务情景对话

交际精品1　商务约会
（林小姐打电话给韦德先生约定在广交会见面。）
　林：喂，韦德先生吗？我是中国福州的林小姐。
韦德：您好，林小姐。我很高兴接到您的电话。
　林：广交会快到了，我想知道您是否打算参加这次春季广交会。
韦德：是的，我们打算参加这次广交会。如能在会上与您见面，我们将非常荣幸。
　林：我也热切希望见到您，因为我们有许多事情和您面谈。不知道您是否有空？能否告知您的日程，以便我们预先做出安排？
韦德：有空，我们将于4月14日至25日在广州。你们什么时间方便呢？
　林：我们将于4月16日至18日在广州。在此期间的任何时候都可与您会面。
韦德：好的。4月17日晚上6点如何？
　林：行，那就4月17日晚上6点在您下榻宾馆的大厅见。您在广州的宾馆预订了吗？
韦德：还没有。你能帮忙预订吗？4月14日开始，共12天。
　林：当然可以。您要订几个房间？您对宾馆有什么特殊要求吗？
韦德：没有。我的同事布朗顿先生将与我同行，所以请预订两个标准间。
　林：好，我们马上办。
韦德：噢，请订方便去交易会的宾馆，因为我们对广州不熟悉，不想每天在来回的路上花太多的时间。
　林：不用担心，我们会尽力的。我想华侨饭店是很好的选择，步行就可到达交易会。您就不必再烦心交通问题。
韦德：考虑得真周到。
　林：别客气。我们此次要谈哪些项目？
韦德：我们想谈谈烧烤炉、烧烤架和烧烤用具。请带上相关的样品。
　林：一定。还有其他的吗？
韦德：我们会带上新品种的样品，比如餐具、开瓶器等。正如您所知，我们经营各种各样的厨房用品和卫浴用品。希望双方之间的合作能一步一步地扩大。
　林：很高兴听到这些。房间预订好后，我会再打电话给您。
韦德：谢谢您来电话，林小姐，再见。
　林：谢谢！再见。

交际精品2　更改约会
（韦德先生打电话给林小姐更改约会。）
韦德：喂，林小姐，我是墨西哥城的韦德。
　林：您好，韦德先生。很高兴又接到您的电话。

韦德:非常感谢为我们预订的华侨宾馆,然而我非常抱歉地通知您,我们不得不取消这个预订。
林:怎么啦,您要取消中国之行吗?
韦德:不,不。我们的访问日程不变。我国的代表团将住在花园宾馆。我们更愿意和全体代表团成员住在一起。
林:明白了。没问题,我将取消您的预订。
韦德:太感谢了,对此造成的不便深表歉意,我为此道歉。
林:完全不必。我们按计划4月17日晚上6点在花园宾馆大厅里见好吗?
韦德:恐怕因未预料之事,我还得推迟约会。
林:没关系。那么,晚上7:30行吗?
韦德:那就说定了。
林:为什么不一起吃晚饭呢?我们想邀请你们一道在花园宾馆进晚餐。我们可以边吃边谈。
韦德:真是太客气了。顺便问一下,贵公司在广交会上有摊位吗?
林:有,您会在交易会上看到我们的新产品。
韦德:您不在期间谁来负责我们的生意和订单的生产呢?请一定保证我们的货物按时发货,因为这些产品的季节性很强,即使是一点延误都可能引起大麻烦。
林:嗯,我的同事会负责的。我在广州仅待三天。乘飞机从广州到我们的城市仅需一小时。我保证你们的订单会按时完工并及时发货。
韦德:十分感谢。我的手机号码是:555-753-9900,24小时开机。有必要时,就打电话给我。
林:好的。我的手机号码是013905622789。
韦德:那我们广州见。祝您快乐!
林:祝您快乐!再见。

交际精品3 行程安排

(薛小姐正在为莫尔先生做出安排。)
莫尔:喂,薛小姐,您好吗?
薛:我很好,谢谢!有事吗?
莫尔:有。您知道,我下周将去参加广交会。我将在那儿待两周以上。在第一期和第二期展会之间有四天的空闲。我到广州很多趟了,因此我可能只好待在宾馆里无所事事。
薛:您打算到其他地方旅行吗?
莫尔:是的,你说得很对。这次我想带夫人一起去。
薛:这是您夫人第一次到中国吗?
莫尔:对。
薛:那您们想去什么样的地方呢?
莫尔:我没有什么主意,尽管我到过中国许多次,但我总是待在广州做生意。
薛:噢,我明白您的情况。您知道中国很大,四天时间在中国旅行是不够的。如果您和夫人喜欢轻松休闲,我建议去海南岛或者桂林,在那儿,你们可享受美丽的大自然。如果你们对历史名胜感兴趣,我想可以去西安。
莫尔:您能大概介绍一下那个岛吗?我们来自内陆国家,更愿意到岛上去玩。

薛：好的。海南岛是中国的第二大岛，在四月份，它的热带气候很温和迷人。您可以在海边享受阳光，在那里玩得开心。

莫尔：好极了。我们该怎么走？

薛：可乘飞机去，仅大约一小时的飞行路程。如果您同意，我可以联系旅行社做出安排，这样可让您的旅行更方便和舒服。

莫尔：真是好主意。能帮我们预订吗？所有费用都由我们负担。

薛：没问题，很高兴能帮助您。我与旅行社安排好之后再发电子邮件告知您有关行程。

莫尔：真不知该怎么感谢才好。

薛：不用客气。再见。

莫尔：再见。

第五章　报价与还价

第一部分　商务情景对话

交际精品1　报盘

（史密斯先生是来自意大利的买家。艾瑞娜小姐是史密斯先生的助理。简是一家制衣公司的销售部经理。他们在谈论价格。）

简：史密斯先生，昨天玩得好吗？

史密斯：噢，很好。我们去了长城，玩得很愉快。

简：太好了！您呢，艾瑞娜小姐！第一次到中国玩得愉快吗？

艾瑞娜：噢，开心极了。

简：既然你们玩得愉快，那么现在该谈生意了吧！

史密斯：好吧。

简：好，现在我们言归正传。您8月24日的邮件提到，您想购买我们的女式上衣。

史密斯：没错，这些是样品的图样。

简：谢谢。女式浴袍，摇粒绒，260克每平方米，单码，数量6,000件。

史密斯：我想，您能否给我们邮件的询价一个答复？

简：当然可以。很乐意报6,000件摇粒绒浴袍，100%全涤，上海离岸价，每件5.90美元。

史密斯：如何包装？

简：每件浴衣套一个塑料袋，每一纸箱装4打。

史密斯：交货期呢？

简：按您的要求，分两批次发货，每批3,000件。第一批的交货期是9月30日，第二批的交货期是10月15日。

史密斯：付款方式呢？

简：与以前的合同一样，即期信用证。

史密斯：非常感谢您的报价，我们一定认真考虑。我们得花些时间核对一下，所以我们能否休息20分钟？然后，我们给您一个答复。

简：好的。

交际精品2 还盘

（他们在洽谈价格，并激烈地讨价还价。史密斯想方设法以最低的价格购买，而简试图说服对方接受报价。）

史密斯：嗯，简，我和艾瑞娜小姐讨论了您的报价。我们觉得有点太高了。

简：能告诉我你们为什么这么想吗？

史密斯：跟您说实话，在来贵国之前，我们接待了另一个制衣商。他们的报价是广州离岸价每件4.50美元。因此，我们不理解为什么要付更多的钱来买您的浴袍。

简：每件4.50美元，真的？

史密斯：真的是4.50美元。

简：真便宜。我猜想您一定从他那儿大量购买了吧？

史密斯：我们买了200件。

简：才200件？

史密斯：嗯，我们对那家公司了解不多，所以我们的订单只是试探性的。

简：对呀，要确认一个生意伙伴是否可靠要花时间的。

史密斯：所以我们向您询价。相信你们不仅可靠，而且价格有竞争力。

简：这点请您放心。

史密斯：不过，显然你们的报价没有竞争力啊。

简：那您认为什么样的价格才算有竞争力？

史密斯：4.50美元，我们付给那家制衣商的价格。

简：噢，这可不行。我们的浴袍比那家要值钱。

史密斯：噢，为什么？

简：因为我们的质量好，质量好的货价格自然要高。史密斯先生，您对这点不会不同意吧？

史密斯：您说的也许有道理。不过，怎么能证明你们的产品比广东那家好？

简：我们获得纺织总会的奖牌，这是证书。

史密斯：噢，谢谢！

交际精品3 达成协议

（双方都做了一些让步，交易终于谈成。）

史密斯：好吧，简，每件5.00美元怎么样？我把价格几乎提高了11%。

简：感谢您为达成协议做出的努力。不过，您的让步恐怕稍微小了点。

史密斯：哎，怎么能这样呢？简，再提价的话，就会把我们逼破产了。

简：别开玩笑了，史密斯先生。作为制衣业行家，您很清楚我们产品的价值比您的还盘要高得多。

史密斯：感谢您的称赞。不过作为一名行家，我觉得报价与市场的主流价格不太相符。

简：恐怕我不能同意这种看法。不过，为了表示我们对一位老客户的诚意，我也把价压低40美分，降到5.50美元一件。您觉得怎么样？

史密斯：非常感谢，不过我得说，这样的价格我们还是付不起。接受你们现时的报价意味着我们将遭受巨大的亏损，利润就更谈不上了。
简：看来这事不好办。这样吧，为了将来的生意，我建议如果您把订单的数量提到1万件，我们把价格定在5.00美元。
史密斯：恐怕我无权做出如此大的让步。我必须与老板联系一下，征求他的意见。
简：行！

（史密斯先生将情况向他的老板进行汇报，20分钟后回到谈判桌前。）
史密斯：同老板联系了一下，虽然有点超出预算计划，还是同意增加数量。
简：太好了。那现在我们谈谈有关交货的一些细节吧。
史密斯：行！

第六章　在中国进出口商品交易会

第一部分　商务情景对话

交际精品1　在中国进出口商品交易会上

（海伦是希腊公司的代表，她在广交会背包展摊上。杰克是乔伊箱包公司的销售员。）

杰克：早上好，欢迎参观我们的展位。
海伦：早上好，很高兴见到您。我是来自希腊的海伦，这是我的名片。我们公司是希腊的主要进口商之一。我想同您谈谈您展摊上的那些背包。
杰克：谢谢。这是我的名片，很高兴能有机会和您面谈。感谢对我司产品的兴趣。我这有些目录，请您先过目。
海伦：谢谢，展摊上的产品都在目录上吗？
杰克：当然。
海伦：是这样的，我们打算进口一批书包。您可以推荐一些产品吗？
杰克：当然可以。这些如何？款号是YX-01到YX-10，本系列产品专为小学生设计。我们的商标采用热移印技术，卡通形象生动，很受小学生们欢迎。
海伦：是用什么面料做的？
杰克：一部分用600D×600D涤纶面料，另一部分用超细纤维。
海伦：能提供更详细的资料吗？
杰克：可以。瞧，这是书包的规格，长16英寸×宽10英寸×厚度5英寸，PVC背胶，U形大口袋，肩带可取下或调节。
海伦：嗯，每款的起订量是多少？
杰克：通常是1,000个。
海伦：最小订单量？
杰克：3,000个。
海伦：我想要看看报价单。
杰克：这就是，给您。
海伦：考虑得真周到。如果您不介意的话，我想先看一下报价单，然后再和您谈。
杰克：好的。再见！

交际精品2　谈论产品

（林小姐是销售部经理，布朗先生是海外客户。）

林：下午好，我姓林，销售部经理。

布朗：林小姐您好，很高兴见到您。

林：幸会，布朗先生。请坐，喝茶还是咖啡?

布朗：方便的话来杯咖啡。

林：好的。您对交易会的印象如何?

布朗：嗯，此次交易会变化真大啊！我参加过三届交易会，发现此次规模大多了，参展也比以前多。

林：是啊，您对什么感兴趣呢?

布朗：有不少呢！我们对您的产品很感兴趣，尤其是童鞋。这些童鞋很时尚，很适合我们的市场。如果质量好，价格公道，我们将大量采购。

林：我们的鞋子有各种尺码，颜色多样。产品在整个生产过程中得通过五道质量检验关，不仅质量上乘，设计也非常新颖，在海外很受欢迎，供不应求。

布朗：不错。

林：您知道，最近国际市场上价格有上涨趋势，我们的鞋子价格随时都有可能提高。对适销您方市场的产品我们专门做了一份报价单。这是报价单和产品目录。

布朗：太好了！请问，你们报盘的有效期一般是多长?

林：15天。我们的价格比其他制造商的开价优惠得多。这一点你可以从我们的价格单看到，所有价格当然要经我方确认后才有效。

布朗：真希望与您建立良好的业务关系，很愿意与您进一步交谈。

林：我也是。

交际精品3　接触客户

（南希是来自美国的采购商。派克是一家电公司的销售商。）

派克：早上好！有什么需要帮忙吗?

南希：可以提供这款冰箱更多的资料吗?

派克：当然可以，请看看我们的宣传册。

南希：谢谢。如果有我们要的型号，价格也合理，我们会考虑下单。

派克：我们还接特殊订单，也就是说，我们可以根据提供的样品及规格生产冰箱。

南希：这些款式看起来很小。

派克：我们在研制此款冰箱时，要解决的问题之一是取消冷冻室。此款单价才50美元。外形设计成动物模样，如熊猫和熊等。

南希：了不起，冷冻室问题解决了，又创造出一个好产品，的确不错。所有的零部件都是在上海生产吗?

派克：是的，我们也做些转包合同，但只在上海。请问，您是哪家公司的?

南希：我来自美国电子产品供应公司。

派克：您愿意去看看我们的工厂或走访一两个转包商吗?

南希：行啊，要是时间允许的话。我星期五要飞回美国。
派克：在此之前我肯定会安排妥当。见见我公司的开创者怎样？您有兴趣同他谈谈即将面世的新款冰箱吗？
南希：这主意不错。说实话吧，我们一直在努力超越我们的竞争对手。过去的几个月里，我们也考虑在中国生产以降低成本。我们的市场部一直在做这项研究，但是他们所提供的数据大部分是间接的。
派克：我想这是您来交易会的原因吧。
南希：没错，我来就是为了与像您这样的行家进行面对面的交流。
派克：明白了，那就马上联系我公司老总。
南希：好，谢谢您。

第七章　商务考察

第一部分　商务情景对话

交际精品1　考察工厂

（美国联合供应公司的总经理伊丽莎白·盖奇女士首次考察黄先生的制造厂。）

黄：很高兴能在我们工厂再次见到您，盖奇太太。您和家人都好吗？
盖奇：都很好，谢谢你！既然我们是老朋友了，请叫我丽莎。我可以直呼你小黄吗？
黄：当然可以，丽莎。您那可爱的儿子汤姆好吗？自从我上次在美国见到他以来，他一定长大了许多。
盖奇：是的，他已经是个高中生了。不瞒你说他是个英俊的小伙子了。
黄：好！盖奇先生好吗？他这次为什么没来？
盖奇：他很好，谢谢。他正忙着呢。
黄：很遗憾，请代我向他转达我的衷心祝福。
盖奇：好的。实际上现在由我全权负责我们之间的业务。
黄：我很高兴和您一道工作。我相信我们之间的合作会令人愉快，并且富有成效。
盖奇：我也这么认为。
黄：可以带您参观一下工厂吗？
盖奇：乐意接受。
黄：您可能知道，是纳米抗菌鞋的生产高峰期，我们的工厂正在满负载生产。工厂的生产能力达到每天1万双鞋。
盖奇：很好，我此行的目的之一就是想了解我们订单的执行情况。产品质量永远是最重要的，而交货期也是一个关键因素，尤其对季节性产品。

（他们一边谈论，一边来到正在生产联合供应公司产品的生产线。）

黄：完全同意你的说法。我确信我们的产品会合符合同规定的标准和您的要求。根据我们的工作日程安排，贵方的订单将按期完工交货。不必担心。
盖奇：你们能同时完成其他客户的所有订单吗？
黄：基本上可以。我们工人现在每天加班两小时，尽管我们必须付双倍的加班工资。

盖奇：如何监控质量？
黄：这里是质量检验区，所有的鞋产品都经过极度严格的质量检测。
盖奇：那我很感兴趣。
黄：成品在流往包装区之前先到这里。产品百分之百都要经过这里检验，次品被扔到这些箱子里，由车间主任和技术员分析问题原因，并找出防止再度发生的办法。
盖奇：那边是产品设计部吗？
黄：是，请看我们的创新纳米产品。我们总是尽力保持产品的新颖性。您对本厂的总体印象如何？
盖奇：哇，好极了！真是眼见为实啊。盖奇先生曾多次告诉我他在贵厂的所见所闻，现在是我亲眼所见。我将向公司报告我的所见所闻，相信在这批产品发货后，后续订单会接踵而来。
黄：太感谢了！

交际精品2　样品陈列室会谈

（博大工艺品公司销售经理金小姐引领一家加拿大公司的布莱恩先生参观样品陈列室。）

布莱恩：样品室真漂亮！
金：谢谢！随意看看，我们的样品室对您完全开放。
布莱恩：谢谢！就像昨晚在我下榻的宾馆房间里向您介绍的那样，我们公司是加拿大的主要工艺品经销商之一。我们经营着品种繁多的工艺产品，总数可达1 500种。其中大多数是从中国进口的，因为中国的工艺品深受我们客户的青睐。
金：贵方寻求特定的工艺品吗？
布莱恩：我想找美术陶瓷、摆设陶瓷、仿古陶瓷等。
金：您算找对地方了，因为我们的主要产品就是工艺瓷器。由于资源丰富、工艺精湛、款式新颖和种类繁多，我们的产品在国内外市场上享有盛誉。
布莱恩：太好了！
金：我们先看看工艺样品，然后坐下来详谈质量、数量、价格及其他事宜。
布莱恩：好的。可以提供一些样品吗？
金：当然可以。准备随身携带吗？如果是的话，我就给您包装起来。
布莱恩：不，样品很重，而我还要到其他地方旅行。您能将它们直接邮寄回我的办公室吗？
金：没问题。但是您必须自付邮费。我可以采用邮费到付。
布莱恩：行，谢谢。这是我们公司的一款新品。您能做个样品吗？我希望能带回公司。
金：我们可在10天内提供复样，您什么时候离开？
布莱恩：星期六，我想时间来不及。可以把复样和样品一起寄给我。我们希望复样能符合这张纸上所描述的所有要求。
金：尽管放心。我相信"良好的开端是成功的一半"这句话，希望我们的复样能为贵公司与我们之间的贸易往来带来一个良好的开端。
布莱恩：希望如此。

交际精品3　投资洽谈

（董先生与一家外国公司的首席执行官瓦特先生洽谈投资事项。）

董：很抱歉，瓦特先生，我们无法向贵方提供您所需要的轴承，因为现在是旺季，我们工厂现已忙得三班倒了。从现在到明年三月份的订单已经满了。

瓦特：很遗憾。但是，我此行的目的不仅仅是要求对我们的订单做最好的安排，而且还想与贵公司讨论我们投资一条新的生产线来为我们生产轴承的可能性。

董：很感谢及时的帮助。但建立一条新的生产线需要很长的时间，我们怎么能使生产能力马上就翻番？

瓦特：我们原先在韩国有一条生产线，由于劳动力成本越来越高，在那里生产的产品失去了竞争力。如果我们将现成的生产线运到这来，花不了太多时间，可在两三个月内形成新的生产能力。

董：这设想倒是令人感兴趣。有实施的详细计划吗？

瓦特：是的。大约需要2周来拆卸和包装这条生产线，还需要另外两三周运输时间和1周报关时间。如果我们抓得紧，可在3周内重新组装和调试生产线。这样一来，生产线就可在年底前投入生产，这就意味着提高生产力，可比坐等现有的生产线生产提早两个月以上。

董：你们有把握在这么短的时间内重建生产线并使其投入使用吗？

瓦特：我相当有把握，因为我们可以带工程师和工人来。他们以前都在这个工厂里工作，对这条线的了解就像了解自己的孩子一样。

董：那这条生产线要如何收费呢？

瓦特：我们不打算就生产线本身收费，我们仅要求这条线专门生产我们的订单。生产线的日常维护应由贵方负责。

董：请让我考虑考虑。

瓦特：我们公司将不再支付我方订单的预付款，因为我们的机器已经抵押在贵厂了。当然在我方订单完成之后，我们将支付全额货款。保证机器运行良好是贵方的责任。我方机器在贵厂使用期间，我们将拥有处置自己财产的全部权利。

董：这很合理。我们将在报关、当地运输和车间安装等方面提供必要的协助。明天我们就召开董事会，并在两日内给您最终的答复。但我个人认为我们的董事会定会批准这项"双赢"的建议。

瓦特：很高兴听到您这么说，期待你们的好消息。

第八章　技术创新和自主品牌战略

第一部分　商务情景对话

交际精品1　商讨产品创新

（尼克松先生正在访问赵小姐的公司，讨论有关产品创新和创自主品牌事宜。）

赵：您好！尼克松先生。再次见到您，非常高兴。

尼克松：您好！赵小姐。收到我们关于所要讨论商品创新问题的传真了吗？为了促进销售，我们公司希望产品在设计、质量等方面进行改进和创新。

赵：是的，那我们就开始讨论了，行吗？

尼克松：当然。我们先从设计入手。贵公司产品进入市场已有些日子了，市场上出现了其他厂家和进口商的模仿产品。为了引领市场，我们想让客户看到新面孔的器具。你有什么好建议吗？

赵：这也是我们所关心的问题。我们已关注此事一段时间了。我们公司正推行技术创新战略，力争创自主品牌。

尼克松：真棒！

赵：只有通过技术创新和创立自主品牌，我们公司才能在激烈的市场竞争中占一席之地。

尼克松：完全正确。

赵：设计师们已经开发了几款新品供贵公司挑选。我们可以在继续原有产品销售的同时，从中选一两款开始，试试顾客的反映。

尼克松：好主意。它们看上去都挺好。我相信新产品会在我们市场热销。为了让我们的产品看上去更起眼，我们公司准备采用新系列的彩套。

赵：印制这些新彩套是没问题的。我们将采用更亮的纸张来印这些新彩套，使它们看起来会更靓一些。

尼克松：我迫切希望看到新包装的创新产品上我们的超市货架。虽然总体上说贵司的产品质量是可以接受的，但我们仍然收到一些顾客的投诉。在此我想再次郑重地提一提质量问题，因为我们不想由于一些很小的质量问题而失去我们的市场和客户。

赵：很感激提醒我们质量问题。事实上，我们一直很重视质量问题。还有，我们公司已经通过了ISO 9000的认证，我们的产品也正在申请CE认证。有了CE认证，我们的产品将以更高的身价进入欧洲市场，这对贵公司尤为有利。

尼克松：很高兴听到这个好消息。最后，很重要的一点是要求将所有工具进行热处理。

赵：从技术角度上讲，这不成问题。然而，它与生产成本有很大关系。如果所有工具都经过热处理，总成本将比现有产品上升20%。

尼克松：我明白，但很抱歉，必须这么做。我们也不想让客户不得不承受更高的价格。

赵：如果是这种情况，我想提个折中的方案。我们将易损的螺丝刀头进行热处理，而不是全部工具。这样既提高工具档次，又保持价格稳定。

尼克松：我个人可以接受。但我无权决定，必须用电话向总部请示批准。不管怎样，我非常高兴所有问题都这么顺利地解决了。感谢贵公司在各方面的友好合作。

赵：不客气。

交际精品2　具体的技术谈判

（陈先生和麦克斯先生之间的技术谈判正进行中。）

陈：麦克斯先生，我们仔细地研究了梯用挂钩的模型和有关图纸。我们很有兴趣与贵方一道开发此新产品。

麦克斯：我很高兴你也感兴趣。现在我该做些什么？

陈：首先，我想谈谈一些技术问题。我们对您的模型进行了测试，发现如果螺丝旋得太紧，塑料夹部分容易弯曲，甚至折断。为了解决这个问题，我们建议用金属部件来代替塑料部件。

麦克斯：从技术角度上说是可行的，但从商业角度上说却不行，因为金属部件外观不如塑料部件那样好看。

陈：明白。我们也许不得不加厚原设计的塑料部件，以增强薄弱环节。

麦克斯：这正是我们所需要的。

陈：动工之前，我们还想了解一下这种梯用挂钩的潜在的市场有多大。

麦克斯：我也没把握。

陈：能告诉我第一次订单能有多少？

麦克斯：这有关系吗？

陈：当然有。正如你所知，生产这个产品的塑料部分，我们必须制作三套注塑模具，每套模具1,000美元。而且，我们还需要五副冲压模，每副200美元。一开始，我们就至少需要投资总共4,000美元。如果订单数量太小，每个产品单价就会很高。

麦克斯：有什么解决办法？

陈：你们要先支付模具款。当您的订货数量累计达到10万件时，我们将从单价中扣还模具的费用。

麦克斯：那就意味着我必须承担4,000美元的风险，直到我售完10万件产品。你能使我的风险降到最低吗？

陈：我想想……好吧，让我们各承担一半的风险。我们公司承担2,000美元，贵公司承担另一半。

麦克斯：太好了！非常感谢！

陈：但请注意既然我们分担了风险，我们就不能再付还你们的那部分，不论将来你们的订单数量是多少。能同意吗？

麦克斯：那当然，你说得很对。我们可以将此写入合同书。

陈：好！就这么定。

交际精品3　商标和专利

（张先生和布朗先生正在讨论电子产品销售合同。）

布朗：经过三天艰苦的合同谈判，这下多轻松啊！很高兴，我们终于谈成了！

张：正如中国话所说的"好事多磨"。在庆祝胜利之前，还有两点需要议一下。

布朗：我的天啊，还有两个"障碍"！

张：不用担心。我们相信解决这两个问题不会有什么困难。

布朗：真的吗？什么问题？

张：正如您在条款11和12中提到的那样，你们的产品在美国享有专利，我们销售时必须使用你们的商标。

布朗：这有什么问题吗？

张：没问题。首先我方需要贵公司提供专利证书和商标注册的复印件，以表明贵公司是这项专利和商标的所有权人。我们还需要有关证据来证明你们的专利和商标仍然有效。

布朗：可以，这些都没问题。我们可以将这些复印件作为本合同的附件。

张：同时，我们尽力建议贵公司在中国申请此商标以保护自己免受侵犯。如果商标被别人注册，那将是很头疼的事。

布朗：非常正确，谢谢你的提醒。我们将立即在中国注册我们的商标。请问，您能帮帮忙吗？因为我们对中国的法律法规不熟悉。

张：当然。但办理此事之前，我们需要贵公司的授权书。

布朗：太感谢了！

张：我们现在可以庆祝生意谈成了。

第九章　包装与质量检验

第一部分　商务情景对话

交际精品1　质量检验

（金星扬声器公司的质检部经理周先生正在向客户、质检代表卡尔太太介绍公司情况。）

周：卡尔太太，欢迎您到我们公司来。

卡尔：您好，周先生。很荣幸访问贵公司。我的老板艾尔伯特·高登先生派我来做质量检验。

周：哦！高登先生是我们公司的老朋友。我相信他一定对你说过我们公司。

卡尔：是的。在开始对我方5406号合同项下货物进行质量检验之前，如能介绍一些贵公司的情况，将不胜感激。

周：为了让您更了解我们的情况，我想简单扼要地介绍一下我们的公司、产品及产品检验。

卡尔：请吧。

周：我们公司是中国主要的扬声器生产厂家之一，生产数百种各种各样的扬声器，主要出口到30多个国家和地区。我们有员工500人，其中包括150名工程师和技术员。每年出口8,000万美元的扬声器。

卡尔：了不起。

周：质量控制部由总经理直接领导，负责所有质量控制有关的事宜。

卡尔：贵方老板重视产品质量至关重要。你们部里有多少人？

周：25人，包括在各车间的15名检验员。

卡尔：他们主要负责什么？或者说他们的日常工作是什么？

周：他们遍布车间的各个角落，检查生产线下来的产品，测试和记录技术参数，提出改进质量和减少次品的建议等。

卡尔：您认为他们在第一线的检验工作行之有效吗？

周：严格说来，是的，行之有效。他们的确形成我们质量控制的第一道防线。从库房中检出的次品非常少。据统计，次品平均比率不到万分之一点五。

卡尔：谢谢介绍。能带我去会见这些质量控制员和检验产品吗？

周：很愿意，让我们去车间吧。

交际精品2　包装

（参观过车间，周先生与卡尔太太正在商谈包装事宜。）

卡尔：你们有效的检验工作给我留下美好的印象。总体来说，我们的合同正在良好有序地进行。我的老板看到我的检验报告后一定会满意贵方产品的。
周：非常感谢。很高兴听到您对我们工作的积极评价。我总是认为质量是生意之门的钥匙。
卡尔：绝对正确！除了刚才在生产线上我提出的问题外，我对扬声器本身没有更多的东西要说。然而，我想强调一下包装对总体质量的重要性。
周：请不必顾虑地告诉我们包装方面的缺点，我们一定尽力改进。
卡尔：好的！首先，包装每个扬声器的塑料袋可以更厚一些，我想这不会贵很多。塑料袋似乎太薄了。在运输和操作过程中，扬声器可能会刮伤很薄的塑料袋。虽然与整个产品的其他部分相比，塑料袋的成本是微不足道的，但却是我们的产品到达顾客手中时的最终包装物。
周：是的。我们将使用双倍厚度的塑料袋来包装贵公司所订的产品。
卡尔：好的。我们要求在塑料袋背面的角落上印上可循环塑料的标志，这是环境保护的要求。
周：我们会印上的。
卡尔：下一个问题是内盒。内盒的尺寸必须一致，太松或太紧都可能损坏内盒。内盒是我们产品在货架上的形象展示。
周：我们将特别注意这一点。
卡尔：最后一点是外纸箱。请不要使用外包装常用的订书钉和塑料打包带。
周：我想这也是出于环保问题的考虑。
卡尔：对啊。今天就先谈到这。
周：感谢您中肯、及时的建议。您的建议有利于我们产品质量提高，这不仅有益于你们，也有益于其他客户。我们一定铭记在心。

交际精品3 商品检验

（周先生和卡尔太太继续商谈商品检验。）

卡尔：周先生，货物发运之前，我们不再派人前来。为此，我们要求对我们订单项下的货物实施商品检验。
周：没问题。我们的出口检验主要是由进出口检验检疫局执行。它在世界上享有很高的国际声誉。
卡尔：我听说过。
周：检验将在发货前5天内进行。进出口检验检疫局在各港口城市都有分支机构，比如在我们的城市，因此进行检验是很方便的。
卡尔：他们采取什么标准呢？
周：如果是法定商检产品，将采用中国国家标准；若非法定商检产品，可采用申请人的商业合同中指定的标准。
卡尔：检验检疫局出具的质量和数量证书将是信用证议付的一份重要文件，可用德文出具吗？
周：不行。通常证书是用中文和英文的。
卡尔：行，英文文本可以接受。当货物到达目的港后，我们可以进行复检吗？
周：理论上可以，但我认为不必要，因为这样可能引起争议。如果你们愿意选择进出口检验检疫局以外的检验机构，对我们来说也可以，因为我们对自己的产品有信心。但检验的费用应由贵公司自行承担。

卡尔：明白。我希望不会发生任何不愉快的事情。真是百闻不如一见，我想我已经完成我此行的任务了。

周：为何不到我们市区转一转，放松一下？

卡尔：谢谢，好极了。

第十章　接受与订货

第一部分　商务情景对话

交际精品1　对产品感兴趣

（希望工具实业公司的总经理刘小姐在波兰波兹南国际展览会上参展。一家欧洲公司进口经理梅森先生来到展位上观看样品。）

刘：您好！我能为您做点什么？

梅森：我对贵公司的100件组合工具感兴趣，您能让我多看一些样品吗？

刘：当然可以。请看这些不同款式的100件组合工具，用途多样。

梅森：好极了。

刘：这种是专业用具，都是用优质钢材制造的，经过热处理，保质期五年。

梅森：这一款呢？

刘：这两款是家用的。是父亲节的上好礼品。

梅森：太好了！哦，我想这款一定是为母亲节设计的喽？

刘：对！是专为女性设计的。瞧，外盒和手柄都用鲜艳亮丽的粉红色。那是女性专用的颜色，不是吗？

梅森：是的，想得真周到。我很喜欢。价格呢？

刘：2.49美元，中国港口船上交货价，这价格基于整货柜的订量。

梅森：我第一次可能订不了这么多。我们从未卖过此产品。对市场而言，这也是一种新做法。让我想想，也许我们可以和其他组合工具拼柜，比如专业工具和家用工具拼柜。

刘：是的。不过，混装产品的生产成本和操作费用要比单一产品高些。

梅森：可以理解，但……

刘：那好，为了与贵公司建立业务关系，我们考虑让步。现报价为每套2.59美元，中国港口船上交货价。最低起订量为500套。

梅森：非常感谢。我回头再来。

刘：这是我的名片，上面有我的手机号和摊位号。欢迎您再来。再见。

梅森：回见。

交际精品2　讨价还价

（刘小姐和梅森先生在展览会上就价格进行谈判。）

刘：很高兴再次见到您，梅森先生。您好吗？

梅森：很好，谢谢！

刘：我们第一次见面至今，已过去两天了。您决定了吗？

梅森：还没呢。贵司的组合工具很好，但与其他公司相比，定价有些偏高。能优惠点，再降一点价吗？比如说每套2.29美元。

刘：坦率地说，我们的价格是比别人高一些，但开辟市场的新时尚和新特色就值这价格，不是吗？而且，我们的质量比其他厂家更优越。

梅森：有道理。那么我们先谈好其他条款，回头在谈价格问题好吗？首先请告知500套的交货期。

刘：大约是我们收到贵公司确定合同和预付款后的30天。

梅森：能否快点，20天行吗？要知道销售旺季将到了。

刘：行。

梅森：哇，您真帮了大忙。那么付款条件呢？

刘：我们一般接受信用证付款。这是我们的惯例。

梅森：信用证付款的费用挺高，并减缓资金周转。我们更倾向电汇付款。

刘：采用电汇付款，合同确定后预付30%，发货前付清余款。

梅森：发货后付清余款可以吗？

刘：恐怕不行。

梅森：哦，还有一件事很重要。请告知包装方式。

刘：正如你两天前见到的样品那样，所有工具都放在粉红色工具盒里。每盒套上四色印刷的彩套，然后包上收缩膜。五盒装一纸箱。贵公司可在彩套上印上公司标志和不同语言的说明文字等。

梅森：很好，就剩下价格问题了。

刘：为促成生意，也表示我方的诚意，我们同意每套降10美分。

梅森：每套2.39美元怎样？

刘：我们各退一步好吗？2.49美元已是我们的底线了。

梅森：成交。

刘：非常感谢。我马上准备合同书。您是在此稍候，还是到四处转转20分钟后再回来呢？

梅森：还是在等吧。这展馆里的各个角落我都踏遍了。

交际精品3　续订单

（*梅森先生向刘小姐下续订单。*）

梅森：您好吗，刘小姐？

刘：很好，谢谢！您呢？

梅森：我也很好，谢谢！我很高兴地告诉您，贵方的产品在我们的市场上销售相当好。贵公司的新理念已受到客户热烈追捧。为了满足对这种组合工具大量的市场需求，我们准备立即与贵方下续订单。

刘：很高兴听到好消息。我们会尽力满足您的要求。

梅森：为了满足高速增长的需求，订量将是上次的三倍以上。请按2,000套的数量报个最优惠价格。

刘：每套2.48美元，中国港口船上交货价。

梅森：这与上次的价格几乎是一样的。
刘：是的，但实际上，它比上次的价格要低得多。
梅森：此话怎讲？能具体解释一下吗？
刘：从上次订货后，情况发生很大变化。我们现面临着至少两方面的压力。正如您所知，从那时起美元对中国货币不断地贬值。仅这一点，我们就已经损失了3%。
梅森：真遗憾。
刘：更糟的是，受国际油价影响，中国国内市场的钢材和塑料价格急剧上涨。而钢材和塑料正是我们的主要原材料。在这种情况下，仍报给你们相同、甚至更低一点的价格，这就意味着在价格上已经给予你们特别的优惠了。
梅森：现在我们了解了贵方的处境，那就不再坚持了。我们接受报价。不过，假如国际油价回落，我们要求价格也自动随之回落。
刘：完全同意。我们希望形势会尽快好转。

第十一章 商务电话

第一部分 商务情景对话

交际精品1　何时才能联系到你！

（上周，孙先生在交易会上认识了林小姐。他想通过电话与林小姐联系。孙先生拨了号码，电话通了。）

总机（*电话录音*）："欢迎致电ABC公司，如果您知道受话人的姓名和分机号码，请按1；如果您想了解本公司介绍，请按2；如果您需要话务员提供服务，请按#键。请不要挂机。"

（孙先生按#字键，音乐响起……话务员接起电话。）

话务员：您好！久等了，能帮您什么忙吗？
孙：我想找林小姐。
话务员：您能告诉我林小姐在哪个部门么？我们公司有好几位林小姐。
孙：嗯……可能是采购部吧。
话务员：采购部。请稍候，我马上帮您接通。

（分机占线。语音提示：对方正在通话中，请不要挂机……稍后，电话通了。）

林：您好！采购部。您是哪位？
孙：您好，嗯……我是鞋料代理商。麻烦叫一下林小姐。
林：我就是。
孙：太好了，很高兴听到您的声音。我是清顺贸易公司的孙先生。
林：孙先生？
孙：哦……我们上一周在材料展销会上见过面。
林：（沉默）……
孙：哦……您对我们的真皮和合成革材料很感兴趣……您让我再和您联系。

林：展销会？没有，我没去过展销会，您可能弄错了。
孙：是吗？对不起，可能我弄错部门了。
林：可能是。我们公司是由技术部负责确认新产品使用材料的。您可能要找技术部的林小姐。
孙：哦……对不起，太谢谢您了！能麻烦您帮我转回总机么？
林：好的。

交际精品2　能帮您带个口信么？
（刘小姐打国际长途电话通知访问团的相关事宜。）
话务员：下午好，中国虎饮料公司。
刘：下午好，我是马来西亚的刘小姐。请转张经理。
话务员：好的，请稍候。
秘书：您好，张经理办公室。
刘：早安。我是马来西亚总部的刘小姐。张经理在吗？
秘书：对不起，他正在开会。我是他的秘书王立。能帮您什么吗？
刘：您好，王立。是访问团参观你们工厂的事。您能帮我转告张经理吗？
秘书：没问题，请讲。
刘：马来西亚的访问团原定周三下午到达。但是由于那个航班临时取消，访问团的行程有所变动。行程得延迟，他们周六下午才能到。请你们相应调整一下接待计划。
秘书：好的。
刘：还有，访问团成员的数目少了5个。他们另有安排。
秘书：好的。我来确认一下：访问团周三不能到达，周六下午才能到达，人数减少，哦，能告诉我确切的人数么？
刘：嗯……总共11人。
秘书：总共11人。
刘：对。谢谢。麻烦请张经理发封电传或电邮给我，以确认他已经得到通知。
秘书：好的。等张经理回来我转告他。他会和您联系的。
刘：非常感谢。

交际精品3　我要投诉
（马先生致电广告部漏播他们的电视广告。）
秘书：早上好！九频道广告部。
马：早上好，小姐。我想找王副总经理接电话。
秘书：您是哪位？
马：亲亲食品公司的马先生。
秘书：请稍等。（对王先生说）亲亲食品公司的马先生找您。
王：您好，马先生。我是王经理。
马：早上好，王经理。是有关我们电视广告的事情。昨晚我们没看到电视剧中间插播我们公司的广告。

王：真抱歉。正想给您打电话。这是我们的过失。我们免费赠送您另外两次30秒钟的广告，好不好？

马：嗯——好吧。什么时段播出？

王：黄金时段。20、21号两天电视新闻之后。

马：您确定么？

王：确定，没问题。

马：那好吧。谢谢，再见。

王：再见。

第十二章　付款方式

第一部分　商务情景对话

交际精品1　要求信用证付款

（来自拿大的客户史密斯先生和来自福建希望进出口公司的陈小姐正在商谈有关付款方式事宜。他们最终达成协议用信用证付款，并安排具体事宜。）

史密斯：我们已经解决了诸如价格、包装、装运等问题，但有关付款方式的问题还需讨论。我们建议用承兑交单的付款方式。你的意见如何？

陈：说实话，承兑交单不可行。因为你们是新客户，如果我们接受你们的条件，我公司就要承受很大的风险。也许今后咱们之间生意往来多了，我们可以考虑托收的付款方式。目前为保险起见，我们还是希望采用不可撤销的信用证，凭装船单据付款。

史密斯：你知道这次的订货量很大。在银行开立信用证时，我们必须付押金和银行手续费。开立这么大金额的信用证费用太大，会增加我们的进口成本。

陈：你们可以与银行协商，看是否能减少押金和其他一些费用。

史密斯：但除此以外，从我方开立信用证到我方客户向我们支付货款通常需要两三个月时间，我们的资金就要被占用。目前经济不景气的情况，可能会给我们带来许多麻烦。所以，是否能灵活一点做些变动呢？你们是否能接受其他付款方式，比如付款交单？

陈：很抱歉，我们不能接受你方要求改变付款方式。我们通常只接受信用证的付款方式。不可撤销的信用证给出口商品增加了银行的担保，我们可以收到该收的款项。

史密斯：真遗憾，你方坚持用信用证支付方式。对于你们而言，信用证付款是最保险的办法，而对我们来说，找银行开信用证意味着额外的费用。

陈：其实，信用证是公平的，对买卖双方都有利。但为了帮助你们摆脱困境，我建议你方先减少一半订单，剩余的继续再订。

史密斯：好吧，我考虑一下。（在电脑上计算并思考一会儿后）好吧，我方减少一半订单。然而，我们还是应该在付款方式上折中一下。你认为是否能接受远期信用证支付方式，允许我们延期付款，比如说见票后60天付款？

陈：一般说来，我们要求凭即期汇票付款。用即期信用证付款在国际贸易中很普遍，但是为促成这次交易的成功，今后获取更多的订单，我们可以考虑你们的要求。

史密斯：谢谢，非常感谢！

陈：我们接着讨论信用证付款的具体事宜吧。能否在交货前30天开立信用证？
史密斯：没问题。我一回去就着手办理开出以你方为受益人的信用证。货何时能做好并装运？
陈：生产厂家可在五月底备齐。
史密斯：因为我方急需这批货，并且要给客户一个明确的交货期，能否说服厂家提前一点交货？比如五月初？
陈：我们希望能满足客户的要求，尤其是像你这样的新顾客。但我们的厂家手头未完成的订单还很多。
史密斯：好吧，我希望你们在收到信用证后能尽快发货。五月至六月是我们的销售旺季，如能尽快装运，将不胜感激。
陈：您尽管放心。收到信用证后，我们会做好必要的准备，在规定的时间内完成装运。
史密斯：太好了。请问，信用证的有效期该是多长？
陈：有效期为装船日期后15天。
史密斯：那你们可提供哪些单据？
陈：除了汇票外，还将提供一整套提单、发票、保险单、产地证书和检验证书。
史密斯：谢谢。多谢你方的合作。

交际精品2　修改信用证

（陈小姐收到相关的信用证，但发现信用证与2345号销售合同有些不符之处。于是，她致电史密斯先生要求修改信用证。）

陈：喂，史密斯先生，我是福建希望进出口公司的小陈。
史密斯：你好，陈小姐。
陈：我于4月8日收到你方开出的信用证。我发现信用证与2345号销售合同有一些不符之处。
史密斯：请说。
陈：首先，货物应按发票金额的110%投保，而不是150%。既然信用证上所有的条款都必须与合同完全一致，那么你方就应该按照合同的条款来开立信用证。
史密斯：是吗？我知道应该是110%，而不是150%。我核对后再通知你们。还有问题吗？
陈：请在"数量"和"150M/T"之间加上"大约"一词。而且，应该是6月15日到期，而非6月5日。
史密斯：我对此深表歉意，这完全是因为粗心大意所致。我会立即与开证行接洽，修改信用证。我们将采取一些措施，以免今后再发生类似情况。
陈：谢谢合作。还有一件事，由于某种原因，五六月份只有两艘船驶往贵国港口，且都是下半月才发船。五月份的舱位已满。现在只有两种选择，展期信用证或允许转船，由你们决定。
史密斯：展证会很麻烦。我会取消"直达轮"条款，将信用证改为允许转船。
陈：非常感谢。希望你们能理解我们的处境，尽快寄送信用证修改通知书以便于装运。

交际精品3　要求其他付款方式

（史密斯先生与陈小姐正在讨论另一订单的付款方式。）

史密斯：陈小姐，我很高兴我们顺利达成交易。虽然你们的价格与马来西亚同类商品相比稍偏高，但由于你方产品质量高，我想再订购，但是，数量取决于付款方式。如果你方能给予较宽松的付款方式，很可能促进我们的贸易往来。能给予更优惠的条件吗？

陈：谢谢贵方的再次订购。一般情况下我们采用信用证的付款方式。您意下如何？

史密斯：你知道，用信用证付款会增加额外费用，我们没钱可赚。能否接受承兑交单付款？

陈：恐怕不行。这种付款方式可能给卖方带来一些麻烦。要知道，国际货币市场很不稳定，美元贬值和对其他货币的冲击，造成了全球市场的极不稳定。

史密斯：那么，你们能不能接受付款交单？

陈：好吧。为了将来长久的生意往来，况且通过上次的交易，我们之间已取得相互的信任，这次就破个例，我们做出让步，50%用付款交单，余款用信用证支付，好吗？

史密斯：好，谢谢通融。我们会增加订单量。

陈：再次感谢贵方的订购，但下不为例。你们最好要在规定的时间内开立相关的信用证。货物一启运，我们即向你们开出即期汇票，相信你们一定会见票即付。

史密斯：我们当然会按常规办事。今天的交流真是令人愉快，富有成果！真诚希望我们今后的交易会不断增加。

第十三章　商务谈判

第一部分　商务情景对话

交际精品1　保险和普惠制原产地证

（布朗太太与供货商王先生正洽谈保险和普惠制原产地证事宜。）

布朗：王先生，既然我们的价格条款是成本加保险费、运费价，那么来确定一下我们的货物该上什么保险。

王：根据通常做法，我们为成本加保险费、运费价上的保险是按发票价格的110%保综合险。

布朗：我们要求不仅投保综合险，还包括罢工险和战争险。

王：我想我们不能保您提及的这些范围更广泛的险种，因为我们合同中的保险费用仅留有0.3%的余地。

布朗：当今世界到处都不太平，我们的船只不得不通过一些敏感地区，在我们国家，罢工也是家常便饭。因此，不得不投保以避免万一遭受损失。

王：我们理解你的处境。但你知道，按国际惯例，卖方对货物只投保惯常险别。如贵方坚持保特殊险，额外的保险费则由买方承担。

布朗：有道理，但我想……

王：坦率地说，我们的价格是目前最优惠的了。我们也不想做亏本生意，尽管保险费在总价仅占很小的比例。

布朗：那该怎么办？

王：简单一点，我们建议你自付特殊险或接受成本加运费价。

布朗：那就采用成本加运费价吧。

王：当然，我们会将保险费从原价中扣除，你方可自行投保。
布朗：有什么区别吗？
王：是有些区别。首先，我们不必就保什么险种而争论。其次，一旦出事，你们理赔更容易，因为你们是在当地的保险公司投的保。再次，双方的信用证也更简单些。
布朗：我们也只好如此了。
王：更改的合同一会儿就好。我们保证在货物装运后会立即通知贵方，以便贵方有足够的时间投保。
布朗：哦，我们还想提醒贵方必须办理普惠制原产地证，这是信用证议付的文件之一。它对我们至关重要，可使我们免交高额关税。
王：我们已写在合同中。为了申请普惠制原产地证，我们还需要一些信息，比如原产地、收货人、通知方、目的港、唛头和消费国等。
布朗：我们公司是收货人，在与我方的承运商做出安排后，我们会告知贵方有关通知方和其他信息。
王：没问题。

交际精品2 独家代理

（贝克先生到访刘小姐的公司，谈判独家代理事宜。）

刘：您好，贝克先生。在我们公司里欢迎您的到访，真是太好了。自从两年前我们在波兰第一次见面以来，贵公司早已成为我们最好的客户之一。
贝克：时光飞逝，但我清楚地记得我们往来始于那款女式睡衣的贸易。在您的鼓励下，我们打开女式睡衣的一个新市场。对此我非常感激。
刘：谢谢。您的电子邮件告知，此行的主要目的是讨论独家代理事宜，对吗？
贝克：完全正确。为了巩固我们已经开辟的市场，我们公司希望获得女式睡衣的独家代理权。
刘：这是一个非常实际和重要的问题。
贝克：正如您所知，我们在欧洲服装行业拥有广泛的商务联系网络和良好的信誉。我们对欧洲市场的情况了如指掌。
刘：很好。
贝克：我司是贵方独家代理的最合适人选。选择我们意味着减少竞争对手，将对贵公司受益匪浅。
刘：我欣赏贵公司对我们新产品的推销所做的努力。据我的理解，贵公司是想要在贵国的独家经销权，对吗？
贝克：不完全对。正如您所知，我国是一个很小的欧洲国家，我们国内的市场是相当有限的，因为我国的人口只有1 500多万，甚至不及贵国的一个省。
刘：嗯，我知道。
贝克：当今欧洲联盟内的各个国家可被看成一个整体，特别是从经济和商务方面来看。商品流通根本没有什么国界。因此要求一个欧洲国家的独家经营权毫无意义。
刘：既然如此，您想如何划定"边界"呢？
贝克：我想是整个欧洲。
刘：我们很想满足您的要求，但恐怕不行。因为我们已经在一些东欧国家销售我们的产品，比如俄罗斯、乌克兰等。将他们从我们的客户名单上划掉是不合适的。我们所能做的是给予现有欧盟内的独家经营权。

贝克：很合理。我们同意将"边界"限定在欧盟内。这是独家经营的协议书草本。请先阅悉，我们下午再议。

刘：好。

交际精品3　销售额和处罚问题

（关于销售额和处罚问题的深入会谈下午继续进行。）

刘：贝克先生，我们仔细地阅读了您的建议书。除了我们上午谈过的涵盖地区外，我们基本上同意独家经营的开始时间、产品范围和其他一些问题。

贝克：好。

刘：在此，我们想就销售额和处罚问题做进一步讨论。虽然我们之间的业务发展迅猛，但与我们销售的其他服装相比，女式睡衣的年销售额还相对较小。我们真切地希望这个市场会比现在大得多。

贝克：这也是我们要求独家经营权的原因。我们有着共同的目的，共同做大市场，双方都赚钱。

刘：贝克先生，我们想确定贵方计划每年的销售量是多少。

贝克：我们认为在初期把销售额定得太高是不现实的，我们可能面临强大的阻力。

刘：为了解决这个问题，达到共同目标，我们为何不定一个渐进的销售额限制？

贝克：好极了！头两年为50万套/年；随后每两年增加25万套/年。我们期望按销售净值获得6%的佣金。

刘：可以。下一个问题是处罚问题，这点似乎对我方不平等。

贝克：您为什么这么认为呢？

刘：条款规定如果我们的产品销往欧盟的其他公司，将受到处罚。如果贵公司向其他公司或厂家购买相同或相似产品却没有相应的处罚条款。我们想在协议书中应加上这部分。

贝克：行，我知道没人能随随便便成功。

刘：为了双方的利益，我们同意指定贵公司为我方的独家代理，期限为4年。

贝克：非常高兴所有问题这么快就解决了。非常感谢您的友好态度和高效工作。我相信我们之间将后的合作会更有成效。

刘：我也很高兴地看到我们的合作顺利健康地发展。

第十四章　签订合同

第一部分　商务情景对话

交际精品1　检查合同草案

（来自英国的商人史密斯先生正与就职于福建万德福进出口公司的陈小姐商讨合同草案。）

史密斯：陈小姐，我昨晚仔细阅读了合同草案。我认为我们已有很大进展。但仍有一些问题需要磋商。

陈：请说。我也认为有必要在列入正式合同前，澄清一些重要条款。
史密斯：首先是包装。这种纸箱用于远洋运输，恐怕不够结实。你们能不能改用木箱？
陈：抱歉。合同规定产品用纸箱包装。况且，纸箱更易搬运，成本更低。
史密斯：好吧，用纸箱，但包装必须经得起粗鲁的装运。那么，你们能采取一些加固措施吗？
陈：没问题。我们会用两根打包带加固纸箱。
史密斯：谢谢。其次是有关付款方式。我想是否能用承兑交单或付款交单？
陈：恐怕不行。大家都知道，这种付款方式可能给卖方带来很大的麻烦。按照我方的惯例，我方希望采用承兑的、不可撤销的信用证，凭装船单据付款。
史密斯：我明白，但开信用证需要支付给银行额外的费用。
陈：对不起，我无能为力。
史密斯：那就用信用证。但我必须再次强调你方要在七月底前完成装运，不得延误。
陈：当然不会，只要你方能及时地开立信用证。
史密斯：一回去，我就立即安排伦敦的中国银行开立相关的信用证，一经开出即传真通知你方。
陈：很好。还有什么问题？
史密斯：品质标准如何规定？
陈：合同中明确规定"品质以卖方提供的第23号样品和说明书的技术标准为准"。关于这一条您有什么意见吗？
史密斯：不，没意见。下一点是有关仲裁。合同规定仲裁在中国进行，但能否在第三国执行？
陈：没问题，因为很少进行仲裁。我希望所有的争议均通过友好协商解决。
史密斯：当然。嗯，似乎我们已讨论了合同草案里所有有争议的问题。然而，您是否能逐项检查一下合同的所有条款，看看还有什么意见不一致的地方？
陈：好的。我准备一下，明早送到你们下榻的酒店，行吗？
史密斯：好，谢谢。

交际精品2　再次检查合同草案

（陈小姐与史密斯先生再次检查合同草案，以确保一切条款都商谈妥当。）

陈：史密斯先生，现在合同已准备好。我们再检查一遍确定是否对所有条款都达成一致意见，好吗？
史密斯：好的。好主意，这样能避免今后的纠纷和索赔。（检查之后）嗯，除了一些小问题，总体还不错。首先，在这儿是不是应该加上这一句"如果一方未能履行合同，另一方有权取消合同"？
陈：行，我会加到合同中。
史密斯：第二点，如果我们以CIF价格条件成交，你们负责投保哪些险别？
陈：我们只负责投保水渍险。
史密斯：你们可以加保破碎险吗？
陈：只要你方愿意承担额外的费用，我方可以接受你方的要求。但我提醒你们索赔只赔偿超过5%的那部分。所以我觉得没必要这样做。
史密斯：有道理。水渍险就行了。

陈：既然保险问题已定下，我们再谈谈其他条款吗？
史密斯：请。
陈：关于包装和运输标志还有问题吗？
史密斯：我同意有关的条款。你方有什么需要解决的问题吗？
陈：喔，我认为漏了"不可抗力"这一条。夏天，我们经常遭遇台风和水灾，生产可能受影响，对合同的执行可能被耽搁。我希望你方不会反对在合同中加入这一条。
史密斯：好吧，如果我们无力与老天爷抗争的话，我们就加上这一条。如果发生了"不可抗力"，你方要尽快通知我方。
陈：会的。谢谢你方的友好合作。希望一切顺利，平安无事。
史密斯：对了，至关重要的一条必须加上，那就是，"必须事先经双方同意，合同方可修改。"
陈：没问题，我会补上。我认为我们现在已对所有的条款达成一致，此合同基本上把我们谈判的内容写进去。但如果在正式合同签订之前发现任何问题，您可以随时和我联系。
史密斯：很好。请问何时能签字？
陈：我希望在下星期一签字，可以吗？
史密斯：可以。再见。
陈：再见。

交际精品3　签订正式合同

（史密斯先生与陈小姐逐条核对合同条款，然后签订正式合同。）

陈：嗯，我想我们之间已没有任何分歧。这是合同，请您再仔细看一下。
史密斯：行，让我们逐条地核对合同条款，商品品名及规格、单位、数量、单价及总金额……（史密斯先生核对完所有的条款之后）我很高兴我们在反复协商之后最终达成协议。该写进去的都写进去了。请问合同有英文版吗？
陈：有，在这，请过目。
史密斯：（史密斯先生看完之后）没问题。
陈：现在一切问题都解决了，可以马上签合同了吗？
史密斯：可以。
陈：请签这。（所有签字结束之后）我们双方都各有两份正式合同。这两份合同由您保存，一份中文版，一份英文版。所有合同文本内容都完全一致。
史密斯：谢谢。祝贺我们圆满达成交易。下一步就是要很好地执行合同。大家都知道，合同一旦签署即具有法律效力。
陈：我相信我们双方都会很重视商业信誉，顺利执行合同。这次交易将促进我们之间贸易的进一步发展。

第十五章　物流配送服务

第一部分　商务情景对话

交际精品1　采访货物配送公司主管

（*李华女士是迅捷配送公司配送服务部主管。当地电视台的记者王先生就迅捷配送公司货物递送服务的主要特点采访了李华女士。*）

王：（面对观众）李华女士是迅捷配送公司配送服务部主管。李华女士，能请您介绍一下贵公司货物递送服务的主要特点吗？

李：配送服务影响着公司贸易的最终结果，并关系着公司的信誉。在这方面我们有很好的声誉。我们对所有的货物提供高质量、可靠、准时的递送服务。

王：那么，贵公司为我们提供哪些货物递送服务呢？

李：我们有适合于紧急货物递送的最快速的加急快递服务。能够确保邮件在两天内送达世界各城市。货物一旦送达，我们还会与对方进行电话确认。

王：除此之外，货物运输还有其他服务项目吗？

李：当然有，除此之外，我们还有特快专递服务，这也是大多数急件递送的理想选择。对于普通货物，我们还有快件服务。

王：那么，具体价格呢？

李：这个不必担心。这三种递送方式能够满足不同客户的需求。我们的价格合理。当然特快专递和快件递送的价格比加急邮件递送更便宜。

王：对于递送服务，最重要的是什么呢？

李：我认为，对于递送服务来说准时与安全是最重要的。服务的质量与货物送达时间长短也同样重要。由于我们高质量的服务，相信我们公司的业务将会迅速发展。

王：谢谢您精彩的谈话。

交际精品2　选择空运

（*比尔是光明公司的工作人员。他打电话给配送部的戴安娜，要求就光明公司运往伦敦的那批货进行空运。*）

戴安娜：配送部。我是戴安娜。

比尔：戴安娜，我是光明公司的比尔。

戴安娜：您好，我能为您做些什么吗？

比尔：请把30箱鲜花两天内从香港运到伦敦。

戴安娜：到伦敦路程很远。但我想应该能满足您的要求。我们可以保证按时送货。

比尔：这批货很急。可能的话，我希望您能考虑空运。希望贵公司能考虑我们的特殊情况。我还想了解一下空运的费用问题。

戴安娜：这需要根据货品的具体情况来定。通常我们按货物的规格、重量、价值来计算运费，有时还要考虑风险。

比尔：我们有30箱鲜花，每箱20千克，0.5立方米。

戴安娜：30箱，20千克，0.5立方米。重量、大小都符合要求。请稍等。别着急。还有足够的时间。如果不出意外，这批鲜花将在后天送达伦敦。

比尔：谢谢您。

戴安娜：运费是每千克4英镑，外加2英镑空运单和21英镑结关。我相信这批鲜花将会准时完好地送达。希望您能满意。

比尔：太好了。谢谢您！

戴安娜：不用谢。如果您有任何问题，请随时与我联系。

比尔：好，再见。

戴安娜：再见。

交际精品3　国际多式联运

（巴里和艾琳在电话中谈论家具运送事宜，他们决定采用国际多式联运集装箱运输。）

巴里：丘比特公司。我是巴里。

艾琳：您好！我是艾琳。

巴里：您好，艾琳！

艾琳：我打电话来是想向您咨询有关我们这个月要从天津运到芝加哥的那30套家具事宜。

巴里：我想，最好还是用国际多式联运集装箱运。

艾琳：我也这么想。集装箱运输安全可靠，而且货也不必转运好几次。

巴里：是啊。我们可以在港口卸货，再用卡车把货送到客户手中。

艾琳：多式联运费用很高吗？

巴里：国际多式联运是一种货物整体运输最有效的运输方式。多式联运经营人负责不同方式的运输全程。它是一种安全和富有竞争性的运输方式。能节省运输费用和时间。因此，运费十分合理。

艾琳：真是太好了。提货单的情况怎么样？

巴里：我们提供多式联运提单。

艾琳：好的。那我们开立信用证时规定需要联运提单而不是通常所用的普通提单。

巴里：行。你想何时发货？

艾琳：我们准备定本周末前的舱位。

巴里：可以，你们的家具备齐了吗？

艾琳：好了，集装箱能拖到我们的仓库吗？

巴里：本周四集装箱拖到您的仓库。

艾琳：太好了！

第十六章　商务会议

第一部分　商务情景对话

交际精品1　筹备会议

（布朗先生正和秘书李小姐讨论有关销售会议的安排事宜。）

布朗：李小姐，我们快速讨论一下销售会议吧？
李：好，我很高兴现在谈论这个问题。
布朗：会议定在这周五下午两点开始，五点结束。而且将会有来自10个国家150名高级经理参加这次会议。你能帮我安排一下吗？
李：当然可以，布朗先生，不过我能不能了解一下你的计划？
布朗：请先寄出正式的会议请柬。哦，要做的事都写在这里了。
李：可以给我吗？我草拟会议通知和会议日程时需要它。
布朗：拿去吧，这是供你参考用的。顺便说一下，请帮我拟一个特别日程表。
李：你是说，你自己还需要一个更详细的日程表，是吗？
布朗：没错。我得主持会议。
李：好的，我明白了。我会认真准备并且在会议开始前送出日程表，以便与会者有时间在会议开始前考虑日程表上的议程。
布朗：很好。你是否想好了比较合适的开会地点呢？
李：是的，会议可以安排在西湖酒店。那里的会议室大小适中。此外，那里的设备齐全，租金合理。
布朗：能告诉我这次会议的预算吗？
李：最多两万元。
布朗：很好。不过在会议开始前，你最好检查一下灯光、空调和投影仪是否正常，还要检查一下水、玻璃杯、烟灰缸、钢笔和纸是否备好。
李：你说得没错。
布朗：顺便问一下，我们还会有几位外宾来参加会议。你做了哪些安排呢？
李：我会安排一位口译员在场。
布朗：那里的会场有同声传译设备，是吧？
李：是的。开会时，与会者也可以依靠同声传译设备。
布朗：很好。另外，你会怎么安排我们来宾就座呢？
李：可是我不熟悉每一位来宾。
布朗：哦，那很容易。我给你写一份来宾的名单。
李：太好了。这样我就可以用这份名单做一个座位安排表，然后再把姓名卡片放在会议桌上。嗯，你希望什么时候供应点心呢？
布朗：在怀特先生报告后的休息时间供应点心。
李：那我们要准备哪些点心呢？
布朗：不如就自助餐吧？
李：好的，我会安排的。如果你不介意，我就着手办了。

交际精品2　会议进行中

（*布朗先生、海恩先生、葛蓝先生、朱比先生、博尔勒先生和葛瑞比先生正在开会。他们在讨论是否要实施一个新项目。*）

布朗：女士们先生们，请注意！请就座。会议准备开始。
海恩：葛蓝先生在哪里？他是要出席会议的。

布朗：哦，他来了。说曹操啊……
葛蓝：对不起，让你们久等了。
布朗：好，所有人都到了。我们开始吧！大家都知道今天我们要讨论什么。明天就要见客户了，从今天到明天的这段时间里，我们一定要想出些有创意的点子。现在，每个人都可以畅所欲言，因为在大脑激烈的思考中无论想法多么愚蠢，都是可以接受的。现在，我们想听听葛兰先生的看法。
葛蓝：啊，我不得不承认我对这笔生意还是有疑问的。这张表显示了我们公司最近的财务状况。从这张表中我们可以很清楚地看到由于通货膨胀率高，我们公司的利润近来在下降。现在销售部购买原材料要支付比原先多一倍的价钱。
布朗：那你是怎么看的呢，朱比先生？
朱比：我对这次的计划没有什么看法。我想海恩先生能否给我们提出什么意见？
布朗：海恩先生？
海恩：我们能否削减成本呢？
朱比：运输费似乎也很高。
博尔勒：这是由于空运费增加了。
朱比：为什么我们不从汉口沿着黄河运送货物呢？那样的话可以大幅度地降低成本。
葛瑞比：恐怕在这方面我的意见与你有所不同。
布朗：你能把这点说得再具体一些吗？
葛瑞比：如果那样的话，会花更长的时间，我们将不得不修改所有的日程安排。
博尔勒：没错。为了确保客户能准时收到货物，我们将不得不提早发货。
海恩：难道不会有所耽搁吗？黄河上运输量是很繁忙的。
朱比：延迟送货肯定会恶化我们公司的公共关系。因为延迟送货而失去客户，这个代价我们可承受不起。
葛蓝：我觉得我们首先要弄清楚启动这项计划要花多少钱，以及在接下来的两三年里我们会有什么样的回报。
海恩：你们都明白，成本问题并不是我们唯一顾虑的。我们这些年一直在等像这样的一次机会。我提议我们马上实施这个计划，这可是一个千载难逢的机会。
葛蓝：我并不是说我反对这个项目，但是在着急做任何决定之前，我们需要做一些核实的工作。
朱比：没错。考虑到目前的市场状况，我们需要更审慎些。
布朗：那么，似乎我们大家都同意这个项目，但是在我们这次会议结束之前，我还要再明确说明一点，如果要实施这个项目，并且要获得成功的话，需要所有人的共同努力。如果我们能使赞助商相信这个项目最终可以让所有的投资人受益的话，那么资金就一定会到位。总之，至关重要的是，所有的部门能够通力合作，确保计划的顺利进行。好，今天就到这儿吧。

交际精品3　做会议记录

（新来的秘书方小姐在询问资深秘书李小姐如何做会议记录。）
方：李小姐，开会时我得做会议记录吗？

李：是的，当然要。会议记录得认真写。
方：你能解释一下该怎么做会议记录吗？
李：好。哦，我随身带着已准备好的开会用的笔记本，你可以看看。
方：谢谢。嗯……这是什么？
李：这是公司的名称……恒星机械进出口公司。然后是……各部门经理会议记录，时间是2006年3月8日，星期四，下午两点半。再下面是……出席人：主席——首席执行官布朗先生。
方：然后在下面留出空白处写经理们的名字，是吗？
李：是的，没错。然后，第一项总是……缺席人表示的歉意。
方：接着是什么？
李：第二项总是……上次会议的记录。上次会议的记录一经阅过，你就可以写上"上次会议的记录已宣读、确认和签署。"
方：已签署？
李：是。当会议记录被确认后，主席就要签字。
方：那么我是不是得把会议上每个人说的每个字都记下来？
李：哦，不需要。这样既难做到也没必要。你只需要把讨论的题目和结果记下来就行了。
方：讨论的结果？
李：一个话题经过一段时间讨论后，通常就有人建议实施。
方：然后呢？
李：然后主席就会问与会者是否赞成这个建议。如果赞成，你就写下"会议同意……"或者"会议决议……"。
方：有什么差别吗？
李：其实没有什么差别。"决议"是一个专门的会议用语。一个建议一经委员会同意就会被叫做"决议"。看，这是上次会议的记录，而这是我的笔记。
方：哦，太好了。我对你做的会议记录很感兴趣：会议决议3月15日不办公。

第十七章　推　销

第一部分　商务情景对话

交际精品1　登门推销

（日升保健品有限公司营销部的露丝，走访一家玩具公司。她正在向玩具公司的杰克推销其产品。）

露丝：早上好，我是日升保健品有限公司的推销员。我们公司是家按摩椅生产厂家。我想占用你几分钟的时间，跟你简单介绍一下我们的产品。
杰克：对不起，我们是一家玩具公司。我们员工要坐在你们的按摩椅上制作可爱的玩具吗？
露丝：你开玩笑吧！
杰克：那么，你能跟我说说到底按摩椅与我们公司有什么关系？
露丝：有，关系还挺大的。最近你们公司的许多员工有颈椎痛和背痛，对吗？

杰克：是的。
露丝：员工工作压力大，且得在流水线旁工作很长时间，难怪他们的身体状况不太好。请问，他们疼痛时通常怎么解决？
杰克：他们下班后会去按摩医院按摩。
露丝：你们公司坐落在市郊，和市里有很长一段距离，是不是？
杰克：哦，是的。我们公司距离市中心约有七公里。
露丝：所以，你们公司的员工治病不方便，是吧？
杰克：没错。
露丝：如果情况真是那样，那么疼痛一定会对你们公司员工的工作效率有很大影响。为什么不试试我们的按摩椅呢？
杰克：是吗？
露丝：我们的按摩椅是用来刺激血液循环和放松肌肉的。
杰克：还有呢？
露丝：按摩椅还可以按摩颈部和脊椎。而且你们的员工也不必走那么远的路去治病。
杰克：不错。我可以试试吗？
露丝：当然可以。（让经理坐在椅子上）
杰克：（过了一会儿）哇，感觉真好。
露丝：如果你们买几台我们的按摩椅，那么你们公司的员工就会省下不少去按摩的钱。
杰克：能演示一下按摩椅怎么操作吗？
露丝：没问题。首先接上电源。在扶手上有一个控制板。
杰克：控制板？
露丝：是的，按"电源"钮来打开或关闭按摩椅。然后按"功能"钮来选择一种功能。这种型号有"揉"和"捶"两种功能。
杰克："揉"和"捶"？现在我感觉好像有一只手在揉我的背。这一定是"揉"的功能。
露丝：是的。（按一下"捶"的按钮）如果你选择"捶"的功能，那么你会感觉好像有人用锤子轻轻地敲打你。
杰克：太好了！
露丝：如果你们的员工不再有这些疼痛，他们会很开心，工作也会更有效率。
杰克：不错。
露丝：同意我的看法吗？对我们的按摩椅感兴趣吗？想不想订几台按摩椅？
杰克：你刚才说的的确很有吸引力。但是我想考虑一下再做最后的决定。
露丝：好，我一两天后再来拜访你。这是我的名片。需要的时候，请给我打电话，好吗？
杰克：谢谢，我会的。

交际精品2　向客户介绍新产品

（朱丽叶在美国从事妇女服装工作。她来和销售经理王先生谈生意。王先生正在与朱丽叶谈论新产品的特点。）

王：朱丽叶，欢迎您来中国。
朱丽叶：我很高兴访问你们公司。希望我们能合作。

王：我也是。朱丽叶，您看过我们的产品目录了吗？
朱丽叶：哦，是的。我已浏览过你上次来信中所附的产品目录和小册子。
王：您觉得我们的新产品怎么样？
朱丽叶：我对你们的新产品印象很好。
王：真高兴。实际上，这是我们刚开发出来的具有创新性的新产品。纱的质量是经过精心挑选的，而且织得很细密。到目前为止已销往海外好几个地区，很畅销的。
朱丽叶：很不错。这种货品有几种颜色？
王：两种标准颜色。您偏好哪一种？
朱丽叶：我比较喜欢深色的那一种，因为那比较适合老年人。
王：我赞同。如果订购量为5,000套或者更多，您可以选择喜欢的颜色。
朱丽叶：这里有样品吗？
王：有的，都在样品室。您想看一下吗？
朱丽叶：好的。
王：带您去样品室吧。
朱丽叶：谢谢。
王：不客气，这边请。（几分钟后）这是我们的样品室。我们公司几乎所有的产品都在这里。
朱丽叶：哦，样品可真多啊。有很多外国客户到这里吧？
王：是的，相当多。他们喜欢时尚，所以每个月我们的陈列品都有变化。
朱丽叶：那么你们公司产品的内销与外销比例是多少？
王：七成外销，三成内销。
朱丽叶：明白了。
王：朱丽叶，请这边走，我们的新产品在那边。
朱丽叶：哦，看看这个。我喜欢这种玫瑰花的图案，让人觉得很温暖很浪漫。
王：是这样的，而且这种材料很好洗。
朱丽叶：真的吗？
王：是的。只要把它放进洗衣机，洗后取出来晾干就行了。不需多费心。
朱丽叶：那很方便的。一码多少钱？
王：一码50元，但还得看订货量。
朱丽叶：这些品种现在有存货吗？
王：因为现在对它们的需求很大，所以目前陈列的产品中只有一些存货，其余的必须等一个星期我们才能供货。离开前，您会下些订单吗？
朱丽叶：嗯……我认为你们的价格比其他公司的价格高，而你们的新产品对于我国的消费者来说是陌生的。你知道的，要开拓一个新市场是不容易的。
王：不错，但是当我们比较价格时，最好先考虑产品的质量，不是吗？同行知道我们的产品质量比其他公司的好。我可以向你保证我们的价格是可行和合理的。所以我们相信我们的产品很有希望得到你们客户的欢迎。
朱丽叶：那么，如果你们可以打折，我会考虑下订单的。
王：好的，如果订购1,000件以上，我们可以打九折。

朱丽叶：好的。我愿意试试你们的新产品。最早什么时候可以交货？
王：这个月底。
朱丽叶：行，但你们必须遵守交货时间。
王：是的，当然。我们一直对出口订单给予优先。您不必担忧。
朱丽叶：那么什么时候可以签约？
王：明天方便吗？
朱丽叶：好的。

交际精品3　谈论广告策略

（朱丽叶喜欢和王先生的公司做生意。现在她正和王先生谈论广告策略。）

朱丽叶：王先生，我对你们的新产品印象很深，想与贵公司做生意。但是现在我关心的主要是产品的促销问题。你知道有很多促销的方法，能否告诉我贵公司对新产品的广告策略？
王：当然可以。我们的产品在这里享有很好的声誉，但是在贵国却是新产品。所以首先要考虑市场定位。我们得进行市场调查，然后决定谁最有可能是产品的消费者。
朱丽叶：说得对。在对产品做广告前，我们应该确定产品的目标消费者。
王：我们认为在介绍新产品时，广告、产品价格和赠送样品都是最重要的。首先我们需要对产品进行广告宣传，必须让消费者熟知我们的产品。
朱丽叶：我同意。
王：我认为下一步就是决定选择哪种媒体以及在什么时候进行广告宣传。
朱丽叶：媒体吗？只有吸引消费者，他们才可能购买。
王：是的，通过媒体。通常会通过两个或更多的媒体宣传产品。做广告的目的是吸引当地消费者对我们的产品感兴趣并保持关注，这样他们才会购买我们的产品。
朱丽叶：你们倾向哪一种媒体呢？
王：我们认为在电视上做广告对消费者购买产品影响更大。比如说，广告商常常请名人做广告使消费者相信其产品值得购买。
朱丽叶：是的。
王：而且电视拥有众多观众，所以通过电视能广而告知。
朱丽叶：但在电视上做广告要花费很大。
王：我认为只要效果令人满意，就值得做。
朱丽叶：听起来很有道理。那么我们什么时候推出广告呢？
王：今年夏初怎么样？
朱丽叶：好啊。我建议除了在电视上做广告，还可以同时利用其他渠道来宣传我们的产品。
王：其他什么渠道？
朱丽叶：通过报纸、杂志、直接邮购、网络以及利用广播来宣传我们的产品，怎么样？
王：太棒了。我们在不同的媒体上做广告，宣传我们产品的与众不同，使更多的人了解我们的产品，改变他们的观念。我们也在尽力推行网上交易。
朱丽叶：当今，网上交易正在成为推销产品的十分流行方式。
王：我们试图找到最行之有效的途径让顾客了解我们的网站和新产品。

朱丽叶：好！顺便说一下，对一种全新的国外产品，我们不能把价格定得太低。否则会削弱产品在消费者心目中的价值。

王：这是肯定的。还有，面对贵国市场上已有的同类产品的激烈竞争，需要召开一个新闻发布会来宣传我们的产品。

朱丽叶：别担心，我会联系一些重要媒体的记者、潜在客户和销售商来参加新闻发布会。

王：太好了！我们最好着手干吧！

第十八章　面试

第一部分　商务情景对话

交际精品1　在接待处

（刘先生刚从大学毕业，正在找工作。今天他将参加一个面试。刘先生朝接待员高小姐走去，高小姐负责接待工作。）

刘：早上好。

高：早上好，先生。我能帮你什么吗？

刘：我是来参加今天早上9点的面试。我前天收到电话，通知我今天来面试。

高：知道了，请问您的姓名？

刘：我叫刘锋。

高：（看了一下名单）哦，是的，您是6号。请到那边坐着等一下好吗？轮到您时我会叫您的名字。

刘：好的，谢谢。

（过了大约二十分钟，高小姐朝刘先生示意。）

高：刘先生，轮到您了。我们的考官在201室等您。这边请！

刘：好的。非常感谢。

高：不用谢。祝您好运。

刘：谢谢。

高：不客气。

交际精品2　在面试中

（刘先生进入面试的房间，人事部经理林小姐及其同事正等着他。）

刘：早上好，我叫刘峰。

林：早上好，刘先生。很高兴见到你，我是人事部的林晴。请坐。

刘：谢谢，林女士。

林：从你简历上看，你刚刚毕业。请谈谈个人情况吧。

刘：我刚从北京大学毕业。我是学经济的，主修国际贸易。

林：在大学里成绩如何？

刘：很好。我学习努力，几乎每次考试都取得好成绩，可以从简历里看出来，我获得了成绩优良奖学金。

林：你知道我们公司是个大型的国际贸易公司，在十多个国家都有分公司。这份工作需要你使用大量英语，因此想知道你的英语水平如何。

刘：我认为很好。我英语口语和书面能力都很强。我已经通过英语6级而且在学校每场考试都取得了好成绩。

林：嗯，从简历上可以看出。你觉得你在学校里受到的教育能够应用到我们公司的工作中吗？

刘：我学的专业与你们公司涉及的领域是对口的。确信可以把我所学的应用到公司的工作中去。

林：你认为你是哪种类型的人？

刘：不晓得你想了解我的哪些情况。嗯，我做事很热心，不喜欢半途而废，那会让我紧张。如果一件事没做完，我会无法专心做其他事情。总之，我想我是一个有抱负、能自我约束且言而有信的人。

林：我很欣赏你这点。你性格外向还是内向？

刘：嗯，我不很确定——也许两者兼有。有时我喜欢一个人独处，但是大部分时间我比较喜欢和其他人在一起，我在大学的社团里非常活跃。

林：你是从众型的，还是领导型的？

刘：我不想领先于别人，尤其是去领导他们。我宁愿和其他人合作，一起努力完成工作。

交际精品3　面试继续进行

（林小姐与坐在她身边的同事交流意见。）

林：你为什么要选择我们公司？我们市有那么多的外贸公司。

刘：贵公司是我们市做事最有效率、最让人称道的公司之一。公司给员工提供了自由、合作的工作环境。我还知道贵公司有一个以老带新的制度，我会珍惜每一个和前辈在一起工作的机会，相信贵公司会给我提供更多的机会学以致用。

林：但你缺乏经验，我为什么要聘用你呢？

刘：没经验不代表没有能力。从理论上讲，我已经学过了国际贸易及其运作原理。坚信我的热情、勤勉以及我的适应能力能够弥补我经验上的不足。我相信我是做这份工作的最佳人选。请给我一个机会以证明我的能力吧。

林：你怎么看待加班这个问题？你知道，我们有时很忙，因此得加班。如果得上夜班，你会不会抱怨呢？

刘：当然不会啦，我认为这很正常。

林：尽管你没有问，但我知道你很想了解薪水的问题。你心中的理想薪水是多少呢？

刘：我可以接受贵公司根据我的资历给予的薪水，但希望公司能根据我的能力，逐渐加薪。贵公司在员工酬劳上有很好的声誉，我相信你们会对我一视同仁。

林：好的。还有问题要问吗？

刘：我什么时候能知道是否被录用？

林：如果被录用，我们会在下周初通知。前三个月为试用期，这是我们的规定。

刘：我理解。

林：那好，很高兴你今天能来，刘先生。

刘：谢谢你给我面试的机会，林女士，希望能再见到你。

林：祝你好运！

刘：谢谢林女士，再见！

第十九章 投 诉

第一部分 商务情景对话

交际精品1 别给我垃圾邮件！
（珍妮登录了一个网站并注册，但万万没料到的是垃圾邮件从此竟源源不断。她把自己的经历向朋友倾诉。）
珍妮：真受不了了！
雪莉：怎么了？
珍妮：我的邮箱里全是垃圾邮件。
雪莉：怎么会这样？
珍妮：逛易趣网上商店的时候，我对一个小店的货很感兴趣，所以就注册了，希望他们告诉我更多的有关它们产品的信息。
雪莉：所以如你所愿，他们就给你提供信息了……
珍妮：对。但后来我不喜欢他们一直向我兜售产品，我很多次请他们别再给我发邮件，每次他们都承诺不再给我发邮件了，可是我还照旧收到他们的邮件。
雪莉：我知道了，你上了他们的钩儿。
珍妮：是的。我发传真、打电话，无数次请他们别再给我发邮件，现在可好，倒好像是我在骚扰他们……
雪莉：我想按照网上的说明，你应该能够自己退出他们的联系人列表吧！顾客不再需要邮件时，商家就不该再寄发邮件。这是商家的义务。
珍妮：我试过太多遍了……他们都是些骗子。这些人就是不愿意那样做。有个人打电话告诉我说"我已经在你打电话的那天把你的名字删除了"，可是一切还是老样子。我昨天又收到了他们的邮件。
雪莉：天哪……真讨厌……那你该怎么办？
珍妮：只能以牙还牙。他们一直骗我，一直让我收到邮件，那我就一直打电话、发传真、发邮件给他们，直到他们不发给我为止。要是他们不想半夜接电话，就别把他们的电话附在邮件上发过来呀，对不对？

交际精品2 商业欺诈
（一位女士致电投诉中心投诉一桩商业欺诈。）
工作人员：投诉中心。请讲。
　某女士：嗯，下午好。有地方投诉可真不错。
工作人员：很高兴能为您提供帮助，女士，您投诉什么？
　某女士：是这样的，我们被地平线旅行社骗了。两年前，我和丈夫参加了他们的一个分时度假推销会。
工作人员：您购买他们的旅行项目了么？

某女士： 怎么可能不买。那些销售代表缠着我们几个小时，好话说尽，想尽办法诱惑我们，他们答应免费赠送我们去维加斯的旅行。最后我就买了他们分时度假的积分。

工作人员： 那你们有没有去维加斯？

某女士： 没有去，旅行只安排在一年中特定的几天。而我们没料到孩子竟会在那几天出意外，最后也没能去成。但最可恶的是最近我打电话预约我的分时度假时，竟然发现我的积分没有了。

工作人员： 怎么回事？

某女士： 我也不知道。本以为我从没用过积分，肯定已经累积了很多，但是他们竟告诉我积分没了，都用来支付会员费了。他们的销售代表从来没对我提过什么会员费。要是提前讲明还要交什么会员费，我才不会签约呢！

工作人员： 好的，我已经把你的投诉记录下来了。我们将会尽快受理你的投诉，把你的投诉转到有关部门。

某女士： 谢谢。我想以后再也不会这么惨了。天下没有免费的午餐！

交际精品3　错装
（施蒂文森向发货方抱怨错装，对方的秘书予以商洽。）

施蒂文森： 早上好，请找业务部的李经理。

秘书： 对不起，他在度假。我是她的秘书，他度假期间，工作暂时由我负责，能帮您什么忙？

施蒂文森： 我是荷兰的施蒂文森。我要投诉。

秘书： 怎么了？

施蒂文森： 我简单地说一下。是关于我们两个月前订的货，货号是1326。我们已经收到货了，可是，开箱才发现，四分之一的箱子里面竟装了其他不同的货品，显然是错装，这给我们造成很大的麻烦。

秘书： 很抱歉，我们会立刻调查此事。如果确实是我方责任，我们一定立刻将替换品发给你们。

施蒂文森： 我们会暂时替你们保管这些错装货品，以待你方处置。但现在是我们所订货品的销售旺季，我们急需替代货品，如果不能在两周内收到替代货品，我们要求取消合同，并退还货款。

秘书： 但即使真的是我方错装，我方发货也不可能两周之内到达你处。

施蒂文森： 既然这样，你们应该以空运替代海运。另外，我们不会承担两种运费的差价。

秘书： 在我澄清事情之前，暂时无法和您讨论替代品的问题。请将检验报告及图片用传真或电子邮件发给我们，我们会尽快通知结果。

……

秘书： 对不起，因为货号混淆造成了错装。既然是我们的问题，我们会按贵方要求空运货品并支付两种运费差价。要知道，货品本身还没有运费贵，但是我们的确需要你们在新市场的支持。

施蒂文森： 生意归生意。感谢你们的合作。

交际精品4　产品质量缺陷

（怀特先生向生产商抱怨货物质量缺陷，当地生产商的代理王先生，承担了相应的责任，并承诺加强质量监控。）

怀特：王先生，对贵公司的产品质量我们一向都很满意。只是这次实在令我感到意外。

王：怎么了？我们的货有什么问题么？

怀特：我们刚刚收到货号为3261的出货。我们发现不良率接近百分之五，远远超过了你们所承诺的百分之二。怎么回事？

王：怎么会呢？每一批货都是依照同样的设计和性能标准生产的且在出货前都是经过检验的。

怀特：眼见为实。这是我们带来的检验报告。

王：（尴尬地）作为你们的代理，我们很抱歉。春节就要来了，厂家要在一个月内赶完所有的货。欲速则不达，可能这批货漏检了。

怀特：那怎么办？

王：我们会马上派人去厂家通知此事，并采取行动改善目前状况。

怀特：那我们的损失怎么办？

王：我们将代表贵方和供应商协商，在最短的时间内让他们做出相应补偿。

怀特：我们希望此事能尽快解决。而且不良率必须控制在2%以内。

王：我们承诺一定会提高质量控制。我们将派有关人员现场监控加强质量控制。为避免类似问题，我们保证更加全面严格地检查货物。

怀特：最重要的是要有一个合格的供应商。如果目前状况没什么改善的话，我们建议你们另外再找一个更好的供应商。

王：没问题。

第二十章　宴会与告别

第一部分　商务情景对话

交际精品1　在酒桌上

（史密斯先生和同事应实业公司刘董事长的邀请去一家饭店赴宴。）

刘：晚上好，史密斯先生。欢迎来参加晚宴。

史密斯：晚上好，董事长。感谢贵公司的邀请。

刘：欢迎你们来！首先，请让我介绍一下我的同事。史密斯先生，这位是王红，我们公司的生产部经理。这位是史密斯先生，美国电子公司的副总经理。

王：很高兴认识您，史密斯先生。

史密斯：认识您我也很高兴。

刘：现在大家都互相认识了，我们坐下来聊聊？

（所有人就座。）

史密斯：听说这里的菜很好。

刘：是啊，这里的菜很好吃，服务也没得比。

刘：史密斯先生，不知道您有无特殊偏好？

史密斯：入乡随俗吧。
刘：我期望今晚点的菜肴你们能够喜欢。
史密斯：我们久仰中国菜肴的大名，正翘首以待呢。
刘：愿意像我们中国人一样用筷子吗？当然，如果你们对使用筷子没什么把握，可以使用刀叉。
史密斯：我试着用筷子吧，但我当心如果我一直用筷子，我只能吃个半饱。所以如果使用筷子有困难我就使用刀叉。

（大家笑。）

刘：你想喝点什么？
史密斯：中国酒。但我们对中国的酒知之甚少，能否给我们推荐一些呢？
刘：当然可以。中国有一些很著名的酒，比如茅台、五粮液、剑南春、孔府家酒等。还有一些很好的红葡萄酒和白葡萄酒，比如张裕红葡萄酒和长城白葡萄酒。您喜欢哪种呢？
史密斯：有人说茅台味道很好。
刘：是的，它是我们中国的名酒之一，确实很好。它喝了不上头。
史密斯：那好，我想尝一下。

（晚餐就绪。）

刘：这是冷盘。请自便，就像在自己家里一样。
史密斯：谢谢。这些都很好吃。
刘：很高兴您能喜欢。再来点好么？
史密斯：谢谢，只要一点点就好了。
刘：来点北京烤鸭吧，这是北京的名菜。
史密斯：好的。喔，真好吃，又嫩又脆，我从没吃过这样好吃的菜。
刘：真的吗？那再来点吧？
史密斯：谢谢，据我所知，中国的宴会有很多道菜，所以刚开始要悠着点。
刘：史密斯先生，您筷子用得很好。
史密斯：多谢鼓励。
刘：来点对虾怎么样？
史密斯：好的，很可口。
刘：您看起来胃口不错嘛，值得喝一杯。为您的健康，干杯！
所有人：干杯！
史密斯：请问，你们中文里是怎么说"Bottoms up"？
刘：我们说"干杯"。
史密斯：那么，我提议为我们的友谊和合作，干杯！
刘：史密斯先生，您学得可真快啊！干杯！
史密斯：这个真好吃，是什么呢？
刘：我不知道它的英文名，但在中文里我们称它为"素鸡"，直译为素食者的鸡。
史密斯：素鸡？真是太好吃了！
刘先生：来点海鲜火锅吧，这家饭店的特色菜。

史密斯：好啊，我很喜欢海鲜。鲜美可口，看上去不错。
刘：是啊，中国菜肴注重色香味俱全。来点饺子好么？
史密斯：饺子是什么呢？
刘：一种里面包着肉馅和菜，用水煮的团子。
史密斯：很有趣，我想来一点。
史密斯：这怪味鸡使我胃口大开。
刘：看来咱俩的口味一样。再来点吧。
史密斯：谢谢，但是我得注意保持体型。

交际精品2　祝酒
（晚宴进行了一个小时，刘董事长清了清嗓子，举杯站了起来，所有人都停止交谈转向她。）
史密斯先生，
女士们先生们：
　　我不想长篇大论影响大家的兴致，破坏今晚的欢乐气氛，但我还是要说几句。
　　今晚我代表本公司非常高兴同史密斯先生及其同事欢聚一堂。正如俗话所说："有朋自远方来，不亦乐乎！"史密斯先生和他的同事来自地球的另一边，我们今晚的喜悦真是难以言表。
　　非常高兴，美国朋友此行富有极大成效——我们签了一份价值3,000万美元的合同并达成长期合作的意向，这为未来的良好关系打下基础。唯一的遗憾就是你们待的时间太短了，我期待着我们再次在中国重聚。
　　我要借这个机会请大家举杯，为我们两家公司的友谊，为我们两家公司的繁荣，也为你们明天旅途顺利。干杯！
所有人：干杯！
（所有人都站立，喝酒并一起鼓掌。）

交际精品3　答谢酒会
刘董事长，
尊敬的来宾，女士们先生们：
　　感谢董事长的美言。借此机会表示我们诚挚的谢意，感谢你们热情的欢迎和款待。
　　虽然我们在这里的时间很短却取得了极大的成果。我们签了一份价值3,000万美元的合同并达成长期合作的协议。更为重要的是，我们和员工们进行接触，和你们交谈，和你们一起进餐、喝酒，与你们讨价还价，与你们同忧愁、共欢笑。我们的尊敬之情由此滋生，我们的友谊由此加深。我确信我们的成效比预期的要好，希望你们知道我们感谢贵方为此所做的努力。
　　明天，我和我的同事将离开这个美丽的城市，但我们会记住这次愉快的旅程。希望有一天你们也能到我们的城市去看看，以便我们能回报你们的热情和好客。
　　现在我提议让我们干杯。为我们的东道主，为你们的健康，当然了，也为我们的友谊和合作。干杯！
所有人：干杯！
（席间响起了热烈的掌声。另一道菜上来了，宴会在活跃的交谈中又进行了大约20分钟。）

Appendix 2 Suggested Key to Practice

（实践操练参考答案）

Chapter 1

I. Complete the Following Dialogues

(1)

1. myself	2. spell	3. names	4. card	5. remember
6. ask	7. really	8. introduce	9. made	10. know

(2)

1. Passport	2. by	3. means/is	4. it	5. declare
6. effects/belongings	7. in	8. please/kindly	9. fruit	10. prohibited

II. Interaction Activities

Task 1

(1) My name is Steve Singer from Sunshine Group Ltd. Allow me to present the representatives of my company to you. This is Mr. Robinson, Chief Executive Officer. He is a very active person and he is really a somebody.

Greeting: A: How do you do?

Response: B: How do you do?

(2) I'd like you to meet our export manager. He has been very successful in his job. What is more, he is never flashy and he is a team player too.

Greeting: A: How nice to meet you.

Response: B: Glad to meet you.

(3) Please let me introduce Miss Howard to you. She is our personnel manager. She is very attractive. The first thing you notice when you meet her is her smile.

Greeting: A: It's a pleasure to know you.

Response: B: I am happy to have the opportunity to meet you.

(4) I take great pleasure in introducing Ms. Morley, our Secretary to you. She is a kind-hearted lady. She is always willing to help others. Greeting: A: I am delighted to meet you. Response: B: It's a pleasure.

Task 2

(1)

A: If I'm not mistaken, you must be Mr. Green.

B: Quite right.

A: I'm glad to introduce myself to you. I am Sandra from New Century Company.

B: Glad to meet you.

A: Welcome to our company. I have often heard of you.

B: I'm happy to make your acquaintance.
A: Thanks. How about your boss?
B: He always talks about you. He has been looking forward to meeting you for a long time.
A: Fine. I am dying to meet him.

(2)

A: What's up?
B: Pretty good. How are you?
A: Fine. Thanks.
B: I am going to Paris on business.
A: Oh! I wish I could go with you.

III. Actual Practice

A: Good morning. May I introduce myself to you? I am Henry Brown from Fruits & Vegetable Corp.
B: My name is Jack Tompkins. I am happy to have the opportunity to meet you.
A: Nice to meet you, too.
B: I'd like to have your telephone number and fax number, Mr. Brown.
A: Here's my name card. Please call me, Jack.
B: Thank you. Here's mine. So your telephone number is (416) 480-480. It's easy to remember, isn't it?
A: That's right.
B: Could you give me some information about your company?
A: Sure. My company is dealing with many kinds of food products. Our products are very popular in the market.
B: What are your main products?
A: Our main products are fresh fruits and vegetables, frozen fruits and vegetables and dried foodstuffs.
B: Good. They are just the products we are after.
A: Let's get down to business.

IV. Creative Discussion

The teacher encourages the students to think and express their ideas creatively.
(No model discussion results are provided for this part.)

Chapter 2

I. Complete the Following Dialogues

1. speak	2. he	3. looking	4. line	5. in
6. professional	7. specializing	8. products	9. interest	10. fall
11. willing	12. direct	13. basis	14. idea	15. adhere

II. Interaction Activities

Task 1

A: I hope you don't mind my asking your opinion.

B: No, not at all.

A: Could you give me some advice about how to get in touch with businessman?

B: From my point of view, nowadays the most effective way to contact is by sending e-mail.

A: To a certain degree, yes, but I think telephoning is more direct.

B: I know what you mean, but sending e-mail is very convenient and cheap.

A: What is your view about sending information by fax?

B: If I were you, I would send an e-mail instead of a fax.

A: That's quite true. Thank you for your help.

B: You are welcome.

Task 2

A: Hey, what's going on?

B: Yeah, not much. I need your good suggestions.

A: What can I do for you?

B: What's your opinion about asking for samples from a new client?

A: Don't hesitate to ask for samples directly from the client.

B: I agree with much of your idea but I am afraid that we don't know each other.

A: It's a common practice to ask for samples from the seller.

B: True enough. What do you reckon I should do next?

A: I'd like to suggest that you make a request soon.

B: I don't entirely agree with you but I'll try.

III. Actual Practice

A: Good morning. Stainless Steel Product Ltd.

B: Good morning. This is David from Canadian Import Corp. Your company has been recommended by Chamber of Commerce.

A: That sounds interesting.

B: Ours is a leading company dealing with the import of steal products. We are importers of high reputation, trading in stainless steel products. As you are the producer, we are very interested in your products.

A: That's quite good.

B: Well. It will be helpful if you give me more information about your business.

A: We are making various kinds of stainless steel products. We have been in this line of business for more than 30 years.

B: Would you be so kind to send us your brochure?

A: Sure. In order to give you a better understanding of our products, we'll send our brochure to you right now.

B: Fine, thanks. As your products fall within the scope of our business activities, we would like to set up business relationship with your corporation.

A: It is a good idea. Establishing direct business relations between our companies will be to our mutual benefit.

IV. Creative Discussion

No discussion results are provided for this part.

V. Debate

The debate is open, so no model discussion results are provided for this part.

Chapter 3

I. Complete the Following Dialogues

(1)

1. interest	2. turn	3. variety	4. quality	5. made
6. market	7. broaden	8. enquiry/inquiry	9. quote	10. basis

(2)

1. a great pleasure to	2. conclude business	3. in particular
4. interested in	5. in the market	6. place an order
7. from stock	8. wouldn't mind	9. be helpful
10. firm offers	11. subject to	12. keep rising
13. in view of	14. in spite of	15. get the ball rolling

II. Interaction Activities

Task 1

A: I wouldn't mind knowing about the information of your air conditioners.

B: No problem. Our air conditioners enjoy good reputation in the world market.

A: We are in the market for your air conditioners.

B: Good. How many are you are going to order?

A: About 30,000 sets for the initial order. Meanwhile, we'd like to inquire about the availability of the air conditioners, that is, a good supply in stock.

B: I am afraid they are out of stock recently because summer is coming.

A: Do you really mean it? You see, we need the goods urgently. Could you do me a favor by turning out more air conditioners for us?

B: In order to set up a good relationship, we'll try our best to meet your requirement as soon as possible.

A: We shall appreciate it if you will do this for us.

Task 2

A: Here is our inquiry list. You will find that the required items including the name of the products, specifications and quantities.

B: Let me have a look.

A: I was wondering if you could offer us competitive prices for digital camera.

B: Thank you for your inquiry.

A: I'd like to stress the important of the competitive prices.

B: I see. You will find our prices very attractive.

A: If the prices are workable, we are planning to place an order with you.

B: Fine. Here are our price lists.

A: We'll look into them.

III. Actual Practice

A: Hello, what can I do for you?

B: Ah, We are keen on your mobile phones.

A: Which models do you prefer?

B: We are particularly interested in Nokia 7260 and Nokia N70. How about the quality of these products?

A: We assure you that they are of superior quality and reasonable in price.

B: What are the terms of prices?

A: We quote FOB, CFR or CIF prices as requested.

B: We need CIF prices.

A: OK. We'll work them out for you soon.

B: Good. When will you make shipment?

A: One month after receiving L/C.

B: OK.

IV. Creative Discussion

The teacher encourages the students to think and express their ideas creatively.

(No model discussion results are provided for this part.)

Chapter 4

I. Complete the Following Dialogues

1. have an appointment	2. am afraid	3. something urgent	4. are filled
5. do me a favor	6. for business activities	7. Got it	8. have a try
9. look at his schedule	10. keep him long	11. a releasing break	12. is available
13. is very kind of	14. is convenient for	15. Let's make it	

II. Interaction Activities

Task 1

A: I am going to pay a business visit to your company.
B: Good. Have you booked your hotel?
A: Not yet. Could you make a hotel reservation for me?
B: Certainly. I'd like to have your business schedule so that we'll arrange everything well for you.
A: It is very considerate of you to say so. I'll send my schedule to you by e-mail as soon as possible.
B: Do you have any special requirements for the hotel?
A: Nothing special. Just make reservation for a standard rooms for me.
B: Let's fix it.
A: By the way, I'd love to visit the natural wonders in China.
B: I recommend you visit Wuyi Mountain, where you will enjoy the beauty of natures.
A: I heard it before. It is a nice option, I think.
B: I am sure you'll have a lot of fun there.

Task 2

A: I'm terribly sorry that I am not able to keep the appointment with you.
B: What's up?
A: I have pressing business to do so I have to put off the meeting.
B: That's all right. Let's make it another time.
A: How about next Monday morning?
B: I am afraid I will be tied up then.
A: Well, When is the most convenient time for you?
B: I'll be expecting you next Monday evening.
A: That's settled.

III. Actual Practice

James: Hello, Mr. Tao. I am going to attend China Technology and Projects Fair next week.
Tao: Wonderful! Glad to have opportunity to meet you.
James: I'm calling to make an appointment with you.
Tao: Could you tell me your itinerary?
James: Sure. I'll stay in your city for a week. The purpose of our meeting is to exchange views with you about promoting sales face to face.
Tao: Pretty good. I'm eager to talk with you.
James: Would Tuesday afternoon suit you?
Tao: Any afternoon except Tuesday. I had a previous engagement.
James: Let's say Wednesday morning, all right?
Tao: OK. Let's make it 9 o'clock at my office.

IV. Creative Discussion

The teacher encourages the students to think and express their ideas creatively.
(No model discussion results are provided for this part.)

Chapter 5

I. Complete the Following Dialogues

(1)

1. nice	2. person	3. correspondence	4. recent	5. visit
6. another	7. out	8. to	9. likely	10. long

(2)

1. unwise	2. on	3. halfway	4. concession	5. reasonable
6. truth	7. quoted	8. really	9. customer	10. have

II. Role-plays

Task 1

Jack: Good morning, Miss Wang, it's nice to see you again.

Wang: Good morning, Jack. How are things going?

Jack: Everything is nice except for the weather. I just can't get over how different the weather is here.

Wang: You are bound to feel that way at first. I hope you'll get used to it soon.

Jack: Yes, I hope so. Miss Wang, I came here to talk to you about my requirements of T-shirt. You see, I told you over the phone yesterday that I'm interested in your T-shirt. I want a T-shirt of 100% cotton, 190 g/m^2.

Wang: I know that, Jack. Therefore, we have specially made out a price-list, which covers those items most salable on your market. Here are our price list and catalogues.

Jake: Well, it seems to me that items No.5, No.8 and No.12 are suitable for our market. But I'm sorry to say that your price is about 8% higher than those offered by other suppliers. It would be impossible for me to push any sales at such high prices.

Wang: I'm sorry to hear you say that. You're probably aware that the costs of raw materials have gone up tremendously during the recent months while our prices for T-shirt basically remain unchanged. I dare say that the prices we offered compare favorably with any quotations you can obtain elsewhere.

Jake: I'm afraid I can't agree with you there. I wish to point out that your offers are higher than some of the quotations I've received from your competitiors in other countries.

Wang: Jack, you are well experienced in this field. You should not listen only to the price, but must take the quality into consideration, too. Everyone in this trade knows that China's T-shirts are not only superior in quality but also attractive in designs and colors.

Jake: I agree with what you say, but the price difference should not be so big. I only ask that your prices be competitive to others. That's reasonable, isn't it?

Wang: Well, to start the ball rolling, we may consider making some concessions in our price. Would you please give me an idea of the quantity you wish to order?

Jack: 20,000 pcs.

Wang: Well, in that case, we are ready to reduce our prices by 5%. This will surely be the highest reduction we can offer.

Jake: I see. That's fine.

Task 2

1. **Jake:** OK, so, we will place an order for 5,000, but we'd like a 10% discount.
   Wang: Sorry, we can only offer you a 5% discount on this order.
   Jake: That's OK, if you can deliver in two weeks.
   Wang: That's fine.

2. **Jack:** We can supply your order. As you are a new customer, we would like you to pay in advance this time. When you've placed more orders, we can start to pay by letten of credit.
   Wang: I'm sorry, but we are not happy about paying everything in advance. We can offer to pay 50%.
   Jack: We'll have to get back to you on that.

3. **Jack:** OK. We'll buy 500 sets from you at that price. Can you deliver them by next month?
   Wang: We can deliver by next month, but it will be more expensive. If you pay the extra shipping costs, we'll deliver.
   Jack: That's OK if you can pay for the insurance.
   Wang: Fine.

4. **Jack:** If we buy more than 500 cases of the Reserve, what discount can you offer us?
   Wang: No discount below 500 cases. But if you buy 1,000 cases, we'll offer 15% less.
   Jack: Let me think about that. Now, if I place an order for 1,000, will you be able to dispatch immediately?
   Wang: I'll try my best.

5. **Jack:** Well, if you get it to us before the Christmas rush, it'll be OK, I take it your prices include insurance?
   Wang: Actually, no, you'll be responsible for that. If you increase your order, then we'd be willing to cover insurance as well.
   Jack: I'll need to do some calculations.
   Wang: Let's look at methods of payment. Since we've not dealt with you before, we'd like to be paid by banker's draft.
   Jack: Well, this is a large order. We've done business with many well-known wine producers by letter of credit.
   Wang: OK. If you agree to pay by letter of credit, then you'll have to pay us within 30 days.
   Jack: That should be fine.

III. Guided Talking

Jack: Could you make an offer for the soccer money box?

Wang: I'd like to. May I have more details about it?

Jack: Well, the style is as the image on the e-mail we sent you. The size is 15 cm / diameter; the material, polyresin and the quantity, 50,000 pcs.

Wang: What about the logo?

Jack: The logo is 2 colors in one position.

Wang: Wait a moment, please, let me calculate it first.

Jack: Take your time.

Wang: Well, the price will be USD 1.20 per piece.

IV. Creative Discussion

An offer is a proposal of terms and conditions of buying or selling a certain commodity. In general, it is the seller who offers the sale of certain commodities to the buyer. Such "Supply" is mostly used.

There are two kinds of offers: firm offer and non-firm offer. A firm offer is made when a seller promises to sell. The seller can not revoke or amend what he has offered during the validity of the offer. Once the offer is accepted by the buyer within its validity, the seller also has no right to alter, change, or revoke it.

A firm offer should be definite, complete, clear and final in its wording. It should include the following: the name of commodity, quality, quantity, and specifications, details of prices, terms of payment, date of delivery and the period for which the offer is valid.

A non-firm offer might contain fewer terms. It is unclear, incomplete and with reservations. Such kind of offer is not binding on the seller. The following expressions can often be read: "Subject to our final confirmation", "The prices are for your reference only" and "Subject to being unsold".

Chapter 6

I. Complete the Following Dialogues

(1)

| 1. name | 2. part | 3. interested | 4. business | 5. catalogue |
| 6. importer | 7. products | 8. market | 9. for | 10. export |

(2)

| 1. delight | 2. newly | 3. product | 4. demonstrate |
| 5. multiple | 6. have | 7. leave | 8. business |

II. Role-plays

Task 1

Question and answer.

A: Good morning, ladies and gentlemen! Welcome to our booth. Today, I take delight in presenting to you one of our newly-developed products to Automatic Drapery System. New look at the whole system, please. The new product incorporates multiple tasks: manual button, remote control and timer automatic control.

B: My name is Tracy Darland. I'm an engineer. Could you specify the function of the remote control and the timer?

A: The remote control can control multiple draperies individually or simultaneously or in different rooms. And this is a unique design of our Your Choice Range. The timer can preset eight times open / close 24 hours. Now, please try our new product.

B: Could I have a set of catalogues of all your products?

A: Yes, of course. Could you leave me your business card, please?

B: OK. I'd also like to have a price list of your product range.

A: Sorry, madam, our quotations vary according to the quantity of the order, so it all depends on how many you orders.

Task 2

Short conversation.

(1)

A: Hello, my name is Bill. Here is my card. I'm a building project contractor. Yesterday, I took part in your demo and found myself particularly interested in your drapery system, Your Choice Range.

B: Thanks. Here is my business card and some of the catalogues of our products.

A: Thank you. I'm now in charge of a construction project of a five star hotel in Spain. The unique design of your remote controller and the advanced technology of your product are just the right fit for the 60 deluxe rooms being built there.

B: Good. Our drapery system is patented for its unique design. The remote controller can be used on drapery in different rooms.

A: That's it. By the way, are you licensed to export?

B: Yes, of course. We were a licensed exporter early in 1960.

A: Wow, an old company with long history. I sincerely hope to establish a good business relationship with you. I'd like to have a further discussion with you.

B: Me too.

(2)

(A is a businessman of a Chinese Trade company and B is a customer.)

A: I understand this is your first visit to our company.

B: Yes, and also my first trip to China. I've always wanted to see with my own eyes China's achievements and now I've been more than rewarded.

A: I see, but I hope you've had a pleasant trip.

B: I did, thank you. Well, come to the point, the purpose of my coming here is to inquire about possibilities of establishing trade relations with your company.

A: Let me assure you of our best attention, Mr. Brown. What's your line of business?

B: Cameras and photographic goods. We are distributors with business branches in most major cities in Britain. Now, we'd like to introduce Chinese-made cameras if your conditions are favorable.

A: We'll see what we can do.

B: There might be few of models we would be interested in, if I could go over your latest catalogues.

A: Here you are. How many copies would you like to have?

B: Ten please. I'd like to airmail some back home.

A: Anything else?

B: Would it be possible for me to have a closer look at your samples?

A: Why not? Mr. Liu over there will take you down to our showroom.

B: Thank you. I'm afraid I've taken a lot of your time.

A: Not at all. Glad to have been of help. Hope to see more of you in future.

(3)

Peter: Good morning. My name is Peter. I'm from the U.S. Here is my business card.

Li: Pleased to meet you, Mr. Peter. My name is Li.

Peter: Pleased to meet you too, Miss Li.

Li: Won't you sit down?

Peter: Thank you.

Li: May I offer you a cup of tea?

Peter: Certainly. I like your Jasmine tea very much.

Li: Well, from your business card, I can see that you specialize in oil-drilling equipment.

Peter: Yes, as matter of fact, we have been in this business for more than twenty years. Mr. Wang from your commercial office in Washington has referred me to you in the hope that I might be of some help in your oil industry.

Li: Currently we have a strong interest in opening up more new oil fields. We could consider buying from you if the technology incorporated in your equipment is advanced and the trade terms favorable.

Peter: I have brought with me a series of catalogs for our latest models. My engineer is accompanying me on the trip. He can meet your technicians and answer any questions about our products.

Li: That's an interesting idea. We shall, first of all, study your catalogs and get in touch with our customers. If they are interested, we'll arrange for further discussion.

Peter: Very good. I'm staying in Beijing Hotel. My room is 315.

Li: We'll let you know their responses as soon as possible.

Peter: Good-bye!

III. Guided Talking

(1)

A: Mr. Brown suggested I get in touch with you.

B: Mr. Robert called me. I'd like to know more about your products.

A: We appreciate your interested. I have some catalogues, and I'd like to have a look then.

B: Thank you. Do they cover all of your products?

A: Yes, everything we export is included.

B: I've heard that you are launching a new style of video camera. Can you tell me more about it?

A: Here is a sample for you to look at. If you have any questions, I'd be glad to answer them.

B: How soon is this product going to be on the market?

A: Well, we are launching it in three weeks'time, on 18th June, but obviously we are starting the publicity campaign before then.

B: I'm glad to hear that. Well, I was much impressed by your booth. I've already seen some items we'd like to order, although I'd still like to study them a bit further.

A: Well, I'm waiting for you to discuss them further.

(2)

B: I've got bad news from Steve about the contract he's been negotiating with Ambros Pty Ltd. He's heard that another company's putting in their own bid in three day's time.

A: Oh, no. We're counting on that contractor. What can we do?

B: Well, we're going to fight it. Our rivals say they'll match us for price and beat our deadlines so we'll have to concentrate on those two issues. Steve says we're going to beat them on every other details, but price and deadlines are the crucial items.

A: Well, you can make the decision to cut prices but, in terms of deadlines, our assembly lines are already working to capacity except at the weekends.

B: I know. I can cut price slightly but do you think you can beat our rival's deadlines?

A: Well, the union meets later this afternoon for their regular monthly meeting. I'll raise this with them as a matter of priority.

B: Can you persuade them to work extra hours at the weekend?

A: Yes, I think so. Can you authorize overtime payment in advance so it's not an issue when I'm talking to the union?

B: Yes, I'll do that once we finish this show. What else?

A: We have to contact Steve so he can tell Ambros that we're going to respond with an improved bid. We've only got two days to prepare.

B: Right.

IV. Creative Discussion

Shows are one of the most effective media for establishing and maintaining customer relations. In an increasing digital age, it is the only medium where buyer, seller and product physically come together—a potential force for business. Show provides a highly flexible environment in which a wide range of sales and marketing objectives can be achieved. Unlike magazines and direct mail, exhibition involves a two-way communication process. At an exhibition, suppliers can physically demonstrate a product's benefits, and visitors can see, touch, taste, smell, hear and judge for themselves.

Shows are a recognized launch pad for new products, and an extremely efficient way to keep up to date with the latest innovations. You can compile a wide range of competitive information on products and suppliers in a concentrated period of time. Decision makers are more likely to name trade shows as an "extremely useful" source of purchasing information, than any other media.

Shows are a rich source of new ideas and applications and as such, play an important role in strategic planning and business generation keep in working closely with sponsoring trade associations and the media to ensure our events are at the forefront of developments. They are also a focal point for industry, attracting a broad cross-section of representatives, from buyers and sellers to trade associations and the media. A full program of associated activities provides a wealth of additional networking opportunities from seminars and social events to competitions and award ceremonies.

Chapter 7

I. Complete the Following Dialogues

(1)

1. simplified 2. tour 3. seeing 4. particular 5. line
6. follow 7. best 8. features 9. place 10. expecting

(2)

1. information / situation 2. agree 3. reputation 4. capacity 5. per
6. peak 7. occupied 8. carrying / turning 9. exert 10. under

II. Interaction Activities

Task 1

A: This is our Design Department. Please look at our revolutionary new nanometer pro-ducts.

B: The up-to-date patterns are very attractive.

A: Our designers always make great efforts to keep the novelty of products.

B: Great! It is vital important that the goods have a new face.

A: Yes. We upgrade our products every year.

B: I believe that your up-to-date patterns will be welcome by the customers at home and abroad.

A: What is your overall impression of our new products?

B: Wonderful! Seeing is believing.

Task 2

A: What is your impression after looking around the plant?

B: While your products are good, the production capacity is not large enough.

A: Yes, we are thinking to enlarge the production scale to produce more and better products.

B: Do you like your production capacity doubled overnight?

A: Doubled overnight? Are you kidding?
B: It's not a joke. What prevents you from expansion?
A: We are out of funds recently.
B: Why not discuss the possibility of our joint investment on your plant?
A: Can you tell me in detail?
B: We provide the existing line in our country. It won't take a long time to disassemble and pack the line. Then we'll ship the line to your plant.
A: That's a good idea.
B: It's not incredible that the new production capacity will come into being soon.
A: I'll think it over.

III. Actual Practice

Tang: Mr. Watt, I am glad to show you around the factory.
Watt: That's very helpful for me.
Tang: What particular products are you interested in?
Watt: I'm seeking for arts porcelain, ornaments for display, imitation antique porcelain.
Tang: Our factory mainly produces ceramic arts and crafts. I am sure our fine porcelain products will meet your demand.
Watt: It sounds nice.
Tang: Here is our showroom. You will find a great variety of porcelain samples in our showroom.
Watt: Oh, you have got a large collection of porcelain samples.
Tang: With rich raw materials, fine workmanship, up-to-date patterns and featuring great varieties, our ceramic arts and crafts enjoy good reputation in the international market. I hope your people will like them.
Watt: Oh yes, Chinese arts and crafts are well appreciated by our customers.
Tang: May I introduce something about our factory to you?
Watt: Well, Don't tell me story. I want to see everything with my own eyes.
(Mr. Watt has looked around the whole factory in high spirits.)
Tang: What's your impression of our factory?
Watt: Wow, excellent! Seeing is believing. I am considering to place an initial order with you soon.

IV. Creative Discussion

The teacher encourages the students to think and express their ideas creatively.
(No model discussion results are provided for this part.)

Chapter 8

I. Complete the Following Dialogues

(1)

1. negotiation 2. agreed 3. about 4. with 5. sold
6. concern / worry 7. attract 8. developed 9. welcome 10. customers

(2)

1. take out 2. don't know for sure 3. do me a favor
4. The aim of 5. promote technical exchanges 6. so far as rights are concerned
7. enjoys the exclusive right 8. is entitled to 9. authorized letter
10. is a must

II. Interaction Activities

Task 1

A: Let's talk about the design and color of the products.

B: Oh, yes. It's high time that we modernized our manufactured goods.

A: Sure. There are many kinds of stationery in the market. To lead the market, we'd like to make our products looked more fancy. Do you have any good ideas for that?

B: Yes. We have paid special attention to it for some time. Our designers have developed some new designs. I'm sure the new designs would show our customers some new faces.

A: Really? Oh, they are all attractive. I believe they will catches the fancy of the customers.

B: And we will use brighten color to print the appearance of our stationery to make them look brighter.

A: That's a good idea.

Task 2

A: We strongly recommend that you to apply for the trademark in China to protect yourself to be offended.

B: Yes, I am thinking to have my manufactured goods registered. Is there better way out?

A: For your information, you should get the related document well prepared.

B: OK.

A: You may contact the Trademark Office to get standard forms to fill out.

B: What about next?

A: To be brief, you go through the formality. If there is no opposition to your application, then registration is approved.

B: Fine. How long will the registered trademark be valid?

A: Sorry, I don't know for sure.

III. Actual Practice

A: First of all, I'd like to introduce the development of innovative products of our company.

B: Go ahead. It's an important step to enter into international market.
A: Our company is adopting innovative strategy. We'll try our best to have our own power brands.
B: It's a good idea.
A: To promote the sale, we have developed some new designs of the products.
B: Got it. Only through innovation and creation of our own power brands can you hold market share in the world market.
A: For your information, we have obtained CE Certificate.
B: Pretty good.
A: With CE Certificate, our new designs will find a ready market in European countries.
B: I'm anxiously looking forward to seeing the innovative products on the store shelves of our supermarkets.

IV. Creative Discussion

Students practise how to make a debate. The teacher encourages Students to have a heated debate and develop as many affirmative or negative statements as possible.

Chapter 9

I. Complete the Following Dialogues

(1)

1. key	2. attach	3. packing	4. damage	5. packing
6. inner	7. hands	8. attractive	9. sales	10. consideration

(2)

1. talk about	2. Could you show me	3. emphasis on	4. outside packing
5. I am afraid that	6. Why not	7. in transit	8. are not convenient for
9. In fact	10. rest assured		

II. Interaction Activities

Task 1

A: Are your products ready for inspection?
B: Yes, quite ready. I'll lead you to look round the workshops and warehouse.
A: Could you tell me something about your quality inspection on the products?
B: OK. We attach much importance to the quality. All products are under strict quality control.
A: It's essential that everyone pay attention to quality.
B: Our own inspectors form the first line of quality control. They spread out every corner of the workshops and packing center.
A: How about their work?
B: Very effective and workable. Few defective products can go to the warehouse before checked out.
A: I see. It's time to start my inspection.

B: I'll ask some workers to help you.

A: Fine. I'll select a few goods at random for inspection.

B: Please don't hesitate to let us know the weak points of work.

A: Actually, your excellent quality control gave me a favorable impression.

Task 2

A: Mr. Green, please don't hesitate to let me know the problems of our goods.

B: Well, I am sorry to tell you some weak points of your packing.

A: Please go ahead.

B: First, I find a few cartons have almost broken before shipment.

A: You mean our outside packing is not strong enough?

B: Yes, since the porcelain are heavy and fragile, the stronger paperboard can reduce the risk of damage in transit.

A: I am sorry about durability of your outer packing. All right. We'll improve the outside packing.

B: I am afraid your poly-bag seems a little too thin. The goods may scratch the bag during transportation.

A: Sounds reasonable. We'll take care of it by using double thick ones.

B: The outlook of inner box should be fit for window display in order to attract customers.

A: Good advice.

B: What are you going to improve the packing?

A: We'll repack the goods and try our best to improve our packing. We promise our future packing will be much better.

III. Actual Practice

1. Sam is going to import a large quantity of sugar from China. Since sugar is a kind of commodity which has got a standard of grade. He may choose "Grade" as a quality standard. Different grades can classify clearly the different quality of goods.

2. Cindy is going to import some arts porcelain and imitation antique porcelain. There are not any specification, grade or standard for such goods. At the beginning of doing business, she'd better ask for samples of these products or she provides the samples for production. The seller will make counter samples for confirmation in this case.

   When signing the contract, she may stipulate "Quality as per Seller's Sample" or "Quality as per Buyer's Sample". The seller should be responsible for delivery goods as the same quality of samples.

3. David is going to import Haier Washing Machine. It has possessed a notable brand name and trade mark. Generally speaking, trade mark and brand name enjoy high reputation in the market. The quality of these products is good and stable. Since Haier Brand is well known at home and abroad, the quality of Haier Washing Machine is certain without asking for seeing samples. Choosing brand or trade mark is proper for David.

4. The products of local flavor or local specialities are suitable for Name of Origin when signing the

quality terms. Therefore the best quality term for Mark is Name of Origin.

IV. Creative Discussion

The teacher encourages the students to think and express their ideas creatively.
(No model discussion results are provided for this part.)

Chapter 10

I. Complete the Following Dialogues

(1)

| 1. from | 2. in | 3. in | 4. to | 5. in | 6. of |
| 7. about | 8. into | 9. outside | 10. like | 11. for | 12. with |

(2)

1. tell something about
2. is superior to
3. It is understandable but
4. assures our customers of
5. is inconvenient for
6. insist on
7. on condition that
8. place a duplicate order
9. push the sale
10. close a deal

II. Interaction Activities

Task 1

A: As far as the offer is concerned, your price is rather on the high side. Could you give us discount of 4%?

B: I am afraid you really don't know how bad the situation is.

A: What's that?

B: We are facing pressures from devaluation of the US dollar against Chinese currency. We lose a lot of money for this reason.

A: Oh, really?

B: Worse still, affected by oil price, steel and plastic prices in Chinese domestic market have increased tremendously.

A: I am sorry to hear that.

B: So it's impossible to allow you a discount of 4%.

A: Will it workable if our quantity will be more than triple, that is, 3 FCL.

B: Good. Large quantity makes discount workable. Shall we meet each other half way? A discount of 2% is the best we can do.

A: Let's call it a deal. I'll place orders with you soon.

Task 2

A: It's time to talk about terms of payment.

B: I think so. As usual, our company accepts terms of payment by confirmed, irrevocable letter of credit at sight.

A: But payment by letter of credit will tied up our capital flow and cause both of us some inconvenience.

B: L/C gives seller protection of the banker's guarantee.

A: It's safe for large amount indeed. Since it is only our trial order, it's not worth opening an L/C for a small order.

B: Sounds reasonable. What do you prefer?

A: We'd like to pay by T/T. It costs less money for bank charges.

B: In this case, we'll make you an exception by T/T.

A: That's a deal.

B: We accept T/T on condition that you remit the payment before shipment.

III. Actual Practice

John: Hey, Mr.Xiao. Compared with the prices of other suppliers, we find your prices of MP4 are much on the high side.

Xiao: In fact, our quality is superior than others.

John: Anyway, your prices are beyond our reach.

Xiao: Let's discuss other terms and conditions before prices, shall we?

John: That's just what I am thinking.

Xiao: Shall we come to terms of payment?

John: Can you accept D/A?

Xiao: We usually accept payment by L/C. That is our usual practice.

John: It is understandable but we insist on payment by D/P.

Xiao: To encourage business, we agree to make an exception by accepting D/P at sight.

John: Thanks so much.

Xiao: We have discussed all details of the trade aside from prices.

John: OK. Let turn to prices again. Could you quote us more reasonable prices?

Xiao: Our prices are carefully calculated so they are our rock-bottom prices.

John: Let me think it over.

Xiao: It's a pity that I can't grant you any further reduction. Actually we have quoted you most favorable price.

John: All right. Let's close a deal.

IV. Creative Discussion

Encourage the students to think actively and express their own ideas creatively during discussion.

(No model discussion results are provided for this part.)

Chapter 11

I. Complete the Following Dialogue

(1)

1. speak   2. Which   3. sorry   4. in
5. message   6. about   7. What   8. as

(2)

1. help   2. have   3. person   4. Just   5. collect
6. charges   7. connect   8. extension   9. accept   10. ahead

II. Role-plays

Task 1

(No suggested keys)

Task 2

A: Hello, this is John speaking. Can I talk to Nicole?

B: Hold on please ... Sorry, she is having a business meeting.

A: Well, when can I reach her?

B: I'm not sure when the meeting will be over. Would you like to leave a message?

A: Er... I'd better talk to her in person. OK, I'll call back later. Thank you! Bye.

B: Bye.

(*Later, John has another try.*)

A: Hello, I'd like to speak to Nicole.

B: I'm afraid she is not available right now. May I know who's calling?

A: This is John.

B: Hello, John. This is Sally speaking. Nicole is out for tea with boss alone (chuckling).

A: What?

B: Ease please, and also with clients. Can I take a message?

A: OK. Nicole and I would have supper together, but I have to make a counter-offer to the trade company and work overtime this evening, so please tell her we have to cancel the date... and I'll date her tomorrow, of course.

B: All right, no problem, I'll tell her as soon as she's back.

A: Thank you.

B: You're welcome.

III. Guided Talking

(1)

A: Hello?

B: Hello. Could I please speak to Mr. Wang An?

A: I'm sorry. He's in a press conference right now. Could I take a message?

B: Yes, please. I'm a clerk in City Bank. I'm calling to tell him that the overdraft of his credit card has exceeded the permitted amount. He should pay the due money, and he'd better go there as soon as possible.

A: OK. I'll give him the message as soon as he's back.

B: Thanks. Good-bye.

(2)

A: Good afternoon. Can I help you?

C: Yes, please. Is Ms. Liu Yifei available, please?

A: I'm sorry, she is on a long-distance call to Paris. Would you like to leave a message?

C: Please tell her I have to cancel our appointment on Friday, and ...

A: Let me get a pen. All right, go ahead.

C: My name is Ma Lin, my number is 13552788900. Could you have her to call me later so that I can arrange a new time?

A: Sure. I'll tell her to call Ma Lin at 13552788900.

C: Thank you. Good-bye.

(3)

A: Hello, Launch Department.

D: Hello, is Zhao Mingmin there?

A: Hold on, please. I'll see if he is available ... Sorry, he's out.

D: Well, Would you like to take a message for me?

A: Certainly, go ahead please.

D: I'm calling to ask about a new band. If possible, let him send me a fax about the relative information tomorrow morning. My number is 87755664, and my name is Qian Kun.

A: OK. ...Mr. Qian Kun at 87755664 ... I'll tell him.

D: Thanks. Bye.

IV. Creative Discussion

The teacher encourages the students to think and express their ideas creatively.
(No model discussion results are provided for this part.)

Chapter 12

I. Complete the Following Dialogues

(1)

1. terms	2. by	3. conditions	4. practice	5. accept
6. against	7. deposit	8. make	9. rest	10. accommodation

(2)

1. satisfactory	2. common	3. importer	4. add	5. expense
6. exporter	7. guarantee	8. on	9. appreciate	10. consideration

II. Interaction Activities

Task 1

John: Now we have settled everything except the terms of payment, would you make the easy terms of payment for us?

Lin: Generally, we only accept payment by irrevocable letter of credit payable against shipping documents.

John: Well, you know our order this time is a total of USD 25,000 worth of the sweaters. To open an L/C for such a large amount is costly, which will add to the cost of our imports. It'll cause us a great deal of difficulty. I wonder if you could accept other kinds of payment such as D/A or D/P?

Lin: I'm afraid not. Our usual practice is to accept payment by L/C only. An irrevocable L/C gives our exports the protection of a banker's guarantee and we'll get the right amount of money.

John: I'm sorry that you adhere to payment by L/C. For you, payment by L/C is the safest method, but for us, the point is to open an L/C with a bank does mean additional expense and tied-up funds.

Task 2

A: I'm afraid I have a complaint to make. According to the contract, you should open the L/C within one month after the signature of the contract. But I haven't received the covering L/C.

B: Sorry for the delay. I'll open the L/C as soon as I return home.

A: I do hope you will open the credit with the least possible delay. As you know, the delivery date is drawing near, we should make the necessary arrangements to effect the shipment in due time.

III. Actual Practice

A: Good morning, glad to see you again. I received your letter of credit on 8th of April. I'm afraid there are some differences between your L/C and Sales Contract No. 2345.

B: Go ahead.

A: First, the letter of credit is at sight instead of after sight. Since all the terms in the L/C should be in full agreement with the contract, you should pay for the shipment immediately after you have received all the necessary shipping documents.

B: Really? I know the letter of credit should be at sight. I'll check it up and inform you. Anything else?

A: The amount of money should be USD 200,000 instead of USD 20,000. What's more, the expiry date should be the 5th of September rather than the 15th of September.

B: I'm sorry for these mistakes, which are caused by our carelessness. I'll approach the opening bank for an amendment to the L/C as soon as I return home. I'll adopt some measures to avoid similar mistakes in the future trade.

A: Thank you for your cooperation. We hope you will understand our situation and let us have your amendment notice as soon as possible.

IV. Creative Discussion

The teacher encourages the students to think and express their ideas creatively.

(No model discussion results are provided for this part.)

Chapter 13

I. Complete the Following Dialogues

(1)

1. insurance	2. classify	3. out	4. on	5. against
6. attention	7. value	8. practice	9. room	10. workable

(2)

1. on	2. effect	3. shipping	4. safe	5. account
6. against	7. with	8. negotiation	9. exempt	10. information

II. Interaction Activities

Task 1

A: May I invite your attention to insurance?

B: Yes, please.

A: What types of insurance should be covered for our shipment?

B: We effect insurance on domestic glassware for 110% of invoice value against WPA.

A: But this kind of insurance is too narrow for the shipment of glassware. For glassware, Risk of breakage is quite necessary. So, please extend the coverage to include Risk of breakage and War Risk.

B: As you may be aware, it's our trade practice that sellers insure the goods against the usual risks. If you insist on additional risk, the extra premium is borne by you.

A: Is there any room for negotiation?

B: I'm afraid that it is impossible, much as we'd like to. We can't break general practice to allow Extraneous Risks by the seller.

B: It makes sense. The extra premium will be paid by us.

Task 2

A: We are pleased to talk over the possibility of being your exclusive agency just now.

B: Yes, As you may be aware, we have well-established marketing channels and we are experienced in machinery and equipment.

A: We appreciate the efforts you made in machinery and equipment sales promotion.

B: I'd like to invite your attention to commission for exclusive agency.

A: As our general practice, we allow a commission of 6% on the net value for sales.

B: We don't think it practical to give us only 6% commission. We have to spend a lot to push sales. I hope you'll increase our commission by 2%.

A: I'm afraid that it won't be possible, much as we want to. Well. In the interests of both sides, we are ready to increase commission by 1%.

B: You said it.

A: Fine. We agree to appoint you as our exclusive agency.

III. Actual Practice

Hong: Welcome to our company. We are glad to talk face to face.

Victor: Mr. Hong, we find your silk products are very popular in Indian market. Both the styles and quality are to the taste of our customers.

Hong: That's fine.

Victor: As we are a large company dealing a lot of different kinds of products, we have rich experience and business connections in Indian market. We know the Indian market like the palm of our hands.

Hong: I see.

Victor: I think you need a good partner to help you to open the Indian market. That's why we are here to talk with you.

Hong: You mean to be our agent?

Victor: Quite right. Don't you think we are qualified for a sole agency?

Hong: Thank you for your kind offer. If you don't mind, we'd like to point out your trade turnover of our silk is still too low to grant you an agent.

Victor: If you appoint us as your agency, we'll double our effort to push the sales.

Hong: Do you have any proposal? If you like to be our sole agent, the volume of sales should at least increase by 20%.

Victor: But at an initial stage, perhaps it's hard for us to reach this goal.

Hong: I'm afraid that it won't be possible, much as we want to appoint you as an agent. How about trying to sell more of our products at an initial stage? When time is ripe, we'll discuss it again.

IV. Creative Discussion

The teacher encourages the students to think actively and express their own ideas creatively.

(No model discussion results are provided for this part.)

Chapter 14

I. Complete the Following Dialogues

(1)

1. draft	2. check	3. corrected	4. except	5. to
6. instead	7. stipulated	8. packed	9. flexible	10. reinforce

(2)

1. signature	2. up	3. contract	4. signing
5. pleasure	6. congratulate	7. transaction	8. conclusion

(3)

1. take some measures
2. on condition that
3. has come to a successful conclusion
4. be responsible for
5. with the consent of
6. is entitled to
7. resort to
8. in conformity with
9. to be signed
10. as per

II. Interaction Activities

Task 1

A: I made a close study of the draft contract last night. It seems to me we've come quite a long way. However, there are still some points which I'd like to bring up.

B: Yes, please.

A: First, about the packing. Is it possible to use wooden cases instead of cardboard boxes?

B: I'm sorry. It's stipulated in the contract that the products are packed in cardboard boxes.

A: Well, carton is all right. Second, about the terms of payment and delivery. We have agreed on the payment made by confirmed, irrevocable letter of credit, payable against shipping documents. But as for delivery, I must stress that you are expected to duly deliver the goods, the shipment should be effected and completed by the end of July. We can't accept any delay.

B: Of course not, as long as you open the covering L/C in due time. Any other questions?

A: No more. But let's check the items in the contract one by one.

B: (*After they have finished checking all the items.*) Since everything is settled, shall we sign the contract now?

A: OK.

B: (*After signing the contract.*) Let's congratulate ourselves that this transaction has been brought to a successful conclusion.

Task 2

A: I think we have reached an agreement on almost all the terms except for some minor points. Do you think it is possible to add the "force majeure"? We often have typhoons and floods in summer, production might be affected and the execution of the contract would be delayed. I hope that you won't object to adding such a clause in the contract.

B: All right. If it's nothing we can do to protest the nature, we'll add it to the contract. In case of "force majeure", you should notify us as soon as possible.

A: I will. Thank you for your friendly cooperation. I hope everything will go smoothly and no disaster will happen.

B: Now, I think it is essential to include this clause, that is, "any modification or alteration to the contract shall only be made with the consent of both parties."

A: No problem, I'll do it. Anything else?

B: Not yet.

A: Please check the draft contract again and if there are any problems, you can contact me at any time and discuss next time.

III. Actual Practice

A: Well, I think there will be no misunderstanding between us at all. Here is our contract. Would you please take one more look before you sign?

B: (*After A has finished checking all the items.*) I'm glad that we've finally come to an agreement after repeated negotiation. Things that should be there are there.

A: Now everything is settled, shall we sign the contract now?

B: Fine.

A: Please sign here. (*After all signatures*) Each has two formal copies of the contract. These two copies are for you, one in Chinese and one in English. They are all in agreement with each other.

B: Thank you. Let's congratulate ourselves that this transaction has been brought to a successful conclusion.

IV. Creative Discussion

Encourage the students to think and express their ideas creatively.

(No model discussion results are provided for this part.)

Chapter 15

I. Complete the Following Dialogues

(1)

1. deliver   2. make   3. possible   4. advance   5. time   6. request   7. meet

(2)

1. postage   2. extra   3. dispatched   4. delivery   5. send   6. receiver

II. Interaction Activities

Task 1

A: In your opinion, which features you think are the most important for Dispatch Department?

B: I believe that high quality of service is of the most importance for Dispatch Department. And you?

A: For me, I will consider shipping charges first. I mean lower cost is important. If we cannot afford it, it's not available.

C: I agree. But I think reputation and reliability of the Dispatch department are very important.

D: I believe security of the cargo shipping is important too.

E: Yes, I'm sure all of you are right.

Task 2

A: I'm sorry to informed you that 30 high definition televisions which was due in Hong Kong on 1st August has not yet arrived.

B: I'll check it immediately. What's the number of your bill of lading?

A: B/L 7696.

B: Well, I'm pleased to tell you that the goods will arrived in Hong Kong the day after tomorrow.

A: Yes? But why the ship has been delayed?

B: The ship was delayed due to the bad weather. I'm very sorry for the delay in delivery and inconvenience it must have caused you. If you have any further questions please contact us at any time as you like.

A: Thank you.

III. Actual Practice

Task 1

Li: Bright Future Inc. Li Hong is speaking.

Wang: Hello, this is Wang Hai from ABC Company.

Li: Hello, Mr. Li. What can I do for you?

Wang: Yes. I'm phoning about our delivery last month and sorry to let you know that there seems to be a mistake. You know that when the components were unpacked and inspected, we found that we ordered 1,000 black and white pairs of shoes but we received only 950 right ones and 50 pairs of white shoes instead.

Li: I'm extremely sorry to hear about your complaints. I can assure that we will replace it immediately. And we can guarantee that it won't happen again.

Wang: It's perfectly all right. Could you tell us when we can expect these 50 pairs of shoes to arrive in our warehouse?

Li: Next Monday. OK?

Wang: Thanks for letting me know that.

Li: You have my sincere apology again. Goodbye.

Wang: Bye now, Mr. Li.

Task 2

A: Dispatch Department. Dhana speaking.

B: Dhana, this is Bill from Bright Company.

A: Yes, Bill. What can I do for you?

B: I'm going to check our request for the early delivery of the goods, 1,000 packages of the LTT fans. What is the earliest time when you can make delivery?

A: I think we can meet your requirement. The earliest delivery we can make is at the end of September. We can assure you that the shipment will be made not later than the first half of October.

B: You know that time of delivery is very important to us. I hope you can give our request your special consideration. The interval is too long. Could we expect an earlier shipment within three months?

A: I'll find out with our home office. We'll do our best to advance the time of delivery. As you know, our manufacturers are full and we have a lot of orders to fill. If you desire earlier delivery, we can only make a partial shipment, maybe.

B: OK. Please let me know whether it is available or not. What about the method of delivery?

A: Most of the products are delivered by train. I believe that the products will reach you in time and in good order and hope they will give you complete satisfaction.

B: Great. Thanks very much.

A: You're welcome. If you have any problems, you can contact me at any time.

B: OK. Bye.

A: Bye.

IV. Creative Discussion

The teacher encourages the students to think and express their own ideas creatively.

(No model discussion results are provided for this part.)

Chapter 16

I. Complete the Following Dialogues

(1)

1. minute	2. agenda	3. checked	4. arranged
5. interpreter	6. seat	7. put	8. successful

(2)

1. admit	2. doubtful	3. tricky	4. bound
5. reckon / think	6. likely	7. expect	8. vote

II. Role-plays

Task 1

A: Good afternoon, ladies and gentlemen. We all know what we're here for. Now we'd like to hear your ideas about the proposed plan, Jack?

B: I think the trade of electronic products is bound to be a booming business in the near future. In addition, we have financial backing as well as an excellent staff. What do you reckon, Tom?

C: I agree with you.

D: It seems to me that our first job is to find out what it's likely to cost us to get started, and what kind of return we can expect over the next two or three years.

E: If we look at the whole picture, the present market may not be so encouraging.

A: OK. Now let's call it a day.

Task 2

A: Is the room ready for the meeting?

B: Yes, I've checked that the lighting, air-conditioning and the video projector are OK, and that water, glasses, ashtrays, pens and papers are available.

A: Good. But you have to prepare the Minute Book and some extra copies of the agenda in case someone else needs it.

B: I've already done that.

B: What about microphones?

A: No problem.

B: Nice work. Well, we'll have several foreign guests to attend the meeting. What have you got then?

B: I've arranged for an interpreter to be present.

A: That's OK. How would you seat our guests, Miss Li?

B: I've prepared name cards to be put on the conference table for guests to sit by.

A: So everything is clear. I hope our organization of the conference will be successful.

B: So do I.

III. Guided Talking

A: Miss Li, I don't know how to take notes at the conference. Could you explain it to me?

B: OK. Oh, I take my notebook ready for the meeting. You can read it.

A: Thank you. Err ..., what's this?

B: This is the heading ... the Heng Xing Silk Trading Company. Then underneath that ... Minutes of Meeting of Branch Managers at 3:00 p.m. on Thursday, 8th, December, 2006, then underneath that ... Present: Mr. White, President, in the chair.

A: And you've left a space underneath to fill in the name of the managers, haven't you?

B: Yes, that's right.

A: Do I have to write down every word that everyone says?

B: No, you just need to make a note of the topics that are discussed and the result of the discussion.

A: The result of the discussion?

B: When a topic has been discussed for some time, someone usually proposes that some action should be taken.

A: Then what happens?

B: Then the chairman asks whether the members agree to the proposal. And if they do agree, you can write down "It was agreed that..." or "It was resolved that ...".

A: I see. Thank you. Miss Li.

IV. Creative Discussion

The teacher encourages the students to think and express their ideas creatively.

(No model discussion results are provided.)

Chapter 17

I. Complete the Following Dialogues

(1)

| 1. hot | 2. attractive | 3. give | 4. up | 5. principle |
| 6. shows | 7. of | 8. arrange | 9. overall | 10. to |

(2)

1. impressed 2. series 3. choose 4. popular 5. meet
6. materials 7. size 8. medium 9. orders 10. let

II. Role-plays

Task 1

A: Welcome to our company, Jack.

B: Thank you for your invitation.

A: Our company has a factory of over 50 years. All our carpets are available for export. Our carpets are 100% wool, fairly thick and very soft. They have been exported to more than 100 countries and regions and are enjoying great popularity in the world.

B: Can I have your catalogue?

A: Here it is.

B: Thank you. (*He glances over the catalogue.*) Can I have a look at your showroom?

A: Sure. This way, please.

(*After visiting the showroom.*)

B: I see that you mainly export handmade carpets. But in many countries, most carpets are machine-made. I suppose machine manufacturing considerably lowers the cost of production.

A: It surely does. But machine-made carpets can't compare with handmade ones in quality or finish.

B: I'm sure of it. How about your designs?

A: We use traditional patterns and also make our new designs.

B: Do you manufacture carpets on customers' requirement?

A: Of course we do. We make designs according to data given by customers.

B: Excellent.

A: Would you like to place some orders?

B: Yes, I'm willing to give your carpets a try.

Task 2

A: I have the pleasure of meeting you again, Mr. Brown. Now what can I do for you?

B: I'm glad to meet you in person. We've been doing good business with each other. I hope our cooperation this time will be further promoted. But my biggest concern now is business promotion. I'm wondering if you could tell me something about your company's advertising campaign for the new product.

A: Well, we think the first thing is what media we should use and when we should place advertisement in the media. Very often in a campaign, two or more media are used together. The purpose of our advertising is to draw foreign customers' interest and keep hold of their attention, so that they may do something in return.

B: What media do you recommend then?

A: We think television is much more effective if it doesn't matter for us to pay a little more money.

B: Well, it's worth doing so long as the result is satisfactory. But when shall we take this advertisement?

A: How about the end of the fall?

B: All right.

III. Guided Talking

A: Good morning, Mr. White. My name is Zhang Hua. I'm from the ABC Company. Here is my name card. I'd like to show you some of our products.

B: Well, we're pretty well established with our regular suppliers.

A: I think I can show you some attractive prices. It won't take long.

B: OK. Can you show me your catalogues?

A: Yes, of course. Here you are. They will give you a good idea of our company's products.

B: Mmm...good. I'm favorably impressed.

A: Nice to hear that. And our new kneepads(护膝垫)are used to eliminate chills, stimulate blood circulation, relax muscles and provide health care for knee joints(关节)and lower limbs. They are especially helpful to arthritis rheum(关节风湿病).

B: Sounds good.

A: In fact, our new product has been sold in a number of areas. They are very popular with the users there.

B: But your price is higher than other companies.

A: If you take the quality into consideration, our price is reasonable.

B: Well, I'd like to give your new product a try, but your delivery dates must be kept.

A: Certainly. You need not worry about it.

IV. Creative Discussion

1. The teacher encourages the students to think and express their ideas creatively.

2. It's an open discussion.

Chapter 18

I. Complete the Following Dialogue

1. Sit down / take a seat   2. resume   3. say something about yourself   4. emphasis

5. scores   6. command   7. proficient   8. choose / decide on

9. notify   10. probation

II. Oral Translation

(*At the interview*)

A: Hello! I'm Peter, personnel manger of our company.

B: Nice to meet you!

A: Tell me about your education, please.

B: I graduated from Shantou University a year ago, and I majored in English language and literature.

A: Do you think you have a good command of English?

B: Yes, I think so. I got high scores in almost every examination. And I also got a good score in the Band 8 Test for English Majors. And I was asked several times to be an interpreter for some companies while I was still a student.

A: What made you choose our company?

B: Your company enjoys a good reputation. And I think working in this company would provide me with more opportunities to use my knowledge.

A: I see. It's been pleasant talking with you. We'll notify you of our decision by next Monday.

B: Thank you.

III. Situational Talks

(Omit.)

IV. Practical Questions and Answers

1. If you want to know whether the appliacant can speak English well or not, you can ask him/her in the following ways:

    (1) Are you proficient in spoken English?

    (2) Do you think you can communicate with other people in English?

    (3) Please tell me something about your English level.

    (4) Do you think you can make yourself understood in English?

    (5) Can you manage an English conversation?

    (6) Why do you think you have a good command of English?

2. If you are asked why you picked their company, you can answer it in this way:

    (1) Your company is an important international company. Working for it, I think I would be able to develop my abilities.

    (2) I think working in this company will provide me with more opportunities.

    (3) I like the job here for it is somewhat challenging but I am looking for a more challenging opportunity.

3. When you are asked why you want to change your job, you can answer like this:

    (1) The work I am doing now lack for potential upward mobility.

    (2) I am looking for a greater challenge.

    (3) There are several reasons. First of all, I am desirous of working with a foreign capital enterprise. Secondly, your company is a new establishment; I think I'll be given more responsibilities. Last, frankly speaking, I wish to get a higher salary.

V. Writing

(Omit.)

VI. Creative Discussion

1. The teacher encourages the students to think and express their ideas creatively. No model discussion results are provided for this part.
2. Mock Interview is open.

Chapter 19

I. Complete the Following Dialogues

(1)

1. shipping advice   2. raw material
3. defective rate   4. tooling   5. labor shortage

(2)

1. counter samples   2. specification
3. substitute   4. equivalent   5. appearance

(3)

1. the delay in shipment   2. on pins and needles
3. at your end   4. attacking / hitting   5. loading work

(4)

1. approval sample   2. The color is lighter   3. the size
4. packing list   5. Some parts

II. Role-plays

Task 1

A: Good morning. ABC Company, may I help you?

B: I want to talk your sales manager, Mr. Chen, please?

A: Sorry, he is not in now. May I know who's calling?

B: This is Steve Smith from the United States. Do you know when he'll be back?

A: Sorry, he didn't leave a word. Do you want to leave him a message?

B: Yes, but may I know whom I'm talking to?

A: This is Lucy, Mr. Chen's secretary.

B: Maybe you can help me. We received the shipment of order no. 002 last week. We found some cartons are broken and some parts are damaged. So, the quantity is not enough now.

A: Do you know the defective percentage?

B: About 2%.

A: Normally, we attach 2% spare parts with the shipment. You can use them as the replacement for the defective parts.

B: Where did you put the spare parts?

A: In the last carton.

B: OK, I'll try to find them.

Task 2

A: What's the problem? Man...you've got a long face.
B: Nothing. Just don't feel happy these days.
A: How come?
B: Well... overtime again and I don't have much time to spend with my girl friend.
A: You must be missing "9 to 5".
B: "9 to 5"? I'd be satisfied with "8 to 6".
A: I can understand, but there is no way out, we work in the "dot com" company, and the job is bound to be fast-paced and demanding.
B: I hate working overtime, anyway.
A: We don't have much choice. Though overtime may give a feeling of despair for many of us, it is a way of life for others today.
B: That's not for me.
A: Come on...remember the old saying? If you don't like it, change it, if you can't change it, change the way you look at it.

III. Conversation Activity

(Omit.)

IV. Actual Practice

1.
(1) I'd like to get pants return and money refunded, they are brand new yet got a hole in them.
(2) Miss, I ordered icy water, but not warm water, would you please change it for me?
(3) Sir, didn't you see the "no smoking" sign over there on the wall? Besides, I have asthma, the fumes are choking me.

2.
(1) Of course, I can. But Mam, this is fresh fruit salad. Are you sure you want it heated up?
(2) Sorry, I didn't mean to disturb you, but I just cannot lower my voice when I get drunk.
(3) I'll get one more at once.

V. Creative Discussion

The teacher encourages the students to think and express their ideas creatively.
(No model discussion results are provided.)

Chapter 20

I. Complete the Following Dialogue

1. to   2. up   3. at   4. for   5. To   6. to   7. at   8. to   9. on   10. to

II. Oral Translation

Task 1

(1) I'd like to propose a toast to our host.

(2) On behalf of all the Chinese present here, I would like to say a few words.

(3) What's your specialty?

(4) May I help you to some more vegetables?

(5) This calls for a drink. To your health, Gan Bei!

(6) This hotpot works up my appetite.

(7) I'm afraid I have to watch my weight.

(8) This kind of food is to his taste.

(9) Thank you for your hospitality.

(10) Well, when in Rome, do as the Romans do.

(11) I wonder if you have a particular preference.

(12) I hope that the dishes this evening will be to your liking.

(13) Please help yourself and make yourself at home.

(14) This kind of wine never goes to the head.

(15) I haven't got the faintest idea of Chinese food.

Task 2

A: Thank you for inviting us to dinner.

B: You're welcome. We are very glad that you can attend our dinner banquet. Let's take our seats.

A: OK!

A: It is said that the food here is delicious and the service is also beyond comparison?

B: Yes. You can have a try. Do you have any particular preference?

A: No, when in Rome, do as the Romans do.

B: Let's have some wine. A drop won't hurt.

A: No, that's enough. I have had a drop too much.

B: Then let's have some more soup. Please don't stand on ceremony.

III. Oral Practice

Task 1

(1) A: Shall I help you to shredded pork with spicy sauce?
   B: Please. I'm fond of it. It's tasty.

(2) A: Help yourself to some sour spicy soup.
   B: No, thanks. I have to watch my weight.

(3) A: Have some more sweet and sour spare-rib, please.
   B: Thank you, but I'm really full.

(4) A: This prawn cooked with soy sauce really works up my appetite.
   B: Really? It seems we have the same taste. Let me help you to some more.

(5) A: Some specially flavored chicken?

B: Just a little, please!

Task 2

(1) A: To our friendship. Bottoms up!
   B: Bottoms up!
(2) A: Here's to your health!
   B: And to yours, too!
(3) A: Now please allow me to propose a toast. This is to your family, Gan Bei!
   B: Gan Bei!
(4) A: I'd like to ask you to join me in a toast to our cooperation. Cheers!
   B: Cheers!
(5) A: This calls for a drink, to your progress in speaking Chinese. Bottoms up!
   B: Bottoms up!

IV. Situational Talks

(1) **Wang:** Good evening, Mr. Brown! Nice to meet you! My name is Wang Gang, I'm the manager of Changyu Company.
   Brown: Pleased to meet you, Mr. Wang! Thank you for inviting us to dinner.
   Wang: You are welcome! Shall we go this way to the dinner table?
(Everybody enters the dining room and finds his own seat.)
   Wang: It's our pleasure to have Mr. Brown and his colleagues here with us tonight. First, let me propose a toast to welcome our distinguished guests from Australia, to the prosperity of our two companies and of course, to your pleasant journey to China. Cheers!
   All: Cheers!
   Brown: Thank you, Mr. Wang. I also like to take this opportunity to express our sincere thanks to your nice welcome and hospitality. Gan Bei!
   All: Gan Bei!
(2) The students can make the welcoming speech and thank you speech according to our sample conversation 2 and sample conversation 3.

V. Creative Discussion

Encourage the students to think and express their own ideas creatively.
(No model discussion results are provided for this part.)